An illustrated History of

BRITISH EUROPEAN AIRWAYS

By Phil Lo Bao

Published by: Browcom Group Plc, Browcom House, Browells Lane, Feltham, Middlesex, TW13 7EQ, England

ISBN 0 946141 398

Distributed in the USA/Canada by: TAYLOR & FRANCIS. IPS, 242 Cherry Street, Philadelphia, Pennsylvania 19106-1906, USA.
Telephone: (215) 238-0392 Toll Free: (800) 821-8312

1st Published 1989

Printed in Great Britain by: Pindar Print London, Browcom House, Browells Lane, Feltham, Middlesex, TW13 7EQ, England

Foreword

By Sir Henry Marking KCVO, CBE, MC

Mr Lo Bao's History of British Airways is dedicated to the memory of his father, but it is more than a remarkable example of filial piety. It is certainly the most complete history of BEA that has been written, but it is probably also the most detailed ever written of any airline in the world. It is not a book for the general reader, but for those with a special interest in aviation it is a useful record.

I was in a good position to see BEA as a whole from the inside and to know the intricacies between BEA and Goverment and others. From May 1949, when I joined BEA, I attended every meeting of the BEA Board (with one exception when I had the 'flu' either as Secretary or as a Board Member, until the British Airways Board was established, after which BEA inevitably lost a good deal of its independence, before its final demise a few years later. To have been privy to all major policy decisions those years was a great privilege to me.

It is now easy to be critical of some of BEA's – and, indeed, of my own – actions. If we were to live our lives over again we would no doubt all try to do some things differently; with hindsight we can all see so clearly what the right course was. But in the real world we have to do our best as we see it at the time, and whatever mistakes may have been made it was by any yardstick a remarkable achievement, as Mr Lo Bao says, that in the short space of 25 years BEA should have grown from nothing to establish itself as "the world's seventh largest airline", the other six all being inside the USA, and "the world's second largest international carrier in terms of passengers flown".

One must remember that in the 1950s and 1960s we were working against a background so different from the 1980s that it is fallacious to judge actions against present-day conditions. During those 20 years BEA, like all-too-many British industries was bedevilled by labour problems (no doubt some of our own making) which interrupted our business and inconvenienced passengers. A monument to British Goverments of the 1980s has been that they have brought about a more orderly and more peaceful climate. In my years as Chief Execulive of BEA I certainly spent more time on industrial relation issues than on any other subject.

Relations between the two Air Corporations were never easy. BEA felt that its very existence was resented by BOAC and that BOAC cherished hopes of an eventual takeover of BEA: Lord Douglas of BEA: and Sir Miles Thomas, who was for some years chairman of BOAC, were not always on particularly cordial terms. The resultant wrangling was against a background of BEA's extremely short average stage lenth, which was only 200 miles. Short stage length operations – when aircraft spend so much time on the ground earning nothing compared with their short-flying-time when they earn money – are notoriously difficult to make profitable; it was in large part the search for longer routes – for instance to Beirut and to the Persian Gulf, – which was, amongst the issues of conflict, understandably acutely irritating to BOAC.

Also during those years as Mr Lo Bao mentions, other mergers in Europe were being considered. The merger of some European airlines into Air Union was mooted and some steps taken towards implementation. They came to nothing, and Lord Douglas had throughout been firmly opposed to BEA's even considering joining. He predicted that the members of Air Union would be quarrelling "like Kilkennny cats", and events proved him right.

As a nationalised Corporation, the BEA Board thought it right to work in collabration with Goverment; some would say under the interference of Goverment. Interference certainly seems to have been the right word for the Minister's action which lead to the resignation of "Pops" D'Erlanger but so far as I know, BEA did not force issues with Goverment and never tried, for instance, to discontinue uneconomic operations in the Highlands and Islands of Scotland, nor wanted to do so. The BEA Board recognised that these air services were necessary to the local communities and, rightly or wrongly, saw it as the nationalised airline's duty to provide them in the absence of any other contenders. Personally, I did not see the collabration with Goverment over these years as amounting to interference in the pejorative sense of that word; Goverment's interference was often helpful to BEA.

During the years covered by Mr Lo Bao's most detailed history three figures stood out: Sholto Douglas, Peter Masefield and Tony Milward. Lord Douglas's strong leadership over 15 years made him a dominating figure in both BEA and in the world's airline industry; Peter Masefield's energy and enthusiasm were vital in firmly establishing BEA in its early years. Incidently, it is thanks to Peter Masefield's insistence that BEA's Annual Reports should be complete and comprehensive that Mr Lo Bao has been able to garner much of the information in his wonderfully complete History. It was these two men who, together with Tony Milward, were successful in welding BEA into a cohesive whole and establishing among its staff an almost family atmosphere which made them fiercly proud of the airline and of their part in it.

The years after the British Airways Board was set up, following the Edwards Committee's Report, were far from easy for its first Chairman, Sir David Nicolson, or any of us, in welding two fiercly individualistic airlines into one airline; David Nicolson was not helped by the lack of support from Ministers and senior Civil Servants. But all that is history, and one can only be proud and glad that British Airways is now such a dominating, successful and highly-regarded player on the world's civial avition stage.

January 1988

An illustrated History of

BRITISH EUROPEAN AIRWAYS

Contents

Introduction

From 1946 to 1947 British European Airways (BEA) was one of the world's leading airlines from many viewpoints. A comprehensive picture of its operations and aircraft is long overdue. This book attempts to fill the gap, and show the airlines slogan of 'Number One in Europe' was really justified. Most areas of BEA activity have been included, though the author has deliberatly left out a detailed consideration of the political reletionship between the Board and the various goverments between 1946 and 1974 to enable a more detailed consideration of operational matters to be given.

With an organisation like BEA, there are likely to be some areas of uncertainty, and some missing information. Anyone who can provide the author with information or corrections is welcome to contact him.

Many people helped me in writing this book. I would like to thank them all. But special thanks must go to Dudley Foy (British Airways Public Affairs Manager), Ron Roberts, Ron Rogers (formerly British Airways Helicopters Penzance now British International Helicopters Penzance), Ian Scott Hill (formerly Chairman of the British Airways Museum Committee), Graham Thorneycroft (RAF Museum Photographic section) and particularly Ron Wilson (British Airways Archivist).

I would like to dedicate this book to the memory of my father, Douglas Lo Bao (BEA and British Airways Station Superintendent Southampton) to whom I owe my interest in aviation and a lot more besides.

P. Lo Bao.
February 1989.

1946

Mix an August morning in 1946, an empty school, a fleet of Vikings and DC-3s and some ex-BOAC staff and you have the beginnings of BEA. Today new airlines are usually launched with a fanfare of publicity, demonstration flights, celebration meals and so on, but the beginnings of BEA on August 1st 1946 went almost unnoticed and there is no precise record of BEA's first scheduled service. It is believed to have been an 08.40 departure from Northolt to Athens, via Marseilles and Rome, flown by a DC-3. The low key start occurred because the routes to be flown by the new airline were already being operated by the BEA Division of BOAC. BEA emerged from that Division under the terms of the 1946 Civil Aviation Act, and took over the existing services.

The origins of British European Airways go back to March 20th 1945, when the war time coalition government published a White Paper, entitled 'British Air Transport' (cmd 6605). This document outlined post war policy for civil air transport, proposing it should be the prerogative of three Public Corporations. The three were: BOAC, which already existed, having been formed by the merger of Imperial Airways and British Airways in January 1939; British South American Airways, to be formed out of British Latin American Airways Limited, and British European Airways. BOAC would fly all intercontinental routes, except those to South America which would be in the hands of British South American. BEA would operate all domestic and European services. A second proposal for the provision of domestic and European air services had been presented to the government by Railway Air Services in October 1944. RAS suggested it should operate a comprehensive network of domestic and European services, to be flown by DH89s, DC-3s and Vikings. The network would be implemented in several phases, and the scheme financed by RAS extending the number of companies that had a financial stake in it. The government did not regard the plan with much enthusiasm preferring the 1945 White Paper proposals, as a result of which RAS ended up being merged into BEA! Following the 1945 General Election, the new Labour government announced in the House of Lords on November 1st 1945, that it would implement the proposals of the White Paper, which it did by introducing the 1946 Civil Aviation Bill.

While this was going on, the RAF commenced limited passenger services to Europe. These were flown by Number 110 Wing of RAF Transport Command from both Croydon and Northolt, using DC-3s. In preparation for the establishment of BEA, the routes were transferred to a specially created BEA Division of BOAC on February 4th 1946. The network linked London with Amsterdam, Brussels, Helsinki, Lisbon, Madrid, Paris, Gothenburg and Stockholm. At first aircraft flew in RAF markings and crews were RAF uniforms. However, from March 4th the aircraft began to fly in BOAC colours, with the crews in BOAC uniforms. The Division added a number of new destinations to its route system during March. On March 1st a weekly service to Gibraltar via Madrid opened; on March 11th a Northolt-Stavanger-Oslo service began, being flown three days a week, and on March 14th the London-Marseilles-Rome-Athens route was extended to Istanbul.

Back at Westminster, the 1946 Civil Aviation Bill finally became Law on August 1st, enabling BEA to begin operations in its own name. The Corporation inherited twenty four DC-3s and eight Vickers Viking IAs from BOAC. Most were technically on lease from BOAC, but gradually the majority had their ownership transferred officially to BEA. The DC-3s and Vikings provided the backbone for the airline's operations for the next seven years, although within seven days of its formation, BEA suffered the loss of one of the DC-3 fleet. G-AHCS crashed while attempting to land at Oslo, killing seven of the seventeen on board and injuring a further five.

The new Corporation's first Chairman was Sir Harold Hartley. He had a long career in civil aviation dating back to 1930 when he became involved in the aviation activities of the London Midland and Scottish Railway. From there he progressed to become Chairman of Railway Air Services, and in 1940 Chairman of the Associated Airways Joint Committee (AAJC). The AAJC had been established by the government to co-ordinate all domestic schedule flying for the duration of the War, from a base at Speke Airport, Liverpool. Having held these posts, Sir Harold was a natural choice to head BEA. His deputy was Air Commodore Whitney Straight, and the airline's Managing Director was Gerard d'Erlanger.

A close up view of operations at Northolt from the visitors enclosure. *(BA)*

Again, both men were well experienced in aviation, with d'Erlanger having served on the Board of the pre War British Airways. The remaining BEA Board Members were:

Sir Patrick Dollan.
(Chairman of the Scottish Advisory Council)
Mr. W.A. Edmenson.
(Chairman of the Northern Ireland Advisory Council)
Mr. I.J. Hayward.
Mr. A.H. Measures.

Apart from the seven man Board, there were two other key posts; Technical Manager and Head of Research and Long Term Development. P.A. Wills was appointed Technical Manager, and he faced an immediate problem -a chronic shortage of spares for the DC-3s. The shortage was so severe that at one time no less than a quarter of the fleet was grounded, requiring the leasing of DC-3s from BOAC on a fairly long term basis (aircraft involved included G-AGHH, 'GHU, 'GIO and 'GIT) and from independent operators on an ad-hoc basis. For example, on November 18th a Skyways DC-3 (G-AGBE) was chartered. Unfortunately the charter did not end as planned, with the aircraft making a forced landing in a French field! Independent airlines found the leasing of aircraft to BEA a welcome source of income, and the practice continued into 1948. Head of Research and Long Term Development was N.E. Rowe. From the aviation point of view he had probably the most interesting job in the Corporation. Over the next few years he was responsible for the establishment of the Helicopter Experimental Unit, the Gust Research Unit, and the evaluation of new aircraft types.

BEA's Head Office was located in what had been a school at Ruislip. The site was literally just across the road from the end of Northolt's main runway, and the noise of low flying Vikings and DC-3s became a part of everyday life for staff working there. It is said that new recruits literally ducked as they sat at their desks, when the loud roar of an arriving or departing Viking or DC-3 shook the window, floor and desk. To begin with BEA was allocated the building only as a temporary measure, with the educationalists keen to get their hands on the school again, especially since it had only been completed in 1939. BEA was equally determined not to let the premises go and a fight developed which eventually went right up to the Lord President of the Council, who ruled in BEA's favour. Bourne School became BEA's permanent Head Office, and remained so until the airline merged with BOAC in 1974. Afterwards it continued to be used by British Airways until December 1985. Harold Hartley quickly decided BEA's symbol would be a flying key, and Bourne School was renamed Keyline House. From there Sir Harold presided over 1,641 staff, 625 of whom had been transferred from BOAC.

BEA had its own Head Office, but it was still dependant on BOAC for a London booking office. BOAC allocated BEA six rooms in its Berkley Square office for the purpose. BEA also needed a town terminal in London, and again BOAC came to its rescue by allowing it to use the BOAC Victoria Air Terminal. The use of Berkley Square and Victoria continued until the summer of 1948, when BEA opened its own sales office at Dorland Hall in Lower Regents Street, and Kensington Air Station was brought into use as a town terminal. Construction of Kensington Air Station had begun on a site in Kensington High Street in 1947, and the terminal was officially opened on May 31st 1948. From there coaches ran to Northolt for each departure, and passengers could check-in at the town terminal, guaranteeing themselves a seat on the flight.

Initially BEA was organised into two divisions, the UK Division managed by Lieutenant Commander G.O. Waters, and the Continental Division under Anthony Milward. The UK Division was based at Liverpool, chosen because it had been the base of the AAJC. The Continental Division operated out of Northolt. There were a number of centralized departments serving both divisions, such as The Technical Department, The Planning Department, The Research and Long Term Development Department and the Policy Department. Plans existed for the formation of a Scottish Division to organise future internal operations in Scotland.

The Continental Division quickly expanded its route system. Prague came on line on August 7th, followed by Hamburg and Berlin on September 1st, Vienna via Frankfurt on September 2nd, Zurich on September 9th and Ankara on September 17th. Hopes of opening services to Warsaw and the Balkan States were thwarted by the reluctance of the governments concerned to give BEA operating rights. September saw the Vikings commence scheduled services. The first scheduled service to be flown by a Viking left Northolt for Copenhagen on the morning of September 1st, the aircraft used being G-AHOP commanded by Captain J.G. James. The next day Vikings appeared on the Oslo and Amsterdam services, while on October 6th G-AHOP began Viking services to Stockholm. From November 1st the type began to serve Gibraltar, Lisbon, Madrid and Prague. It was hoped the Vikings would be able to replace DC-3s on all European services, except for one or two destinations for which the type was technically unsuited.

The Viking operated as a twenty one seater aircraft, in a one class configuration. Seats were arranged in a double row down one side of the aircraft, and a single row on the other. Each seat had its own reading lamp, cold air vent, book rack and stewards call button. BEA began naming the Viking fleet with names beginning with the letter 'V'. As the fleet grew this began to cause a few problems, and some aircraft operated with rather bizarre names. For example: Vampire (G-AHPD), Vagabond (G-AGRW), and even Vilain (G-AIVO). Perhaps the names designed to inspire the least confidence from the travelling public were Veteran (G-AIVD) or Volatile (G-AJDI)! Some incidents were quite in keeping with these unusual names. One involved the failure of a Viking's hydraulics system as it was about to land at Northolt. Because the hydraulics were essential for the lowering of the flaps and undercarriage the event was viewed with some seriousness by the crew. Legend has it that the enterprising steward on board poured all remaining tea, coffee and drink into the hydraulics system to replace the lost fluid. Low and behold, down came the undercarriage and flaps and a safe landing was made. Vikings were rather slow and noisy aeroplanes, and being unpressurized they suffered from turbulence and icing. Flying through the Alps rather than above them was quite normal in winter as pilots sought to avoid icing. From April 1947 BEA began to take delivery of the twenty four Viking 1B. In all, fifty Viking 1Bs were delivered, G-AHPK being the first to arrive on April 15th, and G-AJJN the last on December 13th 1949. As the larger capacity aircraft arrived, the Viking IAs were disposed of generally through the Ministries of Supply or Transport.

While the Continental Division was busy developing its operations, the UK Division was in rather a different situation. The Labour government had decided all scheduled passenger services should be operated by the three Corporations, and that independent operators could only fly scheduled services under associate agreements with the Corporations. Such associate agreements would be exceptions rather than the rule. The 1946 Civil Aviation Act actually stated "It shall not be lawful for any persons other than the three Corporations and their associates to carry passengers or goods by air... upon any scheduled journey between two places, one of which is in the UK". Consequently BEA was faced with having to take over virtually all domestic routes itself, by absorbing the independent airlines currently working scheduled services. The majority of airlines involved were those flying under the AAJC banner, namely Railway Air Services, Great Western and Southern Airlines, Isle of Man Air Services and Scottish Airways. Included in the

Viking IA G-AHOP Inaurgurates commercial Viking services on September 1st with a flight from Northolt to Copenhagen. *(BA)*

take over were the names of several dormant airlines: Highland Airways, North Eastern Airways, West Coast Air Services and Western Isles Airways. Two non AAJC companies were also absorbed: Allied Airways and Channel Islands Airways (CIA). The scale of such take overs was a major one, and far too much to be successfully accomplished in 1946. Consequently the operators were granted permission to continue to fly their own services on behalf of BEA from August 2nd 1946 to January 31st 1947. After that date it was hoped BEA's UK Division would be able to take over the routes, aircraft and staff. The winter programme operated by the independent on behalf of BEA from October 7th was as follows:

Allied Airways
Aberdeen-Shetland. Daily except Sunday.
Aberdeen-Wick-Orkney-Shetland. Daily except Sunday.
Aberdeen-Orkney. Four times a week.
All operated by DH89.

Channel Islands Airways
Guernsey-Alderney. Four times a week.
Guernsey-Jersey. Four services times a day.
Southampton-Guernsey. Three services daily.
Southampton-Jersey. Three services each day.
Croydon-Guernsey. Daily.
Croydon-Jersey. Twice Daily.
All operated by DH89.

Great Western & Southern Airlines
Bristol-Southampton. Twice Daily.
Bristol-Cardiff. Four services a day.
Cardiff-Weston Super Mare. Eight services daily.
Land's End - Isles of Scilly. Four services daily except Sunday.
All operated by DH89.

Isle of Man Air Services
Liverpool-Isle of Man. Five services daily.
Manchester-Blackpool-Isle of Man. Twice daily.
Carlisle-Isle of Man. Daily.
All operated by DH89.

Railway Air Services
Croydon-Liverpool-Belfast. Daily. Commenced November 18th. JU52s were used painted in full BEA colours.
Liverpool-Belfast. Twice Daily.
Croydon-Belfast (direct) Twice Daily.
Croydon-Manchester-Belfast. Twice Daily.
Northolt-Glasgow-Aberdeen. Daily. Commenced on November 18th.
Operated by a mixture of JU52s, Avro 19s, DC-3s and DH89s.

Scottish Airways
Glasgow-Stornoway. Daily except Sunday.
Glasgow-Tiree-Barra-Benbecula. Daily except Sunday.
Glasgow-Campbeltown. Daily except Sunday.
Glasgow-Campbeltown-Islay. Daily except Sunday.
Glasgow-Belfast. Three services a day.
Glasgow-Orkney-Shetland. Daily except Sunday.
Aberdeen-Inverness. Four times a week.
Aberdeen-Inverness-Stornoway. Three services a week.
Inverness-Wick-Orkney. Twice Daily
Wick-Orkney. On Demand.
Operated by DC-3 or DH89.

For the moment BEA's UK Division had no services of its own to operate, but the Division was far from idle, planning the huge task of absorbing the independent airlines in 1947, and co-ordinating their services on its behalf until then.

As soon as BEA was established it began to look into the prospects of new aircraft to replace its existing fleet. At once the airline developed an interest in the Vickers VC2 project, eventually refined into the Viscount. The design had first been submitted to the government in June 1945. It proposed a twenty four seater airliner powered

DC-3 G-AGJZ about to depart from Northolt. *(BA)*

A busy scene at Northolt in 1947, Viking G-AIVJ in the company of DC-3s G-AGIW and G-AGZB, and a Scottish Airlines DC-3 (BA)

by four Rolls Royce Dart turbo-props, capable of flying at 297mph, at altitudes of up to 20,000 feet. The aircraft would be 63'9" in length, with a wing span of 88 feet. The initial design was improved by the end of 1946, to be a thirty two seater aircraft. R.C. Morgan, BEA's Chief Project and Development Engineer, conducted a thorough investigation into the suitability of the type for BEA operations, in the light of which several additional recommendations were made to Vickers to improve the design. One of the strangest was to replace the Darts with two Centaurus piston engines. His reasoning was that piston engines would be more suitable to the short sectors and low altitudes flown on many routes. However the idea was soon abandoned as the technical merits of the Dart engine became apparent. Close liaison with Vickers lead to the project developing into the Vickers V.655, able to carry forty three passengers at 333mph, and in turn it evolved into the Vickers V.700 in 1948, for which BEA eventually placed an order.

A second new type to be evaluated was the Airspeed Ambassador. The project was at a much more advanced stage than the Vickers one, the prototype already being under construction at Christchurch in Hampshire when BEA was formed. The Ambassador was a high winged monoplane powered by two Bristol Centaurus piston engines, and incorporating many modern innovations including full cabin pressurization. It would carry about thiry passengers, having an overall length of 88 feet and a wing span of 115 feet. BEA was not as enthusiastic about the Ambassador, even though the prototype, G-AGUA, made its first flight on July 10th 1947. Eventually it did place an order for twenty of the aircraft in September 1948, perhaps more due to governmental pressure than a total conviction of the aircraft's suitability for its needs.

A third design being considered was the Miles Marathon. BEA was about to inherit a large fleet of Rapide bi-planes and it realized their operational life was limited. The airline considered the Dove, Heron and Marathon as possible replacements, with the government pressurizing it towards the Marathon, a seventeen seat high winged monoplane powered by either four Rolls Royce Mamba turbo-props or four Gipsy Queen piston engines. In December 1946 BEA, again under strong governmental pressure, placed an order for twenty five Mamba powered Marathons to replace the Rapide fleet. It anticipated operating the Marathons in a fourteen seat configuration with the additional space being given over to freight. Up to half a ton could be carried. The order for the Marathon became a long drawn out affair, and the aircraft never entered BEA service. The airline made numerous changes to the details of the order, for example in 1950 BEA instructed Miles that they required aircraft powered by the Gipsy Queen engine, and at the same time reduced the size of the order from twenty five to twelve. Later the order size was cut to seven, and finally in April 1952 BEA cancelled it altogether. It was cancelled because of the high operating costs of the aircraft. Trials with a Marathon in the late summer of 1951 (G-ALUB) showed its operating costs to be £31 an hour, compared with the Rapides of a mere £9-10/-. Given the Rapides made huge losses with those costs there was no hope for economic operations with Marathons. Granted the Marathon's capacity was double that of the DH89, but the small loads on its prospective routes did not justify the higher capacity.

At the same time as BEA placed its original Marathon order, it ordered another new type, the Cunliffe Owen Concordia. Two aircraft were ordered, one to be used for radio research and the other for development flying. BEA indicated that if the type proved successful a larger order may be placed in the future. The Concordia was a tricycle undercarriaged, low wing monoplane, powered by two Alvis Leonides piston engines, and capable of carrying up to ten passengers. The order made even less progress than the Marathon one. The prototype Concordia flew at Southampton in May 1947, and Cunliffe Owen laid

Douglas DC-3 G-AGIP is seen at Northolt during the winter of 1947. *(BA)*

down an initial production batch of six aircraft, two of which were for BEA. But in November 1947 Cuncliffe Owen concluded there was insufficient sales potential for the type, and abandoned the project. BEA never got its Concordias or its Marathons!

BEA did not select a single type to replace the Rapide. Instead Heron Is were purchased for Scotland, and Heron 2s were to have replaced Rapides in the Channel Isles, but for a route swap concluded with Jersey Airlines in 1956. The other bastion of Rapide operations was the Land's End-Isles of Scilly route. There the type soldiered on on until 1964, when it was replaced with the S.61 helicopters.There is a suggestion that BEA might have ordered a much larger fleet of Herons, as replacements for the Rapides, if it had not been for the government pushing the airline towards a Marathon order.

Under the terms of the 1946 Civil Aviation Act BEA was required to establish Regional Advisory Councils. These were designed to help keep BEA in tune with particular regional needs, and to begin with there were two such bodies, one for Scotland and one for Northern Ireland. Later Advisory Councils for both the Channel Isles and England and Wales were established. The Councils in various guises, continued to operate for the next twenty years and provided a very valuable way of keeping BEA aware of regional needs.

The Regional Advisory Councils may have provided an example of success but there were many problems to be faced too. The general economic situation, both at home and in Europe was not good. In particular the airline had to contend with rationing, foreign currency restrictions and considerable limitations on ordinary people regarding travel to Europe. A further difficulty was the continuation of the government's priority booking service to ensure its personnel were always given seats, meaning sometimes the Corporation had to turn away business traffic. The situation was eased in February 1947 when the government ended the priority booking system on most routes, though not those to Berlin, Prague or Vienna.

The most serious problem of all came in December:- the grounding of the whole Viking fleet due to problems with the aircrafts de-icing system. Following several incidents when control surfaces had iced up, the airline felt compelled to ground the type pending modification. From December 8th all Vikings were withdrawn from commercial operations. The chief problem was icing on the tail plane which caused the elevators to become out of balance and made the aircraft very difficult to control. Quite serious modifications were required to the shape and balance of the elevators as well as to the de-icing system itself. Capacity for de-icing fluid was raised to 62 gallons and the dispensing of the fluid over the aircrafts leading edges was also improved. But there was a penalty for the modification. The greater weight meant fuel capacity had to be cut from 750 gallons to 692 to compensate. Vikings remained out of service until April 1947, except for a handful which operated training details from Aldermaston. The withdrawal of the type meant the DC-3 fleet was entirely responsible for the schedules and the fleet was fully stretched. Delays and re-routings were inevitable, and the London-Zurich route was entirely suspended because of the shortage of aircraft, all of which did little to establish a good reputation for the new airline.

1947

1947 began not just with the problems caused by the grounding of the Vikings, but also with the massive task of integrating the AAJC companies. The temporary operating agreements with them, plus Allied Airways and Channel Islands Airways ran out on January 31st. All the operators involved, except for the moment Allied Airways and Channel Islands Airways, were formally absorbed into BEA on February 1st. The take overs by BEA caused a lot of anger and sadness amongst many of the staff of the airlines involved, and the inhabitants of the communities they served. Often senior staff found themselves being offered much lower positions in BEA, and a few were offered none at all. There was some bitterness at what appeared to be the rather high handed and uncaring approach by one or two senior BEA staff in London. Things were particularly bad in Scotland, where residents of the Highland and Island communities feared their special needs would be ignored by BEA's central planners. Allied Airways and Channel Islands Airways tried to remain independent, but despite hard fought battles neither succeeded. The governments of the Channel Islands argued they were outside the scope of the 1946 Civil Aviation Act, and should be allowed to keep their own airline. Whitehall was not impressed and insisted that Channel Islands Airways should become part of BEA. After some heated exchanges the Channel Isles reluctantly agreed, and BEA formally took over Channel Islands Airways on April 1st. Any reluctance on the part of Channel Islands Airways staff to join BEA was soon removed when the Corporation announced its rates of pay. These were found to be considerably higher than those paid by CIA. However many Jersey residents were incensed on April 1st when BEA sent a JU52 to the Island carrying BEA stationary, uniforms, signs and so on. The last JU52 to be seen in the Island had been flown by the Luftwaffe during the German Occupation of the Channel Islands, and the arrival of the BEA machine revived many bitter memories. It was seen as another example of the insensitivity of London managers to local situations. Allied Airways held out a few more days, claiming that as it had never been part of the AAJC it should remain independent. Its battle was no more successful, and on April 17th it was formally incorporated into BEA. The take overs meant BEA inherited ten JU52s, thirteen Avro 19s, thirty nine Rapides, two DC-3s, a DH84 and a DH Moth.

Domestic services were organised into two divisions. The original UK Division was sub-divided into an English Division and a Scottish Division. The English Division was headed by G.O. Waters, and the Scottish by R. McKean. The headquarters of the English Division continued to be Speke Airport Liverpool, while naturally enough the headquarters of the Scottish Division was Glasgow's Renfrew Airport. On February 1st the first domestic trunk route to be flown by BEA, in its own right, was the 13.25 Northolt-Renfrew via Prestwick service. It was worked by DC-3 G-AGYZ commanded by Captain Ramsden. However the Corporation's domestic operations ran into an immediate difficulty - a shortage of serviceable aircraft. Equipment had to be chartered from independent carriers. In Scotland between February 1st and July 31st, Scottish Airlines were contracted to fly many of the services from Renfrew and Prestwick to Northolt using a DC-3, and the Glasgow-Belfast route using a Fokker F.22 (a four engined high winged monoplane).

Improvements on the domestic network came quickly. On March 20th JU52s, which BEA called Jupiters, began a non-stop Croydon-Belfast service with G-AHOF operating the inaugural flight crewed by Captains Moyniham and Yapp. Meanwhile on May 19th the Corporation launched its longest domestic service, from Northolt to Sumburgh in the Shetland Isles, via Edinburgh and Aberdeen. The route was flown six days a week. Also on May 19th DC-3s replaced the Jupiters on the London-Belfast service, operating from Northolt instead of Croydon. The JU52s were relegated to operating Scottish internal services from Glasgow to Inverness or Aberdeen, Orkney and Shetland, and from Glasgow and Inverness to Stornoway.

The fleet of JU52s was inherited from Railway Air Services and Scottish Airways, having originally come from Germany as war reparations. Crews found the type easy to fly, light on the controls and sedate, with a landing speed of just 60mph. Internally the cabin was furnished in royal blue. BEA spent (some would say wasted) £12,500 modifying each aircraft. The JU52 did have its peculiarities, the coiled springs of the undercarriage jangled loudly when taxying, alarming some passengers, and the heating system gave a loud shriek when it was

At Croydon, JU52 G-AHOG prepare's for departure to Belfast *(BA)*

turned on. The shriek was followed by a blast of hot air through the floor vents. Stewards quickly learnt the wisdom of briefing passengers about these peculiarities before the flight, rather than having to try to calm them down once they had experienced the problems! Another difficulty faced in JU52 operations was the dependence on ground power units to start the engines. Outside Glasgow and Edinburgh none of the Scottish stations were equipped with them, meaning at least one engine had to be kept running during turn-rounds. However if bad weather or technical problems forced the pilot to shut down the engines a long wait ensued while a ground power unit was flown out from Glasgow to re-start the JU52. More than one passenger wrote to BEA pointing out how much more reliable the Scottish Airways Rapide service had been. Technically the biggest problem with the JU52 was the chronic lack of useable spares. There were plenty of spares, but most of them were found to be substandard and quite useless. Consequently the airline decided to retire the JU52s from service on August 31st. Retirement of the Jupiters was hastened by a little known incident occuring early in August. On a trip between Kirkwall and Aberdeen the exhaust pipe on one engine fractured, causing carbon monoxide gas to seep into the cockpit almost asphyxicating the crew. The pilot shut down each engine in turn to locate the problem exhaust pipe, but by the time he had found the right engine the atmosphere in the cockpit was getting very foul even with the windows open. The aircraft eventually made a safe landing at Aberdeen, and the failure of the exhaust pipe was traced to the problem of poor quality parts. The last service operated by the type is believed to have been a non-scheduled flight from Glasgow to Liverpool on August 31st. Most of the fleet was flown to Manchester and parked behind the BEA hangar, until the aircraft were taken for scrapping at Warrington.

Among the more unusual work undertaken by the Jupiters was the relief of the Dubh Artach lighthouse off the Scottish west coast. Heavy seas had prevented the keepers receiving fresh supplies for some weeks, so Trinity House chartered one of the JU52s to drop supplies. The aircraft made several slow passes over the islet and on each pass bundles of supplies were dropped. The low flying speed of the aircraft made it ideal for the task.

Another type BEA inherited, and used on some Northern Ireland routes, was the Avro 19. It was not very suitable for passenger operations. Fuselage width was so narrow that it was impossible to arrange seats in rows opposite each other. Instead seats had to be staggered each side of the cabin. If a passenger was unlucky enough to need the toilet he found it tucked away behind a curtain, and it proved to be no more than an elsan. Many unwary passengers barked their shins on the mainspar which passed through the cabin, and the aircraft was noted for excessive vibration and noise. All these problems meant BEA used the aircraft as little as possible, and retired them as quickly as it could. They had ceased to operate passenger services by early 1948, though four, (G-AHII, 'HIK, 'HXL, 'HXM), did soldier on until the early 1950s as training aircraft.

Until May 1947 training was undertaken on behalf of BEA by BOAC at Aldermaston, using Vikings, Avro 19s and DC-3s. On May 1st 1947 BEA and BOAC jointly formed a training subsidiary, called Airways Training Limited. The company would train aircrew, and ground staff, for both Corporations from the Aldermaston base previously used by BOAC. The idea seemed excellent especially as there were many military pilots to be converted to civilian standards, giving the company an additional source of revenue. As it turned out Airways Training was something of an economic disaster, losing £22,303 in its first year of operation. Neither BEA or BOAC could subsidize that sort of loss, and the Corporations quickly realized losses could only grow once the bulge of military pilots had been converted to civilian standards. The new company was closed on September 30th 1948. After the closure of Airways Training BEA took full responsiblity for training its own crews. A small training unit was established, consisting of eight senior Captains, based at Cranfield airfield, using four ex-Airways Training Avro 19s (G-AHII 'HIK, 'HXL, 'HXM). Again it did not prove to be the best solution, as Cranfield was remote from the main operating bases of Northolt and Glasgow. BEA finally concluded the only sensible course was to transfer training to Northolt, and the Cranfield base was closed in October 1949, saving about £30,000 per year.

March 31st saw the end of BEA's first financial year (or to be more correct eight months). The first Report and Accounts was published early in the summer to summarize the financial position of the Corporation and comment on its activities. The document made gloomy financial reading, with BEA making a loss of £2,157,937 in 1946/47. The loss was attributed to a combination of factors including:

a) Severe technical problems and shortage of spares with DC-3s, JU52s and Vikings.
b) Severe winter weather with fog and snow which disrupted operations.
c) The costs of operating such a diverse fleet of aircraft.
d) The costs incurred in establishing the airline and incorporating the AAJC companies.
e) The poor economic conditions throughout Britain and Europe.

The Report and Accounts contained a whole variety of statistical data about the airline's operations. It showed that between August 1946 and March 1947 269,678 revenue earning passengers had been carried, producing an average load factor of 67.9%. If that does not seem many passengers it must be remembered that for most of the time there were no domestic services, and international frequencies were very restricted. 668 tons of cargo and 510 tons of mail were uplifted, and the fleet clocked up a total of 23,200 revenue flying hours. BEA had scheduled 10,191 flights to operate, of which 1,566 were cancelled mainly due to aircraft shortage or weather, and a further 208 were not completed. By March 31st staffing levels had risen to 5,731.

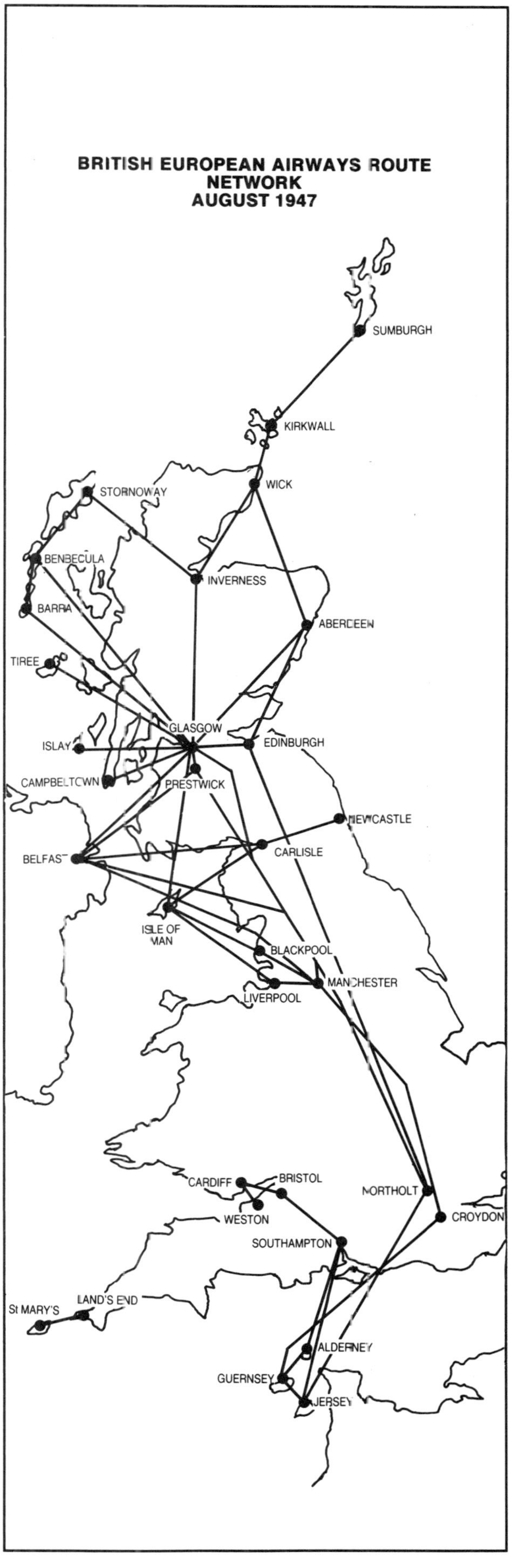

BRITISH EUROPEAN AIRWAYS ROUTE NETWORK AUGUST 1947

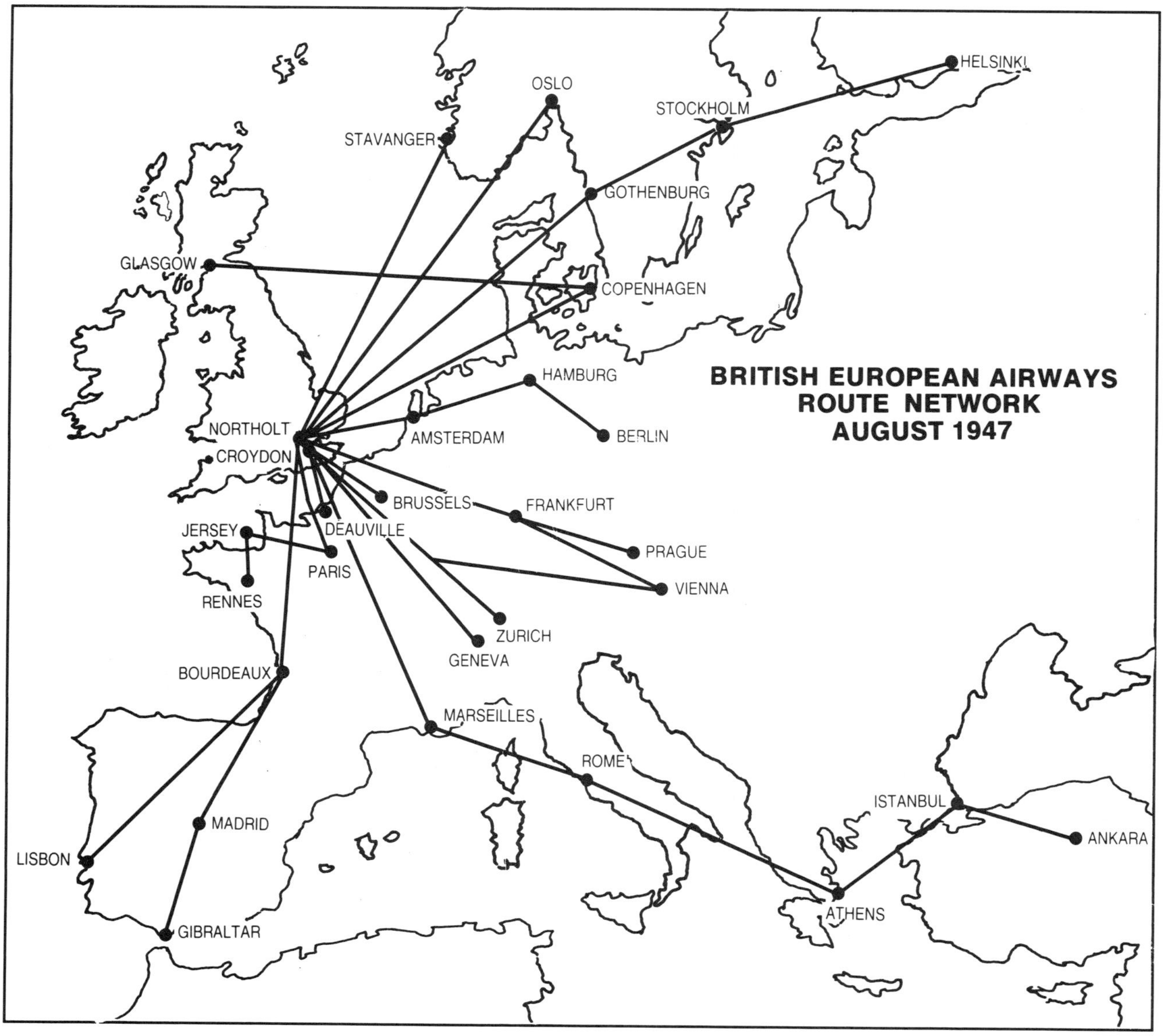

BEA planned to start its first full summer programme of international and domestic service on April 21st, but there were real fears this might be wrecked if the Vikings were not returned to service in time. They were ready for April 21st, but only just. The first scheduled Viking flight to operate, since December 7th 1946, left Northolt on the morning of April 20th, one day before the commencement of the summer timetable, when G-AHPA departed for Oslo. On the same day G-AHPF flew a Prague service. The next day, April 21st, G-AHPM operated a route proving service to Geneva, and on April 22nd G-AHPN recommenced Viking services to Copenhagen and G-AHPO to Madrid and Gibraltar. By the end of May the whole fleet was back in service.

The summer programme was very extensive. On the domestic trunk routes there were nineteen flights a week from Northolt to Belfast, thirteen to Glasgow, six to Prestwick, and six to Edinburgh-Aberdeen-Sumburgh. From Croydon a twice daily DH 89 service ran to Manchester and Liverpool. This route was transferred to Northolt on October 6th, after which it was flown once a day, Monday to Saturday, with a DC-3. Meanwhile services to the Isle of Man ran from Liverpool, Carlisle, Blackpool, Glasgow, Manchester and Belfast. The busiest of these was from Liverpool with up to twelve daily flights, while at the other extreme there was only one flight a day from Ronaldsway to Glasgow. On the Channel Islands network considerable expansion took place. From April 21st the London-Jersey flights began to operate entirely from Northolt, using DC-3s, replacing the Rapide service from Croydon. G-AGIP and G-AHCU both flew Northolt-Jersey services on April 21st. For August, forty two flights a week were scheduled between Northolt and Jersey. However the busiest route to the Channel Isles, at least in terms of the number of flights, were those from Southampton. In August 1947 there were forty four flights a week to Jersey, Forty to Guernsey and two to Alderney, all operated by Rapide aircraft. The summer timetable included the limited use of Vikings on the domestic network. Daily Northolt-Prestwick and Northolt-Glasgow services were scheduled for the type from August 11th with G-AHPK flying the first service. the timetable also showed a daily Glasgow-Belfast Viking Service, operated by the aircraft that had come up from Northolt, although it is not certain whether it was ever flown by Vikings. In the event Vikings did not last long on the domestic scene, and were phased out in favour of the DC-3s in December.

Many other UK routes had high frequencies scheduled for the summer. There were sixty three flights a week between Land's End and the Isles of Scilly, sixty three between Cardiff and Bristol, fifty two between Cardiff and Weston Super Mare, and ninety five between Jersey and Guernsey. Other routes were less frequent, for example there were twelve flights a week over the Belfast-Carlisle-Newcastle route. Carlisle was served by BEA for just one summer, with services being withdrawn on October 6th. Nevertheless for the summer of 1947 it had up to seven arrivals and departures each day, all operated by Rapides.

BEA CARLISLE (August)

Arrivals

E343A	09.20	Isle of Man.
E388A	10.20	Belfast.
E343B	11.50	Isle of Man.
E388N	12.25	Newcastle.
E343C	15.00	Isle of Man.
E388C	16.20	Belfast.
E388P	18.25	Newcastle.

Departures

E343N.	09.44	Isle of Man
E388A.	10.35	Newcastle
E343D.	12.10	Isle of Man
E388N.	12.45	Belfast
E343Q.	15.25	Isle of Man
E388C.	16.35	Newcastle
E388P.	18.45	Belfast

In total the English Division, alone, offered 52,000 seats a week in the summer peak, flying 1,775 services compared with just 457 in February 1947. The Scottish Division scheduled 372 flights a week over its network covering the large cities like Glasgow, Aberdeen and Edinburgh, and small remote Islands like Tiree and Barra.

The European Division was not left behind either. Vikings began to operate the weekly service to Ankara, while Geneva came on line on May 19th with a daily service by the type. BEA began two international services from the provinces, the first being a Glasgow-Copenhagen flight, commencing on August 11th, and flown three times a week by Viking. G-AIVC operated the first service, which was actually from Copenhagen to Glasgow. Traffic returns on the service were very poor, and the airline abandoned the route on December 1st. The second regional international route was from Jersey to Paris. One flight a week was scheduled on Saturdays, flown by a DC-3. BE621A was timed to depart from Jersey at 12.20, with the return trip (BE621N) leaving Le Bourget at 15.20. Like the Glasgow to Copenhagen route, it did not attract many passengers, and BEA decided to suspend flights from October 6th. For the summer the European Division offered a total of 188 weekly flights, most of which originated from Northolt.

Passengers and their relatives, who did not use the BEA coach service from Victoria, sometimes encountered problems in reaching the airport. Part of the problem lay in its name. Despite being called Northolt Airport it was actually sited in Ruislip. Alighting at Northolt underground station was a common, if time consuming, mistake. Passengers and staff alike, found the airport difficult to reach by public transport at evenings and over week-ends, when buses were almost non-existent. Once passengers had arrived at Northolt things were much more relaxed than at a major international airport today. Each flight was checked-in at a separate check-in desk and passengers waited for the aircraft in a small lounge, without the duty free shop and other facilities found in most modern international terminals. Their friends and relatives could wave good-bye from the visitors

Avro 19, G-AGUX, at the English Division Headquarters at Speke. *(J. Stroud)*

BEA's Gust Research Unit flew two Mosquito PR34s. G-AJZE is seen here at Cranfield. *(J. Stroud)*

enclosure, a grass area in front of the terminal, and right by the aircraft.

For the first time in its short life BEA began to operate pure freighter services in the summer of 1947, with the introduction of a Northolt-Prague service, via Brussels, operated by a DC-3 every day except Sunday. The service commenced on the night of August 10th with a departure from Northolt at 00.55, flown by G-AGYZ. It was quickly realized that Prague would not generate much freight once the volume of diplomatic cargo had diminished, and from October 1948 the service operated only to Brussels. From the small beginning BEA slowly established a comprehensive network of pure freighter services.

As the summer programme was gaining momentum, two interesting projects were embarked upon by N.E. Rowe's Research and Long Term Development Unit, the formation of the BEA Helicopter Experimental Unit, and the formation of the Gust Research Unit. On June 26th the BEA Board decided to order five helicopters from the USA; three S.51s and two Bell 47s. Yeovil was selected as the base, since it was the home of Britain's helicopter manufacturer, Westland. The helicopters arrived by sea in the early autumn; and made their first public appearance at Hampden Park in Glasgow on September 28th when S.51s G-AJOR and 'KCU were demonstrated. Exactly what the HEU was supposed to do was uncertain, but BEA felt it essential to be involved in the development of helicopter operations. (A full history of BEA/BA Helicopter operations, written by the author, has been published by Air Britain.)

The Gust Research Unit was set up in collaboration with the Meteorological Office and various government departments to consider the nature and frequency of clear air gusts and sudden violent turbulence at altitudes of over 20,000 feet. Such information was needed to prepare for the operations of Comets and Viscounts. Two Mosquito PR34s were allocated to the Unit by the government. Each aircraft was equipped with weather radar and three accelerometers to measure the gusts. Cranfield was selected for the Unit's base, and both Mosquitos were flown there in January 1948 for the necessary modifications which were carried out by the College of Aeronautics. The first, allocated the civil registration G-AJZE, was delivered to BEA in March, the second, G-AJZF, did not enter service until June. Once again shortage of spares was the problem. 'JZE could only be kept airworthy by 'borrowing' parts from 'JZF. The first experimental flight made by the Gust Research Unit occured on April 22nd 1948. G-AJZE, piloted by First Officer Thomas, flew a Cranfield-Lisbon sortie, in three hours at altitudes varying from 12,000 to 40,000 feet. The aircraft flew at an average speed at 375 mph. Flying the Mosquito was very demanding. A saw tooth flight path was followed with constant changes in altitude. In 1948/49 the Unit flew seventy seven research flights, clocking up 247 flying hours. By January 1949 seven cases of clear air turbulence had been found and investigated by the aircraft. One hazard encountered by the pilots was that the cockpit canopy of the aircraft tended to crack at high altitudes due to the extreme cold, making the remainder of the flight rather cold and draughty! Neither 'JZE or 'JZF were formally owned by BEA, but loaned from the Ministry of Supply. The Corporation did not maintain the aircraft either, that was done by the College of Aeronautics. In January 1950 the Unit was closed down, though it had made its last research flight as early as November 1949. The reason for closure was simple - economy. It had been expected that the programme would go on well into 1950, but government economies meant the funding for the operation was halted, and the Unit closed. The Mosquitos were returned to the Ministry of Supply and eventually re-entered RAF service. The two aircraft had flown 92,300 miles and obtained some useful data on the whole subject of clear air turbulence. However, a complete understanding of clear air turbulence was still a long way off.

Right from the outset, BEA was responsible for assisting a number of airlines to begin operations taking a financial stake in most of them. These airlines were known as associate companies. By May 1947 the BEA associate companies included Alitalia, BEA holding 41% of its shares; Aer Lingus in which BEA had a 30% holding, Cyprus Airways with a 44% BEA holding, Gibraltar Airways in which BEA owned 51% of shares, Malta Airlines with a 34% BEA share and TAE (Greece) in which BEA held 15% of shares. There were also one or two non airline associate companies, the best known of which was International Aeradio. Formed on January 9th 1947 IAL was owned by the government, BEA and BOAC. Its purpose was to provide radio, radar and navigation services at airports. The company proved very successful and has become a major provider of such services world wide. One of the smallest associate companies owned by BEA was the Guernsey Aero Club. BEA obtained control of the organisation in February when it took over Great Western and Southern Airlines, who owned it. Under BEA the Guernsey Aero Club did not function, and its name was added to the list of dormant companies owned by the Corporation. In general, it is beyond the scope of this book to deal in detail with the history of these and the other associate companies, unless they are of particular relevance to BEA's history. In that context, BEA Rapides began to operate the Gibraltar-Tangier route for Gibraltar Airways on August 30th. The service was flown four times a day, with G-AKDX operating the first days schedules. Meanwhile BEA was helping Alitalia equip itself for operations. The Corporation purchased five Lancastrians and a Lancaster which were then modified and delivered to Alitalia later in 1947 and in 1948. Pilot training for Alitalia was undertaken from White Waltham using the Lancaster. BEA's Avro Anson, G-AHBN, was also transferred to Alitalia in 1948.

1947 saw the Corporation experience some changes in key personnel, the most important of which was the arrival of a new Chairman. Sir Harold Hartley retired in 1947, being replaced by Gerard d' Erlanger, formerly Chief Excutive. With his considerable experience it was hoped he might be able to get the airline's financial position into a better state, but he was well aware of the enormity of the task, and said in a Christmas message to the staff: "I cannot venture too far out into the cheerful glow traditionally associated with a white Christmas." Mr d'Erlanger was to be assisted by J.V. Wood, who came to BEA from BOAC and assumed the post of Managing Director. The new management began to take steps to move the airline into better economic health. Their first move was to merge the English and Scottish Divisions into one unit managed by G.O. Waters, which did not meet with the approval of many of the senior staff in Scotland, some of whom resigned from BEA in protest.

BEA Rapide in the airlines earliest colour scheme of silver with red titling. *(BA)*

Another effort at cost cutting was implemented on May 19th, when the Corporation began to charge for in flight catering. It believed its rival would soon follow suit, thereby preventing a loss of traffic to them. A sad miscalculation! Other airlines did not withdraw free catering, and BEA did begin to lose passengers. There was only one answer, to re-introduce free meals, which the airline did on international services in March 1948, and on domestic routes in May 1948.

Perhaps the best remembered areas of cost cutting were the winter schedules and staff reductions. The 1947/48 winter timetable commenced on October 6th and marked the abolition of many domestic routes on the grounds of economy. Those closed for good were Cardiff-Weston Super Mare, Cardiff-Bristol, Bristol-Southampton, Isle of Man-Carlisle, Isle of Man-Blackpool-Manchester, Belfast-Carlisle-Newcastle, Northolt-Prestwick and Prestwick-Belfast. Many would have been suspended for the winter anyway, but BEA made it clear it did not intend to re-open them. Only one of these routes was ever re-opened by BEA; Isle of Man to Manchester, which recommenced in 1951. Other domestic routes were suspended just for the winter, including Northolt-Edinburgh, Croydon-Guernsey, and Isle of Man-Glasgow. Tremendous protests were raised in Edinburgh and Guernsey. The Scots felt indignant that their capital was no longer linked to London, and the people of Guernsey loudly complained that Channel Islands Airways would never have done this to them. BEA learnt its lesson and London-Edinburgh and Guernsey services were not suspended again.

With the suspension of the Croydon-Guernsey link came the closure of the BEA station at Croydon. At one time services to Belfast, Guernsey, Jersey, Liverpool and Manchester had operated from there, together with international services to Deauville and Helsinki via Amsterdam, Copenhagen, Gothenburg and Stockholm. By October 6th only the Guernsey service remained, and when it was suspended (on November 1st) BEA staff were withdrawn. On November 1st there were three departures for Guernsey, at 12.00, 12.05 and 17.00, all Rapide operated, and the last flight was flown by G-AGIF. When London-Guernsey services recommenced, Northolt was used as the terminal. November 1st was not quite the end of BEA involvement at Croydon. In the summers of 1948 and 1949 a Croydon-Deauville service was operated by the airline using Doves leased from Olley Air Services.

International services did not escape pruning either, schedules were considerably curtailed, and one route was axed entirely, the Croydon-Helsinki service. Since April 23rd it had been flown by Consul aircraft leased from Westminster Airways, since traffic did not justify using a Viking. Even the small capacity of the Consul could not save the route and on October 6th it ended. Helsinki was not regularly connected to the network again until 1962. The wisdom of general reductions in international frequencies was more than confirmed by the introduction of further foreign travel restrictions by the government. Even with the cut backs two new routes were launched, London to Malta, and London to Nicosia. The route to Nicosia commenced on October 6th, via Marseilles, Rome and Athens. The Athens-Nicosia sector was operated under charter to Cyprus Airways. Services to Malta began on December 1st, via Marseilles and Rome. Both routes were flown by Viking, and initially operated once a week.

The other major effort to cut costs was the attempt to reduce staffing levels by about 2,000, or approximately one third of the total. To achieve this, local contract staff abroad were made redundant, while at home it was hoped cuts could come by natural wasteage with as few redundancies as possible. The need for staff cuts was well illustrated at Islay in the Inner Hebrides; BEA employed twelve staff there to handle one flight a day in the winter, and fifteen to handle two a day in the summer! The whole business of staff cuts proved very difficult with strong union opposition. Eventually, about 700 staff were made redundant and 1,500 left through natural wasteage. However department managers made such good cases for the replacement of many who had left voluntarily, that in the end staff levels were only reduced from 7,800 to 7,069. The whole matter did little to boost staff morale, especially as there were so many rumours and counter rumours circulating, which the management did little to scotch. In 1949 the whole issue of staff cuts was again tackled, with a little more success.

A final effort at economy was the alteration of the fare structure. Most fares were raised from October 6th by about 15%, but there were a few reductions to generate traffic on certain routes. For example the fare on the Manchester-London service was cut by 4/- single. Some fares on Scottish internal routes were also cut, but once again the States of Guernsey had something to complain about when the airline announced the single fare to Guernsey would rise from £4-5/- to £5-1/-, and that, for a service via Jersey. The States complained that BEA cut its services to the Island and then charged you more for the privilege!

There are many stories about amusing incidents during the early days of operations; so much so that it is difficult to know which to include and which to leave out. One famous Scottish Captain boarded his Rapide, in civilian clothes, with the other passengers, and sat in a passenger seat. After a few minutes he loudly announced that if the pilot did not appear soon he would have a go at flying the aeroplane. Of course no pilot materialized, so he marched up to the Rapide's cockpit, and asked the Radio Operator (who was clearly in league with him) what to do. The Radio Operator showed him what he thought the pilots usually did to make the aircraft fly, and soon the Rapide was airborne. What the passengers felt is not recorded, or perhaps not recordable! Not to be outdone, a certain Jersey based Rapide Captain decided to take the stunt one stage further. He boarded his aircraft in civilian clothes, and carrying a blind man's white walking stick. After sitting in a passenger seat for a while, he began to complain loudly that the pilot was late. He then got up and walked to the cockpit, started up the engines and took off!

1948

The extent of the problems facing BEA were well illustrated by the scale of the financial losses incurred by the Corporation in the financial year 1947/48, the Report and Accounts showed a loss of £3,573,989. Quite clearly there was a long way to go before the airline's economic situation reached anything like stability. Some statistics for the financial year did give a glimmer of hope. Passengers carried had risen to 511,522, with the largest traffic growth being on the European services where there was a 69.8% increase. Freight traffic was up an encouraging 124% on European routes, but only 22% on domestic routes. Of course 1947/48 was BEA's first full financial year, meaning direct comparisons with 1946/47 are a little misleading. Nevertheless traffic returns were improving.

Hoping to build traffic even further, BEA began a cautiously expansive summer programme on April 18th. One new feature included was a non-stop Northolt-Isle of Man service flown daily with a DC-3. There was an increase in frequency on the London-Glasgow services, as well as on routes to Northern Ireland and the Channel Islands. At Land's End, an hourly service to the Scillies was operated on summer Saturdays, except over lunch time. Direct services between London and Edinburg and Guernsey were re-instated. But out went the Northolt-Manchester-Liverpool schedule because of poor passenger loads. Flights ended on April 17th. Between December 1947 and February 1948 the average load on the route had been just five passengers.

The European network included in its summer timetable a new service from Northolt to Nice, with flights operating from June 1st. Nice proved an immediate success and frequencies were quickly increased. Nice became so popular that services routing through Marseilles were all re-routed through Nice from April 1949. Virtually all the international network was now flown by Vikings, except services to Oslo, Hamburg and Berlin. Oslo had been found unsuitable for regular Viking operations, while aircraft using Hamburg and Berlin had to be equipped with RAF landing aids, something present in the DC-3s but not the Vikings. Capacity on the Viking fleet was raised to twenty seven passengers by adding three extra seats, while DC-3 capacity was also raised, from twenty one to twenty eight.

Passengers boarding DC-3 G-AHCT for Jersey in the summer of 1947. *(BA)*

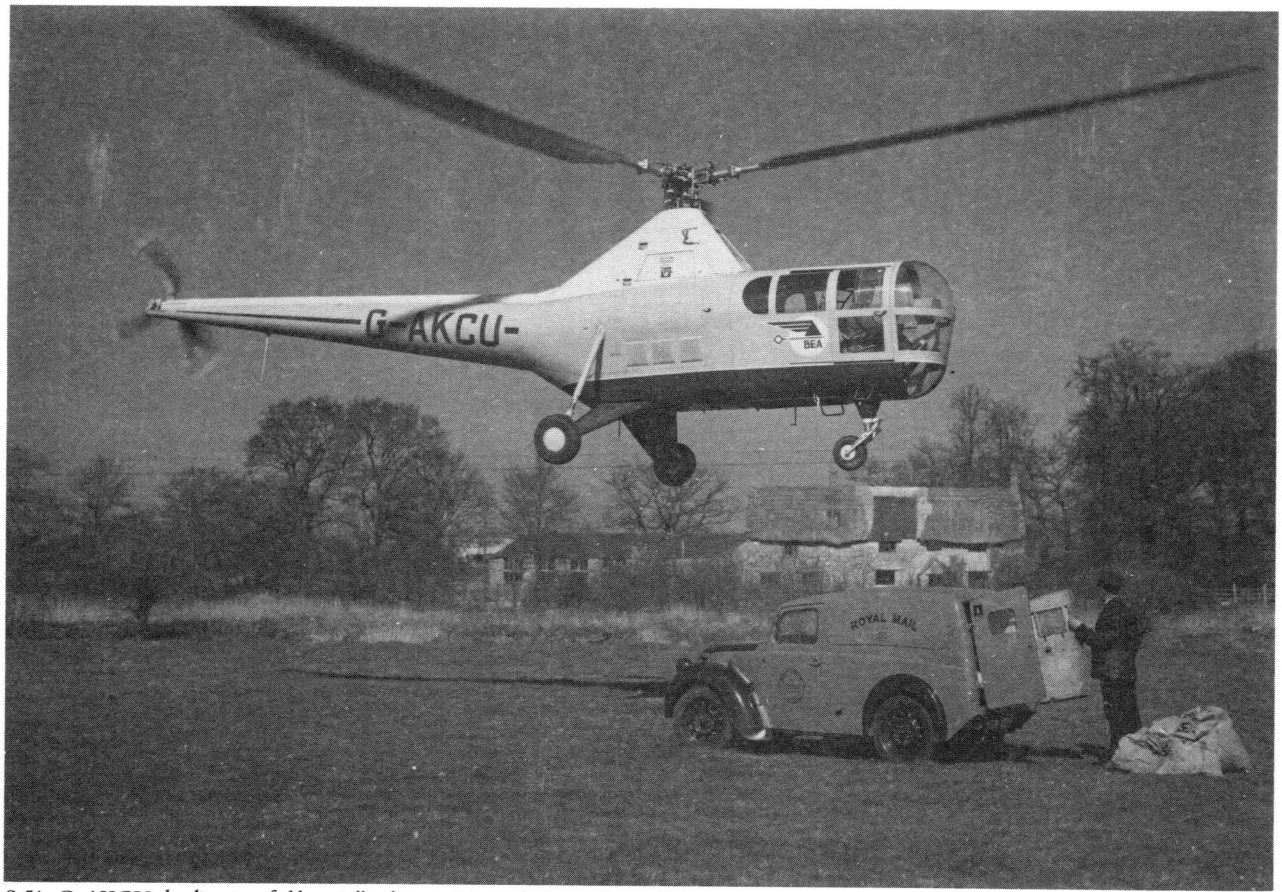

S.51, G-AKCU, landing in a field at Gillingham in Dorset during trail mail flights in 1948. (BIH)

Traffic on both European and internal services did begin to grow and in August the airline carried 84,752 passengers as compared with 77,031 in the August of 1947. In an attempt to improve its image, BEA began issuing passenger comment cards. The cards were issued one day each month, and gave passengers an opportunity to comment on BEA booking facilities, town terminals, airport facilities and in-flight service. Comments lead to the airline providing route maps on board aircraft for passenger's information, and improving the details shown on tickets.

BEA did not always manage to satisfy its customers. One foggy day in 1949, Viking G-AJBY was operating the mid-morning Northolt-Paris service. On arrival overhead at Le Bourget the Captain found the fog far too thick to land, and he diverted to the nearest clear airfield at Abbeville. The lack of customs facilities there meant the passengers could not enter France and continue their journey by road or rail. In fact Abbeville was rather like some of the Scottish airfields, there was just a runway and no proper terminal buildings. 'JBY's Captain decided the only course open to him was to return to Northolt, with his twenty five passengers, to wait for a weather improvement. By the time they got back to Northolt the passengers had been in the air for nearly five hours, yet they had ended up only yards from where they had begun their journey. Many were furious with the Corporation; and one, using BEA's advertising slogan 'BEA takes you there and brings you back', wrote to the airline saying 'BEA takes you there and brings you back but doesn't give you time to do anything in between!'

In the summer of 1948 independent operators began to fly domestic scheduled services under associate agreements with BEA. Many of the routes BEA had abandoned at the end of the 1947 summer season were recommenced by independent airlines under associate agreements. Cambrian Airways began to operate the Cardiff-Bristol and Cardiff-Weston services, while Air Navigation and Trading and Manx Air Services began flights between the Isle of Man and Carlisle. Some routes opened under associate agreements BEA had never flown; for example Air Enterprises began a Cowes-Southampton and Cowes-Croydon service, while East Anglian Flying Services began to operate between Southend and Rochester. Conditions required for the granting of an associate agreement were that the route in question would not hamper BEA's plans for expansion, and that the applicant would operate it for at least two years. In practice many of the routes granted under associate agareements were never flown by the airline concerned as they were totally uneconomic propositions.

The early months of 1948 proved an unhappy time for BEA with three major accidents occurring involving Vikings. On January 6th, G-AHPK crashed at Finebush Lane Ruislip while attempting to land at Northolt in fog. The accident killed one of those on board and injured another eight. Then on April 5th a second Viking was lost. G-AIVP was on a German internal service inbound to Berlin, when it collided with a Russian fighter, killing all those on board. Only days later, on April 21st, a third Viking, G-AIVE, flew into the side of a Scottish mountain in bad weather, injuring thirteen. The incidents provided a further blow to staff morale, and the public image of the airline.

Nevertheless the Corporation looked forward to some newer types of aircraft bringing greater reliability, comfort and safety. An important step was taken in that direction on March 3rd, when the government announced it had granted BEA permission to buy twenty Airspeed Ambassador aircraft. BEA formally signed the order for the fleet on September 20th. There had been a possibility the aircraft would be powered by turbo-props instead of the Centaurus piston engines, but BEA abandoned the idea because of the higher costs, unproven nature of the turbo-prop engines in service, and the lack of adequate ATC facilities at higher cruising levels which would have reduced the benefits from having turbo-prop power. BEA decided to call the Ambassador the Elizabethan. The order was worth £3 million to Airspeed, and the aircraft were to be fitted out as a thirty six seater (later raised to forty nine). Vickers were very unhappy at BEA's decision to buy the Ambassador believing it made an order for their project very unlikely. However BEA was still extremely interested in the Vickers design, and an order did eventually come. The government induced order for the Ambassador was something BEA came to question on many occasions over the next three years. Delay and problem followed delay and problem in the development and delivery of the type, and it did not enter regular BEA service until 1952, although its first service for the Corporation operated in September 1951. The delays were all the more amazing when one realises the prototype had been flying for over a year when the BEA order was placed. The major areas of difficulty surrounded the powerplant, undercarriage and pressurization system. Development was further hampered when a prototype aircraft suffered a heavy landing at Christchurch on November 13th 1950, and had to undergo major repairs to restore it to airworthy condition. It is reputed to have hit the ground two and a half times harder than its designed maximum, causing an engine to break off and some considerable damage to the airframe!

No department was more frustrated with the problems of the aircraft, than the engineers. In 1948 BEA's engineering facilities were located on several airfields. At Northolt all Viking maintenance was carried out in rather unsuitable ex-RAF hangars. There was insufficient space on the airfield for all BEA maintenance requirements, and so DC-3 and Rapide major overhauls were performed at Liverpool, again in rather ill suited accommodation. Such split sites for major maintenance was costly, not the least because many aircraft had to position empty to Liverpool. In an effort to curb costs the engineers proposed that all major maintenance at Liverpool should be phased out, and transferred to Glasgow where a purpose built DC-3 maintenance dock would be built. Glasgow was a more economic proposition than Speke because many more services operated through there, reducing the need for empty positioning flights. The move from Speke to Glasgow was undertaken between January 3rd and March 24th 1949, but it was not until 1950 that the DC-3 major maintenance dock was commissioned. In order to remove the need to position Rapides from either Jersey or Land's End to Glasgow, Rapide overhaul facilities at Jersey were extended to allow the station to provide major checks on aircraft based there and at Land's End. Jersey continued to provide major overhaul facilities for the Rapides until the type was retired from service in 1964.

The Engineering Department was the scene for BEA's first major industrial dispute. Between November 7th and 16th most of the Northolt engineers went on

G-AGIU undergoing maintenance in the Renfrew DC-3 maintenance dock. *(BA)*

DH 89 G-ADAJ was inherited from Scottish Airways in February 1947 and later sold to Air France. (BA)

strike over a new bonus scheme associated with re-organisation of working practices. The dispute caused the cancellation of many services as aircraft went unservicable or were in need of checks, and the airline lost about £90,000 – money it could ill afford to lose. Eventually the bonus scheme was accepted by the staff and proved to be quite successful. On top of the financial blow caused by the dispute came another financial blow, this time caused by the old enemy of aviation, weather. Between November 16th and 30th thick fog caused severe problems to flights from Northolt. On several days it was so thick there were no movements at all, while on other days it hampered early morning and evening operations, adding another £10,000 to BEA's losses due to lost revenue, diversion costs and so on. In the month of November BEA had lost £100,000 through industrial disputes and weather problems!

BEA's close involvement in the life of the more remote areas of the UK was indicated by the establishment of a special Air Ambulance Unit, based at Glasgow, in April 1948. The airline had provided an air ambulance service since February 1947, and by March 1948 one hundred and eighty two ambulance flights had been completed. With such a level of demand BEA decided to establish a full time unit for ambulance work. Under the management of Captain David Barclay, two Rapides, three pilots and three radio officers made up its complement. Day or night 365 days a year, the Unit was on call to serve airfields and airstrips throughout the Scottish Highlands and Islands. Some of the airstrips used were primitive to say the least, consisting of bumpy grass fields without any facilities at all. Inevitably mishaps occurred when using them, for example on January 15th 1949 Rapide G-AHXV tipped over and was severely damaged while landing on the small Orkney Island of North Ronaldsay. After that incident BEA became extremely reluctant to send aircraft to some of the airstrips.

BEA's reluctance to use some of these airstrips was a serious blow to the residents of the small Island communities, as they relied on aircraft for speedy transfer to hospital in Kirkwall or the mainland. The senior Medical Officer in Kirkwall predicted some patients would probably die if BEA did not freely allow ambulance flights into places like North Ronaldsay and Westray. BEA was adamant, and refused to change its mind. Captain Fresson, the then BEA Manager for the Highlands and Islands (and pioneer of air services to Orkney before the war) flew a mercy flight into Stronsay, in DH84G-ACIT, without permission from his superiors in Glasgow. Even though the seriously ill patient was saved several hours of rough sea passage and got hospital treatment more quickly than if a boat had been used, Captain Fresson was severely rebuked for his actions by the airline's senior management, underlining BEA's determination. Captain Fresson had commenced an inter-Orkney Island scheduled passenger service before the war, and the Islanders soon began to petition BEA to re-introduce it. Again BEA was adamant in its refusal. Convenient for the Islanders it might have been, but the financial prospects of such a service were poor and BEA did not see how it could deliberably add to its already large losses. In any case if it were not willing to land aircraft on the Islands for occasional ambulance flights, there was no way it would use them regularly. Not until Loganair began an inter-Island service with Islander aircraft in the late 1960's did the Orcadians get their wish.

A little known aspect of the Corporation's flying activities was the existence of a small fleet of communications aircraft. In England two Austers, a Miles M.28 and an Anson were used. In Scotland a DH84 and a DH Moth provided the airline with its communications needs. The communications fleet was used to take staff to meetings, move crews around the country, and occasionally even ferry a passenger to another airport to catch a flight. The M.28 spent much of its time transporting the Chairman around the various BEA stations. The two Austers, which were based at Speke, were also used for training work, to familiarize pilots of heavy aircraft with light aircraft flying before they converted to Rapides. Another two Austers, G-AGVM and 'HCN, flew for the BEA Flying Club at White Waltham in 1947/48. The luxury of a communications fleet was one that the ailing finances of BEA could not support, and the fleet was gradually withdrawn from service. The Communications Flight had ceased to exist by January 1949. In 1954 BEA nearly had a 'new' communications 'hac' in the form of a DH90 Dragonfly. The DH90 was a scaled down version of the Rapide seating five. In August 1954 F-OAMS (c/n 7529) arrived in Jersey with the intention it should be overhauled by the BEA Rapide engineering unit there and converted into an executive transport for the airline. Unfortunately the plan did not proceed, though exact details are obscure, and the aircraft was eventually flown to Southampton in a Bristol Freighter, where it was rebuilt and flown privately as G-ANYK in 1959.

During 1948 BEA became fully involved in the Berlin Air Lift. Following the cutting of all surface links into West Berlin by the Russians and East Germans, the Allies mounted a massive airlift of supplies to feed the city. Much flying was done by the RAF and USAF, but increasingly civilian operators were involved too, and from August 4th BEA's Charter Department was charged with managing all the British civilian companies involved. By September it was co-ordinating and supervising no less than seventeen airlines flying DC-3s, Halifax ex-bombers, Avro Tudors, Bristol Freighters and Hythe flying boats. On April 1st 1949 BEA created a special Air Lift Division, headed by E.P. Whitfield Manager Germany, to continue managing the British contribution to the airlift, as the task had become too much for the Charter Division with its other responsibilities. Apart from supervising the air lift traffic into West Berlin, BEA continued to fly its own daily passenger service from Northolt to Berlin via Hamburg. The Civil Airlift Division functioned until September 1949 by which time surface communications into West Berlin were again becoming possible.

Apart from this temporary massive freighting operation, BEA was building up its own all-freighter network. By July 1948 the programme of services was as follows:

Northolt-Amsterdam-Copenhagen-Hamburg-London	Five flights a week
Northolt-Brussels-Paris	Three flights a week
Northolt-Marseilles-Rome-Athens	Two flights a week
Northolt-Marseilles-Rome-Athens-Istanbul	One flight a week
Northolt-Bordeaux-Madrid-Lisbon	One flight a fortnight
Northolt-Bordeaux-Madrid-Gibraltar	One flight a fortnight
Northolt-Basle-Zurich	One flight a week
Northolt-Guernsey-Jersey	Seven flights a week carrying newspapers
Northolt-Liverpool-Manchester	One flight a week

DH. 89A G-AKZB was eventually written off at Land's End in December 1961, after joining the fleet in February 1947. (BA)

All these services were flown by DC-3 freighters. BEA had high hopes of winning a major GPO contract to carry mail to Belfast from several parts of the UK, and it converted three more of its DC-3s to freighter configuration in anticipation. However the Postmaster General decided that the carriage of mail by air was too expensive and the contract never materialized. As a direct result of the decision three of the seven DC-3 freighters were returned to passenger operations. One unusual type appeared on a BEA freight service on April 8th, a Halifax chartered from the Lancashire Aircraft Corporation. It flew a Northolt-Marseilles-Rome-Athens service for the Corporation because of aircraft shortages within BEA. Halifax aircraft appeared on BEA cargo flights on a number of other occasions. In 1951 a Halifax, from the same operator, was chartered to fly a Northolt-Rome-Malta freight flight; while on October 17th 1949 a British American Airways Halifax was used on the Athens freighter service.

Though the cargo section of BEA did not succeed with its hoped for mail contract, the HEU did win an experimental contract with the GPO for carrying mail. It had been experimenting with carrying dummy mail loads in Somerset since January 1948. The small Bell 47 helicopter flew a short circuit from Yeovil to Marston Magna, Queen Magna, Sparkford, North Cadbury and Galhampton once a day Monday to Friday. The larger S.51 helicopters flew a longer circuit from Yeovil calling at Sherborne, Gillingham, Blandford, Wimborne, Pool, Wareham, Dorchester, Weymouth, Bridport and Lyme Regis, twice a day on week-days. While the Bell 47 carried no load of any description, the S.51 did carry dummy mail sacks. The two experiments lasted between January 27th and March 7th. The GPO contract was for the carriage of mail over a circuit in East Anglia based on Peterborough, with calls being made at Sheringham, Cromer, Norwich, Thelford, Diss, Harleston, Great Yarmouth, Lowestoft, Beccles, Norwich (again) and East Dereham. Because the work was many miles from the HEU base at Yeovil it was decided to move the base to Peterborough's Westwood Airfield, a move completed in April. An S.51 flew a number of proving flights along the route between May 24th and May 29th, and on June 1st aviation history was made when the HEU flew its first commercial mail carrying flight. The aircraft used was G-AKCU, which carried 63 kilos of mail, and departed from Peterborough at 09.55. Thereafter the route was flown once a day Mondays to Fridays, with a Saturday service between Peterborough and Norwich. The helicopter landed in fields and turn-round times were generally kept to one or two minutes. When the contract came to an end, on September 25th, the HEU had carried 500,000 letters and just over 30,000lbs of parcels. The HEU then began to prepare for a night mail contract for the GPO between Peterborough and Norwich. To gain some experience in night flying, a Monday to Thursday dummy mail flight operated between Peterborough and Downham Market between August 23rd and September 23rd.

Back in the mainstream of airline activity BEA began its winter timetable on October 31st. Most services, both at home and abroad, were curtailed to a more modest level to suit the lower demand in the winter months. Neither Guernsey or Edinburgh lost their links with London, though services from Edinburgh did call at Glasgow, and some of those from Guernsey were via Jersey. The winter timetable included a London-Zurich service, which had been suspended in December 1946.

In 1949 BEA Board reached a vital decision which greatly affected the airline's future; to transfer the London terminal from Northolt to Heathrow as soon as possible. Heathrow was being developed as London's new international airport to replace Croydon and Northolt, and that, plus the limited room at Northolt for further expansion, made the decision to move to Heathrow hardly surprising. Space at Northolt to extend the runway just did not exist, with the close proximity of main roads and buildings; including Keyline House. Furthermore, even by 1949 there was insufficient room on the airfield for all BEA's needs, forcing the airline to use accommodation at White Waltham and later Wembley, to store aircraft spares. The store at White Waltham was closed in 1948 once the new building at Wembley was available. White Waltham was an airfield, but BEA aircraft movements were generally limited to occasional visits from the communications aircraft; for example on January 19th Auster G-AIBR visited from Liverpool, piloted by Captain E.J. Williams, In addition, White Waltham served as the base for the BEA Aero Club. The future move to Heathrow was eagerly awaited. BEA would be able to have all its facilities on one site, in purpose built accommodation. The first step towards the move came in May 1949, when the Corporation announced its new fleet of Elizabethans were to be based at Heathrow where a new maintenance base would be constructed to service them.

Keyline House busied itself with planning some re-organisation of the airline, to be effective from January 1949. The English and Continental Divisions would remain as separate entities, but were to be renamed as British and Continental Services, and, in an attempt to reduce costs some jobs previously carried out by both Divisions would be centralized, especially in the area of finance and accountancy. The English Division's head office at Speke would close and the managers move to Keyline House. To ensure better co-ordination of staff and BEA activity in the various regions at home and in Europe, BEA decided to appoint Area Managers. These men would be responsible for the control of all BEA activity in their area and report direct to the relevant General Manager. Initially they were appointed in Jersey, the Isle of Man and Liverpool, but gradually the idea spread across the whole network. To better cater for Scottish needs, a Scottish Division was re-established but with less autonomy than its predecessor. Accompanying the changes in organisation were some changes in key personnel. G.O. Waters became General Manager with particular responsibility for the British Services, and Anthony Milward became Deputy General Manager, with particular responsibility for Continental Services.

1949

Further major senior management changes occurred early in 1949. The Chairman, Mr d'Erlanger, clashed openly with the government in February, leading to his resignation. The clash was over a proposed Cardiff to Liverpool service. The government gave a high priority to the speedy opening of the route, but the airline felt it to be totally uneconomic and opposed it. In February the Minister of Aviation Lord Pakenham, announced to the House of Lords, that the service would open later in the year despite BEA objections. Mr. d'Erlanger loudly criticised the decision, claiming the government was interfering too greatly in the commercial freedom of BEA. Lord Pakenham would not budge, and Mr. d'Erlanger resigned in protest. He was replaced by Lord Douglas of Kirtleside in March. Then on July 31st, J.V. Wood resigned from the Corporation, partly on the ground of ill health, but because he too objected to the level of government control of the Corporation. Wood was replaced by Peter Masefield, who had been with BEA since January, serving as the Chairman's Personal Assistant.

Sholto Douglas and Peter Masefield were a formidable team to push ahead with the fight for efficiency and profitability, and if the government had hoped either would willingly bow to its wishes, it was quickly disappointed. Lord Douglas had been involved in commercial aviation since 1919, when he had become only the fourth pilot in Britain to gain a commercial pilots licence. While serving with the RAF his great talents were fully exploited, and by 1939 he had risen to become Air Marshal and Deputy Chief of the Air Staff. After the war he became Governor of the British Sector of Germany, before retiring from the RAF and joining BEA, at the age of fifty five. Peter Masefield had a distinguished background in aviation. In 1942 he had been personal adviser to the Lord Privy Seal on commercial aviation matters, and had spent some time in the Air Ministry before joining BEA.

The new team had no easy task and the problems were still immense. To begin with, staffing levels were still far too high and it was imperative to reduce them quickly. Masefield succeeded in doing so, cutting staff from 7,500 to 6,000 in just five months. Many went through natural wastage, but there were some redundancies and the reduction was achieved despite opposition from the unions. Masefield and Lord Douglas began to tackle BEA's problems in other ways too. In 1948 a firm of management consultants had been employed to review the airline's management structure. The report laid the basis for some tighter financial controls, which the new management team was quick to insist on. From 1949 each department and station had to draw up an annual budget of proposed expenditure which was then strictly vetted by Head Office. Those figures had to be adhered to, ensuring expenditure was kept within some reasonable limits.

Apart from staff reductions and better financial control, a vigorous sales drive was launched. Of most significance was the launching of Off-Peak night fares on the London-Paris route from July 29th. The usual return fare to Paris was £14-8/-. The Off-Peak night fare provided for a return of just £10. Travel was limited to the 22.00 departure from Northolt, and the 06.30 from Le Bourget. For the winter of 1949 it was extended to cover departures from Northolt at 08.00, 09.00, 19.30 and 19.40; and from Le Bourget at 08.30, 08.45, 19.30 and 20.30. The fare was instantly popular, and was extended to many other European destinations over the next few years. Another new fare was introduced in October, the Serviceman's fare, which provided cheaper flights for servicemen and their families who wanted to visit Britain from European postings, and applied on services to London from Berlin, Dusseldorf, Malta, Gibraltar and Vienna. Savings were considerable, for example, the normal return fare from Malta to Northolt was £72, but servicemen and their families could travel for just £46-16/-. As part of the sales campaign, an off-line sales office was opened in New York. In November Clive Adams, who had been Traffic Manager for the Continental Division, was appointed BEA Sales Representative USA, working from a small office in New York. The office was not opened to the public, but served travel agents and airlines. This was an astute move as there was a large market in the USA from both businessmen and tourists who wanted to to England, and then onwards from London to Europe. The success of the office is well indicated by the opening of other off-line offices in other parts of the USA and Canada over the next twenty five years. A final feature of the sales drive was the use of a travelling sales exhibition which visited a number of agricultural and county shows during the year. Early in 1950 it was driven to Dover and shipped across the Channel, to undertake a tour of several European cities, including Paris, Brussels, Utrecht, Milan and Frankfurt.

The BEA route map was further extended with the coming of the summer timetable in April. Continental Services opened a number of entirely new routes. A London-Munich service began on June 15th with flights going via Dusseldorf at first, while two days earlier on June 13th, a Northolt-Dinard schedule had begun. The route was flown up to eighteen times a week by Viking. Dinard also received a new service from Jersey which commenced on June 11th, and operated twice a day with Rapides, replacing the weekly Jersey-Rennes flights. Services from the Midlands direct to Europe were commenced on April 11th, with a daily DC-3 flight to Paris from Manchester via Birmingham. The last new route was a short lived German internal service from Hamburg to Hamburg via Dusseldorf and Frankfurt. Operations began on March 25th with a daily flight being made over the circuit by Viking. The route proved quite successful in passenger terms, but was dropped on November 30th for political considerations. BEA was later involved in one other German internal service, not involving Berlin, a Cologne/Bonn to Frankfurt route. Details of that operation had proved very hard to come by. It is believed to have been flown sometime in 1951, but was short lived again for political reasons. On the existing network, services to Prague were increased to six flights per week, all of which now called at Frankfurt in an attempt to boost traffic. During the summer BEA began to fly non-stop services from Northolt to Rome. Previously all flights had called at either Marseilles or Nice. It took the Vikings about six hours to complete a non-stop service to Rome.

At home, frequencies to the Channel Isles were stepped up, with DC-3s flying seven week-day services from Northolt to Jersey, with additional services at week-ends. The popularity of the CI routes is shown by the June loadfactor, 80.5%, as compared with only 58.8% in the previous June. Included in the summer timetable was the controversial Cardiff-Liverpool service. Beginning on April 1st, a Rapide flew from Cardiff to Liverpool with stops at Hawarden (for Chester) and Valley (for Anglesey). Mr. d'Erlanger's opposition to the route was clearly vindicated. Between April and September just six hundred and three passengers used the daily service, yielding a revenue of £1,740. Costs for the operation had amounted to £9,755! Lord Douglas had no hesitation in closing the route from October 1st. Many other difficulties had to be overcome, not the least of which was the apparent forgetfulness on the part of reservations staff, that BEA did not just fly to the Channel Isles from Northolt. One passenger tried to book a seat from Northolt to Guernsey, but was told all flights were full. Nobody told him of the alternative Southampton-Guernsey service. The problem was still around in the early 1970s when the BEA computer listed, as an alternative to the Heathrow-Jersey service, the British Midland flight from Luton, ignoring the BEA service from Southampton. Over the summer a number of independent airlines operated domestic scheduled services under associate agreements with BEA. Seventeen companies were granted associate status to fly schedules over twenty nine different routes, many of which had been flown the previous summer by the same operators.

When it came to the winter programme for 1949/50, there was only one new international route, a daily London-Dusseldorf-Berlin service. Previously flights to Berlin had generally flown via Hamburg. The service was flown by Vikings, which could now operate more easily into Berlin thanks to the improvement of landing aids there. Over the winter months the management's main task was consolidation of existing routes. That was extremely wise, and its success showed in the gradual build up of winter traffic. The Christmas peak was particularly busy, with December 23rd being the busiest day when ten extra flights operated from London to Paris, four to Belfast, three to Jersey and one each to Zurich, Geneva, Nice and Malta. The traffic growth was achieved despite the devaluation of the pound in October, making foreign holidays more expensive and adding half a million pounds to operating costs, as fuel was paid for in dollars.

One area in which stern economies were made was the freighter network. In October 1948 many services had been suspended, including those to Basle, Bordeaux, Gibraltar, Lisbon, Madrid, Prague and Zurich, and more pruning of the freighter network came in 1949. Peter Masefield axed the daily newspaper service from Northolt to Jersey and Guernsey in the spring. It had left Northolt at 05.20, arriving at Jersey at 07.20 after a brief call at Guernsey. Masefield decided the operation was uneconomic and had to go. Also to go was the weekly London-Liverpool-Manchester freighter, meaning BEA worked no domestic scheduled freighter services. Internationally the only freighter routes remaining were London to Brussels, London to Amsterdam, London to Copenhagen, London to Istanbul via Nice, Rome and Athens, and London to Malta via Rome. It was some time before the economic situation improved sufficiently to allow the resumption of expansion in the all-cargo network.

Throughout 1949 the HEU continued its experiments with mail carrying in East Anglia. Between February 14th and 18th of March flights were made at night, carrying only dummy mail sacks, between Peterborough and Norwich in preparation for a GPO night mail contract. Commercial flying began on October 17th when Captain Cameron flew S.51, G-AJOV, from Norwich to Peterborough with the first load of mail. Until April 15th 1950 a daily service was flown Monday to Friday, departing from Norwich at 21.50 and from Peterborough at 01.50 the next morning. Over the time the service operated a 77% regularity was achieved, any delays were generally the result of fog or ice rather than technical problems. Altogether 9,500lbs of mail were carried. The prescribed weather minimum for the operation was a 700 foot cloud base and 800 metres visibility. The closing of the service marked the end of the

HEU's experiments with carrying mail. The operating costs of the S.51, at just over £28 per hour, coupled with its small capacity (only thirty three mail bags), made the operation too costly for the GPO to consider taking up on a regular basis.

When the 1948/49 Report and Accounts was published, it did offer a little encouragement to the airline, recording a loss of £2,763,085 compared with the previous years loss of £3,573,989. This result was achieved without the direct effect of many of the economies made by Douglas and Masefield which had come too late to be included in the figures. The Report and Accounts showed that on March 31st the Corporations fleet consisted of thirty seven Vikings, twenty three passenger DC-3s, five freight DC-3s and nineteen Rapides. They had achieved an average utilization of just over three hours a day each, and flown 29,818 revenue hours. The increasing reliability of the aircraft and their components was indicated in the extension of periods between overhauls, which helped to cut costs. The improvements in times between checks is illustrated in the following table, which applies only to the Vikings and DC-3s:

Flying Hours Between Checks

	Until 1949	**1949**
Check 1	Prior to every flight	Every 24 hours
Check 2	Every 25 hours	Every 30 hours
Check 3	Every 100 hours	Every 150 hours
Check 4	Every 400 hours	Every 600 hours

As the time between checks was lengthened, so the airline was able to get extra revenue earning potential from each aircraft, further aiding the drive towards profitability.

BEA S.51, G-AJOV, approaching Liverpool on a Cardiff-Liverpool service, early in the summer of 1950. *(BA)*

Rapide G-AFRK is pictured at Southampton awaiting a load for Alderney. *(BA)*

History in the Making, Viscount V.630 G-AHRF about to depart from Northolt on the world's first turbine powered commercial air service on July 29th 1950. *(BA)*

1950

BEA's long association with the Viscount project and its predecessors finally culminated in August 1950 in an order for twenty Viscount V.701 aircraft. The V.701 was powered by four Rolls Royce Dart 505 turbine engines, and accommodated forty seven passengers, cruising at 300 mph at heights up to 28,500 feet. Lord Douglas, and particularly Peter Masefield, were keen advocates of the aircraft, seeing it as a major weapon in pushing BEA towards profitability. They hoped that the Viscount would enter service in 1951, however BEA made aviation history before that. On July 29th 1950 BEA operated the world's first commercial flight using a turbine powered aircraft. Vickers lent BEA the Viscount V.630 prototype, G-AHRF, for a month to give the Corporation some experience in turbine operations, and on July 29th BEA used the aircraft to operate a scheduled service from Northolt to Le Bourget. BE329X2 departed from Northolt at midday carrying fourteen fare paying passengers and twelve invited guests, and arrived at Le Bourget fifty seven minutes later having flown at 18,000 feet and cruised at 273 mph. Flying in full BEA livery, 'HRF was commanded by BEA's Captain Raymer who was the first commercial pilot in the world to gain a rating to fly turbo-prop aircraft. G-AHRF then operated a series of flights over the London-Paris route until August 14th. Thirty six return trips were flown, clocking up ninety four hours eighteen minutes of flying time. From August 15th to 23rd the aircraft operated a daily service from Northolt to Edinburgh for the Edinburgh Festival. A further thirty hours seventeen minutes of flying time was logged. In its month with BEA, G-AHRF carried a total of 1,815 passengers, giving them a taste of the future delights of turbine powered flight. Just a few days after 'HRF was returned to Vickers, the prototype Viscount V.700,, G-AMAV, took to the air for the first time. G-AMAV was similar in size to the production model, the V.701, which BEA had ordered. Like G-AHRF, 'MAV was loaned to the airline; in fact on two occasions. The first in 1951/52 was for route proving work prior to the introduction of the V.701s, and the second in 1953 for the famous London to New Zealand Air Race.

While the Viscount was an entirely new fleet development BEA decided to update one of its older aircraft, the DC-3, by cockpit and cabin modernisation. The converted aircraft were to be called Pionairs and have thirty two seats. By installing the latest radio equipment, they could dispense with the radio operator, thus reducing the crew to two pilots. All the American cockpit instrumentation was to be replaced with British equipment, and cabin modernization included new seats, each pair of which were equipped with a reading light and fresh air ventilators. The rear double door, so characteristic of the DC-3, would be taken out and replaced by a single door incorporating built in airstairs. Some aircraft were to retain the larger double door for freight work, and be called Pionair Leopards. An airline wag pointed out that the Leopard was able to change its spots, and this sort of Pionair could change its role from passenger to cargo, so what better name for it than Pionair Leopard?. Cockpit modifications were to be undertaken by Field Aircraft Services using Smiths instruments, and the cabin conversion by Scottish Aviation. The aircraft were flown either to the Scottish Aviation facility at Prestwick or the Field's one at Tollerton for conversion. Initially four aircraft were earmarked to be converted to Pionair standard, although thirty eight were eventually converted, each at a cost of £10,000. Another ten were converted to Pionair Leopard standards for freight work. BEA purchased an additional twenty DC-3s specifically for Pionair conversion.

The proposed timetable for conversion did not go entirely according to plan, partly because of industrial relations problems within Scottish Aviation, and partly due to a shortage of the necessary instruments and other pieces of equipment. These shortages led the airline into some serious scheduling problems in the summer of 1951, a situation made even worse by the late delivery of the Elizabethans. To the planners, it was clear there would be an aircraft shortage, and so the airline purchased four ex-South African Airways Vikings to try to bridge the gap. The four aircraft were bought in 1950, but they needed substantial modifications to bring them up to UK air worthiness standards. The work was carried out by Vickers at Weybridge, and the four were just about ready to help make up for Pionair and Elizabethan shortages later in 1951. They were G-AMGG, 'MGH, 'MGI and 'MGJ. Another four followed in 1952, again to assist with aircraft shortages, these being G-AMNJ, 'MNR, 'MNS and 'MNX.

A fine portrait of G-AJBR on Northolt's passenger apron. (BA)

The first DC-3 to be converted to full Pionair standard was G-ALYF which was delivered to BEA on September 26th 1950. It engaged in several months of crew training and route proving flying, before operating the first commercial flight by a Pionair on January 24th 1951, when it flew a charter for Smiths Instruments from London to Dublin. Regular scheduled operations by the aircraft began on March 21st 1951, when Pionairs began serving the Channel Islands. Prior to the delivery of G-ALYF, BEA had converted three DC-3s to what were nicknamed 'Piotas' – a DC-3 with a Pionair cockpit but a standard rear cabin and no built in airstairs. They enabled crews to be trained for Pionair operations before the type was actually ready. Later the 'Piotas' were converted to full Pionair standard, but which three aircraft were used as the 'Piotas' is unknown.

The name Pionair reflected a new BEA policy, to give each of its aircraft types a class name. The Vikings became the Admiral Class, the Rapides the Islander Class, the Ambassadors the Elizabethan Class, the Viscounts the Discovery Class, and the Marathons, had they ever been delivered, the Clansman Class. Even the HEU's small fleet was not exempt, becoming the King Arthur Class. Each individual aircraft was given a name reflecting the Class, so all the Ambassadors were named after Elizabethan characters, all the Vikings after admirals, all the helicopters after one of the Knights of the Round Table and so on. Only the Rapides names did not reflect their class name, being named after famous personalities not islands. The fleet names were selected from suggestions made by staff in a competition run during the early part of the year.

The gradual success of the efforts of Lord Douglas and Peter Masefield were indicated in the 1949/50 Report and Accounts. Once again the losses had fallen to £1,363,594, a saving of about £1½million over the previous year. 751,512 passengers had been carried, compared with 577,122 in 1948/49, and cargo had risen from 4,426 tons to 6,093 tons. By March 31st 1950 BEA served fifty five stations in sixteen countries, and operating a fleet of ninety two aircraft. 572 aircrew were employed, 194 Captains, 182 First Officers and 196 Radio Operators. A sizeable element of the loss came from domestic services, particularly those in Scotland, which alone accounted for no less than 20% of the total losses. Services to the Isle of Man and the Channel Isles were also uneconomic, with very low loads in the winter. Traffic on these services was roughly double in August what it was in November, yet station costs were not that different. Waterlogging at the three Channel Islands airfields added to the problems in the winter, and flights could be delayed by several days waiting for the airfields to dry out. In 1950 the States of Jersey decided to solve the problem of construction of a hard runway. Guernsey did not follow suit until 1958, and then only after BEA had threatened to withdraw from the Island, if a runway suitable for Viscounts was not constructed. Alderney never did receive a hard runway in the years BEA served the Island, but its problems with waterlogging were less serious than at Jersey or Guernsey.

At the end of March 1950 the most numerous type in the BEA fleet was the Vickers Viking. The airline flew forty two examples in 1950, and they operated nearly all the international services. In total the Vikings flew 63% of all BEA revenue earning services and recorded an average utilization, per aircraft, of just over four hours a day. There were still severe problems with the economics of Rapide operations, mainly because the routes on which they were employed, such as Glasgow to Barra or Guernsey to Alderney, had very low traffic density. The only profitable Rapide route was Jersey to Dinard and that only in the summer. To try to further reduce losses on the Rapides, BEA modified its fleet to a single crew operation by dispensing with the Radio Operator who had been carried in addition to the pilot. Improvements in Air Traffic Control enabled such moves to occur, with the wider provision of VHF R/T.

BEA had established itself as the world's seventh largest airline in terms of passengers carried, the other six were all in the USA. It had a ratio of 66.5 staff per aircraft operated, a ratio beaten by only three other major world airlines. Yet with the average utilization of each aircraft at just under four hours per day there was certainly plenty of room for improving the use of the Corporation's fleet. Peter Masefield reckoned an extra half an hour utilization each day across the whole fleet would produce another £1 million in revenue. He said "if everybody in BEA persuaded just one extra person to fly with us during the coming year, it would mean an extra £70,000 to our revenue account." Staff responded to the challenge; and mothers, fathers, uncles, aunts, grandparents, neighbours and friends were all bombarded with a fly BEA campaign. Passenger figures did begin to creep up, although how much was due to the staff campaign and how much to other factors is a matter of debate.

To encourage extra passengers to fly BEA, a more ambitious summer programme was begun in April, the most obvious feature being the launching of an hourly service to Paris from May 27th. Flights left Northolt on the hour twelve times a day, with an extra three departures on peak days. BEA coined the phrase 'On the Hour every Hour' to advertise the service. BEA estimated the Paris route might produce £2 million in revenue. Such ideas were a little optimistic, it actually earnt £1,186,000 in 1950/51. Two of the daily Paris services operated from Heathrow from April 16th, using Vikings. For the moment they were the only BEA services to use the new airport, and BEA flights were handled by BOAC. BEA did not open its own traffic handling unit at Heathrow until April 1951, but once it did, it began to earn the airline a great deal of money in handling the services of other European operators who had begun to transfer from Northolt. Facilities at Heathrow were even more primitive than at Northolt, with large tents serving as passenger buildings. When it rained everything became a sea of mud, with passengers and staff using duck boards to walk on. However, plans were drawn up to build a large passenger terminal complex in the centre of the airfield, to be in use by 1954 or 1955.

For the summer BEA continued its plans to expand the network both in Europe and at home, with several new services beginning on the dates shown in the table:

April 28th	Glasgow-Manchester-Paris. Operated on week-days by DC-3.
April 28th	Alderney-Gatwick, flown twice a week by Rapide. First flight flown by G-AHXZ.
May 1st	Birmingham-Belfast. Flown on week-days by DC-3.
May 13th	Manchester-Birmingham-Guernsey-Jersey. Operated by DC-3.
May 26th	Northolt-Le Touquet. Operated by DC-3.
July 1st	Glasgow-Perth. Flown by Rapide once daily Mondays to Saturdays.
July 15th	Northolt-Bordeaux. (with road connection to Biarritz). Operated by Viking.

Some of the new routes proved less successful than others. The shortest lived was the Glasgow-Perth Rapide flight, which was abandoned on August 31st because of very poor loads. Perhaps this was because it operated in the middle of the day, rather than in the morning or evening when it could have connected with south bound schedules from Glasgow. Alderney to Gatwick continued only until the end of the 1952 summer season. The route was BEA's first into Gatwick, and the airline had no permanent staff based there. Instead a traffic clerk was sent down from Kensington Air Station to oversee the Rapide's turnround. When the Alderney service ceased, BEA did not use Gatwick again until it became London's second Airport in 1958, though the HEU did nove its base there in 1952.

Out of keeping with the general expansion of the network was the withdrawal of services from London to Lisbon on June 2nd. The explanation was certainly not

BEA purchased this 170 Bristol 170 to carry engines to stranded Elizabethans. *(BA)*

because of poor loads. On the contrary the route was very successful with two Vikings a week. Flights were suspended for political reasons. The Portuguese government felt there was too much British airline capacity on the route because both BEA and BOAC carried passengers between the two cities. So BEA was forced to give up its service, leaving the route to BOAC. The loss of revenue to the airline was estimated as being £25,000. Later in the year the blow was softened a little by the opening of a Northolt-Barcelona route, flown initially on three days a week. It became a money spinner at once and very quickly the frequency was increased to five a week.

BEA's cargo operations were slowly beginning to recover from the severe pruning given to them as part of the earlier economy drive. A great help in the recovery was the winning of a contract from the Ministry of Defence to fly mail and newspapers from London to the British Army on the Rhine. On six nights a week a DC-3 flew from Northolt to Buckenburg (near Hanover), services running from February 3rd.

One of Reggie Brie's (Manager of the HEU) great desires was to experiment with a scheduled passenger service by helicopter. Several potential routes had already been considered, including Bristol to Cardiff and Southampton to the Isle of Wight. The route eventually chosen was Cardiff to Liverpool, via Wrexham. Planning went ahead to open a service in the summer, with BEA believing it would be the first company in the world to fly a scheduled passenger service using a helicopter. Yet just four weeks before the route was launched, Westland ran a passenger service from London to Birmingham to connect the two sites of the British Industrial Fair. The route was flown by a WS.51 between May 9th and 19th and the honour was snatched from BEA. Even so, it launched the Cardiff-Liverpool service on June 1st, beginning the world's first sustained scheduled helicopter passenger service. On June 1st Captain Theilman piloted S.51 G-AJOV from Liverpool to Cardiff carrying three passengers; The Director of Civil Aviation (Lord Packenham), and Lord and Lady Douglas. The optional stop at Wrexham was available from July 1st, although as Wrexham had no suitable airfield the helicopter actually landed in a field at Plas Coch farm. Two services a day were flown by the S.51, but from September the schedule was reduced to just one round trip a day, commencing from Cardiff. Flight E306A left Cardiff at 09.15 arriving at Liverpool at 11.15. The return trip, E307A, left Speke at 13.45, and was scheduled to land at Cardiff two hours later. The fare was £5-10/- return. BEA realized the service could not make money, but experience in schedule helicopter passenger flying was needed even if it was uneconomic. The economics of the service were illustrated between June and September when it earnt £22,611 in revenue, but cost the HEU £24,887 to operate. Flights ceased on March 31st 1951, and the HEU transferred its attention to another scheduled passenger route, Northolt to Birmingham. The end of the Cardiff-Liverpool route marked the ceasing of BEA flying from Cardiff. BEA did establish a small passenger handling unit there in 1952, to handle the thrice weekly Aer Lingus Dublin service. A similar handling unit was established at Bristol, and both lasted until 1959 when Aer Lingus awarded Cambrian Airways the handling contract for their flights. The BEA helicopter service was handled by Cambrian at Cardiff.

During 1950 BEA's associate company – Gibraltar Airways, sought to expand its network by opening services from Gibraltar to Malaga, Seville and Tetuan. The routes commenced on June 2nd, the first service being on the Gibraltar-Seville route, flown by Rapide G-AGEE. Like many services, these routes proved to be grossly uneconomic and were abandoned within three months.

The only other event of note in 1950 was rather a curious one. On August 18th BEA announced it was winding up its Charter Department, and would no longer actively seek ad-hoc charters. The Corporation felt such work did not fit in with its pattern of scheduled operations, and caused too many operational and maintenance difficulties. In future ad-hoc charters would only be undertaken if an aircraft was in the right position at the right time, and could be crewed at no extra cost. The independent operators greeted the news with glee. It did not take BEA long to realize the foolishness of the decision, and a new Charter Department was established a few years later, with BEA aggressively seeking charters. A number of observers of BEA took the decision to abandon charter work as further proof of their view that many of the airline's managers were still trying to run the company like a military unit with a very high degree of rigidity and little commercial flexibility. Such a criticism was often voiced in the first few years of the Corporation's existence, and with so many ex-military personnel in its management there was probably some truth in it. The airline did seem to take some rather dogmatic, commercially dubious decisions on occasions, although as a public corporation its Board was never quite clear about how far decisions needed to be commercially based, or how far it could justify sometimes uncommercial decisions by claiming to be providing a necessary service.

1951

BEA's fifth year of existence began, rather unusually, with the opening of several new routes. On January 1st a major expansion of the German internal network took place, with new services from Berlin to Cologne, Frankfurt, Hanover and Munich. The Berlin-Cologne service continued through to London giving an extra link between Berlin and London, and a Cologne-London service for the first time. Vikings were withdrawn from all German routes except the London-Dusseldorf-Berlin schedule; and six DC-3s were used, instead. From May 8th these aircraft transfered from Berlin's Gatow airfield to Tempelhof which became BEA's Berlin terminal for many years to come. In a move towards improving the service to passengers on the routes, BEA recruited twelve German cabin staff, who all worked out of Berlin. The policy of using at least some German cabin crew on the German internal network continued throughout the remainder of BEA's history.

A second new service commenced early in 1951 was London to Cairo, flown via Nice, Rome, Malta, Tripoli and Benghazi. The sectors from Malta onwards were flown in conjunction with the Malta Airlines. Vikings were used on the weekly schedule. The first flight left Northolt at 07.40 on the morning of January 7th, flown by G-AJBV. It arrived at Malta at 17.00 that afternoon, where it night-stopped. The onward flight to Cairo left Malta the following day at 08.05 and landed at Cairo at 19.30. The service was well patronised by military personnel stationed along the North African coast. In conjunction with the Malta Airlines two feeder services were opened from Malta, Malta to Tunis and Malta to Catania. The Catania service quickly established itself, but the connection to Tunis proved unpopular, and it was withdrawn at the end of the summer. Both routes were flown by Viking. These new routes, and indeed much of the winter programme, were dislocated, late in January, by the grounding of nineteen of the Viking fleet, due to faults with the propellor hubs. Fortunately the fault occured at the slackest time of the year when there was plenty of spare capacity to make up for the grounded aircraft.

The last new route to be introduced in the early part of 1951 was Northolt to Milan. BEA had planned to start services on April 9th, but flights began on February 12th

Services to Cairo began on January 7th 1951, here passengers are seen boarding the inaugural service at Northolt. (BA)

The flagship of the Elizabethan fleet, G-ALZN, in flight (BA)

because the Alitalia service was temporarily suspended. G-AJBR flew the first service, and three flights a week were scheduled. Like the Barcelona route, the airline quickly found this frequency to be inadequate and from April 9th the service was flown daily. Meanwhile on March 21st BEA flights to Prague were finally suspended. The route had never been very well patronized and once the volume of diplomatic and military traffic had diminished the airline could no longer sustain the route. Prague was not re-connected to the network until 1957.

In view of the large number of routes opened early in 1951, it is hardly surprising that the summer timetable contained few new destinations. Internationally there was just one fresh destination, Deauville, linked with Northolt. It was not technically a new route as in the summers of 1947, 1948 and 1949 a Croydon-Deauville schedule had been operated, using a BEA Rapide in 1947, and then Doves leased from Olley Air Services. Traffic did not amount to much and the route was abandoned in September. An international service from Jersey to Paris was re-instated for part of the summer, but it was no more successful than earlier attempts to operate the route, and was given up before the end of the summer timetable.

Domestic services continued largely on the pattern established the previous summer, though Vikings were used on the Northolt-Belfast schedule and Pionairs began a seasonal direct Glasgow-Jersey service. BEA also re-opened an Isle of Man-Manchester service from April 1st. The summer of 1951 proved to be an operational nightmare because of the late delivery of Elizabethans and Pionairs. When the timetable was planned it was expected that several Elizabethans would be in service, however further delays caused by problems with the engines and elevators meant none were available. G-AMAD was delivered to BEA for a time in summer, for route proving flights, but had to return to Airspeed for modifications. Then G-ALZN was loaned to BEA for a similar purpose, and it operated the airline's first Elizabethan service on September 3rd between Heathrow and Paris. Lord Douglas, Peter Masefield and forty five invited guests travelled on the aircraft. Between September 4th and 18th the aircraft was substituted for Vikings on some Paris services, carrying three hundred and fourteen fare paying passengers. On September 19th it too went back to Airspeed for modifications. None of this helped the general operations of the airline, and services timetabled for Elizabethans were operated by Vikings. If the Elizabethan was fully booked it was necessary to substitute two Vikings. Furthermore Elizabethans were scheduled to fly from Heathrow, and the available Vikings were generally at Northolt. Passengers had to be bused between the airports. For those travelling regularly on routes earmarked for Elizabethans, like London-Paris, the journey over to Northolt became an accepted but unwelcome part of the journey.

The lack of Elizabethans was not the only operational problem. The late delivery of Pionairs meant the airline found itself six aircraft short for the summer. Some frequencies had to be reduced, and others suspended. In Scotland twenty two services a week were pruned from the programme, while in Germany the Berlin-Frankfurt, and Berlin-Munich services were suspended. Also temporarily suspended was the London-Oslo service. These routes were re-instated as more Pionairs became available.

One new route, entirely unaffected by aircraft shortage, was the HEU's service from Heathrow and Northolt to Birmingham. Operations commenced at 07.00 on June 4th when S.51, G-AJOV, departed from Birmingham Haymills Rotorstation for Northolt and Heathrow. Unfortunately the S.51 had to divert to Thame Airfield, near Aylesbury, due to bad weather. On June 1st S.51s G-AJHW and 'JOV had flown the route with invited guests. The normal schedule for the route provided for three daily flights, and it was flown until April 9th 1952, by which date the helicopters had carried 1,087 passengers, producing a 58% loadfactor. Though passenger flying ceased on April 9th, a helicopter still operated a once daily service from Heathrow, via Northolt, to Birmingham for freight. Elmdon Airport was used as the terminal for the freighter service instead of Haymills Rotorstation. From the experience gained with the Cardiff-Liverpool, and Heathrow/Northolt-Birmingham services, the HEU concluded that successful passenger operations by helicopters could not be achieved until there was a multi-engined helicopter able to fly in all weathers.

With this in mind it issued a requirement for a thirty five seater multi-engined helicopter able to cruise at 120mph, and cover distances of up to 150 miles. It was hoped such an aircraft could be used on inter-city helicopter services from heliports built near city centres. The requirement, altered on several occasions, was eventually labelled the 'Bealine Bus'. It gradually evolved into a sixty seater able to fly distances of up to 250 miles. Over the next few years several helicopter designs were considered, such as the Bristol 173, the Fairey Rotodyne, the Sikorsky S.56 and S.58, the Piasecki H16 and H21, and the Westland Westminster. Most were too small to meet the BEA requirement and serious consideration was given only to the Rotodyne and the Westminster. Neither helicopter ever entered service with BEA, though the Rotodyne got closest, with the Corporation issuing a letter of intent to purchase six in 1957. The letter was eventually withdrawn in February 1962 because of the helicopter's high noise level, and inadequate capacity; being only a fifty seater whereas BEA wanted a sixty seater. Not until 1970 did BEA think it had found a suitable helicopter in the Sikorsky S.65.200. While only a forty four seater, it did seem ideal for some Scottish internal routes, some CI services, and inter-city routes from London to Paris, Brussels and Amsterdam. An in depth feasibility study of the project was undertaken, and it appeared likely the Corporation would place an order for a number of S.65s. However the ground was cut from under BEA's feet, when Sikorsky announced it had abandoned plans to build the civilian version of the S.65.

BEA sought to increase traffic by providing further Night Excursion fares. In May they were offered on services from London to Amsterdam, Geneva, Nice and Zurich. Fares to Nice were usually £34-5/-, but the new Night Excursion fare of £25 gave almost a £10 saving. In the winter, Off-Peak discount fares were also issued, covering a whole range of destinations, including Copenhagen, Geneva, Oslo, Stockholm and Zurich. Off-Peak fares produced considerable savings, for example 24% on the Stockholm route, and 19% to Copenhagen. Associated with these developments were two new sorts of domestic fares, Student Fares and Off-Peak fares to the Channel Isles. Students travelling between their home and place of study (and vice versa) were able to buy a ticket at 50% of the normal fare, a facility greatly appreciated by those living in the Channel Isles, Isle of Man and Scottish Islands. In a bid to persuade passengers to travel mid-week and not over the week-end peaks, Off-Peak mid-week fares to Jersey and Guernsey were offered, giving savings of up to 25%. They were available on all routes, except the direct Glasgow and Manchester CI flights. A final sales innovation was the offering of discounts to account holders for the purchase of domestic tickets. A 2% discount was given to account holders spending between £200 and £1,000 a year, and a 10% discount applied if over £1,000 was spent. Such discounts were of little value to the holiday maker, but they were appreciated by business travellers who regularly used BEA services.

In preparation for the operation of the Elizabethans and Viscounts, BEA again made aviation history by being the first airline in the UK to order flight simulators. One for each of the two new types was ordered from Air Training Limited on April 13th. The reason for the order

Marathon, G-ALUB, at Northolt, while on loan to BEA for trials. *(BA)*

was pure economy. The introduction of two new aircraft types meant that a large number of valuable flying hours with the new aircraft would have to be given over to training, thereby reducing the ability of the aircraft to make money. The simulators enabled much less time to be spent in training, releasing the aircraft to more profitable activities. Furthermore simulators helped train pilots before the two types were delivered thereby speeding up their entry into service. They provided an exact replica of the aircraft's cockpit and simulated its handling characteristics. Unlike more modern simulators, they did not provide any visual image for the pilots, the cockpit windows being blanked out. The early simulators were not without their problems and critics, and some pilots nicknamed them 'cock ups of mock pits'! Over the next twenty years BEA expanded its Simulator Unit to cover every main type of aircraft it operated. The Elizabethan and Viscount simulators were initially installed at Northolt.

A further project, associated with the coming of the Viscount, was the conversion of two DC-3s to turbo-prop power, by fitting two Rolls Royce Dart 505 engines. It was planned to fly them on freighter services to give both BEA and Rolls Royce operational experience with the Dart engine. The aircraft earmarked for conversion were G-ALXN and G-AMDB, the cost of the work being met by the Ministry of Supply. The modifications were undertaken by Field Aircraft Services at Tollerton. G-ALXN was converted between January and June, while 'MDB emerged as a Dart DC-3 on September 5th 1951. The first commercial service flown by a Dart DC-3 took place on August 15th, when G-ALXN flew the regular freight service from Northolt to Buckenburg carrying 5,500 lbs of mail and newspapers. It was crewed by Captain H.V. Hubbard and First Officer W.J. Ferris. G-ALXN reduced the flying time by a quarter, cruising at 200 mph at 25,000 feet. In subsequent months, crews of other aircraft stared in almost complete disbelief at seeing a DC-3 travelling at such speed and height! Between August 15th and April 30th 1952 the aircraft flew 164 hours on the London-Buckenburg route, sometimes calling at Brussels. On April 20th 1952 they began a second service, Northolt to Paris and Milan. However the days of Dart DC-3 operations were numbered, and early in 1953 the whole project was abandoned. 'LXN and 'MDB were converted back to piston power and modified to Pionair standard. The hours flown by the two aircraft were far below what had been planned because of a shortage of aircrew and engineers, and various technical problems surrounding the engines, de-icing equipment and water methanol injection system. Between August 1951 and September 1952, when most of the flying took place, the two aircraft flew a total of 2,000 hours, and in the financial year 1952/53 'LXN flew 538 hours and 'MDB 668. The experiment did give BEA and Rolls Royce some valuable insights into the ways of the Dart engine.

One new type entered BEA service in 1950/51, the Bristol 170 Freighter. A single aircraft, G-AICS, arrived in August 1950 to be used primarily to carry outside loads that would not fit into a Leopard freighter, and convey spare Centaurus engines to Elizabethans stranded abroad with engine failure. Its career with BEA turned out to be very short lived. In the financial year 1950/51 it flew just

Dart Dakota G-AMDB is seen at Northolt. *(BA).*

204 hours and earnt a mere £9,500 in revenue. It carried no Centaurus engines because the Elizabeths were not in service. In fact it was never to carry them, as early in 1952 BEA decided it was uneconomic to keep 'ICS, and the airline leased it to Silver City Airways on a long term lease. The lease to Silver City began on June 10th 1952 and continued until Silver City purchased the aircraft on May 12th 1957. Part of the agreement stipulated that Silver City would make a Bristol 170 available to BEA at short notice to transport a spare engine to any stranded Elizabethan. So reliable did the Centaurus prove, once the Elizabethan had settled down in service, that the assistance of Silver City was rarely, if ever, needed. BEA nearly had a much larger fleet of Bristol 170s. The 1946 the airline ordered fourteen, eight for passenger carrying called Wayfarers; and six for cargo. Adverse economic conditions within the airline meant the order was subsequently cut to just one, G-AICS. The registrations G-AICM and G-AICN were reserved for the first aircraft of the original order, though they were not taken up by BEA.

1951 saw the start of some new all-freighter services, flown by the Pionair Leopard aircraft, not the Bristol 170. From March 12th the airline flew a six times weekly night mail service from Manchester to Belfast, the service becoming a regular feature of BEA operations, lasting well into British Airways days. Shortages of Pionairs in 1951 meant the Corporation lacked sufficient aircraft to fly the route, and for much of the year it was flown by a DC-3 chartered from Air Transport & Charter. Lack of freighter aircraft lead BEA to lease capacity from other operators too. Sivewright Airways DC-3s worked the twice weekly London-Nice-Rome service until Sivewright went into liquidation in March 1951. Then Scottish Airlines aircraft were chartered for this and other routes. Apart from the Manchester-Belfast route two other new cargo routes were opened London-Dusseldorf-Vienna-Linz-London, and London-Lyons-Milan. Linz, Vienna and Lyons proved to be unpopular destinations and were soon dropped from the network, while Milan became a major cargo destination, with services expanding over the years to several flights a day. Linz and Lyons were never again served by BEA either on a freighter or passenger service, though Cambrian Airways did begin a London-Lyons service with BAC I-IIs in the 1970s.

Another aircraft to appear in BEA colours in 1951, was the De Havilland Heron prototype G-ALZL. The airline loaned the aircraft for trials on its Channel Islands services for the period August 4th to September 2nd. During that time it was used mainly on the Northolt or Southampton to Guernsey and Jersey services, although it did operate a few services into Alderney, making it the largest BEA fixed wing aircraft ever to visit the Island. Whilst with BEA in the Channel Isles, G-ALZL flew thirty four journeys and carried a total of 481 passengers. 'LZL also visited both Land's End and St. Mary's in the Isles of Scilly, again being the largest fixed wing aircraft in BEA colours to visit the Scillies. The airfield at St Mary's was even smaller than that at Alderney. Experience gained with the Heron was instrumental in BEA placing an order for two Heron IBs in 1954 for use in Scotland; and subsequently in 1955 for two Heron 2s for use on services into Alderney. However, the Heron 2s never flew for the airline, since services to Alderney were handed over to Jersey Airlines in April 1956 as part of a route swap between the two airlines.

A most unusual, and little known fleet project, considered by BEA in 1951 was to use the giant Bristol Brabazon airliner on the London-Paris route. The Brabazon had become something of a white elephant, and the airline wondered whether its large capacity could be usefully employed on the high density Paris service. Indeed on May 30th an MP even asked a question in the House of Commons about the project. Needless to say the rather grand idea came to nothing. The economics of operating just one Brabazon on such a short trip were simply awful, and the Brabazon ended up being scrapped.

A fleet project which did materialize was the conversion of most of the Vikings from twenty nine to thirty six seaters. The decision was part of the Corporation's plan to offer tourist class (later called economy class) accommodation on its European routes. Until 1951 all flights had been of a first class standard, but the Board believed this was not ideal. Often routes were too short to benefit from luxury service, and many passengers simply wanted to fly from A to B as cheaply as possible. So the decision was taken to provide tourist class international services, which would be operated by the Viking aircraft, hence the conversion scheme. The conversion included an updating of the aircraft's cockpit, with the installation of more modern instrumentation and radios. The newer radios, in turn again removed the need to carry a Radio Officer. The cost of each conversion was roughly the same as that for the Pionairs, about £10,000 per aircraft. The airline hoped the extra capacity plus the tourist fares could enable each of the converted Vikings to earn about an extra £35,000 a year. Most of the conversion work was undertaken by Scottish Aviation, with the first thirty six seater Viking being delivered to BEA on July 15th 1952.

The operational costs of the Viking was the subject of Peter Masefield's Brancker Lecture in 1951. The Brancker Lecture was an annual event given to the members of the Institute of Transport, and Masefield was invited to give it in 1951. In a long and complex lecture Masefield showed that the Vikings maximum profitability was achieved on routes of about 460 miles. Unfortunately for BEA, he pointed out, most of its Viking routes were much shorter, London-Paris being just 215 miles! Only a very high volume of traffic could compensate for the problem, which often was not forthcoming, or at least occured only in the summer months. Masefield showed that in 1950/51 the Viking had earnt £1,106,100; yet the operating costs for the type had been £1,098,100, meaning the aircraft earnt BEA just £8,000 in profit. The Vikings operating costs were broken down as follows:

29.6% on station costs, ground handling and staff pay.
18.0% on engineering.
11.7% on fuel and oil.

9.5% on aircrew pay and costs.
9.0% on administration.
8.9% on sales.
6.8% on landing fees.
5.6% on customer services, such as in flight catering.
1.6% on other costs.

Peter Masefield concluded BEA could never hope to earn a respectable profit if it had to rely on the Vikings. He suggested the coming Elizabethan heralded a brighter future with its higher capacity, shorter journey times and cheaper operating costs. But until the Elizabethan was available BEA had to soldier on with the Vikings.

One thing BEA did not soldier on with was its organisational structure. From January 1st 1951 it finally scrapped the British and Continental Services Divisions and re-organised Operations into seven departments:

The Commercial Department, headed by Philip Lawton, dealing with sales, reservations and market research.

The Traffic Department under G.O. Waters, dealing with all apsects of traffic handling.

The Flight Operations Department managed by Captain James, responsible for the recruitment, training and management of aircrew, and Operations Staff.

Aircraft Movements and Schedules Department under A. Milward, which concerned itself with scheduling and the production of timetables.

The Engineering Department controlled by Beverley Shenstone.

The Finance and Property Department under R.L. Weir.

The Administrative Department, managed by J. Tyzack.

BEA hoped the new structure might simplify management and reduce costs. One other important change occured in 1951, when John C. Henry retired as head of the airline's Public Relations Unit. He was replaced by W. Simpson who had been responsible for BEA's dealings with the press since 1948, making him the ideal choice as Head of PR. The Public Relations Unit had a vital job to perform. It dealt with customer complaints, and relations with the media. An efficient PR Unit was absolutely essential for the well being of the airline.

As the re-organisation was being put into practice the Engineering Department eagerly pressed ahead with its plan for a purpose built engineering base at Heathrow to replace the facilities at Northolt and Renfrew. A design was drawn up which provided initially for a five bay pre-stressed concrete building, costing about £2 million to build. The design included the very latest in aircraft maintenance technology and would be capable of performing major overhauls on the Elizabethans and Viscounts when they entered service. It was quickly decided to add another five maintenance bays to the building.

Even with all these developments BEA was still small enough to be a family concern. Staff on most stations and in most departments knew each other, and as there were in total only about 7,000 of them the airline was still able to retain a corporate spirit. Many stations in the remoter areas were quite literally family affairs. Station Superintendent Sumburgh (Shetland) was J. Black. He had one assistant to help him handle services, his daughter Marie. At Campbeltown, Station Superintendent Macreachy was also assisted by his daughter, and the same situation existed at Barra. Many of the staff at the remoter stations had worked in aviation for many years. Mr Black had been at Sumburgh since 1936, Mr Macdonald at Benbecula since 1938, but the record went to Mr Macreachy who had worked at Cambeltown since 1932. Staff with such a wealth of local experience were invaluable to the airline, and similar situations existed in the Channel Isles and Isle of Man.

Heron 1 prototype, G-ALZL, at Liverpool, in BEA markings. *(BA)*

1952

The 1951/52 Report and Accounts was eagerly awaited by staff and government alike. All were anxious to see how effective the economies and sales drive of Lord Douglas and Peter Masefield had been. When the Report and Accounts was published the figures were rather disappointing. The losses had actually risen from £979,267 to £1,459,131; though for the first time for total passengers carried by the Corporation in one financial year exceeded one million, at 1,135,579. Much of the reason for the loss lay in the shortage of aircraft over the summer of 1951, and the resultant loss of traffic and increased costs. Also to blame were a rise in staff wages and a general increase in airline operating costs. The new management team were far from happy. Lord Douglas said in the Report and Accounts "If all British people flying over the route network served by BEA had flown on their own national airline alone, the deficit would have been eliminated two years ago." The Commercial Department was certainly doing all it could to persuade people to do just that. In 1952 it offered an even cheaper fare on the London-Paris route; the Night Tourist Fare of £6-10/- single and £9-15/- return. Travel was restricted to departures after 20.00 or before 08.00, and the fare came into operation from October 1st. One departure each way was provided at this fare, leaving Northolt at 20.00 and Le Bourget at 08.00 the next morning. Viking G-AMNJ operated the first Night Tourist flight on October 1st. The Commercial Department sought to expand domestic traffic over the trunk routes from London by offering week-end returns. The fare was set at £8 and available for travel on the London-Glasgow or Edinburgh services. It provided a useful boost to traffic levels over the traditionally slack week-ends. In an attempt to boost sales and give the airline a higher public profile, new Sales Offices were opened in Liverpool, Glasgow, Paris, Cannes, Hamburg, Zurich, Geneva, Milan, Vienna, Nice and a number of other cities.

The Report and Accounts revealed that on March 31st 1952 BEA operated a fleet of forty nine Vikings, six Elizabethans, thirty eight Pionairs, eight Pionair Leopards, two Dart DC-3s, eighteen Rapides, a Bristol Freighter and several helicopters. It gave comprehensive details of the hours flown by each type:

Hours Flown by BEA Aircraft 1951/52

Type	Hours Flown	Average Utilization (hours)
Viking	83,952	5.5
Elizabethan	116	.92
Pionair	45,746	4.19
Pionair Leopard	8,062	4.79
Dart DC-3	157	.65
Rapide	11,840	1.70
Bristol 170	1,003	3.03
S.51	739	1.16
Bell 47	not given	

Prospects did begin to look a little brighter for 1952 with the final introduction of the Elizabethans to passenger services on a regular basis. The first commercial Elizabethan service in 1952 operated on March 13th to Paris, using aircraft G-ALZS. From March 13th to 26th the type operated several Paris services on an ad-hoc basis, and on March 27th Elizabethans began a twice daily scheduled service over the route, with G-ALZP flying the first flight. From June 16th the type began a daily luxury first class service to Paris, called the Silver Wing Service, reviving memories of Imperial Airways days. The fare for the luxury service was £15-19/- return, compared with the normal tourist fare of £11-14/-, and the Night Tourist fare of £9-15/-. The Silver Wing service left Heathrow and Le Bourget at about midday. At midday on June 9th G-ALZX operated a Silver Wing service for invited guests, and then on June 16th the same aircraft began the regular Silver Wing service.

The Elizabethan was one year late entering BEA service, but the airline quickly pressed the new aircraft into service on several more routes: On April 20th G-ALZV flew the first Elizabethan service between London and Milan, and on the same day Elizabethan services to Vienna via Zurich began with a flight operated by G-ALZR. From June 7th the aircraft began to serve Nicosia via Rome and Athens. The Athens-Nicosia sector was operator under charter to Cyprus Airways, making that company only the second airline in the world to fly the Elizabethan. With the coming of the winter and the

Cargo being loaded into Pionair Leopard G-AMNV at Heathrow, with no less than seven other Pionairs in the picture. *(BA)*

larger number of the type in service, further new destinations were added to the Elizabethan's network. On October 26th Stockholm, via Copenhagen, began to be served by the type, G-AMAD flying the first service. The next day a direct London-Stockholm Elizabethan schedule was operated, subsequently flown three days a week. However, even now, Elizabethan operations did not go entirely smoothly, with many technical delays occuring, and it was nearly a year before teething troubles with the aircraft were finally ironed out.

Apart from the arrival of the Elizabethans the summer timetable contained details of a new London-Basle service. Schedules to Basle began on May 2nd, Viking G-AJJN flying the first service under the command of Captain Bailey. Meanwhile a Manchester-Zurich direct service began on April 20th, and Helsinki was briefly restored to the route network. The 1952 Olympic Games were held there and for the duration of the Games, in July, BEA operated a Viking service from Northolt to Helsinki, G-AMGH flying the first service. The special service was used by several nations to get their Olympic teams to Helsinki, including Great Britain. Finally BEA began a new route for the Malta Airlines and Gibraltar Airways, from Malta to Gibraltar via Tunis and Algiers. Flights commenced on June 19th using a Viking, and were scheduled to be flown once a month. Traffic was so poor that the route was given up after the September flight. On the domestic scene London-Manchester services were re-commenced on a twice daily basis with Vikings.

Despite the arrival of the Elizabethan BEA's share of traffic on many international routes was far from good. In the summer BEA found it was carrying only 29% of traffic to Switzerland, 28% to the Scandinavian countries, and 19% of traffic to Amsterdam. The airline concluded that the main problem seemed to lie with the continued use of Vikings on many of the routes, while competitors were using more modern, comfortable and quieter aircraft. It was really only the coming of the Viscount, coupled with the wider use of tourist fares that remedied the situation.

A new hardship to face BEA was a fuel shortage. In May there was a strike in America by 9,000 oil workers. It lead to a world wide shortage of aviation fuel, as most of it was refined in America. The problem lasted from May 12th to June 8th and the government was forced to intervene to ensure the best use of available fuel. Supplies to airlines were limited to 65% of the previous months fuel used, hitting BEA hard. 1,554 flights had to be cancelled, while many others were combined or re-routed. Considerable inconvenience was caused to the public, and BEA lost a significant amount of revenue through no fault of its own. But there was yet another blow, connected with fuel, when the government raised the fuel tax levy on aviaiton fuel. The levy was charged at 1/10$\frac{1}{2}$d per gallon on domestic services, but the government raised it to 2/6d in the spring, further adding to BEA's bills, and making the finances of domestic operations even worse.

One bright spot in the summer was the appearance of the Viscount V.700 prototype, G-AMAV. The aircraft was loaned to the Corporation for route proving flights. They commenced on August 25th with 'MAV flying a London-Rome-Athen-Nicosia flight. It carried six crew and seventeen representatives from BEA, Vickers and

Rolls Royce. Over the months it clocked up 550 flying hours before being returned to Vickers in February 1953. No commercial loads were carried by 'MAV on these route proving flights.

During July the Board announced an order for a new type, the Bristol 171 helicopter. The Bristol 171 was the first British built helicopter to be ordered by the airline, and could carry up to four passengers at 95 mph for up to 175 miles. Two '171s were ordered, to replace the S.51s which were sold off in 1953/54. Prior to the delivery of the '171s BEA loaned a prototype (G-ALSR) from its manufacturer, The Bristol Aeroplane Company. G-ALSR remained with BEA until just after the Corporation's own '171s (G-AMWG and 'MWH) had been delivered, meaning briefly the airline had three Bristol 171s in service.

BEA's HEU was experimenting with the use of the South Bank site near Waterloo Bridge, as a possible city centre heliport in London. On July 28th S.51, G-AJOR, made several landings there to allow the authorities to measure noise levels and obstruction clearances. However the site was not authorized for regular use, the City of London authorities being unwilling to allow single engined helicopters to fly into the city centre. That lead BEA to consider using a barge moored on the River Thames, although nothing came of the idea, and London had to wait for the opening of Battersea Heliport in 1959 before it got a city centre heliport. Between 1952 and 1959 BEA was occasionally allowed to use the South Bank. In 1955/56 it was even allowed to make regular use of the site for a scheduled service from Heathow, but under stringent restrictions. The HEU faced great problems with all its helicopter operations due to the high cost of helicopter flying. Something of the problem was indicated by the fact that rotor blades had to be replaced after 150 flying hours, and a new set of blades cost £6,000 a time. In 1952/53 S.51 G-AJOV flew a total of 450 hours, meaning three sets of blades had to be replaced, costing the airline £18,000; while S.51 G-AJOR and Bell 47 G-AKFB also flew sufficient hours to require one set of blade replacements each. The HEU had a total bill £30,000 just in replacement costs for rotor blades!

Just prior to the opening of the winter schedules, BEA ended Rapide operations in Scotland, except for the route to Barra and the air ambulance service. Pionairs replaced Rapides on all routes apart from Barra. Barra had no airfield, the aircraft landing on the beach at Northbay when the tide was out, making it unsuitable for Pionair operations. Until October 1st Rapides had flown the Glasgow-Campbeltown-Islay route, and the Glasgow-Tiree route. On that day Pionairs took over the services. The first scheduled Pionair flight into Campbeltown and Islay was operated by G-AGIU, while G-ALXL operated the first Pionair flight to Tiree. Tiree became a stop on the Glasgow-Benbecula-Stornoway route, as there was insufficient traffic from and to Tiree to justify a Pionair service in its own right. The withdrawal of the Rapides meant BEA was able to sell off nine more of the type. Three Rapides remained based in Glasgow for the air ambulance service and schedule to Barra. The latter was far from demanding with only two flights a week being operated, one on Monday and the other on Friday. The schedule showed it took one hour thirty minutes to fly to Barra, but only one hour twenty minutes to get back. Were the westerly winds really that strong?

The winter schedule itself contained no new routes, but right at its outset, on 30th October, the airline carried its five millionth passenger. Winter operations were often affected by fog, and things were especially bad in 1952. Fog descended in November and caused havoc right through into December. The problem caused 2,029 BEA flights to be cancelled, and countless others were diverted from Northolt and Heathrow to Birmingham, Manchester and Bournemouth. The airline lost another £25,000 through this problem. BEA had for a long time

Bristol 171 G-AMWH at Southampton. *(P.Marson)*

Elizabethan G-ALZY at Blackbushe diring F.I.D.O. demostrations in November 1952. *(BA)*

been campaigning about the need to install FIDO at Heathrow. FIDO was a fog dispersal system, developed in the Second World War, which worked by burning petrol along each side of the runway. On November 11th the airline took part in a FIDO demonstration, to prove its point. Elizabethan G-ALZY and Viking G-AHPM joined a BOAC York (G-AGJC) to make a number of landings at Blackbushe, using FIDO, in thick fog. The landings were made quite successfully, but the Ministry of Aviation never took up the idea of using FIDO at commercial airports, believing there were safety implications for a passenger aircraft landing between two rows of burning petrol!

A new experience for BEA in 1952 was the operation of a Royal Flight. On November 26th Elizabethan G-AMAB carried the Duke of Edinburgh to Malta, returning via Rome; where the Duchess of Kent was picked up on December 2nd. Afterwards BEA became a regular Royal carrier, indeed the RAF thought so highly of BEA's services, that it placed a contract with the airline to provide catering for all Royal flights on both civil and military aircraft.

At Heathrow the long anticipated maintenance base was nearing completion in the early part of the year. On March 17th BEA began the massive task of moving its engineering headquarters from Northolt into the new facilities. The Heathrow Base consisted of 458,405 square feet divided into ten bays, five coming into use in 1952 and the rest in 1953. Each bay had its own aircraft access door from the apron, and a fully equipped maintenance dock. The first bay to be ready for use was the Elizabethan dock. The move from Northolt was completed by April 17th, though some electrical and instrument workshops remained at Northolt for the time being. The new Base quickly ran into problems with the staff. Lack of canteen facilities and poor public transport caused considerable discontent, but after a while the problems were rectified. The Heathrow Base was to be used for Viscount and Elizabethan maintenance only, with Pionair and Viking major maintenance conducted at Renfrew, where a new Pionair Check Three dock was opened on October 13th. Viking maintenance was transferred from Northolt to Glasgow during March and April. The move was only a short term measure as the airline was planning to withdraw the Vikings from operational service by the end of 1954. Concentration of Pionair and Viking overhauls at Glasgow was not without economic penalties. It was a long way for aircraft to position, especially those operating in the Channel Islands or on the German internal network. Operations staff tried to minimize such costly positioning flights by scheduling aircraft, needing maintenance, to operate services into Glasgow.

In 1952 BEA made what was a rather unusual purchase for an airline - a new fleet of buses to carry passengers from Kensington Air Terminal to Northolt and Heathrow. The new buses were built by Park Royal coach builders as one and a half deckers carrying thirty seven passengers. They entered service in 1953, and were to become a familiar sight in and around London for many years to come.

A final event of note in June 1952, was the opening of a hard runway at Jersey. It was 4,000 feet long and overcame, once and for all, the waterlogging problems faced in the winter months with the old grass runways. To mark the occasion a flying display was held, and BEA contributed to the static display of aircraft:- Viking G-AMNJ, Elizabethan G-ALZV and Dart DC-3 G-ALXN. The existence of hard runway enabled the airline to operate both Vikings and Elizabethans into Jersey. Elizabethans did eventually serve the Island regularly, but Vikings only made rare appearances.

1953

During 1953 the remaining Elizabethans were delivered, the last to arrive being G-ALZN on March 31st, and of course more BEA stations began to receive Elizabethan services. On April 17th Elizabethan services from London to Manchester commenced with G-AMAC flying the first service. From April 19th the aircraft began flying several other routes: London to Amsterdam (first flight by G-ALZX), London to Brussels and Dusseldorf (first flight by G-AMAF), London to Amsterdam and Hanover (first flight by G-ALZT) and finally London to Amsterdam and Hamburg (first flight by G-ALZY). At the beginning of October Elizabethans appeared on a number of other routes, including London-Amsterdam-Cologne/Bonn from October 4th (first flight by G-ALZY), London-Nice-Malta from October 7th (first flight by G-ALZZ) and two routes from Manchester, to Paris via Birmingham and to Dusseldorf. The first Elizabethan to fly the Manchester-Paris route was G-ALZX on October 5th. The next day the same aircraft inaugurated Elizabethan flights between Manchester and Dusseldorf. At last, much to the relief of engineers, Operations staff and the travelling public, the Elizabethans began to overcome their teething problems and provide regular and reliable service. They proved popular with aircrews and passengers alike.

However the popularity for the Elizabethan was totally eclipsed by that for the Viscount. The first Viscount to be delivered to BEA was G-ALWE on January 3rd. It returned briefly to Wisley on February 11th for a formal naming ceremony performed by Lady Douglas. G-ALWF and 'MNY were delivered in February and G-AMOG in March. Between January and April these Viscounts made a number of route proving flights, fequently setting up flight time records. On January 22nd G-ALWE flew from London to Cologne in the record time of one hour ten minutes, while on March 19th 'LWE flew to Zurich in just one hour forty seven minutes. Further flight time records were established once the aircraft had entered commercial service, for example, on May 1st G-AMNY flying a scheduled London-Geneva flight completed the journey in one hour thirty one minutes, while 'LWE completed a schedule to Copenhagen in two hours twenty six minutes on July 1st.

The first commercial Viscount service was a rather

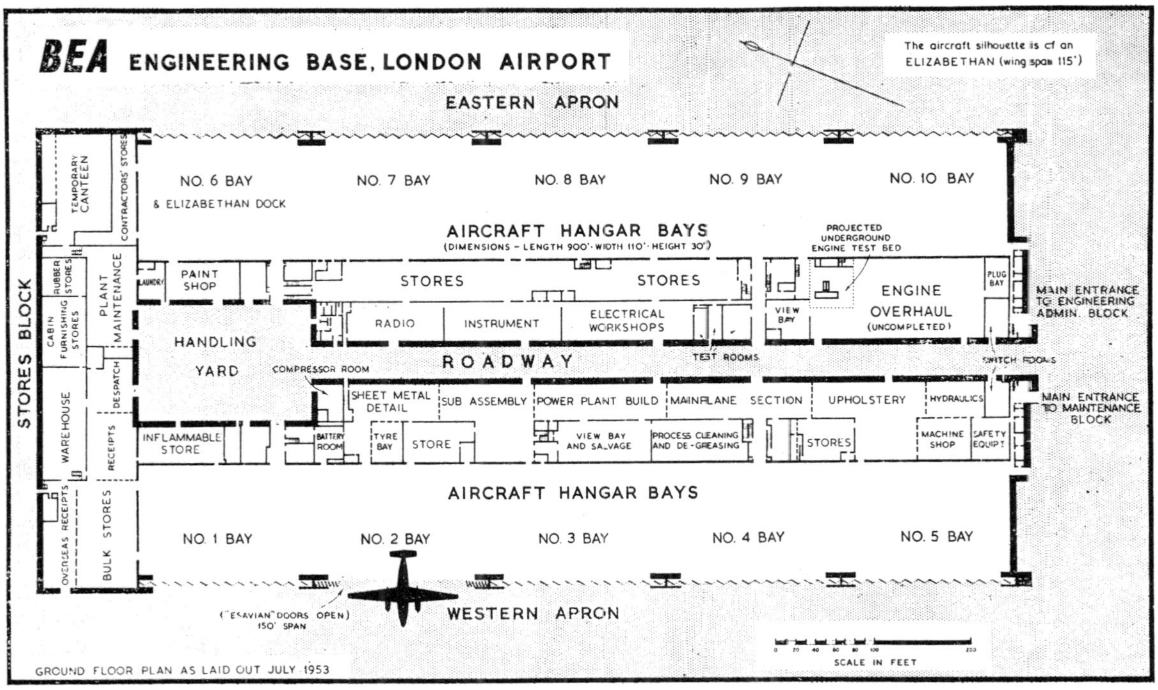

An early visit to Geneva by Viscount V.701 G-AMNY. *(BA)*

unusual affair. A Viscount, G-AMOG, was substituted for a Pionair Leopard freighter to operate a scheduled freight service from London to Nicosia, via Rome and Athens on April 2nd. Several other scheduled freight flights were flown over the route, and the Heathrow-Istanbul route, by G-AMOG over the next few weeks. Finally on April 18th commercial passenger services by Viscount began, with G-AMNY, piloted by Captains Johnson and Wilson, flying a Heathrow-Rome-Athens-Nicosia service. In accordance with normal operating procedure the Athens-Nicosia sector was flown under charter to Cyprus Airways, making the airline the second in the world to operate a commercial Viscount flight. It will be remembered it was the second to operate Elizabethans in similar circumstances. Following this, Viscounts were placed on many routes:

19th April	London-Rome-Athens-Istanbul. First flight by G-ALWE.
25th April	London-Zurich. First flight by G-ALWE.
1st June	London-Geneva. First flight by G-AMNY.
1st July	London-Copenhagen-Stockholm. First flight by G-ALWE.
17th July	London-Glasgow. First flight by G-AMOB. Viscounts were used on this route on an ad-hoc basis only for some time.
6th October	London-Milan. First flight by G-AMNY.
6th October	London-Geneva-Milan. First flight by G-AMOB.
1st November	London-Frankfurt. First flight by G-AMOD.
1st November	London-Belfast. First flight by G-AMOD.

The Belfast service was an all first class luxury service called the Ulster Flyer. The schedule provided for an evening departure from Heathrow with the aircraft night-stopped at Belfast and returning to London early the next morning. Unfortunately the inaugural flight went astray because of thick fog at Heathrow, and the first Belfast-London Ulster Flyer, flown by G-AMOD, had to divert to Manchester. The use of the Viscounts significantly cut flying times. Time savings were typically demonstrated on the London-Frankfurt service. The Viscount cut fifty minutes off the Viking's scheduled flight time, and fifteen minutes from the Elizabethan's. The Royal Family tasted the delights of Viscount travel for the first time on May 14th, when G-AMOB carried Princess Margaret to Oslo, the first of a whole line of BEA Royal flights using Viscounts.

Inside the Viscount the colour scheme was grey and red, which may have been restful but was certainly not bright! The large oval windows were very popular with passengers who flocked to use the new type which was comfortable, quiet and quick. To fly Viscounts BEA had forty eight pilots by May 1953, and a further thirty were earmarked to begin conversion courses in September. The courses involved thirteen or fourteen hours of 'flying', though twelve of those were in the simulator where BEA calculated it saved about £1,000 per pilot on training costs. Competition was intense to be chosen to fly the Viscuont, and Captain James, Bailey and Johnson (the selection team for Viscount aircrews) had a hard job selecting applicants. Engineers, too, found the Viscount to be a delight. Of particular pleasure for them was its low slung engines which could be worked on without the need for high scaffolding or clambering over the wings. Mr J.J. Gubbins, BEA's Manager in charge of Design and Procurement of Equipment, designed a whole range of Viscount maintenance equipment. Best known was the engine servicing cradle that could be moved around, with an engine in it, by just one engineer. The cradles were built by Bramber Engineering Limited. Engineers were instructed on Viscounts under the supervision of R.J. Jauncey, Viscount Type Engineer.

At the same time as BEA was preparing to introduce the Viscount, it demonstrated its faith in the type by placing an order, on February 11th, for twelve larger eighty six seaters, designated the V.801. BEA regarded the '801 as ideal for its high density routes to Paris, Amsterdam, Brussels and Dusseldorf, however the increased capacity of the V.801 meant its cruising speed dropped to under 300 mph. BEA was not entirely happy at that prospect and engaged in consultations with Vickers and Rolls Royce about the possibility of improving engine performance. Out of the talks emerged a new specification issued by Vickers, the V.802, able to carry seventy one passengers at 325 mph using Dart 510 RDa6 engines. On April 14th 1954 BEA cancelled its order for the V.801 and ordered twelve of the V.802s instead. The '802 had a fuselage length of only three feet more than the V.701, passenger capacity being raised mainly through moving the front bulkhead forward and the rear bulkhead backwards.

With the rising standard of living more people were taking holidays in the sun. To cater for them BEA began a Northolt-Palma service on May 15th, Viking G-AIVK flying the inaugural service. Due to the Viking's limited range a refuelling stop was made at Bordeaux. As Majorca developed into a major holiday resort for the British public, BEA's services expanded, and by the early 1960s several flights a day operated from London, as well as several a week from Manchester and Glasgow. On October 4th BEA resumed services to Lisbon, with Viscounts, at an initial frequency of one flight a week. Apart from the routes to Palma and Lisbon, the summer saw the beginning of international tourist class services and fares. From April 1st 90% of the airline's international capacity was sold as tourist class with substantial fare reductions. For the moment the Viscounts operated in an all first class configuration, but the other types provided tourist class accommodation, with the Vikings being specially adapted for the role. Viking operations that summer were not without problems. Between May 2nd and September 9th all Vikings which had flown over 9,000 hours were grounded for spar modifications, affecting fifteen of the BEA fleet, and inevitably there was some disruption to services. How thankful the airline was that the problem had not occurred the previous summer. Some of the Vikings had already been grounded for a few days in April, for modifications to their seats. BEA began phasing out the type as the Elizabethans and Viscounts entered service, and between April 1953 and June 1954 thirteen were sold, and another thirteen were placed into storage awaiting sale.

To facilitate better control of reservations the Corporation installed its first mechanical reservations system on March 3rd. It was a far cry from the sophisticated computer technology of the late '60s and early '70s but it did improve the service. The system, called 'Flightmaster', was capable of displaying seat availability on up to 32,000 flights. The old reservations system, using boards and pieces of paper, was quite unable to cope with the scale of BEA activity by 1953. At least the reservations staff could have their windows open on a windy day! With the old system that was a risk they could ill afford, as on occasions the wind blew the pieces of paper off the boards causing havoc! In the summer BEA replaced Kensington Air Station with a new terminal at Waterloo. The new terminal could handle 2,000 passengers and twenty coach departures an hour. It was a little closer to Heathrow than Kensington Air Station. On average, coach journey times were reduced by fifteen minutes. The terminal was officially opened by the Minister of Aviation on May 19th, and came into regular use on May 21st. Waterloo was to be only a temporary town terminal for BEA, as the land on which it stood was earmarked for the eventual building of the National Theatre. In readiness for a future move, BEA obtained a piece of land on the Cromwell Road to become its new town terminal site when Waterloo had to be vacated.

Surprisingly enough summer traffic levels were quite healthy despite restrictions of foreign travel and a foreign currency allowance, limiting the amount of foreign currency allowed to be taken out of Britain. From February 1952 until March 1953 it had been set at £25 per person per annum, but in the Budget it was raised to £40 helping the airline a little. Foreign currency restrictions encouraged people to take holidays in Sterling Area countries such as Malta, Cyprus, Gibraltar; and of course at home, in the Channel Isles and Isle of Man. Traffic to the Channel Isles boomed, and to cope with demand the airline scheduled Elizabethans on the London-Jersey route at week-ends over the summer. By the end of the year BEA had carried 320,000 passengers to the CI, most of whom had travelled on the London-Jersey/Guernsey or Southampton-Jersey routes.

With a Conservative government in power it was inevitable that there would be some changes in the legislation regarding commercial aviation. They occurred in 1953, with the government removing BEA's monopoly on scheduled services within the UK. Independent airlines no longer required associate agreements with BEA to fly scheduled services. Now, subject to licencing, they were free to operate their own services and many jumped at the chance. By the summer of 1954 twenty independents were flying domestic scheduled services, some in direct competition with BEA, like Don Everal's service from Birmingham to Jersey. Eventually BEA faced competition on the domestic trunk routes and some international services.

BEA's associate company, Gibraltar Airways, had been flying its schedule across the Straits of Gibraltar to Tangier using Rapides for many years, but the DH 89s were getting old, and the build up of traffic was exceeding their capacity. From October 5th Gibraltar Airways began to use a BEA Pionair for the service. G-AGHP flew the first days schedule for Gibraltar Airways, and thereafter a Pionair was based at Gibraltar to maintain the link with Tangier. The aircraft was changed once a month. The value of using the Pionair was indicated in the financial turn round experienced by Gibraltar Airways. In 1953 it made a loss of £603, but in 1954 - the first full year of Pionair operations - that was turned into a profit of £4,127.

BEA's own finances were brought to public attention on July 30th with the publication of the 1952/53 Report and Accounts. The loss was £1,459,131, slightly up on the previous year. Given the problems of late delivery of aircraft, fuel strikes, currency restriction and fuel tax surcharges, the result was not unexpected. The Report estimated the fuel strike and currency restrictions had cost the airline £1,200,000 in lost revenue. Lord Douglas was understandably disappointed, however, he could at least derive a crumb of comfort, these were exceptional problems which would probably not recur. Passenger traffic had risen by 23% to 1,400,122; though the overall load factor had fallen from 66.9% to 64.5%. The Report detailed the following statistics concerning the revenue earnt by each type, and its operational costs:

	Average Revenue per Aircraft	Average cost per flying hour
Elizabethan	£150,000	£164
Viking	£130,000	£80
Pionair	£95,000	£63
Pionair Leopard	£60,000	£51
Rapide	£8,000	£14

The high cost per flying hour of the Elizabethan reflected the initial problems the type had suffered. The Viking operating costs too were quite high, due to the increasing age and consequent technical difficulties with the type.

The Engineering Department, fully established in its new Heathrow premises, was extremely busy. The scale of its activity is demonstrated by the number of checks it performed on aircraft in 1952/53:- 2,968 Check Ones, 396 Check Twos, 229 Check Threes, 169 Check Fours and 12 Check Fives. The Check Five was a temporary check on the Elizabethan and Viscount fleet, phased out once the types had settled down into service. The overhauls continued to be performed after a specific number of flying hours, and by 1953 these were as follows:

	Check 1	Check 2	Check 3	Check 4	Check 5
Viking	60	305	610	1,200	-
Pionair	60	305	610	1,200	-
Elizabethan	55	105	210	410	800
Viscount	85	155	310	620	1,200
Rapide	55	205	410	800	-

One major task undertaken by the engineers in 1953 was the virtual rebuilding of Elizabethan G-ALZO. On July 10th the aircraft was engaged in training at Blackbushe, and was severely damaged in a heavy landing. It was dismantled and taken by road to Heathrow, where it was repaired. 26,000 man hours later the aircraft returned to service!

As far as the Helicopter Experimental Unit was concerned, 1953 was a quiet year. The London-Birmingham freighter route continued, with the Bristol 171 entering service on July 13th. The other major event was the chartering of two S.51s by the government, to assist in flood relief operations in Holland during February and on February 4th Captains Cameron and Crewdsen flew the S.51s to Holland via Lypmne and Antwerp, where they remained until February 11th. While in Holland they rescued seventy six people and carried doctors and supplies to those cut off by flood water in about twenty villages. The two aircraft flew a total of forty five hours on the task. Later in the year one of the S.51s was used at Blackbushe to assist in the calibration of the new Decca 424 Approach Surveillance Radar. The helicopter, flown by 'Jock' Cameron, is reputed to have landed within five yards of the selected spot on several approaches made under radar control.

In October 1953 a London to New Zealand Air Race was organised. BEA decided to enter with the backing of Vickers, to advertise the airline and the Viscount. Vickers loaned BEA the Viscount V.700 prototype, G-AMAV, which was still painted in full BEA colours. The team to crew the aircraft were:
Peter Masefield. Team Manager.
Captains W. Ballie, A.S. Johnson, S. Jones. Pilots.
R.H. Chadwick. Navigator.
I.A. Dalgleish and E.H.S. Bristow. Radio Operators.
Also on board were two representatives from Vickers, John Profumo (Deputy Minister of Civil Aviation) who acted as steward, and Raymond Baxter of the BBC. G-AMAV left Heathrow, wearing race number 23, at 16.40 on October 8th and arrived at Christchurch New Zealand at 09.23 on October 10th. The 12,365 mile journey had been flown in forty hours forty three minutes, at an average speed of 316 mph. Stops to refuel were made at Bahrain (fourteen minutes), Colombo (nineteen minutes), The Coco Islands (twenty two minutes) and Melbourne (fifteen minutes). The Viscount was entered under the Transport Handicap Class, and was the first to arrive in its class. The Royal Aero Club placed it second, because of the vast speed advantage it had over its rivals, a KLM DC-6, and a Royal New Zealand Air Force Hastings. Once out in New Zealand, Vickers took the opportunity to demonstrate the Viscount to interested airlines both there and in Australia. Further demonstrations occurred as 'MAV made a leisurely journey home, and in total it was shown off in thirty one different cities. Orders eventually followed for Viscounts from New Zealand, Australia, India and Pakistan. Naturally BEA gained some free publicity at each stop. This was not the only time G-AMAV ventured abroad in BEA colours. In May 1953 the aircraft made a sales tour of Uganda, Kenya and India, again full BEA livery.

The Heathrow that G-AMAV flew out of on October 8th was gradually developing into London's main airport. Progress towards the new central area terminal was continuing, and the access tunnels to it from the Bath Road were finished. The tunnels ran under one of the main runways, which had been closed while they were dug. By October 1953 most European airlines had moved to Heathrow from Northolt, and BEA was busy handling many of them. The Corporation's own services were building up from the airport with the fuller use of the Viscounts and Elizabethans. Heathrow proved a useful diversionary airport for Northolt, having much better landing aids, which often made it useable when Northolt was closed by bad weather.

1954

The Viscounts began to bring a new era of confidence to BEA. The airline found it was winning back some of the traffic lost to its European rivals over the previous two or three years because the Viscount was so popular. On the Swiss routes BEA's total share of traffic had declined to only 30% by 1953 with the stiff competition from Swissair's Convairs. Viscounts began to redress the balance, and by the end of 1954 the Corporation found its share of traffic had risen to 41% and it continued to rise. The same story occurred on several other routes, like London-Amsterdam and Brussels, as well as some of the services to West Germany. BEA's faith in the Viscount was clearly paying off. Passenger liking for the type continued to be high, with some passengers actually being willing to for go an earlier service if the later flight was Viscount operated.

Deliveries of the type continued, twenty being in service by March, and the Viscount route network was further expanded. On January 2nd Viscount services to Madrid began with G-AMOL being used for the first flight, while G-AMOF flew the inaugural Viscount service to Palma on January 10th, and G-AMOH to Barcelona on January 13th. In April the Viscounts began to fly the non-stop London-Stockholm service, and the London-Dusseldorf-Munich-Athens schedule. For the summer season Viscounts flew some of the international routes from the provinces. On April 11th they replaced Elizabethans on the Manchester-Birmingham-Paris route, and on April 13th the Manchester-Amsterdam-Dusseldorf schedule. Use of the Viscounts on continental routes from Manchester meant the aircraft also flew some London-Manchester services as positioning flights.

The glittering success of the Viscounts almost overshadows any other changes in 1954. Yet developments there were. For a number of years BEA had arranged a coach service between Bordeaux and Biarritz in connection with the London-Bordeaux flights. Because the coach link had become well patronised BEA decided to open a direct London-Biarritz operation, beginning on May 28th when Viking G-AJBP inaugurated the route. Biarritz would be served in the summer only. Perhaps the real claim to fame of the new route was that it was the last new international service to be inaugurated by a Viking. A second new route began on April 11th, when an Elizabethan opened a twice weekly link between London and Naples. BEA already served Naples, with a service from Malta begun in 1953. Elizabethans replaced Vikings on the German internal network and on the Malta-Tripoli-Benghazi-Cairo route. BEA hoped the greater use of Elizabethans on the German services would encourage traffic, although it was not to be, because the East Germans began to relax restrictions on surface travel through East Germany into West Berlin. BEA had always relied on the difficulties of surface travel to boost its loads into Berlin, but now loads fell by 25%, leading to economies in schedules, staff and premises. The effects of the East German move were still being felt by BEA in 1955/56, leading to the suspension of the Berlin to Munich and Frankfurt routes. Passengers travelling on certain routes benefitted from the wider use of Night Tourist, Fares which were extended to cover flights to Hamburg, Malta, Milan, Palma and Rome. £13-12/- could be saved on the normal day time fare to Rome, by flying Night Tourist, and £5-3/- by a similar fare to Palma.

One route flown in the winter of 1954, which had previously been a summer only service, was Manchester to Zurich. Winter services commenced on December 17th using Viscounts. Passengers were mainly those going abroad for winter sports holidays, and not a few returned with arms or legs in plaster! The winter was not a very good time for Viscount operations, with the type suffering three accidents in an eight week period. On October 24th G-AMNZ suffered a partial undercarriage collapse when landing at Rome. On December 12th G-ALWF encountered the same fate when landing at Blackbushe on a training flight As if that were not bad enough, the very next day, G-AMOB repeated the incident almost exactly, as it slithered to a halt on its belly at Blackbushe. All three aircraft were soon returned to service thanks to the skill of the Engineering Unit.

Passengers travelling to Hamburg in the winter found themselves flying on a Pionair Leopard freighter. A limited number of passenger seats were fitted to the aircraft to enable it to accommodate passengers as well as freight. Apart from the newspaper service flown to the Channel Isles in 1947/48, it is believed this was the first BEA service to operate in a part passenger/part freight configuration. It was a taste of things to come in the

1960s, when some Viscounts and Vanguards operated in mixed configuration. The passenger capacity on the Leopard was really too low for the Hamburg service, and by 1956 a daily all-passenger Pionair schedule was operating, via Colgne/Bonn.

1954 was an important year for the HEU. On January 14th the London-Birmingham all-cargo service was finally abandoned, but on June 15th a new passenger schedule was commenced, Heathrow-Southampton-Northolt-Southampton-Heathrow. One flight a day worked over the route on week-days only, and Bristol 171 G-AMWH flew the inaugural services. When Northolt closed as a BEA station, on October 30th, the Southampton-Northolt sector was abandoned, and a single round trip between Heathrow and Southampton operated. The schedule provided for a 13.05 departure from Heathrow, with the helicopter arriving at Southampton at 13.55. The return left Eastleigh at 14.15. Connections were possible from and to Glasgow, Edinburgh, Aberdeen and Belfast, as well as several European destinations. On October 6th BEA ordered two Westand WS.55 helicopters for the HEU at a cost of £54,000. The first, G-ANFH, saw service on December 22nd, when it operated the Southampton schedule. After that the WS.55 replaced the Bristol 171s on most of the flights to Southampton. Like the previous passenger routes tried by the Helicopter Experimental Unit this one was not an economic success, and was abandoned in April 1955. The HEU helicopters continued to be engaged in a number of research programmes, including the calibration of various systems of helicopter cockpit lighting, and heliport lighting, and the Bell 47s were kept active on training work for both BEA and other operators. BEA trained four of its own pilots to fly helicopters in 1954, as well as three pilots for the Ministry of Aviation. These pilots then proceeded to check out BEA's! Keeping the HEU cost BEA £92,070 for 1954/55, mostly covered by a grant of £80,561 from the Ministry of Aviation. The HEU qualified for an annual Ministry grant because of its experimental work. The helicopter fleet was reduced to five aircraft in 1954 following the sale of the last

One of the farthest points on the network, Istanbul, with V.701 G-AMON. *(BA)*

remaining S.51 (G-AJOV) and the return of Bristol 171 (G-ALSR) to Bristol Aeroplane Company at the end of its lease. The five were: one WS.55, two Bristol 171s and two Bell 47s. A second WS.55 was on order.

By 1954 BEA's staffing levels stood at just under 9,000 and included in the total was a new grade, the Flight Clerk. There were seventy one Flight Clerks by the end of 1954. They were in effect flying traffic clerks. On board the aircraft they acted as cabin attendant to the passengers, which really amounted to no more than giving the safety briefing, since they were never used on routes where there was any catering service. When the aircraft landed, the Flight Clerk assisted local traffic staff with the turnround. The aim was to reduce the number of traffic staff required at smaller stations, and Pionair services in Scotland and the Channel Isles were crewed by Flight Clerks. The largest single group of staff were the engineers, numbering some 3,000. Of these nearly 2,000 were located at the Heathrow Base, and another 700 or so at the Renfrew Engineering Base. The remainder were scattered round the network at home and abroad. It was BEA's practice to station engineers at most of its destinations, the number depending on how busy a particular airport was. Abroad, except at the busiest stations like Rome, Paris and Berlin, there was generally only one engineer - usually in permanent residence - but sometimes on detachment from a pool of travelling engineers based in London. At most stations in the UK there were several engineers, except in the Scottish Highlands and Islands which were without engineers, apart from Inverness and Kirkwall. The senior engineer at each station was given the official title of Station Engineer, even if he was the only engineer! Each Station Engineer held a small stock of spares for the types of aircraft using his station, but any serious defects usually meant an urgent telex to London for spares to be flown out on the next available service of any airline. Sometimes aircraft would be chartered to fly out spares, or even a BEA aircraft sent with urgently needed bits and pieces. Nowhere was unserviceability more feared than at Barra's beach airstrip. If the Rapide (or later Heron) went unserviceable a real rush at Renfrew ensued to get spares flown out before the tide came up!

Ever keen to improve its load factors, BEA launched a number of improvements to the standard of service offered to passengers on board its aircraft. One was to extend the scope of its named all first class luxury services, the most popular of which was the already existing Siliver Wing lunch time flight to and from Paris, departing from London at 13.00 and Le Bourget at 12.30. The service was still flown by Elizabethan, but such importance was placed on it, that its departure was usually personally directed by BEA's Senior Traffic Officer (Deputy Station Manager) Mr Kent, who saluted the departing aircraft leather gloves in hand. On the flight passengers were treated to a slap up lunch consisting of Champagne, Scotch salmon, lamb cutlets and pears in port wine, followed by cheese and biscuits and coffee. The success of the service lead BEA to extend the idea of all first class luxury flights to other popular routes. In 1954 a Monday and Thursday Viscount service, again called the Silver Wing service, was launched to Lisbon. Departure from Heathrow was at 10.15, and from Lisbon at 15.30. By 1954 luxury named services were also operating on some of the domestic trunk routes. The Clansman flew from London to Glasgow each evening, returning the next morning, while the Ulster Flyer operated on the same pattern to Belfast. Later the Chieftan Service was added, to serve Edinburgh. By 1956 BEA had tried another three international destinations for the luxury all first class service, Brussels received a daily Silver Wing Service with departures from Heathrow at 12.45 and Brussels at 14.05; Madrid had the Madrid Flyer on Mondays and Fridays, and Palma the Majorca Flyer on Saturdays and Sundays. All were Viscount operated, except the Brussels Silver Wing service, which was flown by Elizabethan. These experiments were not altogether successful, with the Brussels, Madrid and Palma services ending very quickly. The Paris Silver Wing flight lasted longest, being dropped in 1958 when Viscount V.806s were introduced offering first and tourist class accommodation on all services. The domestic luxury services managed to survive a little longer, but by March 1960 they too had ceased; passengers being, for the most part, unwilling to pay the higher fares for such short periods of luxury.

A further customer services improvement, was the beginning of cabin announcements to passengers through a cabin address system, replacing the older method of the steward shouting above the engine noise. No such refinement existed on the Pionairs though, and the author can still picture the Flight Clerk standing at the top of the cabin rushing through the announcements before the engines were revved up! In November BEA began a system enabling passengers to pay for their tickets by instalments, a sort of higher purchase. Tickets could be paid for over a six, twelve or twenty one month period. To cover the costs of the scheme passengers were charged an extra 1% above the fare for the flight. The idea proved a useful money spinner and over the summer of 1955 BEA estimated it had earnt an extra £100,000 by offering payment by instalment. The winter of 1954 saw yet another sales drive, but with a difference. The salesmen used were aircrew. With a less demanding flying programme in the winter, several Captains were detached to spend two weeks at a time on the road selling BEA. Forty pilots took part in the scheme, but it was not repeated. Perhaps the pilot's expense claims were a little higher than those of the humble sales rep! In 1954/55 BEA had a surplus of aircrew, and no new pilots were recruited in either year. Instead the airline was able to second some pilots to other operators and ten were seconded to Lufthansa, two to Iraqi Airways, three to Trans Australian Airlines and four to British West Indian Airways. They were all employed on Viscount crew training for the airlines.

An unexpected boost to BEA's revenue came as a result of the national rail strike between May 18th and 29th. Freight traffic on many domestic routes boomed and the airline picked up some lucrative freight charters, especially for the carriage of national newspapers. Vikings and Leopards flew a series of newspaper charters from

Northolt to Exeter and Cardiff during the strike. Ninety seven BEA flights were made, and the Corporation co-ordinated another four hundred and four flights by various independent operators.

1954 was an important year in the history of BEA because it marked the retirement of the Vikings and the closure of Northolt as a BEA station. By April 1st BEA had only eighteen Vikings left in service (G-AHPS, 'IVB, 'IVD, 'IVF, 'IVI, 'IVJ, 'IVK, 'IVL, 'IVM, 'MGG, 'MGH, 'MGI, 'MGJ, 'MNJ, 'JBR, 'JBY, 'JDI and 'JJN). Another fifteen were in store awaiting a buyer (G-AHPP, 'HPR, 'IVN, 'JBM, 'JBN, 'JBP, 'JBS, 'JBT, 'JBU, 'JBX, 'JCE, 'KBH, 'MNR, 'MNJ and 'MNX). The summer timetable included Viking flights from London to Barcelona, Biarritz, Bordeaux, Balse, Dusseldorf, Gibraltar, Madrid, Munich, Naples and Rome, plus domestic Viking flights from Northolt to Belfast, Glasgow and Manchester. The winter timetable, commencing on October 3rd, contained no scheduled Viking services, although the aircraft did fly some services as extras or substitutes for other types for the month of October. The last commercial Viking service is believed to have been operated by G-AHPS early in October. Retirement was officially set for October 31st, and on October 30th two flight operated from Northolt to mark the occasion. Both were local flights from and to Northolt, G-AIVK, flown by Captain Riley carried a party of pressmen, while G-AIVI commanded by Captain James carried a selection of BEA staff and the Chairman. Between 1946 and 1954 BEA had operated no less than eighty different Vikings, but not at the same time. Together they had flown 414,000 revenue flying hours and travelled sixty five and one half million miles. The aircraft had carried nearly three million passengers for BEA, and earnt the airline £35 million. It had done more than any other type to establish BEA as a major airline in those early days, even if by 1954 it was rather slow and uneconomic. Buyers for the retired fleet were not numerous, and a number of Vikings were cocooned at Heathrow for some time awaiting sale. The last two, G-AHPS and G-AIVF, were not sold until February 29th 1956.

On October 30th, the day G-AIVI and 'IVK operated their farewell flights, BEA closed down its station at Northolt. International services had all transferred to Heathrow by October 3rd, and cargo flights had moved early in October, leaving Northolt with only domestic flights. They too were transferred to Heathrow on October 31st. The final days programme for Northolt on October 30th was:

Northolt Departures 30.10.54.

08.05	BE902	P.32	Manchester/Glasgow.
08.25	BE660	P.32	Jersey.
08.45	BE920	P.32	Edinburgh.
09.05	BE904	P.32	Glasgow.
09.15	BE542	P.32	Belfast.
10.10	BE718	P.32	Guernsey.
10.25	BE664	P.32	Jersey.
12.05	BE906	P.32	Glasgow.
13.20	BE672	P.32	Jersey.
14.50	BE724	P.32	Guernsey.
15.20	BE676	P.32	Jersey.
15.35	BE550	P.32	Belfast.
16.05	BE908	P.32	Glasgow.
17.05	BE678	P.32	Jersey.
17.05	BE910	P.32	Manchester/Glasgow.
18.20	BE924	P.32	Birmingham/Edinburgh /Glasgow.
19.00	BE684	P.32	Jersey.

Northolt Arrivals 30.10.54.

09.35	BE653	P.32	Jersey.
12.05	BE659	P.32	Jersey.
12.05	BE925	P.32	Edinburgh/Glasgow /Birmingham.
12.45	BE903	P.32	Glasgow/Manchester.
13.35	BE717	P.32	Guernsey.
14.35	BE663	P.32	Jersey.
15.05	BE545	P.32	Belfast.
15.20	BE907	P.32	Glasgow.
18.20	BE673	P.32	Jersey.

In addition there were the two local flights by the Vikings, and several aircraft positioned from Northolt to Heathrow, the positioning flights continuing into the next day. The fewer number of arrivals than departures is the result of several flights normally scheduled to land at Northolt being re-routed to Heathrow to save positioning flights between the two airports. The honour of the last scheduled service into and out of Northolt, fell to Pionair G-AHCZ commanded by Tommy Froggatt. It made the last commercial BEA arrival at Northolt when it touched down from Jersey as BE673 at 18.20. Forty minutes later Captain Froggatt taxied 'HCZ away from the apron on flight BE684 for Jersey, marking the end of an era. The final BEA aircraft to fly out of Northolt was a Viking, which positioned to Heathrow on the 31st October. Between 1946 and 1954 BEA carried 3,777,000 passengers on its services from and to Northolt, and handled another million and a half passengers for other airlines. Centralization of operations at Heathrow made technical and economic sense; but it was a sad day for those who had worked at Northolt since 1946 to see G-AHCZ vanishing in the early evening darkness towards Jersey. The only BEA presence at Northolt after October 31st was an engineering instrument workshop, and eventually that too moved across to Heathrow. Northolt remained an operational airfield with the RAF.

While all this was going on, it was rather ironic that BEA was involved in a planning tribunal for the development of Gatwick as London's second airport. It was quite plain Heathrow would be insufficient to handle all future traffic for London, and the government was keen to develop a second airport. Gatwick was the choice and BEA fully supported the idea. Back at Heathrow, the central area with its new passenger facilities was not yet operational and passengers were dealt with in a motley collection of prefabricated huts. Still, they were at least one step up from the tents used previously. The central area finally came into use on April 17th 1955, and the honour of the first flight to use it fell to the 07.30 BEA departure for Amsterdam, flown by Viscount V.701 G-AMOA.

1955

If 1954 will be best remembered for the withdrawal of the Vikings and the closure of Northolt, 1955 will stand out because the airline announced its first ever profit. The finances for 1954/55 recorded an overall profit of just £63,039. Very modest perhaps, but at least it was a profit, and Lord Douglas's team had achieved their goal of wiping out the traditional losses. To what did they attribute the profit? Mainly to the effect of the Elizabethans and Viscounts which allowed BEA to compete with its European rivals. But there were other helpful factors too, such as the closure of Northolt allowing the airline's London operations to be centralized on one site; the withdrawal of the Vikings; the run down of the Rapide fleet; and very effective financial management. Of course the rise in passenger traffic must not be ignored either, overall passenger traffic was up 18.8%, and of especial comfort was the growth of traffic over the lean winter months.

All very exciting, but the Board was anxious to avoid staff becoming complacent. The profit margin was so slim that without careful management and great effort by the staff the dreaded losses might easily return. A call was issued for staff to redouble their efforts, which seemed to pay off, since the airline managed to make a profit for the next six financial years.

With the success of this first profit under its belt, BEA forged ahead with another phase of growth. Several brand new services were commenced:

London to Salzburg.	Launched on April 22nd by Pionair. (G-AGJZ flew the first service)
London to Ajaccio.	Launched on April 23rd by Elizabethan, as a stop on the Malta route. One flight a week operated, G-ALZZ operating the first flight.
Glasgow to Guernsey.	Launched on June 4th, by Pionair. A seasonal Sunday service.
Manchester to Milan	Launched on June 16th by Viscount. (G-AMOG flew the first service)
London to Cairo	(Via Munich and Athens). Launched on August 17th, by Viscount.
London to Vienna (non stop)	Launched on October 4th by Viscount, flown twice weekly.

The Salzburg route is worthy of note because it was the last European service from Heathrow to be launched by a Pionair. Indeed the Pionair continued to operate the service until 1958, making it the last international passenger flight out of Heathrow flown by the type. The launching of the Ajaccio service did not go entirely according to plan, as the aircraft (G-ALZZ) developed a technical fault while over France, and the pilot elected to divert to Le Bourget for repairs. Not a very auspicious start to BEA services to Corsica.

Not to be outdone, the HEU joined in with its own new passenger schedule during the summer. From July 25th the Unit flew a WS.55 on eight round trips a day between Heathrow and the centre of London. The site chosen was the South Bank which BEA helicopters had used previously. G-ANUK operated the first trip which took thirteen minutes, and cost £1-15/- single. When the winter came, flights were reduced to four round trips a day. Because the WS.55 had to follow the course of the River Thames it had to be fitted with floats and have an extra silencer fitted to reduce engine noise. The weight penalty of the floats and silencer reduced the maximum passenger load to five, meaning that even if all the trips were full a loss of £322 per day occurred! The HEU was not being reckless with BEA's small profit. It was well aware of the problems, but launched the service because it wanted some experience of flying regular services into a city centre. The Heathrow-South Bank route terminated on May 31st 1956, by which time the WS.55 had carried 3,833 passengers. Most were simply joy riders anxious to see London from the air or experience helicopter flight, though a few businessmen did use it to reach the centre of the city quickly.

Up in Scotland, services were improved with the delivery of two De Havilland Heron IBs. The aircraft had been ordered to replace the Rapides on services to Barra and on the air ambulance work. They were delivered early in the year, and named in a special ceremony at Glasgow on March 18th. Each was given the name of a medical pioneer, G-ANXA being named Sir John Hunter, and 'NXB Sir James Simpson. After the naming ceremony, they flew a party of invited guests around the

Herons replaced Rapides on the Scottish Air Ambulance Service, and flights to Tiree and Barra, here G-ANXB is illustrated next to Rapide G-AHKS. *(BA)*

Glasgow area. Even before the ceremony they had begun to work for the airline, with G-ANXB flying its first ambulance charter on March 4th. Passenger operations began on April 1st, after which the airline sold off its Rapide contingent at Glasgow.

At first Heron schedules were not very demanding. A week-day morning service was flown to Tiree, replacing the Pionair which had previously called there on its way to Benbecula. BEA was very glad to be able to withdraw Pionairs from Tiree because the low loads to the Island made the stop very uneconomic. Once at Tiree the Heron continued on to Barra's beach landing strip on three days a week, before returning to Glasgow again via Tiree. An evening service was flown to Tiree on some days, and that was the extent of the Heron schedules. In the winter the programme was even less strenuous, with a three days a week service to Tiree and Barra being the sole schedules flown by the type. Because the beach was used at Barra, landings could only be made at low tide, and a strange note was found in the timetable warning passengers to check the timings of Barra services as they were liable to 'alteration subject to weather and tide conditions at Barra'. The note continued to be displayed in every BEA domestic timetable up to its last, and was surely a unique feature of the timetable compared with those of international rivals!

Over the next few years Heron schedules were slowly built up, especially following the delivery of a third aircraft, G-AOFY in time for the summer season in 1956. One of the three remained on permanent air ambulance standy, the second worked the routes to Barra and Tiree, and the third became involved in a more demanding route pattern as BEA tried to improve the service it offered in the Highlands and Islands. From June until the end of August it night-stopped at Stornoway to provide an early morning Stornoway-Inverness-Glasgow flight. In the middle of the day it flew north to Inverness and Wick, and finally operated an evening Glasgow-Inverness-Stornoway service. The early morning and evening services to Stornoway proved very popular with the residents of the Isle of Lewis enabling them to make day trips to Glasgow and Inverness, and BEA continued the service in the summer of 1957. The loss of G-AOFY on September 28th 1957 meant the schedule was not flown in subsequent summers. On September 28th G-AOFY answered an air ambulance call out to Islay in very bad weather. Whilst trying to land the Heron crashed into the sea, killing the pilots and the nurse on board (Sister Jean Kennedy). BEA never replaced the aircraft, and Heron schedules reverted just to the Tiree and Barra run. The route was flown six days a week right through to Barra in the summer, and to Tiree only each evening. In the winter five flights a week went out to Tiree, with three going on to Barra.

Schedules remained at this level until the summer of 1968, when a direct Glasgow-Barra flight was flown seven days a week, making Barra the first Scottish Island to have Sunday service, something most other Islands resisted. Tiree was served by a morning flight on six days a week, and an evening one generally on three days only. For the summer of 1970 the Herons stretched their wings to serve Campbeltown and Islay, at the modest level of one flight a week to each place, flown on a Friday evening.

Air ambulance flights made up much of the Herons work. On average they flew two hundred and fifty ambulance flights a year, and carried about three hundred patients. Most calls came from the Western Isles and Islay, but occasionally the aircraft had to fly mercy missions to Orkney and Shetland in the north. Trips to the Northern Isles usually transferred patients to Aberdeen, whereas those to the Western Isles and Islay flew patients to Glasgow, or sometimes Inverness. The service was available twenty four hours a day, every day of the year. Responsibility for calling on the air ambulance rested with the local doctor, and BEA staff at the stations involved were always on call. Most calls seemed to come in the middle of the night, in the middle of a gale, or on Christmas Day! The costs of operating the vital link were reckoned to be about £12,000 a year. BEA did not pay, however, the money was provided by the Scottish Health Service. The Heron was equipped with two stretchers and always carried a nurse from a Glasgow hospital. The nurses all received some special training to familiarize them with the medical equipment carried by the Heron.

By 1972 the Herons had been in service for nearly twenty years, and BEA began to think about a replacement for them, a far from easy task. Apart from the need to be suitable for the easy loading of stretchers, the replacement required a fixed undercarriage, as the salt from Barra's beach would play havoc with any aircraft with retractable undercarriage. Any replacement would also have to be rugged, a requirement made essential by the nature of Barra's landing strip. Plenty of advice was available to pilots from local residents, the best remembered being not to land unless the seagulls legs were visible. If their legs were not visible it meant they had sunk into the sand, and so might the aircraft! Sometimes Herons did get stuck in the sand, and pilots were instructed not to stop the machine on the sand, except above the high water mark. On one occasion G-ANXA got firmly stuck in the wet sand. The airfield's fire tender came to the rescue only to get stuck itself. The quick thinking of Kitty Macpherson, the Station Superintendent at Barra, saved the day. She loaned the local distillery's tractor and hauled the Heron out just in time to escape a soaking by the rising tide. The fire tender was not so lucky, and could be seen bobbing at anchor in Northbay that evening! After careful thought BEA placed an order for three Britten Norman Trislanders, but the temporary demise of Britten Norman meant the order was never confirmed, and instead the Corporation decided to buy two Short Skyliners in 1972, they arrived in time for the summer programme in 1973, and the Herons were retired. The last scheduled service was operated over the Barra-Tiree-Glasgow route by G-ANXB on March 30th. From April 1st the Skyliners took over. When the Herons retired BEA handed over responsibility for the air ambulance service to Loganair, who used Islander aircraft. The two Herons were overhauled at Glasgow and stored awaiting sale. The last Heron flight to operate under the 'Bealine' callsign occurred on June 18th 1973, when Captain Montgomery flew G-ANXA on a C of A test flight following its overhaul. Both aircraft were eventually purchased by Peters Aviation of Norwich, with G-ANXB being delivered on October 25th, and G-ANXA on November 20th. Prior to delivery to Peters, G-ANXA spent about twelve weeks on lease to Sierra Leone Airways in Freetown West Africa. 'NXA was ferried out to Freetown from Glasgow by a BEA crew; who returned it to the UK at end of the lease, flying the Heron from Freetown to Peters Aviation base at Norwich. From BEA's point of view the Herons had been ideal for their task, but the finances of their operations were rather frightening. Records show the aircraft required a 125% load factor, or seventeen passengers, to break even. Given the maximum capacity of the aircraft was only fourteen passengers, each flight, even if fully loaded, made a loss!

Back in 1955, while passenger services were

At the South Bank on July 25th 1955, G-ANUK unloads passengers from LHR. *(BIH)*

booming, things were not quite so rosy on the cargo side of operations. BEA decided to make a big effort to attract a lot more cargo. A major advertising campaign was begun, and cargo traffic did begin to grow again. To be quite honest, some of the growth resulted from unusual factors, like another rail strike in June, which put tremendous pressure on cargo facilities at Heathrow, as everyone wanted to send their cargo by air. In one week the Cargo Unit handled 800 tons, about one fifteenth of its normal annual total. Meanwhile in December the freighter services received a massive boost with the carriage of Christmas mail. 945 tons of Christmas mail were flown, about one eighth of the total volume of mail shifted in a year. The most important mail route was Manchester to Belfast over which several extra mail freighters were scheduled during the Christmas rush.

At Gatwick a successful winter was also being experienced by the HEU. In October it won a useful contract with the Ministry of Defence for Civil Defence work. The contract required a helicopter to visit many parts of the UK and consequently BEA decided to purchase a third WS.55, registered as G-AOCF. The work lasted right through the traditionally lean winter months and continued until September 1957, by which time the helicopter had flown 227 hours for the Ministry and carried 1,400 passengers. As the contract neared its end, one of the three WS.55s (G-ANUK) was sold off.

Many of BEA's passenger and freight schedules to Europe were thrown into confusion during the winter months thanks to a strike by French Air Traffic Control staff which becan on November 10th and lasted right through until January 1956. The effect of the dispute was not simply felt on the services to France, but on those overflying France too. The result was delays, cancellations and re-routings to hundreds of flights to Spain, Gibraltar, Portugal, Italy and so on. To have such disruption over the busy Christmas period caused the airline severe difficulties. By January 1956 the Corporation estimated the dispute cost it about £100,000 in lost revenue and extra costs incurred by delays and re-routins.

In the late summer the first major change to the airline's senior management for several years occurred, with the resignation of Peter Masefield, who left the airline to become Managing Director of the Bristol Aeroplane Company. To him must go much of the credit in bringing the airline into a profitable state, and it was fitting he should leave in the year that the first profit was recorded. Lord Douglas appointed Anthony Milward as Chief Executive in his place. Milward had been in BEA since the beginning and was well suited to the task, being known as a fair man, a humourist, and a man with a determination that BEA's fortunes should continue to prosper. In May 1956 he joined the Board.

G-AMKE displays the built in airstairs so characteristic of the Pionair. *(BA)*

1956

In August 1956 BEA celebrated its tenth birthday. In those ten years it had carried about twelve million passengers, nearly 100,000 tons of freight and earnt £113 million in revenue. The Corporation was quite determined the anniversary should not go unmarked; and in contrast to the launching of BEA in 1946, there was a considerable amount of publicity and celebration, culminating in a lavish lunch given by the Board at the Savoy Hotel on August 1st, where chief guest was Harold Watkinson MP, the Minister of Aviation. Other celebrations included a ball at the Albert Hall, and a public display at Heathrow showing how things had progressed over the ten years.

From the mid 1950's onwards BEA began to extend its influence in the UK aviation scene by acquiring a financial stake in several independent airlines. The first airline to be involved was Jersey Airlines. In 1955 the Corporation purchased 25% of the Jersey company's shares, and R.L. Weir was nominated as BEA representative on Jersey Airlines Board. With this formal association between the two carriers, it was not long before they undertook an evaluation of their routes to the Channel Isles. From the review an agreement to swap certain routes was reached on March 9th. BEA agreed to transfer to Jersey Airlines all its services to Alderney (Guernsey-Alderney, Jersey-Alderney and Southampton-Alderney) as well as its direct Guernsey-Southampton flights. In return, Jersey Airlines gave up its direct Jersey-Southampton service leaving BEA as the sole operator on the busy holiday route. Also included in the swap was the Jersey/Guernsey-Dinard service. For some time BEA and Jersey Airlines had been co-operating on the service, and in the winter the two airlines operated on alternate days. Now BEA gave up the route entirely in favour of Jersey Airlines. Overall the deal suited the Corporation well, as it enabled BEA to withdraw entirely from the tiny Island of Alderney. With a resident population of under 2,000, flights to the Island had never made much money. Two Heron 2s, (G-AORG, G-AORH) which BEA had already ordered to take the place of the Rapides on the Alderney services, would be delivered straight to Jersey Airlines.

BEA services to Alderney ceased on April 20th 1956, all flights that day being flown by Rapide G-AKZB, piloted by Captain Stokoe. He flew three services to Guernsey and one to Southampton. The final BEA departure from Alderney was at 15.20, with flight BE873 to Guernsey. Once the flight had gone the airline closed its small traffic handling unit at Blaye Airport, and its sales offfice in Victoria Street St Annes. Most of the staff of four were transferred to Jersey Airlines who commenced operations the next day, but BEA Official-in-Charge at Alderney, Freddie Farmer, left the Island to become a Duty Officer at the London Air Terminal. His sadness at leaving the peaceful Island for the hustle and bustle of London can only be imagined! Since BEA had taken over the Alderney routes from Channel Islands Airways all services had been flown by Rapide, and frequencies were never very extensive. The average summer gave the Island twenty eight flights a week to Guernsey, Jersey and Southampton, and the winter eighteen to Guernsey and Southampton. Because the airline's staff was very small, holidays or sickness often required a BEA official to travel from Guernsey to help out. Sometimes he found his travelling companion on the aircraft was a Guernsey Policeman who was going up to Alderney for a fortnights spell of law enforcement. The Island, at that time, had no resident police, although law enforcement generally meant a running battle with the residents over the closing time of the sixteen pubs! One over zealous PC was thrown into the harbour one night for trying to shut the pubs at 10.30pm.

On April 20th, in accordance with the agreement with Jersey Airlines, BEA gave up its Guernsey-Southampton services, and Jersey-Dinard flights. It was still possible to fly from Guernsey to Southampton on BEA by travelling to Jersey and changing aircraft. The wisdom of giving up the route was later greatly questioned, as Jersey Airlines and its successor companies developed it very successfully. The last service from Southampton to Guernsey (BE740) departed at 14.35. Meanwhile at 16.15 the last Rapide (BE374) left Dinard for Jersey. Dinard remained a seasonal station with the summer service to London continuing. However BEA aircraft were frequent visitors to Dinard in the winter on crew training flights, and diversions from Jersey or Guernsey.

The end of the Alderney and Dinard services marked

the final demise of scheduled Rapide operations in the Channel Isles, enabling a further three Rapides to be sold off. As a result BEA's Rapide fleet was reduced to just three aircraft, all based at Land's End for the Scillies route. Rapides did still pay visits to Jersey and Southampton as all major checks on the aircraft were performed in the airline's Jersey hangar, and the aircraft would position to Land's End via Southampton (and later Bournemouth) to clear customs. The positioning flights were sometimes flown by Jersey based pilots who enjoyed the change from their normal routines. Whether the pilot was from Jersey of Land's End, the positioning flight was often treated rather light heartedly. Low flying was frequently the order of the day, and it was not unknown for a pilot to swoop over the house or farm of a friend on the way down through Cornwall.

Apart from the agreement with Jersey Airlines, BEA entered a formal operating agreement with Cambrian Airways in 1956, although two airlines had already been informally linked, as Cambrian's Managing Director, Kenneth S. Davies, was a member of the BEA Board. The agreement, signed on May 9th covered operations between Manchester/Liverpool and the Channel Isles, and Manchester and Bristol and Cardiff. Under the terms of the deal, BEA gave up flying the seasonal Liverpool-Jersey route and Cambrian became the sole operator. Cambrian would in future run a Manchester-Bristol and Cardiff service in co-operation with BEA. In the winter it was timed to connect with a Cardiff-Jersey service giving a link from Manchester to Jersey, and enable BEA to drop its once weekly winter direct service from Manchester to Jersey. In 1958 the link between the Welsh and British airlines went a stage further, with BEA purchasing a 33% share holding in Cambrian. Eventually Cambrian became a fully owned subsidiary of BEA and was integrated into British Airways, losing its own identity to the regret of many.

As BEA purchased shares in Jersey Airlines and Cambrian, so it reduced its share holding in the Irish national airline, Aer Lingus and reached a new operating agreement with it. Since 1947 Aer Lingus had operated all the scheduled services between Eire and the UK explaining why BEA did not fly to Dublin. The agreement was due to run out in March 1957, and the two airlines and their governments negotiated a new one under the terms of which BEA reduced its share holding in Aer Lingus to 10%, and Aer Lingus was granted traffic rights to pick up passengers at Manchester for several European cities, like Amsterdam. In return BEA received the long hoped for demand of being able to operate scheduled services from London, Birmingham and Manchester to Dublin, services commenced in April 1957.

For 1956 three new international routes were opened from London:

May 17th.	London to Venice Twice Weekly by Viscount. (First flight by G-ANHD)
June 15th	London to Bergen. Weekly Night Tourist service by Viscount. (First flight by G-ANHE)
October 17th.	London to Tel Aviv, via Cyprus. Twice weekly by Viscount.

One other new International route was Birmingham to

Viscount V.730 G-AODH at Belfast Nutts Corner. The aircraft was on lease from Fred Olsen. *(BA)*

Dusseldorf. Birmingham was added as a stop on the Manchester-Dusseldorf flight from April 23rd, with Viscount G-AMOD operating the first service through Birmingham. Viscounts replaced Pionairs on the London-Gothenburg-Oslo route from April 25th. Meanwhile the route network to the Channel Isles was extended in June, with the opening of a seasonal Belfast-Jersey non-stop service flown on Saturdays and Sundays by Pionair.

At the height of the summer BEA's HEU commenced yet another experimental passenger route, a feeder link between Birmingham's Elmdom Airport and Leicester and Nottingham. Services commenced on July 2nd, using the WS.55 helicopters. A twice daily schedule was offered Mondays to Saturdays, with flights connecting with the Birmingham-Paris midday link. For the winter flying was reduced to a once daily round trip. The helicopters landed at specially prepared heliports in Leicester and Nottingham, and commencement of the service had been delayed serveral months by problems over getting planning permission for the building of these sites. On November 10th the last flight over the route took place, partly because of poor loads and partly because of the shortage of fuel caused by the Suez crisis. The Suez affair had a serious effect on the whole of BEA operations because it produced a serious shortage of aviation fuel, leading to the government imposing a fuel tax surcharge as a way of rationing supplies. The surcharge cost BEA about £300,000 which it sought to counter by adding 1/- supplement to all fares. The difficulties caused by Suez lead BEA to suspend its services to Cairo and the route remained suspended until 1957, although when it was resurrected only the service via Munich and Athens operated. The North African link to Cairo was never resumed, though aircraft still flew as far as Benghazi.

After the abortive Birmingham feeder service, the HEA gave up experimenting with helicopter passenger services until a more economical helicopter design became available. Instead the Unit concentrated on charter work, crop spraying and training. It employed five pilots and twenty nine ground staff, most of whom were engineers. In 1957 its Manager, Reggie Brie, retired and was replaced by Captain 'Jock' Cameron who had been a pilot with the Unit since it was formed in 1947.

Over the summer BEA made use of Elizabethan aircraft on the Heathrow-Jersey route on a regular basis. One Elizabethan flight was scheduled each day of the week arriving at Jersey at 21.05. The aircraft night-stopped and returned to London early the next morning. On Saturdays and Sundays additional Elizabethan services operated, and there was a real hope that Viscounts would soon come to the Island because the Jersey government decided to extend the runway to accommodate a fully loaded Viscount. In Scotland an effort was being made to boost traffic to the Western Isles by the introduction of an early morning Heron service from Stornoway to Inverness and Glasgow. An evening flight operated in the reverse direction. BEA also put on an evening Pionair from Glasgow to Benbecula on Monday, Friday and Saturday. Though the Stornoway service was popular, the evening Benbecula one was not and was dropped in 1958. BEA did try to boost traffic to Benbecula again in 1959 by the provision of a direct Inverness-Benbecula service on three days a week, with an equal lack of success. Services to Benbecula were then maintained by a daily except Sunday Pionair service from Glasgow, and another from Stornoway.

In 1956 BEA began to fly some of the German internal services with a leased DC-4 aircraft. Due to aircraft shortages, BEA chartered a DC-4 from Air Charter Ltd to operate some of the Berlin-Hamburg and Hanover schedules. Three DC-4s were used at various times, G-ANYB, 'OFW and 'OYK. The lease of Air Charter DC-4s continued until October 1958 by which time BEA had sufficient Viscounts to fly the services involved. Aircraft shortages were not confined to the passenger network, there was a shortage of freighter equipment as well. To overcome the deficit the airline began to charter Vikings or DC-3s from Eagle Airways to operate its London-Amsterdam-Copenhagen-Hamburg-London freighter. The use of Eagle equipment lasted from April 23rd 1956 until late 1957. On November 10th 1956, Viscounts made their first appearance on a regular basis on freight services. The type was used to fly a twice weekly service from London to Milan.

Viscounts were still proving a great success and asset to BEA. Each aircraft achieved an average utilisation of about 2,400 hours per year, and on January 18th BEA carried its one millionth Viscount passenger. Only sixteen months later, on April 22nd 1957, the two millionth Viscount passenger was clocked up. On July 30th, the final V.701 (G-AOFX) was delivered to the airline. BEA had taken delivery of twenty seven V.701s, and was the worlds largest Viscount operator. The Queen made her first Viscount flight in the middle of June, when she flew in G-ANHC to Oslo. She was accompanied by Princess Margaret and the Duke and Duchess of Gloucester, BEA soon became much more regularly involved in carrying members of the Royal Family thanks to a complete re-organisation of Royal Family travel arrangements. The government announced, in April, that the RAF's Royal Flight would in future only operate short range trips, and BEA and BOAC would be used for Royal trips to Europe and beyond. Consequently BEA set about designing a special royal interior to be installed in the Viscount used for the Royal flight. Confidence in the types safety to carry the Royal Family, and indeed anybody else, was demonstrated on January 2nd when G-ANHF made an emergency landing at Bordeaux on just one engine, following fuel contamination. There were a few airliners about in 1956 capable of achieving a similiar feat.

Early in 1956 BEA announced an order for a further sixteen Viscounts, the new V.806. The '806 was to be powered by an uprated version of the Dart, the RDa 7.Mark 520, making it faster than the V.802, though its operating weight was similar. BEA planned to operate the '806 in a mixed first/economy configuration, with fifty eight seats. This version of the Viscount was the last to be ordered by the Corporation. The airline did take an option on the V.840, and expressed an interest in the

G-ALZY at Heathrow's North Side. *(BA)*

projected V.870, an eighty eight seater, although neither were ordered and the Vanguard was purchased instead. The order for the V.806 was placed in January. Seven months later, on July 20th, BEA placed an order for twenty V.951 Vanguard aircraft, to be delivered to BEA in 1959/60. The Vanguard had an all up weight of 135,000 lbs, and a capacity for eighteen first class and one hundred and nine economy class passengers. It was to be powered by the Rolls Royce Tyne turbo-prop engine. BEA ordered the aircraft for its high density routes, both in the UK and abroad. In July 1958 Vickers announced an improved version of the Vanguard, the V.953, with a higher all up weight, of 142,000lbs, and a passenger capacity of one hundred and thirty five. BEA considered the '953 a better prospect than the '951, and wanted to transfer its order from '951s to '953s. Unfortunately it was not a simple matter, because by mid 1958 Vickers were well on the way to completing the first six V.951s for BEA. So the airline amended the order to be six V.951 and fourteen V.953. Both aircraft were noteable for their double bubble type fuselage, and large freight holds. In order to accommodate the type at the Heathrow Engineering Base a new extension was required. BEA announced plans for that during the later part of 1956, amounting to almost doubling the floor area from 500,000 square feet to 958,000 square feet. Construction began in October 1956 with completion scheduled for 1960 ready for the Vanguard. The Engineering Base had already become filled to capacity with the transfer of Pionair major maintenance from Glasgow between June and August 1956. All major overhauls were undertaken at Heathrow, except on the Rapides which used Jersey, and the Herons which were dealt with in Glasgow. To ease pressure at Heathrow facilities at Manchester and Glasgow were improved to allow both stations to perform Check Ones on Viscounts.

Lord Douglas and Anthony Milward were well pleased with the financial results for the year 1955/56. The airline recorded a profit of £603,614. Most of that came from the contribution made by the Viscounts and to a lesser degree the Elizabethans; Viscounts contributing £1,138,605 in revenue, and Elizabethans £558,721. An all time high load factor was recorded of 69.4%, and 2,224,747 passengers were carried. 1955/56 was the first financial year in which BEA had carried more than two million passengers. A most encouraging sign was the growth of traffic on domestic trunk routes:

Growth in Domestic Passenger Traffic

	1954/55	1956/57
London-Glasgow	92,347	133,087
London-Belfast	77,887	109,606
London-Manchester	41,684	65,928
London-Edinburgh	29,167	61,264

Unfortunately not all domestic routes showed such a healthy picture. Irish Sea routes to the Isle of Man were causing serious concern, producing a loss of £400,000. The problem, as with all holiday routes, was the great diversity in traffic between the summer and winter. On the Manchester-Isle of Man route the ratio of passengers carried in the summer to the winter was 25:1. Scottish internal routes provided further problems being totally unviable. However there was little BEA could do about that. As a public corporation it had a duty to provide such socially necessary routes even at the expense of profit.

1957

In the late 1950s most major European airlines were becoming increasingly interested in jet travel, and naturally enough BEA was anxious not to be left out. A three year fleet plan, published in September, acknowledged the need for a small fleet of jets by 1960 to operate the longer routes, and a jet specification was drawn up. It required an aircraft capable of seating one hundred passengers, cruising at 600mph, with a range of 1,000 miles. From the specification two choices presented themselves to BEA, the Bristol 200 and the De Havilland DH121. Initially BEA favoured the Bristol 200 project, but eventually the DH121 was found to be technically superior. BEA began to pursue the design proposal with great seriousness. The DH121 could not be in use before 1963, but the airline believed it needed an operational jet by 1960. Consequently BEA decided to order six Comet 4Bs as a stop gap measure until the DH121 was ready. The order was formally placed with De Havilland on March 28th 1957. The Comet 4B was powered by four Rolls Royce Avon jets, and carried up to one hundred and two passengers in an economy class mode, or eighty seven in a mixed first/economy configuration. Cruising speed was about 500 mph, and deliveries were to begin in 1959. The order was later increased to fourteen aircraft, and by the time they began to arrive BEA found it badly needed them, not on the longer routes, but on some of the shorter European sectors where other airlines were operating new jets like the Caravelle.

The 1957 fleet plan considered in detail the future of the existing types in use. Elizabethans were to be withdrawn from service during 1957 and replaced by existing Viscounts. Pionairs would go by 1960, being replaced by Viscount V.701s, the V.701s being converted to a sixty seater aircraft and fitted with built in airstairs. Viscount V.802s and V.806s would take over from the V.701s and the Vanguards supplement the 800 series Viscounts. A grand scheme, but needless to say it did not entirely work out in practice. The Elizabethans did begin to be phased out in 1957, with five being sold during the year, but the type continued into 1958. For the summer of 1957 the Elizabethan schedules were concentrated mainly on routes to Malta, calling for twenty two flights a week between London and Malta, some via various intermediate stops and some direct. Four weekly flights were also worked by the Elizabethans between Malta-Tripoli and Benghazi. Other international schedules by the type were limited to a four times weekly service to Bordeaux and Biarritz, a twice weekly Night Tourist service to Barcelona, a thrice weekly Night Tourist service to Rome, and a daily Heathrow-Cologne-Hanover service. On the domestic network Elizabethans were scheduled to operate only to Jersey with ten flights a week.

Plans to replace the Pionair by 1960 again did not succeed, and the type was still flying passenger service until May 1962, and Vanguards entry into service was seriously delayed due to a series of technical problems with the aircraft.

The fleet plan did, however, achieve its goal with regard to the Viscount V.802s. In the early months of 1957 the type began to be delivered to BEA, the first to arrive being G-AOJD on January 11th. G-AOJC followed on January 19th and 'OJE on the 26th. The first commercial service by a Viscount V.802 occurred on February 13th with G-AOJD flying forty seven passengers from Heathrow to Glasgow. On February 15th the first international flight by this mark of Viscount took place, when G-AOJD flew twenty six passengers from Heathrow to Amsterdam. On February 18th G-AOJF flew the first V.802 service to Paris, and other destinations received the type during the remainder of the year: Zurich on June 1st, Copenhagen on July 1st, and by September: Belfast, Dublin, Dusseldorf, Frankfurt, Geneva, Hamburg, and Nice. Right at the end of the year BEA received its first V.806, G-AOYH. It arrived at Heathrow on December 23rd, although the V.806s did not begin scheduled operations until the following year.

While 1957 saw the delivery of the twin new marks of Viscounts, it sadly saw several serious accidents with Viscounts. On March 14th V.701, G-ALWE, crashed on approach to Ringway Airport Manchester. Metal fatigue caused a flap failure, leading to the aircraft hitting the ground and bursting into flames. Twenty two people were killed, including several on the ground. After the accident all the V.701s were grounded while their flap system was checked for fatigue, the first and last time the Viscount fleet had ever been grounded. However fatal accidents with Viscounts were not over. G-AOJA crashed

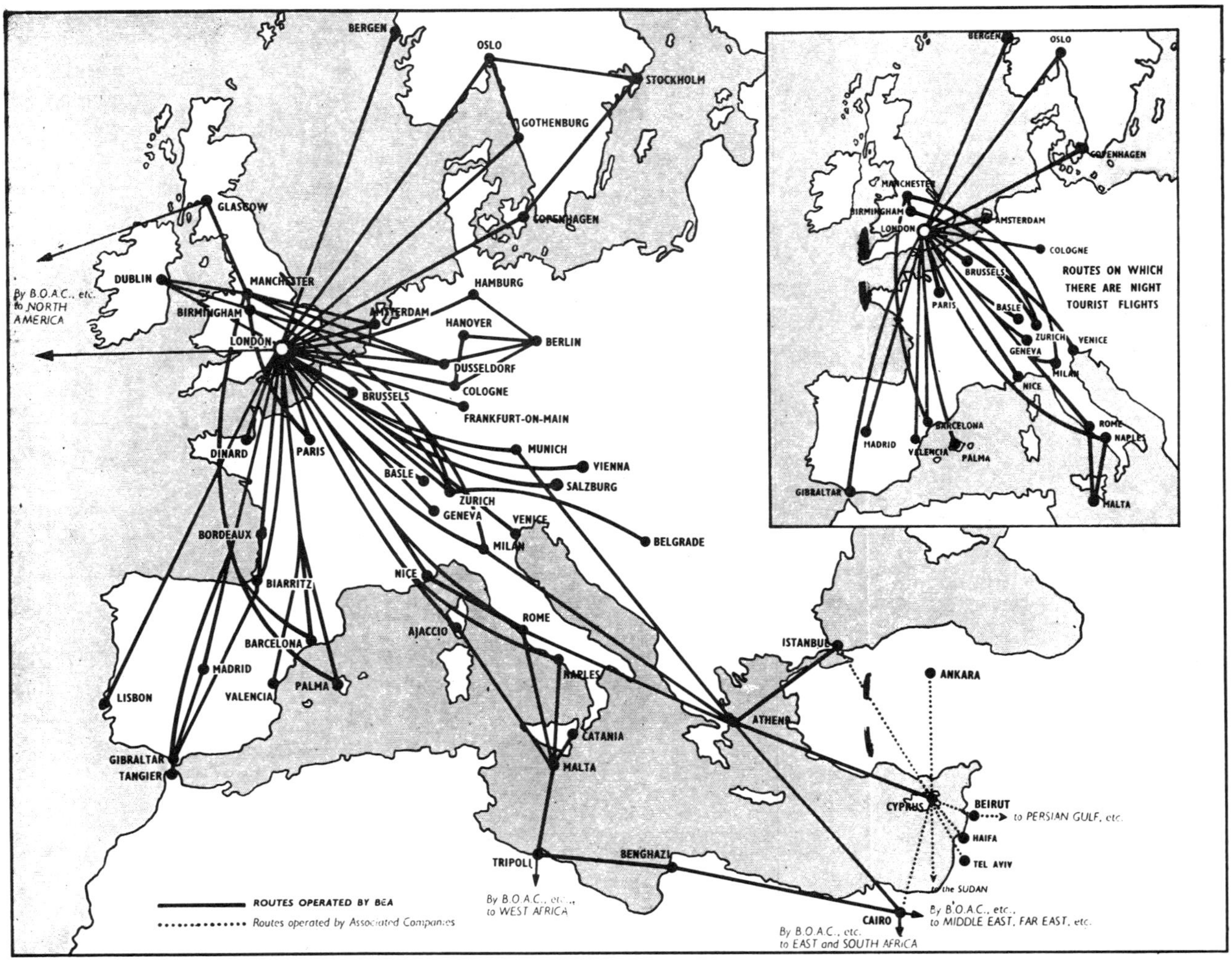

when attempting an overshoot at Belfast on October 23rd, killing the five crew and two staff passengers on board. This time the aircraft was not to blame, but a combination of bad weather and pilot error. Even that was not the end of troubles with the Viscounts, on November 17th G-AOHP, operating a freight service to Copenhagen, suffered a three engine failure just prior to touchdown and crashed short of the runway. Happily two crew escaped with only injuries, though the aircraft was written off. BEA purchased several more Viscounts to make up for these losses. G-APJU was ordered to replace G-AOHP, and G-APIM replaced G-AOJA. A third aircraft (G-APKF) was ordered to replace G-AOYF which crashed, prior to delivery to BEA, while on a sales tour at Johannesburg during the autumn.

In 1956/57 BEA began to earn significant amounts of money from selling seats to inclusive tour operators. Inclusive holidays (transport and hotel accommodation) were becoming increasingly popular in the mid 1950s, and BEA cashed in on the boom by selling seats on scheduled services to the tour operators. Palma, Barcelona, Gibraltar, Switzerland and Northern Italy were the main destinations, and the airline received £1,123,000 from IT sales. As yet BEA did not operate any whole aircraft charters for inclusive tour operators, something still several years off. However BEA soon found there was a negative side to the growth of package holidays, independent airlines began to cash in on the growth by offering holiday organisers cheap rates for whole aircraft charters. Travel companies snapped up such deals and BEA began to see a decline in holiday passengers carried on scheduled services to the resorts. The problem was to multiply over the next twenty years. Even in 1957 a foretaste of the problem was experienced, with charter airlines carrying 27% of the total number of passengers between the UK and Spain, and 21% of the total number to Munich and Austria.

The most significant development in BEA scheduled operations in 1957 was the beginning of scheduled services to Eire. Operations began on April 14th, when the first London-Dublin service was flown by G-AOHI. The next day Pionairs began a Birmingham-Dublin schedule, and on April 16th Viscounts began to fly to Dublin from Manchester. Two services a day operated from Heathrow to Dublin, and three a week each from Manchester and Birmingham.

Several other international routes opened in 1957:

May 3rd.	London-Valencia. First flight by Viscount G-AMOB. A Night Tourist service.
June 4th.	London-Belgrade, via Zurich. Once weekly by Viscount.

June 16th. Manchester-Barcelona. A Night Tourist service by Viscount.
October 7th. London-Prague. G-AMOA operated the first flight on this re-introduced route.

Passengers travelling to Brussels benefitted from Viscount travel from June 1st, having previously had to fly on the Elizabethans. Viscounts knocked fifteen minutes off the journey time. The same day the Elizabethan was supplanted by the Viscount on the London-Dusseldorf schedule, reducing flying times by twenty-five minutes, and on October 8th the same type change was made on the London-Malta schedules. The longer route to Malta made the faster speed of the Viscount most noticeable, cutting journey times by over an hour.

Domestically, 1957 was a year of consolidation; with only one new seasonal service being opened; from Aberdeen to Jersey, via Edinburgh, operated on a Sunday by Pionair. The departure and return of the Jersey service were the only movements at Aberdeen on a Sunday and the airfield had to be opened specially for them, thereby increasing BEA's costs and ensuring the route did not survive beyond 1960. Overall, however, summer traffic was booming both at home and in Europe, and on August 22nd BEA carried its 15 millionth passenger. During August the airline carried over 400,000 passengers, the highest monthly total so far achieved. The carriage of such a large number of passengers in a single month was quite a feat considering none of the airline's fleet had a passenger capacity of even sixty seats, and the average was more like forty.

The design of the 1957 summer timetable caused something of a political storm. BEA decided to remove the Union flag from the front cover of the timetable, which caused several Conservative MPs to protest, and one raised the matter in the House of Commons suggesting BEA was being unpatriotic. In explanation Anthony Milward said "There must always be countries, of which the Near East is an example, who do not appreciate literature embodying the Union Jack. Our expensive timetables, instead of being prominently displayed, are therefore hidden behind competitors publications. Our decision is dictated soley by commercial sense".

Timetable covers were not the only issue to be faced in the summer of 1957. The airline found itself with a severe shortage of aircrew. Indeed at one time it seemed likely services were going to be cancelled because of insufficient pilots to fly them. The problem was eased by the RAF agreeing to early release for some pilots due for discharge. Several ex-RAF pilots were recruited into BEA and given a twenty two week training course to suit them for civilian flying with the Corporation. Between 1957 and 1958 BEA recruited a total of one hundred and two extra pilots from military sources. At the same time the airline opened the new flight simulator building at Heston. The building housed the two Viscount simulators and the single Elizabethan simulator. Together the three simulators clocked up 1,600 hours of use in 1956/57, saving BEA thousands of pounds in flight training costs. In October 1957 BEA began a new scheme for recruiting and training ground staff, called the General Apprenticeship Scheme. About ten school leavers would be recruited annually and given a three year training course in all aspects of the airline's commercial, traffic, operations and sales procedures, interspersed with time at college studying for the National Certificate in Commerce and membership of the Institute of Transport. The GA Scheme, as it quickly became known, was very popular with school leavers and competition for places was always intense.

British European Airways new London town terminal was opened on October 6th, and at the same time the temporary terminal at Waterloo was closed. The new

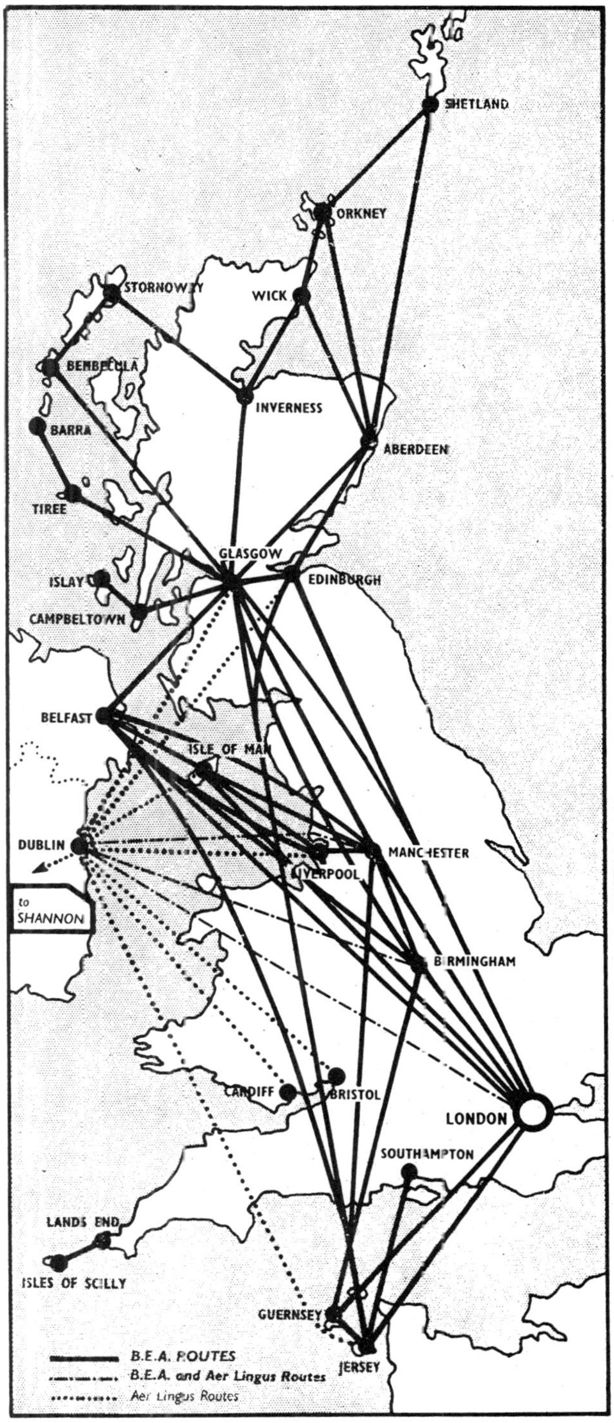

location in Cromwell Road, was called West London Air Terminal and construction had begun in 1956. Originally it was intended to use the building as the town terminal for BEA, BOAC and the British independent airlines flying out of Heathrow. In the end the terminal was designated solely for use by BEA. The Corporation planned a multi-storey building, housing, not just the town terminal facilities but also many of the airline's departments and offices at present scattered all over London. Principal among these was the Reservations Section which would be allocated considerable space at WLAT. Initially, however, only a temporary building was erected on the site, and it was this structure which was brought into use on October 6th. Construction of the permanent building began later, the first phase of it being ready for occupation in July 1960. The site of the terminal in Cromwell Road was well placed for links with the underground system being close to Gloucester Road station. Because West London Air Terminal was closer to Heathrow than Waterloo, BEA expected coach journey times to be up to fifteen minutes quicker. Coach trips out to Heathrow were becoming an increasing problem as road traffic built up, and it was not uncommon for departures to have to be delayed because the coach had got stuck in the traffic. Some discussion was held with British Rail over the possibility of running a rail service to Heathrow from either Victoria or Waterloo but the talks did not reach any definite conclusion, and the airport did not get a rail link until the 1970s, and then by underground train.

Financially the results for 1956/57 were not as good as those of the previous year. A profit was recorded, but of only £216,770, two thirds down on 1955/56. With the Suez Crisis and general economic situation it is rather surprising BEA managed to record a profit at all.

Competition of a new sort was faced by BEA in 1956/57, low cost 'Aircoach' services, operated by a independent airlines, such as Hunting Clan and Skyways to Cyprus, Gibraltar and Malta. Fares were kept low by using high density seating, offering few catering facilities on the flights and providing only one class accommodation. The carriers were aiming mainly at servicemen and their families who might want to return to the UK for holidays, or to visit service units in these places. BEA had offered a special serviceman's fare for some time, but the new fares undercut even those, and the airline did begin to face a small but significant traffic loss because of the 'Aircoach' services. The competition was the first to be experienced on European routes from British independent operators. BEA naturally faced competition of a sort from European rivals, however such competition was usually limited, since it was normal for BEA and the particular European national carrier to operate services under a 'pooling' arrangement. Under such arrangements fares were fixed between the two, profits shared, and frequencies worked out in co-operation. In some ways this benefitted the travelling public as it meant tickets were interchangeable and timings complementary, but in other ways it did not. Fares were kept higher than they might otherwise have been, and neither BEA or its partners had a great deal of incentive to try to provide a better quality service.

Elizabethan G-ALZR is clearly the object of some interest. *(BA)*

1958

A further round of agreements were concluded between BEA and several other airlines in January and February, including one with Cyprus Airways. From January 26th BEA undertook to operate all Cyprus Airways flights using two Viscounts, replacing Cyprus Airways own fleet of DC-3s. Cyprus Airways had considered buying a small fleet of Viscounts, but the planners concluded it would be more economic to charter BEA Viscounts and thus avoid the costly process of owning its own fleet. Because of the agreement, BEA aircraft began to appear far beyond their normal territory. On February 2nd a BEA Viscount opened Cyprus Airways new service from Nicosia to Kuwait, Bahrain and Doha. BEA continued to fly the route for Cyprus Airways for several years to come, spreading the BEA flag where it had not been seen before. The Viscounts used were regularly rotated, and aircraft were permanently stationed at Nicosia.

A second agreement was reached with Cambrian Airways. As already noted the two airlines had an operating agreement in existence, but on February 7th the links between the two carriers were made closer by BEA purchasing one third of the share capital of Cambrian Airways. With this link the airlines began to work closely together. BEA acted as sales agent for Cambrian, and began to handle the Welsh airline's aircraft at places like Jersey, Guernsey and Manchester. Sir Arnold Overton and Mr P.C.F. Lawton were appointed as BEA representatives on the Cambrian Board. However, things did not go well for Cambrian in 1958. In December the airline reported a loss of £53,473 for the year, but unlike BEA, Cambrian could not sustain such a loss and consequently the airline closed down operations for the winter and laid off most of the staff. Early in 1959 it concluded a further agreement with BEA to lease Pionairs from the Corporation (G-AHCZ, G-AGIP and G-ALXL) to re-commence operations. They were leased to Cambrian at the give-away rate of £7 per flying hour. At the end of 1959 arrangements were made for the three Pionairs to be purchased by Cambrian, and BEA actually credited the rental charges paid by Cambrian against the purchase price! Without such generous aid it is most unlikely Cambrian would have survived.

Next in line for an agreement was BOAC, who had been eager to gain rights to carry passengers between London and other European capitals its aircraft called at, such as Rome, Madrid and Paris. BEA and its eye on a greater share of traffic to Beruit, Tel Aviv and Cairo. A deal was reached whereby BOAC gained rights to carry passengers on some European sectors, while BEA obtained a greater share of the traffic to the Near East. The last agreement was with Aeroflot, the Soviet Airline. Negotiations between the British and Soviet governments, BEA and Aeroflot had been going on since 1955 concerning the establishment of services between Moscow and London. The talks proceeded very slowly each side being very wary of the other, but eventually on 26th February 1958 a formal agreement was reached, providing for four services a week to be operated, two by BEA (via Warsaw or Copenhagen) and two by Aeroflot. Flights were to commence in 1959, although a BEA Viscount made a proving flight to Moscow on February 18th 1958. The trip was flown by G-AOHO, which became the first BEA aircraft to land in Moscow when it landed at Vnukovo Airport.

During 1958 several landmarks in Viscount operations were clocked up. On January 27th the Viscount V.806 entered commercial service, when G-AOYH flew a London-Amsterdam schedule. The '806s soon began flying to other European cities on scheduled services: Geneva and Zurich from May 6th, Oslo and Stockholm from July 15th and Paris and Nice during August. By August 2nd the fleet of V.806s had all been delivered with the exception of G-APOX, which was built out of the parts salvaged from the crashed G-AOYF, and did not arrive at Heathrow until April 11th 1959, making it the last Viscount to be delivered to BEA. A second Viscount landmark occurred on February 19th when BEA carried its three millionth Viscount passsenger, and a third followed on May 1st as the airline began to operate mixed class services with the '806s. The V.806 operated with sixteen first class and forty two economy class seats to offer passengers a choice of class. Mixed class services were introduced on the Paris route, replacing the old Silver Wing service, and on some flights to other European destinations including Nice, Geneva, Zurich, Oslo, Copenhagen and Stockholm. The last

The end of an era, passengers disembarking from G-AMAF on the occasion of the final Elizabethan service, June 30th 1958. *(BA)*

Silver Wing service to Paris was operated by Viscount V.802 G-AOHU on April 30th.

The arrival of the Viscount V.806s heralded the final retirement of the Elizabethans. June 30th was the day on which the type made its last flight for BEA, with one aircraft flying a round trip between London and Hanover, via Cologne/Bonn. G-AMAF worked the service, the timings of the last sectors of which were:

Hanover	Depart 13.55
Cologne	Arrive 15.05
Cologne	Depart 15.35
Heathrow	Arrive 17.40 BE467

The prompt delivery of the new Viscounts allowed BEA to retire the Elizabethans a full month earlier than expected. In their career with BEA the Elizabethans had carried 2,430,000 passengers and flown 31 million miles. The aircraft had achieved an overall load factor of 64.5%. The early years were well remembered for the technical problems and resulting delays, but once the type had settled down it provided sterling service and supported the Viscount in bringing BEA into profitability. Although never as popular as the Viscount, the Elizabethan did prove a popular aircraft to travel in, with its high wings and large windows providing the passengers with splendid views.

The long awaited opening of Gatwick as London's second airport occurred on June 9th, with Her Majesty the Queen performing the ceremony, after which the first commercial movement occurred, flown by a BEA Pionair, G-ALXK, which departed on a charter to Jersey. BEA activity at Gatwick was to centre around Channel Islands services. In 1957 the airline had decided to transfer most of the London-Jersey flights, and all of the London-Guernsey ones to Gatwick when it opened. The decision was partly made to reduce pressure on facilities at Heathrow, and partly because Gatwick was a little closer to the CI than Heathrow, saving about ten minutes flying time. With the fast rail link from Gatwick to Victoria, BEA considered the airport an ideal London terminal for CI flights. From June 9th BEA scheduled up to seven Pionair flights a day from Gatwick to Guernsey, and up to fourteen flights to Jersey, flown by a mixture of Pionairs and Viscounts. Jersey was still connected to Heathrow with a twice daily Viscount service, mainly for the benefit of those wishing to make inter-line connections. The new BEA station at Gatwick had one hundred and thirty seven staff, and quickly proved itself a useful diversionary point for Heathrow. Between October 1958 and March 1959 staff at Gatwick handled 257 BEA aircraft diverting from Heathrow and another 230 aircraft of other operators. In 1958 BEA decided to make some cautious moves to run international services from Gatwick the following summer. The airport itself was the latest in aviation architecture, incorporating a finger pier around which the aircraft were parked.

Apart from the opening of services from Gatwick, the summer timetable included a new international route:- from Heathrow to Warsaw. From April 8th a twice weekly Viscount service flew to the Polish capital, with G-AMOB operating the first flight. Viscounts were now operating just about all BEA's international routes. Pionairs still flew the London-Salzburg service, a monthly London-Gibraltar flight via Biarritz (which was really a positioning flight to change the aircraft at Gibraltar operating the Gibraltar-Tangier route); and a three times weekly Birmingham-Dublin schedule. The rest of the Pionair fleet concentrated on Scottish services, the CI network and second line domestic services out of Manchester and Birmingham. These and all other BEA services were controlled by a central Operations Office at Heathrow, and sub units at Jersey, Glasgow, Berlin and Rome. To facilitate better control of operations a new Operations Control Centre was opened at Heathrow on April 28th. Situated in the Queen's Building it had a large display board recording all BEA movements at Heathrow, and those of foreign airlines handled by the Corporation. Some details were also displayed concerning BEA operations outside London. Each type had its own Operations Controller who had overall responsibility for movements of the type, making any decisions necessary regarding aircraft changes and so on.

BEA's staff faced many headaches in the summer of 1958. Between May 5th and June 20th there was a strike by London Transport drivers, meaning the normal coach service from WLAT was suspended as the coaches were driven by London Transport drivers. BEA arranged a temporary coach link between Feltham railway station and Heathrow, and passengers reached the airport by taking the train to Feltham and joining the coach. During the strike no less than 110,000 passengers used the temporary link. The dispute meant passengers could not check-in at WLAT, further increasing the pressure on the already over stretched check-in facilities at Heathrow. The lengthening and resurfacing of the runway at Birmingham's Elmdon Airport caused additional difficulties for BEA. The task took from May 11th 1958 until May 6th 1959, and for much of the time Viscounts were unable to use the airport. Hence Pionairs had to be substituted and schedules adjusted.

The need for extra Pionairs to fly the Birmingham routes, and the loss of several aircraft in accidents in 1958/59 created an inevitable shortage of aircraft. BEA responded to the situation by leasing aircraft to operate many of its freighter routes, thereby releasing its own aircraft to fly passenger services. Most aircraft were leased from Dan Air. From May 25th 1959 Dan Air DC-3s were chartered to fly the London-Glasgow-Manchester-London cargo route for a two year period. DC-3G-AMSS was the first Dan Air aircraft to appear on the schedule, however it was Dan Air Yorks which were the most commonly chartered equipment. In 1959 they worked the Monday and Wednesday London-Milan cargo route, and in 1960 took over the Manchester-Glasgow route from the DC-3s. BEA also contracted Dan Air Yorks to operate two flights a week to Paris and one to Brussels beginning in 1960. By that time it was a shortage of Vanguards that required the use of Dan Air aircraft. Prior to 1958/59 Yorks had made occasional appearances on BEA cargo services, for example in December 1951 a York had been chartered from Eagle Airways to operate at least one London-Nice-Rome-Athens cargo working. Even with the use of Dan Air aircraft BEA still needed more capacity in 1959, and for a time a Skyways DC-3 was chartered to fly the twice weekly London-Frankfurt-Dusseldorf-London cargo route. Dan Air Yorks eventually took over that in 1960. The use of Yorks continued until early 1962, by which time the three Argosys were operational. Four Yorks appeared on the BEA contract, G-ANTI, 'NTJ, 'NTK and 'NXN.

1958 was a bad year for accidents to BEA aircraft. The first occurred on February 6th and is possibly the best remembered of all BEA accidents. Manchester United Football Club had chartered an Elizabethan to bring them back from a game in Belgrade. The aircraft (G-ALZU) called at Munich to refuel on a typical Bavarian winters day of snow and ice. On departure 'LZU failed to become airborne and could not be stopped in the remaining length of runway. It overran the end of the runway and crashed with the loss of twenty three lives, another twenty one being injured. Some of Manchester United's, and England's, best soccer stars were killed or maimed. The Accident Report blamed the pilot, Captain Thain, for not having checked the upper surface of the aircraft's wings for ice. However, he insisted that it was not his fault and take off had been prevented by slush on the runway hindering acceleration. It took him twenty years to

First away from Gatwick after its opening by the Queen on June 9th 1958 was BEA Pionair G-ALXK. *(BA)*

Another leased Viscount, V.745 G-APNF, displaying slightly unusual titling. *(BA)*

vindicate himself, although once his name was cleared he did not return to flying but lived quietly running a chicken farm. As the nation and airline were coming to terms with the loss another occurred. On April 28th Viscount G-AORC was chartered by BOAC to fly to Prestwick to collect some stranded London bound passengers. On approach to Prestwick 'ORC hit some high ground and was written off. The five crew escaped, although they were all injured. Pilot error was undeniably the cause, the crew having misread the altimeter by 1,000 feet.

Less than a month later (on May 16th) Pionair Leopard G-AGHP was lost on a freight flight from Rome, via Nice to London when it broke up in severe turbulence near Chateney (France) killing all three on board. There was yet one more serious incident; a mid air collision between a BEA Viscount (G-ANHC) and an Italian Air Force F.86 fighter which occurred on October 22nd, during a London-Rome flight. The collision took place at 23,000 feet and the Viscount plunged into the ground, out of control, killing all those on board. The F.86 pilot managed to eject safely. The accident highlighted the need for much close co-operation between civilian and military Air Traffic Controllers.

The most apparent feature of the winter timetable, effective from November 1st was the replacement of the Pionairs and leased Air Charter DC-4s by Viscounts on the German internal network. The Viscounts were an immediate success, traffic growing by up to 60% on some routes. Viscount V.701s were usually used, and several of them (G-ALWF, 'MOB, 'MOK, 'NHA, 'NHB, 'NHD, and 'OFX) had been modified for high density operations with up to sixty three seats and built in airstairs. Viscounts also took over the Gibraltar-Tangier and Madrid service for Gibraltar Airways, ending the need for the monthly Pionair positioning flight from Heathrow to Gibraltar. A new aspect of the winter programme was the offering of even cheaper weekend return fares on domestic trunk routes from London to Edinburgh, Glasgow and Belfast. The fare was set at £8 return for travel on a Saturday or Sunday, and the ticket was valid for a stay of up to eight days. Almost overnight there was a 25% leap in weekend loads, and by the end of the first full year of weekend cheap fares there had been a 50% improvement.

The winter did not spare Operations and traffic staff from still more troubles. Once again the weather was the culprit with severe fog affecting the London area between November 1958 and February 1959. It was the worst winter weather BEA had faced since the winter of 1948/49. But weather problems did not just confine themselves to the London area with fog affecting services to Birmingham, Manchester and Glasgow. By February 1959 BEA estimated that the weather had cost £250,000 in lost revenue and diversionary expenses. Operations staff daily faced the problem of having aircraft out of position, crews in the wrong place and passengers stranded, underlining the value of having some automatic landing equipment to enable aircraft to land even in the worst fog. The DH121 project included such a facility, but it would be many years before BEA could make full use of it. One accident was directly attributed to the weather. On Christmas Eve, a Viscount (G-AOFX) was diverted from Heathrow to Bournemouth. The weather at Hurn was flyable, but only just, and aircraft missed the runway and landed on the grass alongside. Luckily nobody was hurt, and the Viscount was only slightly damaged.

With all these problems, few people in BEA can have been very sad when Big Ben chimed midnight on December 31st. Surely 1959 would not be such a difficult year?

BEA

1959

1959 did indeed prove to be an exciting year for the airline, although there were inevitable troubles. Most of the excitement was generated by BEA entering the jet age, and the Corporation's first Comet, G-APMA, made its maiden flight at Hatfield on June 27th. Towards the end of the year the type began to be delivered to Heathrow. The airline had to make extensive preparations to enter the jet age. Crews needed to be trained, engineers licenced, traffic and operations manuals written, and so on. Crew training began with several BEA pilots spending some time with 216 Squadron, RAF, who flew Comet 4s. Once trained, the pilots returned to BEA and began to train the Corporation's own aircrews. Pilots converting from one type to another had to undergo a training course of several weeks, and take an Air Registration Board examination. In 1958/59 378 BEA pilots took such exams (but not all for Comet conversion courses). The pass rate was 93% indicating the high quality of BEA training and the calibre of its crews.

The first Comet to be delivered to BEA was G-APMB which arrived on November 9th. A week later G-APMC was delivered too, and plans were laid to fly a series of route proving flights, to commence on December 1st with a proving flight from Heathrow to Nice. But modern technology was beaten by that ancient phenomenon fog! A second proving flight was laid on for December 4th on the Heathrow-Oslo route. Yet again plans were dashed, not by fog but political considerations. Several days before an Air France Caravelle had visited Oslo, leading to a storm of protest over the noise it made. The Norwegian Parliament was due to debate the issue of jet noise on December 4th, so BEA thought it wiser not to add fuel to the fire by sending a Comet. On December 5th proving flights finally did begin, when G-APMB flew a round trip to Moscow. In Moscow there were no problems over public protests about aircraft noise, or anything else for that matter! Over the next few weeks the two Comets visited Warsaw, Stockholm and Zurich. In the early part of 1960 Comets began to carry commercial loads, being substituted for Viscounts on an ad-hoc basis, though it was not until April 1st 1960 that regular scheduled operations by the type began with G-APMB flying a Tel Aviv-London service, via Athens and Rome. It took that long for regular Comet services to commence because of an industrial dispute with pilots who demanded an extra £700 a year and a two hour reduction in the working day for flying the aircraft. BEA did not agree, and the type was virtually grounded in the early part of 1960, until the dispute was settled by arbitration.

Before the Comets had even entered service, the airline ordered its second generation of jets, the DH 121. On August 12th 1959 BEA signed an order with Hawker Siddeley for twenty four of the type. The order was the result of a lengthy period of evaluation and consultation between the manufacturers and BEA. Very careful thought went into the design, even down to the offsetting of the nose wheel to give extra baggage space. The '121 later named Trident 1C (a name chosen as the result of a staff competition), would be able to cruise at 600 mph for 1,000 miles, carrying eighty passengers in a mixed first and economy class configuration, or one hundred passengers in an all economy class mode. Three Rolls Royce Spey jet engines powered the type, and they would be powerful enough to allow the aircraft to be ferried on two engines, to save the cost of keeping spare engines at out stations or freighting them out. Tridents were to be equipped with automatic landing equipment for landing in bad weather, and an Auxillary Power Unit (APU) in the tail. APUs reduced dependence on ground equipment, and allowed the type to operate into airfields where ground power units did not exist. The order was valued at £28 million, and BEA wanted the type to be in service for 1963. The tailor made design of the Trident 1C may have been excellent from BEA's point of view, but it made the aircraft very difficult to sell to anyone else. In an effort to make the Trident more marketable Hawker Siddeley launched the Trident 1E. The 1E incorporated a number of improvements over the 1C, especially in performance, and it did obtain a handful of sales mainly in the Middle East. Most of the 1Es built eventually found their way into the BEA/British Airways fold.

In the course of 1959, the Vanguard like the Comet was making progress towards entry into commercial service. The prototype, G-AOYW, made its maiden flight on January 20th, when it flew the short distance the Vickers factory at Weybridge to the Vickers test airfield at Wisley. On April 22nd the first production Vanguard for BEA, G-APEA, made its maiden flight at Weybridge. It was the only Vanguard to be painted in BEA's current colour scheme, since the airline had just announced a new scheme and the rest of the Vanguard fleet were painted in that. The new colour scheme consisted of a black line along the cabin side, with a white cabin top, and a grey or silver underside. The wings were painted red, and the new Corporation symbol of a red square with BEA's initials inside it in white, was painted on the tail, and at the front and rear of the black strip. A small Union flag appeared on each side of the forward fuselage. The name 'British European Airways' which had appeared along the cabin roof was removed. That, coupled with the great reduction in the size of the Union Jack, caused some protest from a number of Conservative MPs, who signed a House of Commons motion "deploring the action of BEA in drastically reducing the size of the national flag on its aircraft, and the deletion altogether of the words 'British European Airways!' The new scheme spelt the end of BEA's old flying key symbol, the red square taking its place, meaning Keyline House had to be renamed. It was called Bealine House, and BEA aircraft began to use the radio callsign of 'Bealine'. One final feature of the new look, was the removal of the practice of naming individual aircraft. The last aircraft to receive a name was Comet G-APME, named John Tebbutt.

Vanguards G-APEA, G-APEB and G-APED flew several sales tours for Vickers prior to delivery to BEA, visiting Canada, the USA, the West Indies and a number of African states including Sudan, Nigeria, South Africa, Egypt and Rhodesia. As all three were painted in BEA colours the airline received some free advertising. BEA planners were busy preparing for the Vanguard to enter commercial service on July 1st 1960, yet just as with the Elizabethan, technical problems delayed the introduction of the type, though not by quite as long.

Fleet development did not end here. BEA was keenly interested in two other types. First was the Argosy freighter which was purpose built and capable of carrying 9,300lbs of cargo, compared with the Leopards 6,500lbs. The aeroplane was powered by four Rolls Royce Dart engines, and fitted with cargo rollers to allow pallets to be moved inside the aircraft. The Argosy had two large, hinged, loading doors; one at the front and one at the rear, which speeded up turn-round times by allowing incoming cargo to be off loaded from the rear door, while outbound

Vanguard V.951 G-APEA seen at Heathrow during a pre delivery visit. *(BA)*

cargo could be loaded simultaneously through the front. The prototype Argosy flew at Bitteswell on 8th January (G-AOZZ), and BEA cargo experts looked longingly at the aircraft. It represented a considerable advance on the existing Pionair Leopard freighter in terms of speed, capacity and crew comfort. However, it was not until 27th April 1961 that the BEA Board finally decided the airline could afford the luxury of such specialized freighters, placing an order for three Argosys. Development of the Argosy had proceeded so far by then, that the aircraft were able to be delivered to BEA later in 1961. The second type to be evaluated by the Corporation was the Handley Page Herald. BEA was well aware that the remaining days of passenger flying by Pionairs was limited and it was anxious to find a replacement for the type to operate the low density routes in Scotland. It was no use simply substituting a Viscount as several of the airfields involved were too small to accommodate a fully loaded Viscount. The cost of improving airport runways to allow them to take Viscounts was considered to be too great at the time. BEA viewed the Herald as a possible Pionair replacement in Scotland. Deciding the aircraft was well suited to such work, it made arrangements to lease three Heralds from the Ministry of Supply. On June 11th 1959 the Ministry had announced it was to buy three Heralds from Handley Page to encourage development of the aircraft, and BEA's need for three aircraft fitted in well with the Ministry's plans.

Apart from issuing a letter of intent to purchase six Rotodyne helicopters on January 7th (which was withdrawn in February 1962), the HEU was busy with charter work in 1959. A wide variety of charters were flown, the majority being crop spraying charters. A Bell 47, and later a WS.55, were fitted out with crop spraying gear on a semi-permanent basis. Crop spraying work was carried out all over the country, with East Anglia being the most common location. The helicopter was supported by a large van which carried an engineer, and a supply of fuel and spares. So successful was the work that Fred Charlton, the HEU Senior Engineer, developed a plastic crop spraying boom to fit onto a WS.55 during the year. The HEU took delivery of a new helicopter in April, an Agusta Bell 47 G-APTH, which was named Sir Lucan.

For the summer of 1959 two new international destinations were added to the BEA network. The first was London-Klagenfurt. A seasonal twice weekly service via Munich was launched on June 1st and ran until October 1st. The second destination was Moscow to where services began on May 14th, operating twice weekly via Copenhagen. G-AOYS commanded by Captain McLahhan flew the first service. Passengers were charged £142-4/- first class and £118-16/- economy class for travel to Moscow, and the airline even offered a package holiday there for three nights costing £120. The break even load factor for the Moscow service was 51%, which BEA realised was unlikely to be achieved very often in the short term. The service was as much a status symbol as a money maker at the beginning. Flying into Moscow did present problems. As Russian Air Traffic Controllers did not always speak English, the flights had to carry an interpreter to translate ATC messages. Furthermore, the Russian winter weather was very harsh. If Moscow was snow bound the aircraft had to divert back to Copenhagen, there being no other Soviet airfields open for western civilian use. Captains had to take on a lot of fuel in case of a lengthy diversion. Fortunately with the low loads this was not a great problem. Staff, too, had to be issued with special winter clothing. BEA's Representative in Moscow faced another problem, was his flat bugged? It was best to assume it was, and the only safe place for a conversation was reckoned to be in the bathroom with all the taps turned on! There was perhaps no stanger place for BEA management meetings.

On the German internal network BEA re-introduced the Berlin-Frankfurt services with two daily flights, using a Viscount. It quickly attracted passengers, and many extras were laid on to cope with demand. By now seventeen of the Viscount V.701s had been modified to sixty to sixty three seaters, and were fully employed on the German network and services into Jersey. Guernsey's government still held out against building a hard runway, so Pionairs continued to reign supreme there. To cater for the increased levels of traffic on many routes, the Viscount V.802s were modified for high density operations. Capacity was raised from fifty eight to sixty six and even seventy one if no catering facilities were required. In order to obtain more IT and holiday traffic, the airline slashed its inclusive tour charter rates by 25%, and issued 300,000 copies of a booklet called 'The Happiest Holiday of All'. The booklet promoted various destinations, and needless to say concluded that part of a happy holiday included flying with BEA.

In line with plans made in 1958, BEA began to operate a small number of international services from Gatwick Airport. Two routes were opened, to Dinard and to Cologne and Hanover. The Dinard service was flown daily between June and September by Viscount and became a regular seasonal feature of BEA Gatwick's work until the end of the 1963 season. However the Gatwick-Cologne-Hanover route did not live up to expectations. Beginning on May 15th a once daily schedule was flown, but loads were so poor that it was abandoned at the end of October. BEA found passengers were not prepared to travel down to Gatwick when other flights used Heathrow. It appeared inter-line passengers would not put up with an hour and a halfs coach trip between the two airports. Nevertheless for the summer of 1959 Gatwick was a very busy station, handling sixty flights a week to Jersey, forty seven to Guernsey and the daily Dinard and Hanover flights. Apart from its own services BEA Gatwick handled flights for several other operators including the Royal Canadian Air Force. But traffic at Gatwick was much less than it is today, and handling revenue was not very great.

The airline earnt itself some extra revenue by chartering to TAP a Viscount to operate their services from Lisbon and Oporto to London. The aircraft operated in normal BEA colours and with BEA crews, but wore a small TAP sticker near the main door. The charter arrangements began on June 9th, and provided for three flights a week to Lisbon, with one of these calling at

Oporto en route. G-AOHH seems to have been most regularly used, wearing a TAP sticker on a semi-permanent basis. This was the first of several agreements between the two airlines, which continued until TAP had suitable aircraft of its own to fly the routes. During the year BEA negotiated an agreement with the Greek airline, Olympic Airways. Olympic had ordered Comet 4Bs, and it contracted BEA to provide crew training and maintenance for its aircraft. A traffic agreement provided for BEA and Olympic to operate direct flights from London to Athens, from where flight radiated out to Turkey, Cyprus, Egypt, Israel and the Lebanon. Some days BEA aircraft would fly a particular route onwards from Athens, and other days Olympic would. An Olympic Comet from Paris and Frankfurt was timed to arrive at Athens to connect with the onward flights.

The end of the summer season marked the retirement of Pionairs from international passenger services out of Heathrow. The last international scheduled service to be flown by a Pionair occurred on Thursday October 29th, when one of the fleet operated a round trip to Salzburg. The aircraft left Heathrow at 09.55 and arrived back at 20.05, although which aircraft flew this historic service is unknown. Pionairs continued to operate some domestic services out of Heathrow, and flew one remaining international passenger route, from Birmingham to Dublin.

Although BEA was primarily an airline there were many departments within the organisation not directly related to flying, one being the Corporation's Medical Service. It had a surgery in the Engineering Base at Heathrow, and in 1958/59 it dealt with 37,000 patients. Treatments given ranged from immunisation against various diseases through to on the spot treatment for those injured working on the Base. The Service employed several Doctors, whose duties included providing basic first aid courses for cabin staff, and regular refresher courses. Research into various medical problems concerned with civil aviation occupied much of their time, covering such diverse issues as special winter clothing for staff at Moscow, radiation hazards to crews from aircraft weather radars, and environmental conditions in offices. The Unit checked the quality of food and drink served on BEA aircraft at home and abroad, and supervised the carriage of sick and invalid passengers. In 1958/59 over two thousand such passengers were carried, including one hundred and fifty two on stretchers, and fourteen in 'Oxycots'. 'Oxycots' were cots with a built in oxygen system for the use of seriously ill children. Outside London BEA had sixty four GPs it could call on in emergencies, for example to give crews medical examinations after an accident. The Medical Service gave keen support to the establishment of a BEA sports ground near Bealine House. A thirty acre site was purchased by the airline in the summer of 1959, enabling BEA sports teams to play 'home' fixtures at last. The Medical Service also supported the Corporation's decision to stop giving passengers boiled sweets prior to take off. Since 1946 sweets had been offered to passengers to stop their ears popping, but with more modern aircraft this was no longer necessary from a medical point of view, and the practice was stopped, much to the displeasure of many passengers, not just the children!

With the size of BEA's fleet the quantity of work that fell to the Engineering Unit was considerable. In 1958/59 BEA engineers performed the following number of checks:

Type	Check 1	Check 2	Check 3	Check 4
Viscount V.806	241	27	15	-
Viscount V.802	308	27	27	19
Viscount V.701	318	29	21	22
Pionair	623	85	39	40
Elizabethan	47	5	5	2
Heron	30	2	-	3
Rapide	35	7	3	1

All Check Threes and Fours were performed at Heathow, except for those on Herons which were done at Glasgow, and Rapides, which were carried out in Jersey. Check Ones and Twos were generally performed at Heathrow, though some were done at Manchester, Glasgow, Jersey, and Berlin. The standard of work achieved by the airline's engineers was extremely high, gaining BEA a very high reputation with other carriers. In 1959 the Engineering Department made 25,000 square feet of the Heathrow Base available to the Royal Aeronautical Society Historical Aircraft Collection, to enable them to work on restoration or building replicas, of early aircraft which were being prepared for exhibition. It was quite an intriguing sight to go from a Viscount undergoing a Check Four to a collection of Bleriot, Farnham, Fokker, and Avro bi-planes all under the same roof. The Base was becoming a popular place to visit, especially with schools and aviation enthusiasts. In 1958/59 no less than 5,250 people were shown around.

July 1959 marked the fiftieth anniversary of the first crossing of the Channel by aircraft, and the Daily Mail decided to celebrate the anniversary by holding a London to Paris Air Race, on July 19th. The starting point would be Marble Arch and the finishing line the Arc de Triomphe. BEA decided to enter the race, with an eye for some publicity. Suitably clad in suits and bowler hats, its team of thirteen were rushed from Marble Arch to Northolt in a London Transport double decker bus and then Underground train. At Northolt they boarded Comet G-APMA, which BEA loaned for the occasion as it had not yet been delivered. The Comet flew to Le Bourget, and the team completed their journey in a taxi. The Arc de Triomphe was reached in one hour and one minute, winning the airline the team prize of £1,000. The overall winner of the race, using a military jet, completed the course in just forty one minutes!

During the course of the year rumours began to circulate concerning a possible merger with BOAC. They were some ten years premature, but were fuelled by joint talks between the two Corporations on ways they could co-operate with each other. Such rumours were really never entirely silenced and continued to surface from time to time, despite vigorous denials by the management of the two airlines.

BEA

1960

If 1958/59 did not produce particularly successful financial results 1959/60 certainly did. The airline's financial postion showed a remarkable turn round, with the profit rising from £233,000 to £2,086,000, making 1959/60 BEA's most successful financial year to date. The improvement was the result of three main factors: firstly a growth in domestic passenger traffic, secondly an improvement in the world economy, and lastly development of inclusive tour traffic. Domestic passenger traffic showed a rise of 23%, with the largest growth being recorded on the London-Manchester route, where passenger carried lept by 57%. Passengers were being turned away from some services, something the management of 1947 would have found hard to believe! The general economic recovery helped international passenger traffic to record a less spectacular but welcome growth of 14%. On the IT scene the fare reductions introduced in 1959 proved their worth, producing a 60% growth in IT traffic for the airline. 1959/60 saw 1,356,617 IT passengers carried, compared with only 84,537 in 1958/59. Spain was the most popular IT destination, followed by Southern France, Italy, Austria and Switzerland.

The Report and Accounts showed BEA employed 1,449 Air Crew, 746 of whom were pilots, 119 Radio Operators and 584 cabin staff. The pilots flew an average of 575 hours each during 1959/60, and the cabin crews 632 hours. These men and women crewed BEA's ninety nine aircraft, and another 11,000 or so ground staff supported the operation. Eighty two stations at home and abroad received BEA services ranging from Sumburgh in the Shetland Isles to Tripoli in North Africa. At all the domestic stations BEA had its own ground staff, managed by a Station Superintendent, usually assisted by a Senior Traffic Officer. Some stations were extremely small; Barra in the Western Isles had just one BEA official, Station Superintendent Miss Macpherson, who incidently was BEA's only female Station Superintendent. Miss Macpherson did almost everything at Barra, from reservations, through passenger check-in, load control, meeting and boarding the aircraft, and even checking the beach to see if it was dry enough to allow the Heron to land! Abroad, BEA services were generally handled by the national airline of the country concerned, though BEA maintained handling units at several places, such as Paris, Rome, Athens, and Berlin. Once again each station

Comet 4B G-APMD on the apron at Heathrow shortly after delivery to the airline. (BA)

had a Station Superintendent, or a BEA Representative, who were generally English. Most other overseas staff tended to be locally recruited.

It had become traditional for BEA to launch an all out sales drive in the early months of a new year and 1960 was no exception. The sales drive had a dual thrust, the cutting of fares and opening of new sales outlets. The airline planned an ambitious scheme to reduce fares by between 15% and 20% between 1960 and 1961. In some cases reductions were even higher, up to 40%. New Night Tourist fares were introduced to Portugal and Greece, while the day return fare between London and Paris was cut from £16-16/- to £14-19/-. On Channel Islands and Isle of Man services fares were reduced for travel on Mondays, Fridays and Sundays to lessen the traffic peak on Saturdays. Finally domestic Off-Peak fares were available as London-Belfast, Edinburgh and Glasgow services. The Off Peak fares were considerably cheaper than normal tickets, but they were only available on late night or early morning flights. Several new off-line sales offices were opened during the year, including ones in Los Angeles, Exeter and Florence. The Los Angeles and Exeter offices were not open to the public but the Florence office was also a normal public booking office. As well as new off-line sales offices, BEA opened several new public booking offices in various cities including Klagenfurt and Bordeaux, and a number of existing offices were modernized too.

From April 1st Comets began to fly regular services. The table below shows the date on which scheduled Comet services began:

April 1st.	London-Nicosia (in co-operation with Cyprus Airways).
April 1st.	London-Tel Aviv.
April 1st.	London-Moscow. Inaugural flight operated by G-APMD.
May 1st.	London-Warsaw.
May 14th.	London-Zurich.
June 1st.	London-Copenhagen. Inaugural flight flown by G-APMD.
June 5th.	London-Malta. Inaugural flight flown by G-APMD.
June 5th.	London-Nice. Inaugural flight flown by G-APMD.
July 1st.	London-Oslo-Stockholm. Inaugural flight operated by G-APMA.
August 1st.	London-Frankfurt. Inaugural flight flown by G-APMC.

Quite why G-APMD operated so many of the inaugural flights is a mystery. At the end of 1960 nineteen stations on the network received scheduled Comet services, and BEA gradually began to win back some of the traffic lost to other operators who had introduced jets on their routes before BEA. This was particularly noticeable on the London-Frankfurt and London-Nice services, where BEA had been losing traffic to Pan Americans Boeing 707s, and Air Frances Caravelles respectively. BEA still suffered from traffic losses on other routes where it was unable to fly jets, the most serious being London to Paris, thanks to Air France making much greater use of Caravelles. BEA hoped the shortness of the route might mean passengers were not so easily lured onto jets, as they actually knocked only ten minutes off flight times. A vain hope! To the travelling public jets were the way to travel and passengers began to desert BEA services for the Air France Caravelles. Comets were certainly not ideal to use on such short routes, being designed for economic operation on longer sectors, but BEA quickly realized it needed to use them on the Paris route if it was not to lose much of its share of traffic. Thus in 1960/61 the airline increased its order for the type. On July 19th a further three Comets were ordered, and, realizing that a similar problem would occur on a number of other short routes two more Comets were ordered on December 22nd, and another two on January 20th 1961.

The target date for the commencement of commercial Vanguard flying was July, and in the early part of the year preparation went ahead towards that goal. Vanguard G-APED flew a series of route proving flights to places like Paris and Brussels notching up two hundred flying hours as it did so. At the same time schedules were published showing Vanguard operations were to commence on July 1st, and everything seemed well on target until.... out of the blue problems developed with the Tyne engines. In the course of a bench testing session at Rolls Royce, a Tyne engine suffered a compressor blade fracture and failure. Such a fault could be very serious if it occurred on an aircraft, and Rolls Royce recommended all Tyne powered aircraft should be grounded until the engine design could be modified. BEA now faced real difficulties. The Vanguards could not be ready for July 1st, meaning schedules had to be rewritten and extra aircraft obtained to cover the gaps. The Vanguard could seat nearly double the load of a Viscount, and for every Vanguard schedule fully booked, two Viscounts would have to be substituted. For example, the London-Paris route was scheduled for seven daily Vanguard flights from July 1st but that required eleven or twelve Viscount trips. BEA had some spare Viscount capacity itself, but nowhere near enough, so two Viscounts were chartered from the Norwegian operator Fred Olsen. Both were type V.779s, the two aircraft in question being LN-FOH which was allocated the British registration of G-APZP, and LN-FOM which became G-ARBW. BEA had chartered Fred Olsen Viscounts before. Between 1955 and 1957 shortage of capacity had lead the airline to charter two V.736s. Some additional Viscount capacity was created by releasing Viscounts from freight work, and replacing them with a leased Dan Air York, and many Viscount services to Jersey were replaced by an Ambassador again leased from Dan Air. The airline managed to get through the summer, but not without considerable difficulty, and much adverse reaction from passengers. For many it was history repeating itself. Less than ten years before, they were able to recall a similar situation when BEA was seeking to introduce the Elizabethan.

By October 1960 Vanguard G-APED had been fitted with the modified Tyne engines, and began a rigorous programme of flight testing which lasted seventy five hours. It was successfully completed and at last a Certificate of Airworthiness was issued on December 2nd. G-APED did not arrive at Heathrow until January 1961, but two more Vanguards were modified and delivered to the airline just as the year was ending, G-APEE arrived first on December 3rd, and 'PEF on the 13th . They immediately began crew training refresher courses and sufficient crews were available for the type to make a limited entry into service on December 17th; when G-APEF, commanded by Captain Johnson, operated a London-Paris service in place of a Viscount. Two days later G-APEE flew a London-Zurich service in the morning, followed by an afternoon flight to Geneva, again both as Viscount substitutions. 'PEE remained in Geneva until December 21st to allow the crew a rest period, then it positioned empty to Dusseldorf and flew a scheduled Dusseldorf-London flight. Meanwhile 'PEF operated the first domestic Vanguard service on December 20th by flying a round trip to Glasgow. Over the next months the type continued to be used on an ad-hoc basis, but on March 1st 1961 it entered regular services on the Paris route.

The summer programme featured a pooled London-Gibraltar service, with Hunting Clan. The arrangement began on April 18th, providing for BEA to operate several Viscount flights a week on the route, and Hunting Clan to operate once or twice a week. On July 1st Hunting Clan became British United Airways, but the agreement continued for many years, and was extended to cover services to Malaga. It was the first pooling agreement BEA had made with a British independent carrier. A new route for 1960 was a London and Malta to Alghero (Sardinia) flight. BEA already called at Ajaccio in Corsica on certain London-Malta flights, and Sardinia was added on the same basis. Services commenced on June 5th with one Viscount flight a week calling at Alghero from London en route for Malta, and one on the reverse service. The first aircraft to call at Alghero was G-AMNZ. A second new service linked London and Turin. The licences to operate into Alghero and Turin were some of the last granted to BEA by the Air Advisory

WS.55 G-ANFH is seen displaying its crop spraying boom. *(BIH)*

Council. Under the terms of the 1960 Civil Aviation Act all new licence applications were to be heard by a new body, the Air Transport Licencing Board. The terms of reference for the Board reflected Conservative government policy by requiring it to look favourably on applications from independent operators for both domestic and international routes. Here was the first hint of coming competition for BEA on some of its major routes.

BEA operations into Guernsey came up to date with the arrival of the Viscount in the late summer. The States of Guernsey finally decided to construct a hard runway in 1959, which was formally opened on August 1st 1960; being 4,800 feet in length. BEA began immediate Viscount services to the Island. On August 1st Viscount G-AOFX arrived at Guernsey at 09.20 from Jersey, to become the first of the type to land there. It remained on the ground for most of the day, departing at 16.30 on a scheduled flight to Gatwick. Initially loads had to be limited to forty four passengers because one end of the runway was not yet hardened enough to be used. Thereafter Guernsey operations were flown by a mixture of Viscounts and Pionairs, though it was not to be long before the Pionairs were to be retired from Channel Islands flying. On October 1st BEA carried its ten millionth Viscount passenger, meaning nearly half the total of twenty five million passengers carried by BEA since formation in 1946 had been flown on Viscounts, and indicating the scale of BEA's use of the type as well as its popularity with passengers.

When the summer programme ceased on October 31st Pionairs were withdrawn from services out of Heathrow and from the Irish Sea network covering Liverpool, the Isle of Man and Belfast. The last scheduled Pionair flight out of Heathrow was operated on October 31st by G-AGZB. Under the command of Captain Griffin it was scheduled to fly a round trip to Birmingham. The event went somewhat wrong, as in bad weather 'GZB ran into a ditch on landing at Birmingham. The Pionair was only slightly damaged, but the south bound service had to be cancelled, providing a rather inglorious end to BEA Pionair operations from Heathrow. Pionairs now only appeared at Heathrow on occasional extra flights from Jersey and Guernsey, and when going into the Base for Checks. Pionair Leopard freighters still flew from London, although on a decreasing scale with the additional use of Viscounts and the coming of the Argosys. The longest freighter route still to be Leopard operated was the Heathrow-Rome flight, via Nice outbound, and Milan in bound. It operated on Wednesday, Friday and Sunday, leaving Heathrow as BEFO6 at 02.30. After a night-stop at Rome it returned to Heathrow, departing Rome at 10.10 on Monday, Thursday and Saturday. The call at Milan was made on request. BEA services to Milan transferred from Malpensa to Linate airport on November 1st. Malpensa was thirty miles from the city whereas Linate was only five making it much more convenient. Malpensa continued to be used for diversions when bad weather closed Linate.

BEA was beginning to face a new problem at Heathrow, jet noise. To curb excessive disturbance to local residents the Airport Authority decided jets could onlt use three of the (then) possible eight directions for night take offs, and pilots were instructed not to run up engines to full power before commencing night take offs. Restrictions gradually extended to a curb on the number of night take offs by jets and elaborate noise abatement procedures to be followed after any take off day or night were introduced. By 1973 BEA had only one jet departure after 23.00, a 23.10 Trident to Malta on four days a week. The Corporation made greater use of Vanguards, especially in the late 1960s to get around the restrictions, as turbo-props were exempt from them.

With the vast increase in traffic using Heathrow, the airspace around the airport was becoming increasingly congested. In the morning and evening peak periods aircraft had to hold for up to an hour awaiting clearance to land at Heathrow, and those delays severely disrupted BEA schedules. Airline schedulers actually built in a small allowance of time on many services into London to take account of the problem, explaining why the timetable showed some flights into London taking longer than the outbound trip from London. While congestion was worst at Heathrow, it was by no means the only airfield affected, indeed airspace generally was becoming over crowded, reflected in the rising number of 'near misses'. The danger was highlighted on August 11th when, at Rome, a Viscount (G-AMOP) had to take violent evasive action to avoid colliding with a Boeing 707 as it was about to land. Thirteen people in the Viscounts were seriously injured. A strange accident occurred on January 5th at Malta. Viscount G-AMNY made an emergency landing with a hydraulics failure. A safe landing was made, but as the aircraft tried to taxi off the runway to the civil apron the brakes failed and it ended up colliding with the control tower! The two pilots and two passengers were slightly injured, and the pulse rate of the tower controller is reputed to have trebled! BEA lost another Viscount, G-AOHU, at Heathrow on January 7th. The aircraft was operating a scheduled service from Dublin, when its nosewheel collapsed on landing. A fire broke out and the aircraft was burnt out although thankfully there were no injuries.

On September 20th the Helicopter Experimental Unit was honoured for its work in helicopter development by Bell Helicopters, who awarded BEA a Helicopter Pioneer Award. In a ceremony at Gatwick, Lord Douglas received the award from General John Schweizer. The HEU's General Manager, Captain John Cameron, also attended the Ceremony. In 1959/60 the HEU activities were summarised as follows:

Aircraft Fleet	Charter Flying (hours)	Development & Training Flying (hours)
Two Westland WS.55	443	156
One Bristol 171	321	5
Two Bell 47	482	59

Much of the charter flying, especially for the Bell 47s and WS.55s continued to be crop spraying.

BEA

1961

Compared with other years, 1961 was rather quiet for the airline. One of the few major events was the retirement of Pionairs from operations on the Channel Islands network. Scheduled Pionair operations into Jersey and Guernsey ceased on March 31st, with the last service being between Jersey and Guernsey, operated by G-AGNK. However a Pionair (G-AGNK) was retained at Jersey for some weeks to act as a standby aircraft and to operate a number of extra services over the Easter period, particularly on April 3rd and 4th. The withdrawal of the Pionairs meant BEA could no longer fly into Southampton, as the airfield still had only a grass runway making it unsuitable for Viscounts. The Southampton-Jersey route had been the second busiest Channel Islands route for many years, and the Corporation was reluctant to have to move out. To keep a link between the South coast and Jersey BEA decided to open a service from Bournemouth (Hurn) to Jersey with Viscounts. Flights to Southampton were supposed to cease on March 31st, and begin from Hurn the next day. However difficulties over Customs facilities at Southampton meant services ended on Sunday March 19th. The last departure from Southampton was BE754 at 17.20, flown by G-AHCX commanded by Captain Draper. To illustrate how popular the route was, all thirty two seats were filled. From March 20th to 31st the Pionairs operated into Hurn, as did the freighter service operated by Leopards on Wednesday and Sunday. The first Viscount service into Hurn occurred on the afternoon of April 1st. BE8656 arrived at Hurn from Jersey at 14.30, operated by G-ANHF. Over the summer of 1961 up to twenty three Viscount flights a week were scheduled between Jersey and Hurn. Bournemouth was never as popular as Southampton, and by 1965 only thirteen flights a week were timetabled for the summer. Hurn did prove a useful diversionary airfield for Heathrow, and in the winter months the small traffic unit there, headed by Station Superintendent Tom Williams, was supplemented by extra staff from Heathrow. Once or twice there were so many diversions that the facilities at Hurn were totally swamped. On the record day for diversions twenty seven flights arrived at Hurn, all to be handled by BEA, within one and three quarter hours! With only three sets of passenger steps, aircraft were dealt with one by one, and

Displaying its elegant features, Vanguard V.951 G-APEB at the 1960 Farnborough Air Show. *(BA)*

Comet 4B G-APMG arriving at Rome. *(BA)*

some passengers had to sit on the aircraft for several hours before they could be disembarked.

As Pionairs were being withdrawn in the Channel Isles, their use was being curtailed in the Scottish Highlands and Islands. From April 1st, Viscounts replaced Pionairs on the routes to the Western Isles of Benbecula and Stornoway, and on March 29th BEA announced it would receive three Herald aircraft to replace Pionairs on remaining Scottish services. With so many Pionair services being taken over by other types, BEA was able to drastically reduce its fleet of the aircraft from twenty-five in January 1961 to seven by December. They were: Pionair G-ALXL, and Pionair Leopards G-AHCU, 'HCX, 'LTT, 'MDB, 'MNV and 'MNW. By May 1962 the fleet was further reduced to just four Pionair Leopards G-AHCU, 'LTT, 'MNV and 'MNW.

For the summer of 1961 a number of new European services were commenced.
These included:

London-Oporto.	Commenced on April 1st.
London-Budapest via Prague.	Commenced on April 1st, but produced poor loads and Budapest was dropped from the network on 31.10.62.
London-Palermo.	Commenced on June 1st, as an intermediate stop on the London-Malta service. Flown once a week in each direction by Vanguard.
London-Stavanger.	Commenced on June 1st, flown by Viscounts, on a seasonal basis only.

Cairo was re-introduced to the network with a service from Nicosia, operating in conjunction with Cyprus Airways. Like Budapest, Cairo failed to generate much traffic and the route only ran until the end of October. The key problem was that the Egyptian government did not lift its restrictions on foreign travel by nationals.

By March seven Comets were in service linking London with nineteen destinations mainly in the Middle East and Eastern Europe. The value of jet travel was plainly illustrated on the London-Athens route. In 1951 it had taken a Viking twenty three hours to reach Athens, with a night-stop en route in Rome, now the Comet could do it in four hours. BEA Comets took over from Viscounts on the TAP London-Lisbon route from April 1st. In order to make maximum use of the leased Comet, TAP also used the aircraft to fly onwards from Lisbon to Madeira, the first and only time BEA aircraft appeared at Porto Santo Airport, except on IT charters. Comet G-ARJM operated the first service into Porto Santo. The Comet charter to TAP lasted until 31st October 1962, by which time TAP had taken deliver of its own jets, three Caravelles.

On May 18th BEA put the first of the larger (in terms of passenger loads) Vanguard V.953s into commercial service, with G-APEG flying a London-Paris schedule. For the summer the Vanguards were timetabled to fly to Paris, Madrid, Gibraltar and Malta (some calling at Rome, or Naples, or Palermo) some of which were new destinations for the type. Domestically, Vanguards flew four flights daily between London and Belfast, four to Glasgow and two to Edinburgh. Throughout much of the summer BEA services to Edinburgh were disrupted by the lengthening and resurfacing of runway at Turnhouse. Flights were transferred to East Fortune aerodrome, one and a quarter hours road journey from the city centre. Facilities at East Fortune were primitive to say the least, and the Corporation was very relieved to be able to return to Turnhouse when the work had been completed.

The arrival of modern aircraft like the Comet and Vanguard did not end the practical joking of some pilots.

A Vanguard Captain once stood at the bottom of the forward airstairs of a Vanguard welcoming passengers to the flight and inviting them to visit the cockpit during the journey. Once they had all boarded he quietly slipped away to his own aircraft on a nearby stand, leaving the aircraft's actual Captain quite unaware of what had happened, and to face a constant stream of uninvited guests to his flight deck!

Although Comets and Vanguards were getting most publicity, Viscounts still performed sterling work on domestic and international routes. Indeed it was the Viscount which carried the BEA flag to its furthest point, Doha in the Persian Gulf. Under charter to Cyprus Airways BEA Viscounts operated a three times weekly service on Tuesday, Thursday and Saturday from Nicosia to Doha, via Beruit, Kuwait and Bahrain. The days of Viscount operations over the route were numbered though, with Comets taking over the schedule from October. BEA Comets did not see service for very long in the Gulf, because on 29th March 1962 Cyprus Airways gave up the route thanks to falling loads.

In the spring the new Air Transport Licencing Board (ATLB) began to function, and immediately several independent airlines applied to fly routes presently flown by BEA. Most applications came from Eagle and BUA, and the hearings lasted well into 1962. BEA naturally objected to the requests, opposition being ably put by Henry Marking the airline's Solicitor. Over fifty licence applications were made by the independents, and eventually the ATLB decided to award twenty two of them, including licences to both Eagle and BUA for services from Heathrow and Gatwick, respectively to Belfast, Edinburgh and Glasgow. BEA immediately appealed with the appeal hearings beginning on April 9th 1962. They lasted eleven days, although to BEA's great disappointment its appeals were quashed on all but two routes. The airline's gloom was reflected in the 1961/62 Report and Accounts: "These new airlines rights will mean yet more empty seats on the market. It will now be the more difficult for the airline to hold down fares let alone reduce them".

On a brighter note, 1961 was a good year for BEA Royal Flights. On no less than six occasions various members of the Royal Family travelled on special BEA flights:

January 11th.	Princess Margaret travelled to Oslo in Viscount G-APOX.
April 29th.	The Queen and Prince Philip flew by Comet to Alghero, and the aircraft picked up the Queen Mother there and brough her back to London the next day.
May 5th.	The Queen and Prince Philip accompanied by the Duke and Duchess of Gloucester flew by Comet to Ancona (Italy) via Rome.
May 9th.	The Queen and Prince Philip were brought back from Italy, on a Comet from Turin.
May 25th.	The Duke and Duchess of Gloucester returned home from Crete to Heathrow in a Comet.

The aircraft used were fitted with a luxury interior to accommodate the Royal party, although often the rear of the cabin was left in its ordinary configuration to cater for the press and Court officials who accompanied the Royal visitors. The carriage of the Royal Family was very effective publicity for the airline as there could be little better publicity than seeing the Queen boarding a BEA aircraft on television.

A far cry from the comforts of the Royal Flights were the comforts, or to be more exact lack of them, on freighter aircraft. The only comfort afforded to the crews of the Leopard freighters was a lavatory. Things did begin to improve in November with the arrival of the first Argosy. The type was pressurised and even provided

First into Bournemouth Hurn Airport, Viscount V.701 G-ANHF inaugurates Viscount services into Hurn from Jersey on April 1st 1961. *(BA)*

The large cargo doors are clearly visible on Argosy G-APRN as it unloads at le Bourget. *(BA).*

facilities for hot food to be stored for the crew. Still, things were not as grand as on BOAC's freighters, where a steward was carried to wait on the flight deck crews. The first Argosy, G-APRN, began to operate on an ad-hoc basis on the London-Milan route on November 17th, and once a second aircraft had arrived, G-APRM, a regular four times weekly London-Milan schedule was commenced. Early in 1962, with the third Argosy (G-AOZZ) in service the type began to fly more routes. From January 8th, Argosys flew a daily London-Manchester-Glasgow route, and from January 30th daily services to Copenhagen, Dusseldorf, Frankfurt and Paris. By May 1962 all freighter services were flown by Argosy, except London-Amsterdam and Zurich, and Manchester-Belfast which were Viscount operated. For a time in 1961 the Amsterdam route had been flown by a DC-3 leased from Derby Airways, beginning on February 2nd when G-AMSX commanded by Captain Milsom worked the schedule. Derby flew the route until the middle of the summer.

The Argosy brought BEA freighter operations into the modern world, giving the airline the ability to carry a much wider range of loads than the Leopard permitted. Special handling vehicles were delivered to BEA to enable pallets to be loaded straight from a lorry onto the aircraft. The lorries could also off load pallets and deliver them straight to the customer. They caused a few problems in Jersey and Guernsey where some of the roads proved rather narrow for them, as a BEA driver in Jersey found when he tried to deliver some cargo to Channel Television's transmitter, demolishing the wall at the entrance to the narrow lane. Argosys did not appear in Guernsey until May 1963, when G-AOZZ inaugurated a twice weekly service from London, although Jersey had been handling the type since April 1962.

On May 19th BEA and BOAC opened their new purpose built aircrew training school at Hamble near Southampton. The opening ceremony was performed by the Duke of Edinburgh. The College was established to train recruits for a commercial flying career with both airlines. Most of the intake would be selected from school leavers, though some were recruited from university graduates. The first intake of thiry four students arrived at Hamble on September 9th, and all but three of them were designated to serve with BEA. The cost of training a pilot at Hamble was about £4,000, £1,000 to be paid by the government, £1,000 by the pilot himself by deductions from his salary once trained, and the remainder by the airline. Until the first pilots were ready BEA still faced a shortage of aircrew and to fill the gap, the airline mounted a recruitment drive in Canada, employing thiry pilots from the Royal Canadian Air Force and Trans Canada Airlines (later Air Canada). Back at Hamble flight training was undertaken using a fleet of Chipmunks and Apaches. Later the Chipmunks were replaced by Cherokees. A small number of Chipmunks were retained for aerobatic training. The Apaches were later superseded by Barons.

Once a pilot had completed his Hamble training he joined BEA as a Second Officer, and underwent type training to qualify him for the aircraft he would fly. Flight training for those destined for the Viscounts, or for existing BEA aircrew converting to the type, was undertaken at Jersey, Dinard and Gatwick. Comet, Vanguard and Argosy training was conducted from Stansted or Prestwick. At Stansted, BEA established a small full time handling unit to deal with training details, with eighteen engineers. Much initial training for the type conversions was done on the BEA flight simulators which covered Viscount, Vanguard and Comet aircraft. A simulator for the Trident was on order. The scale of simulator use is shown from the statistics for their use in 1961/62. 7,300 simulator hours were 'flown', which enabled actual flying time in aircraft to be cut to 2,300 hours; two thirds below the requirement necessary if the simulators had not been in use.

No amount of training could entirely remove accidents with the Corporation suffering three major incidents during the year. On November 27th a Viscount, (G-AOYH) departing from Munich, ran into severe turbulence. Two of the crew and thirteen passengers were injured, and the Captain made an immediate return to Munich, where the aircraft landed safely. Less than a month later, on December 12th, Rapide G-AKZB came to grief while landing at Land's End inbound from St Mary's in the Scillies. It overran the airfield after its brakes locked on wet grass. Damage was considerable, and the engineers decided 'KZB was beyond economic repair. The most serious of the spate of accidents came on December 21st, far down the line at Ankara. Comet, G-ARJM, was getting airborn en route for Nicosia with twenty seven passengers and seven crew on board, when it stalled and dived into the ground. All the crew and twenty of the passengers were killed, and only one of the seven remaining passengers escaped serious injury. At first pilot error was suspected, with theories that the pilot must have climbed too steeply inducing the stall! But careful investigation found the fault actually lay with the instruments, which misled the crew into thinking the angle of climb was shallower than it actually was.

BEA's sales staff took an important step into the technological age in August 1961, by ordering a computer to handle reservations. BEA wanted the computer to be ready for use by 1964, enabling reservations to be handled much more speedily. Many prospective passengers were heartily tired of trying to 'phone the airline and finding lines engaged for long periods of time, and without a doubt reservations had been lost because of this. The new computer would speed up the booking system, meaning that the telephone ought to be answered more quickly. The airline intended to locate the computer at West London Air Terminal, and centralize all reservations there. As a stop gap measure, an attempt was made to reduce the time taken to answer 'phone calls by installing some extra phone lines at Dorland Hall. Delays in answering the 'phone had also put many travel agents off booking passengers on BEA, since for each ticket they sold they had to contact BEA first. Agents often found it quicker to 'phone another carrier. To deal with the problem BEA began a new system whereby agents could sell seats without direct reference to the airline on any services except those in the height of the summer. Travel agents then periodically advised BEA of the bookings they had made. The policy of giving sales offices a new look continued, with face lifts being given to offices as far apart as Stornoway and Lisbon. One other change in the reservations structure occurred, with the ending of domestic return fares. Returns could be purchased simply by buying two single tickets. One all to rare occurrence was a number of fare reductions. Much to the disappointment of businessmen these were not on the European routes, but in Scotland, the Isle of Man, and the Channel Isles. Reductions of up to 30% were offered, the only catch being that travel must occur in the middle of the week. Once again, the purpose behind the reductions was to try to even out traffic levels by discouraging weekend travel.

Since 1946 BEA had owned shares in the Italian carrier, Alitalia, and had assisted the airline in commencing operations. The remaining shares in Alitalia were finally sold off in 1961. However the two airlines maintained a very close relationship. Services from Rome, Naples and Milan to London were pooled, and each handled the others flights at London, Milan, Turin, and Naples. BEA did not need the services of Alitalia at Rome, as it maintained a joint handling unit there with BOAC. BEA also sold off its share holding in Jersey Airlines in December.

Passengers using some of the Corporation's services travelled on two unusual types during the summer, the Bristol Britannia, and the Douglas DC-7C. Throughout April and May BEA used chartered BOAC Britannias to fly some services from London to Copenhagen and Nice. The Britannia charter resulted from late deliveries of the Comet jets. Three Britannias were used at various times, G-AOVG, 'OVP and 'OVT. The 10.30 (BE742) service to Copenhagen was generally Britannia operated, as was the 17.00 (BE104) Nice service. Britannias were joined by a DC-7C in April. The DC-7C flew a daily flight from London to Zurich (BE568 departing LHR at 11.50), and a daily trip to Frankfurt (BE604 departing LHR at 17.20). It is quite likely that some of these services may have been flown by the Britannias not DC-7s. Once again the shortage of Comets was the cause. Later in the summer, because of a shortage of Vanguards, BEA leased further DC-7C capacity from BOAC. The DC-7 operated four round trips between London and Le Bourget, with departures from Heathrow at 10.00 (BE340), 14.00 (BE348), 18.00 (BE356) and 22.00 (BE364). The aircraft were used between June and the end of August. No records remain to indicate which of the BOAC DC-7Cs were used. For the summer of 1961 Paris was linked with Gatwick, not with the mighty DC-7, but the humble Viscount. A once daily round trip was provided with departure from Le Bourget at 13.00 (BE407) and from Gatwick at 15.00 (BE408). What was notable about the service was not the loads it produced, they were very slim, but the demanding schedule for the aircraft involved. It began its day at Birmingham, and worked the following sectors: Birmingham-Glasgow-Birmingham-Le Bourget-Gatwick-Le Bourget-Birmingham-Glasgow-Birmingham. Airline schedulers certainly seemed to know how to get the most out of their aircraft in those days!

An unusual angle on Argosy 101 G-APRM as it lands at Heathrow. (BA)

BEA

1962

There is a well known saying that 'all good things must come to an end.' The truth of the saying was felt by BEA at the end of March 1962, when the airline's accountants calculated it had made a loss of £1,488,065 for the financial year 1961/62. A red balance sheet was something the Corporation had not had for the last seven years, and there were plenty of explanations for it. To begin with too many flights had been scheduled for the summer especially in West Germany and on the domestic network. Aircraft flew half empty and losses soared. Then revenue from off-line sales offices was found to be far below expectations, while introductory costs of bringing Comets, Vanguards, Heralds and Argosys into service produced a bill of £3 million. Another factor was the decline in traffic on some key European routes as foreign airlines made ever increasing use of jets. London-Paris continued to be of greatest concern, with a steady loss of traffic to Air France Caravelles. Equally worrying was a 6% fall in loads to Frankfurt, due to Pan American flying a daily Boeing 707 on the route. Finally, BEA felt the costs of several industrial disputes and a crop of winter weather problems. The most serious industrial problem was a strike by Ministry of Aviation baggage loaders at Heathrow in December 1961. At least BEA would have more control over that situation in the future as the airline took over responsibility for ramp handling from the Ministry on April 1st 1962. 627 staff, 242 vehicles, 100 sets of passenger steps and 33 airside coaches now became BEA's possessions! Apart from the December dispute, fog in the same month caused severe disruption to schedules, a thousand flights being cancelled. In January the fog turned to thick snow and more costly delays and cancellations.

In a vigorous attempt to overcome the financial crisis BEA took several steps. New off-line sales offices were opened in several parts of the world to try to boost BEA traffic. One opened in Sydney under J.A. O'Shea, another in Johannesburg run by J.H.B. Richards and a third in Toronto managed by A. Mills. A thorough review of all scheduled services was undertaken resulting in the decision not to re-open flights from London to Ajaccio and Budapest, and to close the London-Belgrade and Birmingham-Amsterdam flights. Services in the Channel Isles, Isle of Man and Scotland were all pruned, and talks with Cambrian Airways began over the possibility of handing over all the Irish Sea services to them. The last cost cutting exercise involved the sale of some of the Viscount V.701 fleet. Ten aircraft were sold to the Brazilian carrier VASP, being delivered in August. (For the record the ten were G-AMOB, 'MOD, 'MOF, 'MOI, 'NHA, 'NHB, 'NHD, 'NHE, 'NHF and 'OFX.) At the same time BEA finally dispensed with Radio Operators on its aircraft, partly as an economy measure and partly due to better Air Traffic Control facilities and aircraft radio equipment. Radio Officers were all offered other jobs with the airline, some retraining as pilots, but most joining Traffic or Operations Departments.

As a consequence of the losses of 1961/62 and the continued economic difficulties only one new route was opened in 1962, a Comet service to Helsinki, via Stockholm, operating four times weekly. Comets continued to be introduced on a number of existing routes, such as London to Madrid and Paris. Services by Comet to Paris commenced on October 28th, and helped to improve BEA's competitive position. The use of sophisticated jets like the Comet did produce problems for the airline on occasions. One day in 1962 a Comet, en route from Heathrow to Gibraltar, was forced to divert to Seville because of bad weather at the Rock. Seville was not a regular port of call for BEA, and on arrival it was found there was no suitable ground power unit for a Comet. An attempt to start up using its own batteries failed, leading to a further fifteen hour delay while the batteries were recharged. At least this sort of hiccup would not recur once the Tridents were in use, as they were fitted with built in Auxillary Power Units.

By the summer Vanguards were flying nearly all the services on the trunk routes from London to Belfast, Edinburgh and Glasgow. They produced a 21% traffic growth on routes to Scotland, and a 16% growth on the Belfast service. The aircraft gave a larger cargo carrying facility, enabling cargo carried on the Scottish trunk routes to rise by 20%, and on the Belfast by 66%. For the first time Vanguards made a limited appearance on the London-Isle on Man service. On Saturdays BE7024, which left Heathrow at 11.45 for Ronaldsway, was Vanguard operated. The return sector, BE7027, departed from the Isle of Man at 13.25. Viscounts continued to fly the non-stop London-Isle of Man service on other days.

Herald G-APWC on a rare visit to Heathrow in May 1962. Note it is still fitted with under wing fuel tanks from its South American Royal Tour. (BA)

Internationally the Vanguards began to make an impact on the high density routes, especially those from London to Barcelona, Dublin, Gibraltar, Malta and Palma. During the year traffic to Spain and Gibraltar rose by 30%, and to Malta by 16%, all largely due to the influence of the Vanguard. Vanguards replaced the Viscount on the weekly London-Alghero-Malta schedule, with G-APER operating the first Vanguard service into Alghero on Saturday July 7th. All this work gave the type a very high utilization of about eighty hours per aircraft per week over the summer peak. The Vanguard proved quite a success story for BEA in many respects, particularly with its fuel efficiency and versatility. However, just as with the Trident, the type proved hard to sell to other customers. There was only one other order, from Air Canada. The reason was not that the Vanguard was too closely tailored to BEA's requirements, but because jet travel was becoming so popular that passengers did not want to travel on unfashionable turbo-props. Hopes of the Vanguard selling as well as the Viscount were not fulfilled. Only forty three Vanguards were built compared with over four hundred Viscounts. BEA found the Vanguard to be of greatest value on routes where its rivals did not use jet equipment. Where they did, the Corporation soon found itself having to replace Vanguards with Comets or Tridents to keep its share of traffic.

BEA had hoped to begin flying the Handley Page Heralds on the Scottish Highland and Island routes at the beginning of the 1961 summer programme. But several events delayed their entry into service by a year. These included development problems, and delays in delivery of Series 200 Heralds to Jersey Airlines. Handley Page approached the Ministry of Supply (who were to own the three BEA Heralds) to ask if they would object to the leasing of the first aircraft destined for BEA (G-APWB) to Jersey Airlines, pending the delivery of its own Series 200 aircraft. The Ministry agreed, and 'PWB went to Jersey instead of Glasgow. The second Herald ('PWC) was delivered to BEA in January 1962, but instead of entering scheduled services, it departed to South America in company with the Handley Page demonstrator aircraft (G-APWA). The pair were used by the Duke of Edinburgh for a lengthy tour of South America. The type was selected because it was ideally suited to operate into the small and high airfields along the Duke's itinerary. The two Heralds were away in South America between February 9th and April 5th, and were crewed by BEA pilots and Cabin Staff. Two BEA engineers accompanied the aircraft, as did a number of Handley Page pilots and ground support staff. The Heralds were modified to incorporate long range fuel tanks under the wings, High Frequency Radios, and Oxygen systems. G-APWA, which was painted in full BEA colours, was fitted out as the Duke's aircraft with a VIP interior, while G-APWC remained in normal airline configuration. BEA's Operations Department, assisted by BOAC and IAL, provided all airfield planning and routes for the thirty eight landing grounds visited in eleven countries. After the trip the Duke, who often flew G-APWA himself, sent the following telegram to the Chairman: "The two Heralds gave excellent service throughout my tour of South America."

Back in Scotland preparations went ahead for the opening of Herald services in the Spring of 1962. G-APWB was returned from Jersey Airlines, re-painted in full BEA colours, and flown north to Renfrew. It arrived in Scotland on March 10th. G-APWD was delivered on April 30th, and G-APWC after its South American adventure arrived on May 28th. The first commercial Herald service in Scotland operated on April 16th, when G-APWB flew a Glasgow-Sumburgh service, calling at Aberdeen, Wick and Orkney. With the arrival of the third Herald, BEA finally retired the Pionairs from service. By May only one route remained Pionair operated Glasgow-Campbeltown-Islay. The last commercial BEA Pionair service operated over the route on the morning of Saturday May 19th. The schedule for the historic flight was as follows:

Islay Depart	10.25
Campbeltown Arrive	10.45
Campbeltown Depart	11.00
Glasgow Arrive	11.35
Flight Number	BE8679.

The aircraft used was Pionair Leopard G-ALTT. To mark the occasion, prior to 'LTT's departure outbound to Islay, all the types used by BEA in Scotland were lined up on the apron at Renfrew for a photograph. In the line up was a Vanguard, Viscount, Herald, Heron and G-ALTT. With the arrival of BE8679 at Renfrew a chapter in BEA history closed and the Pionairs were retired. The type had served with BEA as either the DC-3 or Pionair continually since August 1st 1946, had carried 8½ million passengers and flown an amazing 97 million miles.

The summer timetable for the Herald called for one aircraft to fly a Glasgow-Campbeltown-Islay service each morning except Sunday. It then flew to Sumburgh via Inverness, Wick and Orkney, and returned to Glasgow via Aberdeen. The second aircraft left Glasgow at 09.40 and proceeded to Sumburgh via Aberdeen, returning to Glasgow via Orkney, Wick and Inverness. On Monday, Friday and Saturday it flew an evening service to Islay via Campbeltown, arriving back at Glasgow at 19.50. The third Herald operated a Glasgow-Edinburgh-Aberdeen-Wick-Orkney and return service. The winter schedule was roughly the same, with the exception that there was no evening service to Islay, and a second service to Sumburgh only on certain days. A Glasgow-Aberdeen late evening service was soon added to the Herald's programme, the aircraft night-stopping at Aberdeen, and returning to Glasgow early the next morning.

By the summer of 1965 the Herald schedule had been developed to quite an intensive level. In the peak of the summer (June 26th to September 4th) the programme was as follows, all flights being daily except Sunday unless otherwise shown:

Aircraft One
Aberdeen (06.45) - Edinburgh-Glasgow (08.30).
Glasgow (09.10) - Edinburgh-Aberdeen-Wick-Orkney (12.35).
Orkney (13.40) - Aberdeen (14.30). Monday, Friday and Saturday only.
Aberdeen (15.00) - Orkney (15.50). Monday, Friday and Saturday only.
Orkney (16.35) - Wick-Aberdeen-Edinburgh-Glasgow (20.10).
Glasgow (20.45) - Edinburgh - Aberdeen (22.20).

Aircraft Two
Glasgow (09.30) - Inverness-Wick-Orkney-Sumburgh (13.40).
Sumburgh (14.30) - Orkney-Wick-Inverness-Glasgow (18.10).
Glasgow (18.45) - Belfast (19.35). Daily except Saturday and Sunday.
Belfast (20.10) - Glasgow (21.00). Daily except Saturday and Sunday.

Aircraft Three
Glasgow (10.00) - Campbeltown-Islay (11.10).
Islay (11.30) - Campbeltown-Glasgow (12.35).
Glasgow (13.10) - Aberdeen-Sumburgh (15.25).
Sumburgh (15.55) - Aberdeen-Glasgow (18.10).
Glasgow (18.50) - Campbeltown-Islay (20.00).
Islay (20.20) - Campbeltown-Glasgow (21.25).

Unlike the Herons, which never operated outside Scotland in BEA colours, the Heralds did make occasional forays beyond the border. In 1965 they flew an evening service from Glasgow to Belfast, taking fifty minutes for each sector. The longest service BEA Heralds ever flew was a Glasgow-Jersey direct service, operated once a fortnight during the peak of the summer. Under the flight

In its more normal enviroment, G-APWC takes on a load at Kirkwall. *(BA)*

BEA ORGANISATION - 1962

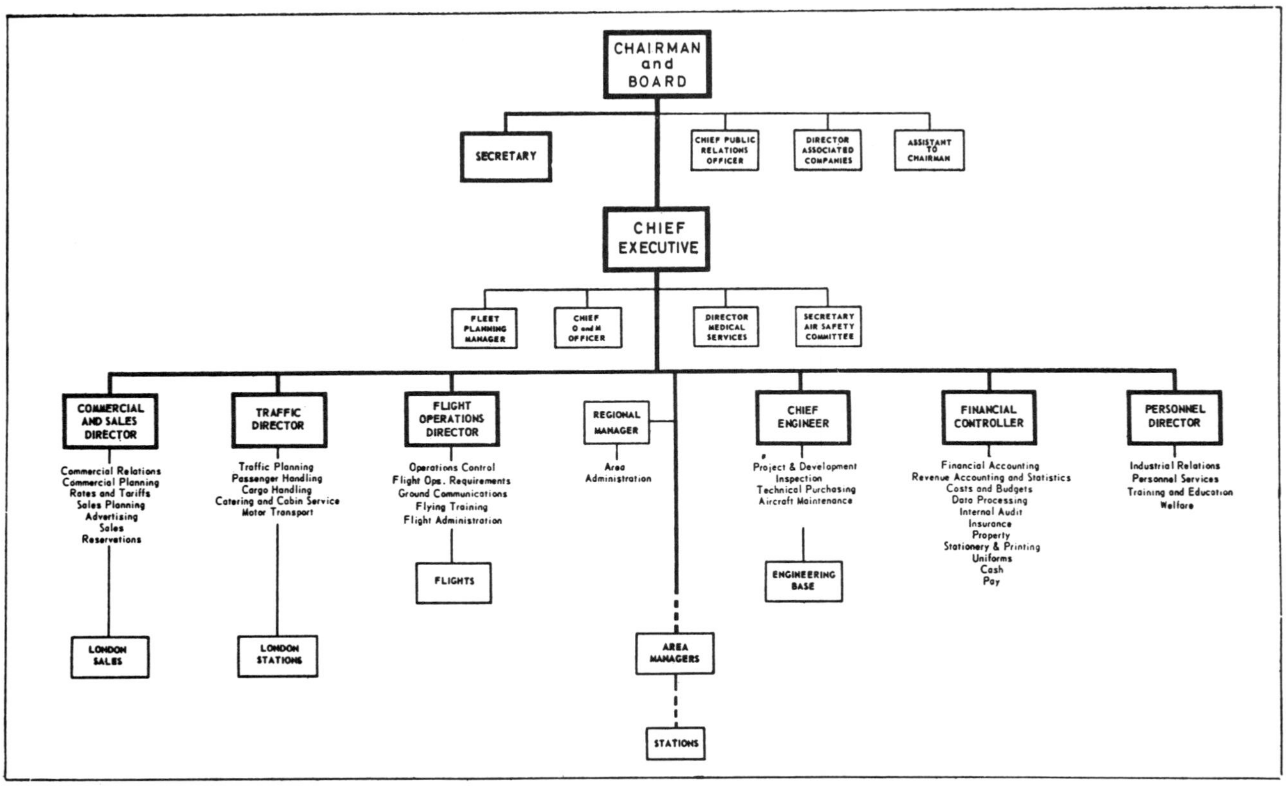

number BE3738A the aircraft would arrive in Jersey at about 15.00. Forty five minutes later BE3739A left for Glasgow. The Herald took about two and a quarter hours to fly between the two points. As well as being the longest trip flown by the type, it was the only one flown on a Sunday, and the only one to offer any catering facilities. Given the utilization of the Heralds in the summer and the maintenance requirement in the winter, ad-hoc charters were rarely undertaken. One of the few that did was on May 24th 1962 when G-APWC, on its way back from South America, flew Princess Alexandra from Heathrow to Stockholm and back. The only other non scheduled activity was occasional air ambulance flights when Herons were not available. The Heralds often carried stretcher cases on scheduled flights, their wide rear door and low sill height making it easy to load stretchers.

In many ways the Herald was an ideal aircraft for the routes it flew. Its performance meant it could carry a full load even out of Sumburgh, and the low sill height removed the need for elaborate ground handling equipment. Heralds were very popular with cargo handlers because they were so easy to load. A great variety of cargo was carried to the Scottish Islands including mail, newspapers, medicine and much else. When television first came to the Orkneys, BEA Heralds flew 8,000 TV sets from Aberdeen to Kirkwall. Return trips also carried a variety of cargo, including fresh lobsters, and knitwear. The high wings allowed the passengers an excellent view of the Highlands and Islands as they passed over them. The great disadvantage of the Herald was the cost involved in supporting just three aircraft. Maintenance equipment and spares were needed, engineers had to be licenced and crews trained. BEA was anxious to standardise its fleet as much as possible to reduce costs, and concluded the Herald would have to go, once runway improvements were made at Orkney, Islay and Sumburgh to accommodate Viscounts. Even so at Sumburgh Viscount loads would have to be limited to about forty six, due to the difficult nature of the approaches to the main runway. The Ministry of Aviation had the necessary improvements completed by the end of October 1966, and the Heralds were withdrawn and returned to the Ministry of Supply who sold them to Autair. The final day of Herald operations was Monday October 31st 1966, with the last flight operating over the same route as the last BEA Pionair flight four years before, Islay to Glasgow via Campbeltown. The aircraft (G-APWB) departed from Islay as BE8679 under the command of Captain Burnett at 11.30, arriving at Campbeltown fifteen minutes later. At 12.05 Captain Burnett lifted the Herald off the runway at RAF Campbeltown with thirty four passengers bound for Glasgow. The airlines two officials on duty at Campbeltown, Station Superintendent William Macpherson, and Senior Station Assistant Archie Gilchrist saluted as the aircraft made a final low pass over the airfield. Thirty minutes later it was back at Glasgow.

Summary of Herald Flying Hours 1962-66

	1962/63	1963/64	1964/65	1965/66	1966 (1.4 to 31.10)
G-APWB	989	1.534	1,611	1,508	724
G-APWC	1,120	1.525	1,642	1,374	736
G-APWD	1,152	1.564	1,615	1,545	756
TOTAL	3,261	4.623	4,868	4,427	2,216

Back in 1962 preparations for the introduction of the Trident fleet were gaining momentum. The first Trident, G-ARPA, made its maiden flight at Hatfield on January 7th, and by March 1963 no less than five aircraft were flying both from Hatfield and Khartoum, where the types abilities to operate in hot conditions were evaluated. There were certainly problems with the design particularly with the wing flaps and leading edge droops. They took some time to sort out, but were nothing compared with the teething problems experienced with the Elizabethans and Vanguards. After the first flight of G-ARPA, Lord Douglas said of the type: "BEA's hopes lie with the Trident in the same way as ten years ago the future lay with the equally revolutionary Viscount. It is the very last word in short service jet transport and is specially designed for our particular network". The Trident's automatic landing system was being tested, installed in an RAE Varsity at Bedford. The Varsity successfully made several fully automatic landings at both Bedford and Heathrow during the December fogs to demonstrate the value of the system. To equip Tridents with autoland was reputed to have cost BEA about £10 million.

For several years BEA had been keen on building up regional services from Birmingham and Manchester to Europe. One of the difficulties was the poor terminal facilities at Manchester, and the airline was very glad when a plan was announced, in 1961, to build a brand new terminal incorporating the latest features of pier gates. Construction of the terminal was completed by the autumn of 1962, and the building was officially opened by the Duke of Edinburgh in October. The first BEA aircraft to use it was Vanguard G-APEH operating a flight from London. The new facilities provided separate piers for domestic and international services, and put Manchester well and truly on the aviation map.

One route soldiering on in the same way as it had done since 1947 was the Land's End-Isles of Scilly link. In 1962 BEA still maintained a fleet of three Rapides specifically for it (G-AGSH, 'HKU and 'JCL.) No other fixed wing type in BEA service, apart from the Herons, were capable of operating from the small airfield on St Mary's which explains why the Rapides were still in service. Even the Heron, had it been used, could only fly into St Mary's, with a restricted payload. The Land's End-Scillies link was completely divorced from the rest of the BEA network and was largely self supporting. Headquarters were at St Just aerodrome, where there were four pilots, four traffic staff and five engineers. At St Mary's there were four traffic staff to handle services, the firemen acting as baggage loaders as they did at Land's End. In the summer the Rapides maintained an hourly service on a Saturday between 08.00 and 19.00. On other week-days there were eight or nine flights. One aircraft flew the schedules, while a second provided standby cover and operated extra flights at peak times, which were generally timetabled at similar times to the scheduled services. The third Rapide was usually found in Jersey being maintained. Reservations for the route were controlled by a small office at Wharf Street in Penzance, staffed by two sales officers; one of whom, Ron Rogers, still works in BIH Reservations at Penzance today. Station Superintendent Land's End/Scillies was Geoffrey Waite, and operations at St Mary's were managed by

Vanguard G-APED pictured at Palma Airport. *(BA)*

Official-in-Charge, Henry Casley. 1962 marked the twenty fifth anniversary of schedules to the Scillies, services having begun on September 13th 1937 using DH Dragons. Twenty five years on, BEA began to give some thought to replacing the aged Rapides. It concluded the only answer lay in the use of a helicopter because of St Mary's small airfield, and in 1962 the HEU carried out an evaluation of the Boeing Vertol 107, the Bristol 192 and the Sikorsky S.61 as possible equipment. The S.61 was selected as most suitable, and on August 1st 1963 the BEA Board decided to order two of them; one for the Scillies service, and the other for charter work.

Passengers flying on BEA services from London faced one serious problem in 1962, a protracted strike by airline electricians in April and May. The strike followed an attempt to change their working procedures and lasted seven weeks. It had little immediate effect, but eventually over eight hundred flights were cancelled, and the airline lost £300,000 in revenue. The dispute was eventually settled by arbitration.

The number of aircrew required to operate BEA's aircraft was considerable. On April 1st 1962 the airline employed no less than 796 pilots. Generally each pilot was assigned to fly only one type, though the helicopter pilots did fly all the helicopters. Within the larger fleets of aircraft there were several 'Flights' of aircrews each 'Flight' being managed by a Flight Manager. In charge of all the 'Flights' was a senior Flight Manager who acted as chief pilot for the particular type. The exact breakdown of aircrew between types is shown below:

	Captains	**First/Second Officers**
Comet	60	95
Vanguard	80	133
Viscount	192	166
Herald/Pionair	11	8
Heron	6	5
Rapide	4	-
Helicopters	4	2
Total	374	422

In America, National Airlines had just launched the 'Shuttle' concept - a high frequency walk on service where seats were guaranteed without the need for prior booking. BEA took more than a passing interest in the idea, and considered a similar type of service might be possible on the domestic trunk routes, and the London-Paris sector. Lord Douglas announced in September that the Corporation was planning a walk on, no frills, service from London to Glasgow and Paris, to begin in 1963. In fact it was nearly fifteen years before British Airways launched the shuttle, and Lord Douglas's announcement seemed to be more political than commercial. BEA was anxious to win its appeal to the ATLB over licences already granted to the independents on the Glasgow route, and the announcement was designed to add weight to the BEA case that it was providing the best and most suitable service.

Cargo loads increased considerably in 1962. The results for 1961/62 had been poor, with cargo loads actually falling, but in 1962 loads began to pick up very well. The use of the Vanguard and Argosy did most to boost them, giving a higher capacity and much faster service. So much did loads grow that the Heathrow Cargo Unit began to reach saturation point. Between November 18th and 24th 1,400 tons of cargo passed through Heathrow; a record for one week, and proof of the need for a new purpose built cargo building which was still several years away. One unusual cargo carried during the autumn of 1962 was 20 ten gallon drums of Watney's Ale, which a Vanguard shipped out to Gibraltar to stop a local pub running dry! With the possibility of Britain joining the Common Market (EEC) BEA began to look into the potential benefits and problems EEC membership might bring its cargo activity. A conference, of senior airline cargo managers, was held at Gibraltar to discuss the issue, but their discussions proved rather premature, as the British bid to join the EEC was firmly rejected by the French. Another avenue of discussion concerning the EEC was whether BEA should join the proposed Air Union. Air Union was to be the joint airline of the Common Market countries. BEA quickly decided not to join, and the 1962/63 Report and Accounts explained why: "Our view is that BEA's scale of operation is sufficiently large to make it unnecessary for the Corporation to become a member of a large airline consortium. Indeed the present balance of advantage appears to BEA to be against joining Air Union." Once again such discussion was rather unnecessary, since not only did the British bid to join the EEC fail, but Air Union itself never got off the ground, except for some technical collaboration between the national airlines involved.

Apart from the issue of Air Union, an old rumour began to circulate in 1962 - that BEA and BOAC would be merged by the government. Indeed when the bid to join Europe failed, it was suggested the government may merge the two, to make a single British airline better able to compete with Air Union. Lord Douglas had always been against a merger, and he sought to publically dismiss the idea. Whether there was any truth in the rumour is unclear. What is plain is the ideas of merging never really disappeared and rumours surfaced from time to time over the next few years. In 1963 they had reached such proportions that Lord Douglas published a comprehensive denial of them in the Chairman's Page of an edition of the BEA Magazine. He showed how the interests of BEA and BOAC were too diverse to make a merger sensible; profits generally made by BEA could not offset losses generally made by BOAC, and a merger would in the end save only a very small amount of money. Furthermore he pointed out a single airline would be too large, employing 38,000 staff. Such size would be more likely to decrease efficiency with the whole concern becoming too impersonal and staff losing any sense of belonging, or pride in the company. He ended his article by suggesting BEA staff in a merged airline might well be regarded as junior to the ex-BOAC staff. After the eventual merger in 1974 much of what Douglas predicted occurred. and he almost deserves the title of Prophet! Unfortunately he had died by 1974, and the arguments were lost under the determination of the government to act.

BEA

1963

In April 1963 the Viscount celebrated its tenth birthday in operation by BEA, while the Comets and Vanguards were settling into their third year of flying. Certainly the Comets, and to a lesser degree the Vanguards, were the more glamorous aircraft in the fleet, but the Viscount was still earning 41% of BEA's total revenue. As the tenth birthday of the Viscount fleet was celebrated, the original Viscount V.701s were withdrawn from service, the type flying its final revenue earning services on March 31st. The remaining '701s were sold off mainly to Cambrian Airways and Channel Airways. Since they had begun flying for BEA the 701s had managed to carry 6 million passengers, and had been responsible for opening many new routes.

The withdrawal of the aircraft was accompanied by BEA ending services to the Isle of Man. Under a new agreement with Cambrian, BEA transferred its routes to Cambrian, who purchased a fleet of Viscount V.701s from BEA to operate them. Initially Cambrian purchased five aircraft (G-AMNZ, 'MOG, 'MOL, 'MON, and 'MOP) and their crews were trained by BEA as part of the deal. The routes transferred to Cambrian were: Heathrow-Liverpool-Isle of Man, Heathrow-Isle of Man (direct), Liverpool-Isle of Man, Belfast-Isle of Man, Belfast-Liverpool, and Manchester-Isle of Man. That meant the end of BEA operations at Liverpool as well as the Isle of Man. Neither Liverpool City Council or the government of the Isle of Man were very happy at the turn of events. The Liverpool City Council felt snubbed by the national airline and believed the future of their airport would suffer. The Manx government were fearful that Cambrian's service might prove short lived if profits were inadequate. Cambrian sought to assure the Manx government this would not be the case, and promised a better service than BEA had provided. BEA had willingly given up these routes because of their unprofitability, so how could Cambrian be so optimistic? The answer lay in its lower salary scales, greater staff flexibility and lower depreciation costs of the aircraft.

BEA services to the Isle of Man ceased on the afternoon of March 31st. The final flight left Ronaldsway at 18.22 bound for Liverpool, operated by Viscount G-AOJB under the command of Captain Charters. BEA's traffic handling units at both Ronaldsway and Liverpool were closed, and Cambrian took over most of the staff involved. BEA Duty Officer Liverpool, Harold Ayres, became Cambrian Station Superintendent Liverpool, and BEA Senior Traffic Officer Ronaldsway, Frank Gawne, became Cambrian Station Superintendent.

A significant event in the early months of 1963 was the opening of BEA's new catering building at Heathrow. The new building, on the north side, was officially opened on February 3rd. It was a three storey affair, capable of producing up to eight thousand meals a day. Catering was a major area of activity by BEA. Each day it used, on average: forty two Ox tongues, several hundred four pound loaves, twelve gallons of fresh double cream, three hundred gallons of milk and half a ton of potatoes. In a typical week passengers ate their way through a thousand chickens, sixty to eighty ducks, forty or so turkeys, twelve York hams, three hundred cooked hams thirty odd sides of beef, four hundred pounds of fillet steak, forty pounds of Caviar..... Chief Chef Gus Pfeifer was certainly busier than many hotel chefs. Apart from catering facilities the new building contained offices for cabin staff reporting and briefing. 1963 was a key year for BEA catering activities because apart from the catering building, the airline also set up a new subsidiary company jointly with Fortes, called Airport Catering Services. ACS took over from BEA airport buffets at Manchester, Edinburgh, Jersey and at West London Air Terminal, and the Fortes buffets at Heathrow and Gatwick. ACS freed BEA from direct involvement in the provision of buffet facilities, but still gave it a share in their profits! ACS formally began operations on September 8th, and quickly expanded its activity to open new buffets at Hurn, Glasgow, Exeter and Leeds/Bradford.

To encourage sales for the 1963 summer season the Corporation produced a new booklet called 'The BEA Holiday Planning Guide' giving information on the booking of holidays abroad, including BEA's schedules. At the same time a new booklet for winter holidays was being printed to encourage traffic to Southern Germany, Austria and Switzerland. Britain was not neglected either, with a new departure being the publication of booklets to promote holidays in Britain, issued in European countries. Reservations staff were still waiting for the computer to help them with their work, but the computers' manufacturer had encountered many problems in producing exactly what BEA had in mind. Eventually the airlines patience was exhausted and the order was cancelled. Instead a new order was placed with Univac for a system similar to that used in the USA by several airlines. The deal was signed on November 14th, and provided for the delivery of two computers. BEA had decided it needed to duplicate the system in case of failure.

BEA continued to show itself at the forefront of airline development by introducing the Standby Fare, in April. To begin with it was available only on services from London to Edinburgh and Glasgow. Using the fare a one third discount over the normal fare was possible, the condition being that no prior booking was permitted with the passenger simply turning up at the airport to be carried only if there was a spare seat. So popular were Standby Fares, that they were soon extended to cover London to Birmingham and Manchester and eventually to many other domestic routes too. Perhaps their popularity was partly the result of a 5% to 10% increase in normal domestic fares to help cover costs! Abroad, BEA sought to generate more traffic on its Middle Eastern routes by cutting fares to Beruit, Cairo and Tel Aviv. Attention was also being given to the problem of 'no shows', passengers with firm reservations for a flight who simply did not turn up at the airport. The issue became so serious that on some flights, which were shown as fully booked, up to 40% of the passengers just did not turn up at departure time. BEA believed the major problem lay with passengers who booked several months in advance, and then changed their minds without telling the airline. From April 1st any booking made more six weeks prior to departure had to be accompanied by a deposit, and the balance of the fare had to be paid no later than six weeks before travel. If a passenger still did not turn up, BEA reserved the right to charge him a 'No Show' fee, of a percentage of the fare. Passengers soon got wise to the fact BEA was reluctant to enforce the fee, and the attempts to deal with the issue of 'no shows' met with little success. Another tactic used by many carriers, BEA included, was to deliberately overbook flights (book more passengers than there were seats) in the expectation that some passengers would not turn up. Normally it worked quite well, but there were occasions when all those booked did turn up leaving perhaps ten or so passengers with no seat. The airline's reputation inevitably suffered especially with those passengers who thought they had a firm booking but found they were without a seat.

The summer programme incorporated the first Rail-Air Link to Heathrow. From April 1st passengers arriving at Watford Station from the Midlands and the North could travel direct to Heathrow by coach to join their flight. In 1965 the scheme was extended to cover Reading Station, and a few years later Woking too. The coach links were initially operated by BEA and British Rail jointly, but eventually they were contracted out to private coach firms. From April 1st BEA returned most of its London-Jersey and Guernsey services to Heathrow from Gatwick. The move was the result of considerable public pressure, with Gatwick being far less popular than Heathrow not the least because Heathrow offered such superior inter-line connections. Many of the staff at Gatwick were returned to Heathrow from whence they had come in 1958. The summer programme from Gatwick was very limited, with only seven weekly services to Guernsey and twelve to Jersey, all operated by Viscounts. However more and more airlines were using Gatwick, and the BEA handling unit was able to make up for some

V.806's G-AOYS and G-AOYP at Glasgow Abbotsinch in 1966 *(BA)*

Vanguards provided BEA with excellent service, especially on high density routes. G-APEA is caught lifting off at Heathrow. (BA)

of the loss of its own aircraft, by handling other operators. The return to Heathrow meant the re-introduction of Heathrow to Guernsey services. The first scheduled direct flight between the two points since June 1958 left Heathrow at 11.20 on April 1st (BE3308), and returned from Guernsey at 15.50 (BE3319). The aircraft operating the service also flew the midday Guernsey-Gatwick link.

Down at Gibraltar, Gibraltar Airways took what many thought was a rather backward step. It replaced the leased BEA Viscount with a leased Dakota (G-AMFV) on the short trip across the Straits to Tangier. The DC-3 began flying in April. G-AMFV had been previously owned by BEA, who sold it to Cambrian in June 1960. BEA now repurchased the aircraft and dry leased it to Gibraltar Airways; making BEA once again the owner of a DC-3, less than a year after the Corporation had retired the last of the type from its network. G-AMFV continued to operate the Gibraltar link until 1970, though it never flew so much as one hour for BEA itself. At the other end of the Mediterranean BEA and the Malta Airlines concluded a new ten year operating agreement, under which the Malta Airlines services from Malta to Rome, Tripoli, Catania and London would be flown by BEA aircraft. The deal covered the period to just past the target date for Malta's independence. One sector not involved was Malta to Benghazi, because Malta Airlines decided to abandon the route. The last flight left Benghazi on March 30th (MN239) for Tripoli and Malta, using a BEA Viscount.

For the winter BEA began a non-stop Heathrow-Aberdeen Viscount link, from November 1st, with a daily departure from London in the evening. The aircraft night-stopped at Aberdeen and flew the south bound leg early the next morning. London-Aberdeen flights were not entirely new. Until 1955 a Pionair had flown a London-Edinburgh-Aberdeen service, and after that the airline offered a connection to Aberdeen via Glasgow. What was new, however, was the fact that the 1963 service was direct. Of even greater significance was the beginning of competition on the London-Glasgow route from November 1st, with flights by British Eagle. Initially Eagle flew the route with ex-BOAC Britannia aircraft, but eventually it purchased BAC I-IIs which entered service in 1966. Eagle's programme was extended in 1965 to include services from London to Belfast and Edinburgh. The beginning of Eagle's service provided BEA with a real challenge and the Corporation began to lose a small but valuable percentage of traffic to Eagle.

The autumn marked an event which greatly pleased the airline's crews, the opening of Belfast's new airport at the ex-military airfield at Aldergrove. Belfast's existing airfield at Nutts Corner had been something of a nightmare to pilots with its dreadful weather record, (suffering especially from cross winds), and its relatively short runways. True to the last, weather robbed Nutts Corner of its final BEA service when low cloud and drizzle forced the last flight into Nutts Corner, a Vanguard from Heathrow, to diver to Aldergrove, on September 24th. The next day, Aldergrove formally came into use, although the opening ceremony performed by the Queen Mother did not occur until October 28th. Also opened in the Autumn, was the permanent building at West London Air Terminal, which the Duke of Edinburgh declared operational on November 6th. The modern multi-storey building contained check-in facilities and a waiting lounge for passengers on the ground floor, together with facilities for various airline administrative activities on the other floors. A great deal of space on the upper floors was to be given over to the Reservations Units computer. Hand in hand with the opening of WLAT went an order for a fleet of Routemaster double-decker buses to replace the old one and a half deckers in carrying passengers out to Heathrow. The new buses could seat fifty seven as compared with the thirty seven of the existing fleet, and towed a baggage trailer. On arrival at Heathrow the baggage trailer would be taken direct to the aircraft, saving the time of off loading baggage from the coach and re-loading it on a truck.

Developments in the BEA Engineering Unit focused on two issues in 1963, the extension of flying hours between overhauls and the beginning Progressive Maintenance. The greater reliability of components and the new system of Progressive Maintenance enabled the flying times between engineering checks to be raised:

FLYING HOURS BETWEEN CHECKS

	Check 1	Check 2	Check 3	Check 4
Comet	200	1,070	-	6,420
Vanguard	200	870	-	5,100
Viscount	200	1,070	2,140	3,200
Argosy	145	1,125	-	3,000
Herald	145	1,620	-	3,200
Heron	65	350	700	1,400
Rapide	100	300	600	1,200

Progressive Maintenance was really the key to the extension of hours between overhauls. It required the replacing of individual components after the component had flown a certain number of hours. Replacement occurred whether or not the part was defective. By using the scheme the need for major checks was reduced, and the airline was able to dispense completely with Check Three on the newer types of aircraft in the fleet. When a component was replaced it would be overhauled in the relevant workshop, and in turn it replaced a similar component on another aircraft when its time was due.

During April 1963 BEA made what may have been its most unusual staff appointment, an honorary bagpipe player. Robert Crabb, formerly a Pipe Major with the Second Batallion Scots Guards, was enlisted to play at special occasions. He made his debut on April 20th when he piped passengers aboard the first Comet service to Venice. He subsequently appeared at various functions and events to add a touch of colour. At the other end of the hierachy the BEA Board consisted of the following members on April 1st:

		Date Appointed	Term to Expire
Lord Douglas	Chairman	14.3.49	31.3.64
Sir John Keeling	Deputy Chairman	24.7.47	Indefinite
A. Milward	Chief Executive	1.5.56	30.6.64
Lord Balfour		1.7.55	30.6.64
S. Kenneth Davies		12.3.51	11.3.64
Sir Walter Edmenson		16.12.46	15.12.63
Sir Giles Gutherie	Chairman BOAC	1.4.59	31.3.65
A.C. Ping		1.4.49	2.12.65
B.S. Shenstone	Chief Engineer	10.10.60	9.10.63
R.L. Weir	Financial Controller	1.4.59	31.3.64

Apart from these gentlemen there were a number of other key personnel who were not Board members, including Cyril Herring then Personnel Director, Captain Jimmy James Flight Operations Director, P.C.F. Lawton Commercial and Sales Director, Henry Marking Corporation Solicitor and E.P. Whitfield Traffic Director. The hierarchy had been together for some time, and that stability and helped BEA towards greater efficiency and profitability.

Being the national carrier, BEA frequently carried VIPS, and was always eager to get some publicity from such occurrences. Henry Berry, BEA's Public Relations Officer, saw great advertising potential when the Beatles were carried from London to Paris. The first three letters of the word Beatles were, of course, the initials of BEA. Harry had the letters 'TLES' painted on a board in white on a red background and planned to get the Beatles to hold it alongside the BEA logo on the aircraft's door. The plan almost backfired, because weather problems lead to a last minute change in three of the Beatles travel plans. However Harry Berry did succeed in getting Ringo Star to oblige by holding the painted board alongside the BEA logo on a Vanguards front door when he passed through Heathrow the next day. The airline was gratified to find the pictures of the stunt appearing in many newspapers and magazines.

For much of the summer the HEU's WS.55, G-AOCF, was based at Land's End to assist with the setting up and evaluating of the Decca Flight Log, which the coming S.61s were to use as a main means of navigation. While down in the area, 'OCF demonstrated the value of helicopter travel as a life saver. On July 20th, 'OCF and its pilot Dave Eastwood, were on the ground at St Mary's in the Scillies. A Mayflower Air Services Rapide crashed when attempting to take off from St Mary's bound for Plymouth, and its pilot, Captain Cleife (who was the airline's Managing Director) was seriously injured and burnt. He was only saved from being burnt alive by the prompt action of a BEA fireman who cut him free from the blazing wreckage. The medical care Captain Cleife required was far beyond that available at St Mary's small hospital and it was plain he could die if he did not receive attention promptly. Even though en route weather conditions were marginal, Dave Eastwood offered to fly him, in the WS.55, to Penzance Hospital; where he was able to receive the necessary aid. Had the helicopter not been at St Mary's Captain Cleife would probably have died. As it was, after a long illness, he eventually recovered.

1964

The static nature of the management team changed early in 1964 with the retirement of Lord Douglas. He handed over as Chairman to Anthony Milward on March 31st. In turn Milward was succeeded as Chief Executive by Henry Marking. Lord Douglas had served as BEA's Chairman for fifteen years and seventeen days; in which time aided first by Peter Masefield and then by Milward, he had brought the airline into a sound financial situation. In his career he saw BEA transformed from making an annual loss of over £1 million into a generally profitable Corporation. Financial results for his final year as Chairman, 1963/64, showed the airline had made a record profit of £3,030,000. Lord Douglas had made a name for himself as a most determined man. Examples of his tenacity in standing up to the government abound ...... the decision to abandon the Marathon ... to abandon the Cardiff-Valley-Liverpool service .... to order the Viscount .... the list was endless. As a gesture the Board allowed him to keep his official car (a Bentley) when he retired, and the airline's staff gave him a most unusual retirement present - a garage to keep it in! Lord Douglas lead a quiet life in retirement until his death in 1969.

Anthony Milward was a BEA man through and through. He had worked for the Corporation from the beginning, having served as General Services Manager, Manager Continental Services and eventually Chief Executive. His appointment from within the airline demonstrated the government's faith in the abilities of the present senior management. Milward was determined to continue the policy of Lord Douglas, for whom he had a very high opinion saying: "He was a very good Chairman in every sense. He was forthright, able, with a good brain. He had the confidence of those around him." The selection of Marking as Chief Excutive was Milward's first act. Marking, too, had worked for BEA for a long time, having been recruited by the Legal Department as a solicitor in 1949, and progressing to become Corporation Solicitor. On his promotion to Chief Executive he joined the Board, as did P.C.F. Lawton the Sales Director and Captain A.R. Glen. Lawton's and Glen's seats on the Board were created by the retirement of Sir Walter Edmenson who longest serving Board member, and the departure of Beverley Shenstone to become Chief Engineer of BOAC. Shenstone was succeeded as BEA's Chief Engineer by Ken Wilkinson, who did not immediately become a Board member. Before passing on from management changes there is one more to record, Ian Scott Hill replaced E.P. Whitfield as Traffic Director. Scott Hill's experience in aviation went even further back than most, having worked for Imperial Airways. As all these appointments were made from within the airline it did not take long for then new team to settle down.

Lord Douglas's retirement coincided with a very prosperous period for cargo operations. In 1963/64 freight carried jumped by 19% to a total of 58,259 tons, and the growth prompted BEA to decide to order a further five Argosy aircraft. The new Argosys were the AW222 model, an improved version of the existing aircraft, with a larger loading door enabling pallets of 108 inches in width to be accommodated. Those were the size of pallet used by BOAC and many other international carriers, and the AW222 was deliberately designed to accommodate them, allowing pallets to be transhipped from BOAC straight onto BEA aircraft. The load of the new Argosy would be 13,650 lbs compared with the 9,300 lbs of the older model. BEA's engineers found an ingenious way of saving money on the purchase, by fitting the fleet with the same mark of Dart engines used by the Viscount V.806 fleet. BEA calculated it had saved about £500,000 by taking the step. The existing Argosys were taken back by Hawker Siddeley in part-exchange for the new aircraft; and the order, worth £4 million, was signed on September 21st. One new all-cargo route was opened in 1964, London to Gothenburg. From November 1st a thrice weekly Argosy service began to call at the Swedish city. Because of the industrial nature of the area, Gothenburg quickly justified its inclusion in the network, and by 1970 no less than five Merchantman flights a week landed there, which in capacity terms equalled about eight or nine Argosy trips. Domestic cargo traffic was still sluggish and from November BEA cut domestic bulk cargo rates in an effort to improve things.

The ordering of the new Argosy fleet may have been important, but of far greater significance was the entry of the first Trident ICs into commercial service. The first Trident to be delivered was G-ARPG, which landed at Heathrow on February 19th. G-ARPH followed on March 25th and 'RPF on March 31st. By the end of the year twelve of the twenty four on order had been delivered. One, G-ARPB, was leased back to Hawker Siddeley for development flying mainly for the autoland system. One of the initial three Tridents to be delivered to BEA was used for crew training at Stansted, where it was flown by the Duke of Edinburgh, who expressed great interest in the type. A major step towards the introduction of the aircraft ocurred on February 28th, when Lady Douglas officially named the type 'Trident' in a ceremony at Heathrow. G-ARPG was used for the occasion. The Trident was earmarked for use on scheduled services from April 1st, but the first commercial Trident flight actually occurred on March 11th, when G-ARPG replaced a Comet on a London-Copenhagen flight, to the delight of the passengers. The first scheduled Trident service took place on the morning of April 1st when G-ARPG left Heathrow for Zurich at 09.50 operating flight BE564. After that the type began to operate on other routes too:

London-Copenhagen	Eleven flights a week from April 1st.
London-Frankfurt	Seven flights a week from April 1st.
London-Geneva	Eighteen flights a week from April 1st.
London-Zurich	Seven flights a week from April 1st, fourteen a week from July 1st.
London-Nice	Seven flights a week from June 1st.
London-Rome	Seven flights a week from July 1st.
London-Milan	Seven flights a week from August 1st.

For the winter the Trident appeared on some or all of flights to Brussels, Barcelona, Helsinki, Munich, Prague, Stockholm, Valencia, Venice and Vienna. Just like Viscounts, a decade before, the Trident proved immensely popular with passengers. On the London-Frankfurt route, to give a typical illustration, loads rose by 10% as soon as the Tridents appeared. Being rear engined the Trident was a lot quieter than other types, and this caused a few passengers to enquire rather anxiously if everything was 'OK' because they could not hear the engines. Some teasing of new cabin staff also took place, with pilots asking new stewardesses to go back to the back of the cabin to see if they could hear the engines as the crew were afraid they might have stopped. On March 20th BEA placed an order with Plessey for flight data recorders for the Tridents and all the other aircraft in the fleet too, except Rapides. The recorder would be a valuable aid in helping to investigate the cause of accidents. The flight data recorder, or 'Black Box' as it is usually known, records details of the aircraft's course, speed, height and so on on magnetic tape.

Scheduled services by the Tridents were not the only improvement to services. For the first time BEA began to fly non-stop Comet services to Tel Aviv, with two direct flights a week beginning on April 1st. Until April 1st all Tel Aviv services had made at least one stop en-route, usually in Athens. Services to Palma were expanded by the launching of a thrice weekly Glasgow-Palma route via Manchester; and in Germany a new service linked Berlin with Bremen using Viscounts on a twice daily basis. The route opened on April 1st with departures from Berlin at 06.55 and 19.00 and from Bremen at 09.00 and 21.10. In an attempt to keep costs low at Bremen, the Station Engineer was also made Station Superintendent. It was the first time the Corporation had taken such a step, and its success prompted the repeat of the idea at Stuttgart a few years later.

On April 1st BEA launched its own inclusive tour holiday programme, operated by a subsidiary company called Silver Wing Holidays. BEA had been selling seats to tour operators, but with the buoyancy of IT travel it decided to cash in on the whole activity by selling package holidays as well. The first brochure offered a limited range of holidays to Spain, but it was soon expanded and from that small beginning BEA developed a major involvement in IT work.

At the beginning of the winter timetable, which was a usual November 1st, BEA opened a new direct London-Berlin service. One flight a day by Viscount was scheduled, leaving London at 11.25, and returning out of Berlin at 15.45. The Viscount took about two and a half hours for each sector.

In the course of the year, the airline found itself once again the innocent victim of international political problems, this time at Gibraltar. The Spanish had long claimed sovereignty over the Rock, and in 1964 they started a series of moves to press their claim. To begin with they caused difficulties for those wishing to cross from Rock into Spain, forcing BEA to cancel coach service from Gibraltar Airport to the Costa Del Sol, resulting in a 10% fall in passenger traffic into Gibraltar. Over the next few years things got progressively worse, the border was eventually totally shut, and restrictions were placed on aircraft landing at the Rock. Elsewhere, traffic began to decline on the previously prosperous route to Nice because of competition from BUA who began a new London-Genoa service in 1964. BEA had applied for the licence and even appointed a Representative in Genoa, but the ATLB awarded the route to BUA and the BEA representative became an off-line sales officer. BUA took a significant amount of traffic from the BEA service to Nice once the Genoa route got going.

Over the summer Vanguards made a limited appearance on services to Jersey. A Vanguard (G-APEF) had visited Jersey on a route proving flight on November 13th 1963, and from June 1st 1964 the type was scheduled to operate a weekly service from London on a Saturday afternoon. Its capacity, at roughly double the Viscounts, proved useful in accommodating the week-end traffic peak. In subsequent summers Vanguards flew more London-Jersey services, and began to appear on routes from Jersey to Birmingham, Gatwick and Manchester.

Undoubtedly the most nostalgic event in 1964 was the withdrawal of the Rapides from the Scillies route marking their final retirement from BEA. Rapide flights ended on May 1st, the S.61 helicopter taking over the route the next day. The first S.61 flight from Land's End to the Scillies was flown by G-ASNL commanded by Captain Cameron. The three strong Rapide fleet was sold to British Westpoint Airlines, marking the end of an era. Rapides had served continually with BEA since 1947. On Friday May 1st, five scheduled services were timetabled for the Rapides, being flown by one aircraft, G-AHKU piloted by Ron Hurcombe. The last scheduled departure from St Mary's for Land's End was at 16.30, and G-AHKU arrived at Land's End just twenty minutes later. But the very last Rapide flight out of the Scillies was flown by G-AJCL, operating an ambulance charter, costing the local Health Authority the grand sum of £13-2/-. Flying the Rapides to the Scillies was demanding to the very last. Strong winds made it a bumpy exit from BEA service, and Captain Hurcombe arrived at the party held to celebrate the retirement of the Rapides and coming of the S.61s, complaining how much his arms and legs ached from trying to hold the aircraft steady in the wind. Captain Hurcombe must have suffered something of a culture shock because following the retirement of the Rapides he was transferred to Vanguards!

The weather caused some disruption to the events of May 1st. A Viscount had flown a party of senior staff and journalists down from London to witness the withdrawal of the Rapides and introduction of the helicopters. Given the small size of Land's End airport, the Viscount had landed at St Mawgan near Newquay, and the two S.61s had collected the party from there and flown them on the Land's End and later St Mary's. The plan called for group to return to St Mawgan in the evening by S.61. However as departure time from Land's End approached, the weather deteriorated and the new BEAH Manager at Land's End, Captain Perkis, was anxious to avoid having his two helicopters stuck at St Mawgan and thus unable to commence service the next day. Reluctantly the guests were dispatched to Newquay by coach, a trip of about two hours, compared with less than half an hour in the S.61. Since 1947 Rapides had flown 384,000 passengers to the Scillies, on 77,500 flights, although that was only a fraction of the total number of passengers and flights

BEAH S.61 G-ASNM on the small Channel Island of Sark in February 1966. *(Guernsey Press)*

operated by Rapides over the whole BEA network.

Hours flown by BEA Rapide Fleet 1962-64

	1962/63	**1963/64**	**1964/65**
G-AGSH	669	677	95
G-AHKU	711	620	71
G-AJCL	690	642	2
Total	2,070	1,939	168

For a while the S.61 operated from Land's End aerodrome, but BEA was having a new heliport built just east of Penzance, on an old rubbish tip at Eastern Green. Construction of the ten acre site was completed in time for the helicopter to transfer there on September 1st.

With the arrival of the S.61, BEA's Helicopter Experimental Unit was entirely re-organised. It was considered inappropriate for an organisation operating an established service with a large twin engined helicopter to be called an Experimental Unit, so a new associate company was created; BEA Helicopters Limited. BEAH formally came into existence on January 1st, with Lord Balfour as Chairman and Captain Cameron as Managing Director. As it now flew two S.61s, BEAH decided to reduce its remaining fleet from two WS.55s, one Bristol 171 and two Bell 47s, to one WS.55 and a single Bell 47. These helicopters, and one of the two S.61s, continued to find work in a variety of charter activities, including contracts with the Police to watch traffic flows on the M6; charters to TV and film companies and crop spraying. BEAH had its eyes on a new source of income for the S.61s: support work for the exploration rigs drilling for oil and natural gas off the coast of East Anglia. With that in mind a new company was established, jointly with Okanagan Helicopters of Vancouver; called International Helicopters. Each of the parent companies provided an S.61 for the operation, and BEA purchased a third aircraft for the task (G-ATBJ), whilst Okanagan supplied CF-OKY which was allocated the English registration of G-ATFM. Unusually it was flown across the Atlantic. Normally S.61s were dismantled and shipped across. International Helicopters was constituted right at the end of 1964, and operations began to support Shell rigs from a make shift heliport in Lowestoft Docks on July 9th 1965. The association with Okanagan did not last long. There were a series of wrangles between the Canadian carrier and the British authorities, which did not directly involve BEA and Okanangan decided to dissolve their partnership. Late in 1965 BEA bought out the Okanagan share of International Helicopters, including their S.61 G-ATFM.

Apart from the establishment of BEAH and International Helicopters, a number of other changes occurred with BEA's associate companies. On March 31st the Corporation finally sold off its remaining shares in Aer Lingus. BEA had owned 40% of Aer Lingus shares. But as the Irish airline had become more firmly established the holding had been gradually reduced, until in 1964 only 2.7% of Aer Lingus shares were BEA owned, and they were now sold. At the same time BEA obtained a financial interest in the British independent, BKS Air Transport, by purchasing a 30% holding in the company. P.C.F. Lawton and A.C. Ping were appointed as BEA directors on the BKS Board. Eventually BKS, later renamed Northeast Airlines, became a fully owned BEA subsidiary and part of British Airways Regional. BKS had been founded in 1952, and by 1964 operated a range of scheduled passenger services from Leeds/Bradford and Newcastle to the Channel Isles, Belfast, Dublin and London. It flew a mixture of DC-3s, Ambassadors, HS748s, and a single Britannia. The Britannia fleet was later raised to four aircraft.

Although the Reservations Department had been the first BEA section to order a computer, it was the engineers who were the first section of the airline to actually acquire a computer. A CT 1300 was delivered to the Heathrow Base during 1964 to be used to keep track of components in store and the life span of aircraft components. The computer was a very necessary piece of equipment if the Progressive Maintenance system was to work efficiently. In 1964 the Engineering Unit opened new instrument workshop in Heathrow, enabling BEA to perform nearly all its own instrument maintenance. As such work required a totally clean environment staff employed in the work shop had to wear specially designed anti dust clothing, and the air was continually changed with an advanced air conditioning system. In general terms BEA engineers had good cause to be happy. For a number of years they had been involved in industrial disputes over pay and conditions, but in 1964 Milward and his team concluded a new industrial relations agreement with them, giving much better rates of pay and working conditions. In return the engineers agreed to give up certain demarcation issues and to generally improve efficiency.

1964 ended with one very small step towards an eventual merger with BOAC. The Medical Services operated by each airline were merged into a single unit under an ex-BEA Doctor, Graham Taylor. The move made sound economic sense because the two separate medical services had virtually duplicated each other. In its last year of separate existence, the BEA Medical Unit had carried out 4,000 consultations, 167 pre-entry medicals for pilots, 425 medical courses for cabin staff and 928 cabin staff refresher courses. The Unit supervised the carriage of 3,510 invalids, which sometimes required no more than a special briefing to cabin staff, but at other times involved making oxygen available for the passenger, some of whom were carried on stretchers. A further move towards closer co-operation between BEA and BOAC occurred in the first few weeks of 1965, with the announcement that the BEA Staff College at East Burnham would in future be shared with BOAC. The College had been set up in 1960 to provide management courses for airline personnel. BEA would use it for five months of the year, BOAC for another five, while over the two summer months of July and August it would be let out to other firms.

BEA

1965

1965 opened with BEA seeking to improve the quality of in-flight service offered on its aircraft. First, from January 1st, passengers were allowed to smoke cigars and pipes as well as cigarettes. The airline had previously considered pipe and cigar smoke to be too offensive, but better aircraft ventilation allowed the change. Secondly, the Catering Unit was geared up to provide special meals for passengers, like vegetarian meals and meals for those requiring a special diet for religious reasons. At least twenty four hours notice was required, but the facility was greatly appreciated by many. Ordinary food for economy class passengers was upgraded too. Out went the (often stale) slab of fruit cake, and in came open sandwiches as the standard snack. Full meals for economy passengers were also improved. The Corporation hoped the changes might help the airline regain some of the traffic lost to other airlines. First class passengers were not neglected either. Service was extended to offer passengers free drinks, more comfortable seats, their own bus out to the aircraft, and a choice of meals on board. One member of the aircraft cabin crew would be allocated solely to first class passengers. However at roughly double economy class fares, the first class passenger might expect a little extra! Finally the airline introduced a new class of passenger –the CIP, or Commercially Important Passenger. CIPs were businessmen who regularly flew first class. They were given special attention, and a separate lounge at Heathrow was provided where they could wait prior to departure.

All these developments created problems for cabin staff. The increasing use of jets reduced journey times considerably. Many European cities were little more than

Trident 1C G-ARPG prepares for the first commercial service on the 11th March 1964. *(BA)*

an hour away from London. Yet improvements in cabin services meant the cabin crews had to fit much more into a shorter journey. To serve passengers a full meal and give first class and CIP passengers that bit extra attention became quite literally a race against time. Almost as soon as the 'Fasten Seat Belts' sign had been extinguished after take off the cabin crew were busy serving drinks, orders for which had been taken while the aircraft was taxying out for take-off. Then the meal would appear and by the time it had been cleared away the aircraft was often just about to land at its destination. The job of the cabin crews was (and still is) a hard and demanding one, lacking the glamour of the similar job in BOAC. BEA had always insisted on the highest standards of personal appearance by its cabin staff, but with the other in-flight improvements even more rigorous standards were required by the airline. As BEA began to carry more foreign passengers, the airline realized the need to provide cabin announcements in foreign languages. Consequently pre-recorded in flight announcements gradually began to appear on flights in the language of the country of destination. Staff, too, were encouraged to learn foreign languages, and those who could pass a proficiency test were allowed to wear a small flag of the nation whose language they spoke, on their uniform jacket shoulder. They received a financial reward for their linguistic abilities, of 50p per week for each language spoken!

On the ground the quality of service was improved in several ways. On August 1st a new coach service between Heathrow and WLAT was launched – the Executive Express. The bus ran direct from the aircraft steps to WLAT, in connection with peak time arrivals from Aberdeen, Belfast, Edinburgh and Glasgow. It was available only to passengers with hand baggage, but saved the businessman the extra time of having to go through the terminal building to catch the coach. A coach service ran in the opposite direction too, from WLAT direct to aircraft departing for Aberdeen, Belfast, Edinburgh and Glasgow. In the first week, a thousand passengers used the Executive Express. Several developments occured, at Heathrow, to try to improve punctuality, chief among which was the introduction of Traffic Dispatchers. Each movement would be allocated a Dispatcher, who had the task of co-ordinating all the traffic services required to ensure an on time arrival and departure. The Dispatcher was equipped with a mobile office, in the form of a Bedford van, and had a radio to keep him in constant touch with Load Control, the Departure Gate and so on. To make it easy for staff to identify the Dispatcher, he wore a red top to his uniform cap, earning the officials the nickname 'Redcaps'. A large number of Dispatchers were required and staff were recruited from all over the network to do the job. The beneficial effect of the 'Redcaps' was soon felt with an increasing number of on time departures.

A fresh difficulty encountered at Heathrow was terminal building congestion. All BEA European flights operated from Number One Europa Building, as did the flights of most of the other European operators. Domestic services departed from Number Two Britannic Building, a small area on one end of Number One Building. Eagle services were crammed in there too, and the Terminals just could not cope with the volume of traffic using them. In 1965 it was decided to construct a new building, to be called Terminal One, for the almost exclusive use of BEA. Other operators could then fit more comfortably into the Europa building, which would be renamed Terminal Two. Terminal One was to be ready for May 1969, but once construction began other problems arose, particularly a shortage of aircraft stands caused by the building work. Aircraft were parked over a very much wider area leading to delays in getting steps and other ground handling vehicles to arrivals. There were just too many scattered stands to allow the airline to leave a set of steps at each. BEA decided to press the airport authorities to allocate a group of stands for its sole use to minimize the difficulty. Initially that was refused, and it took until 1967 to get the matter resolved in BEA's favour.As the year ended, one new BEA building did open at Heathrow, a Motor Transport Base on the north side. It came into operation on November 16th, and included a fully equipped garage to service ground equipment, as well as a control centre to co-ordinate vehicle movements and requirements. Only the Cargo Unit was awaiting a purpose built facility, and plans were underway to meet that need too.

BEA's Reservations Service finally got its computer in the early months of the year. The system, called 'Beacon' (BEA Computer Network) came into use at 15.00 on April 17th. It was programmed to handle reservations on nearly all BEA services, except those in the German internal network and some domestic services. The coming of the computer meant reservations staff moved from Dorland Hall to WLAT, where two hundred and sixteen sales positions were provided. In the first full week-day of use, the computer handled 9,000 phone calls, 7,000 telex messages, and sold 22,000 seats on BEA services. Computerization made BEA reservations much more efficient, yet the airline was still not satisfied. Phase Two of 'Beacon' was launched, aiming to link sales offices directly into the computer, and to hold more information about each booking.

The Corporation's route structure was widened in the course of 1965 by the opening of a selection of new routes:

London to Shannon	Commenced on April 2nd, initially with three Viscount flights weekly, but increasing in the summer peak to six Vanguard services weekly.
London to Corfu	Commenced on April 3rd, with one Comet service a week. After calling at Corfu the aircraft continued on to Athens.
London to Dubrovnik	Commenced on May 1st with a single Vanguard service on a Saturday. Flights left London at 23.15, and returned from Dubrovnik at 03.50 on Sunday

morning.

Berlin to Stuttgart — Commenced on June 1st, with a daily Viscount flight. The service left Berlin at 18.30 (BE1771) and Stuttgart at 21.00 (BE1778).

After June 1st passengers travelling on the number one international service, from London to Paris, were flown in Trident aircraft. Virtually all the services on the route featured Trident travel, although the type was not ideal for the short sectors involved, with the Vanguard still being a much more economic proposition. Nevertheless the need to be competitive forced BEA into the move. Overall the Trident was fitting into the BEA network very well and by June fifteen aircraft were operating, flying to eighteen destinations from London. The type was averaging a load factor of 63% proving its popularity with passengers. In July Tridents first appeared on services from the provinces to the Continent, when Tridents replaced Viscounts on the daily Manchester-Paris flight. The summer schedules included improvements in services from the provinces to Barcelona. The previous summer a Manchester-Birmingham-Barcelona flight had operated with considerable success. BEA decided to increase the capacity on the route for the summer of 1965 by providing a direct Manchester-Barcelona service on Mondays, Thursdays and Sundays, and a direct Birmingham-Barcelona flight on Monday and Friday. The routes were both Viscount operated, and took place at night.

BEA's confidence in the Trident was shown by its order for a new mark of Trident, the Trident 2. The order, valued at £30 million, was for fifteen with an option (never taken up) for another ten. The Trident 2 was to be a long range version with a range of 2,400 miles, enabling it to fly non-stop on any BEA service from Heathrow. It would be fitted with ninety four economy class seats, and powered by an improved version of the Spey engine giving it 21% more power than the rather underpowered Trident 1. Trident 2s were to replace the Comets on long haul services.

Trident history in the summer of 1965 had one more significant landmark, the achieving of the world's first ever fully automatic landing by an aircraft on a commercial service. Development of the Trident's autoland system had been going on for many years. By June 1965 no less than six hundred trial autolands had occurred in various weather conditions. Now the system was used, in good weather, on a commercial flight. On June 10th G-ARPG was operating BE343 from Le Bourget to Heathrow. It had eighty passengers on board, and was crewed by Captain Eric Poole, Flight Manager Development, Captain Tom Atkins, Trident Training Captain, and Captain M. Mitchell. The aircraft made a fully automatic landing at Heathrow, and each passenger was presented with a small momento. Captain Poole recalls "although I was completely confident, my pulse rate was perhaps a little faster than normal." Needless to say the aircraft, with it triplicated autoland system, made a perfect touch down and aviation history had been made. It took several more years of development flying before the system could be used on commercial flights in bad weather.

The sleek lines of Trident 1C G-ARPB at Heathrow. *(BA)*

At the other end of the BEA network, in Scotland, the Heron aircraft plodded on with their ambulance duties and scheduled flights. On April 30th Captain David Barclay, who was senior pilot on Herons and had been involved with the Air Ambulance Unit since its inception, retired. David had been flying in Scotland since 1935, joining BEA in February 1947. He had flown 2,000 of the 5,500 air ambulance services operated by the Corporation, and many of those whom he had taken to hospital gathered at Tiree and Barra to wish him well as he piloted his last flight, a Heron scheduled service from Glasgow to Barra via Tiree, and return. G-ANXB was used and staff at Tiree and Barra made official presentations to the Captain. There were many informal ones too. For the occasion the Heron carried a Stewardess, which was not normal, but David's daughter was a BEA stewardess and accompanied him on his last flight. Men like David Barclay were legends in their own right, and their vast amount of flying experience in all kinds of weather, contributed greatly to aircraft safety in these remote areas.

On July 23rd, BEA carried its 50 millionth passenger, Mrs Hazel. She was presented with a bouquet and a cheque for Fifty Guineas. It had taken BEA fourteen years to carry its first 25 million passengers, yet the second 25 million had been flown in only five years, indicating just how much traffic had grown. There was little else to be happy about over that summer. The schedules were almost wrecked by an industrial dispute with the pilots. Aircrew had submitted a claim for higher wages and lower hours which the management refused. The situation quickly worsened, with a fifty five point list of grievances being issued by the pilots. They demanded BEA remove the grievances, and when it refused a twenty four strike was called. Fortunately last minute negotiations temporarily solved the problem, with the airline agreeing to pay an immediate 5% rise and hold talks on the list. Unfortunately the problem did not go away and was to dog operations for several years to come. Even more sad was the loss of Vanguard G-APEE on the night of October 27th. The Vanguard was flying the late evening Off-Peak service from Edinburgh to Heathrow with twenty nine passengers and seven crew on board, when it crashed at Heathrow killing all on board. Weather conditions were poor at the time, with some fog, and 'PEE had already made two approaches and overshoots. On the third attempt the aircraft hit the runway as it tried to overshoot and caught fire. It was the first fatal accident to affect Vanguard operations, and the Enquiry concluded that the chief cause was pilot error.

An issue of a different nature confronted BEA in 1965, the government decision not to restrict the volume of inclusive tour charter flying by independent airlines. On February 17th the Minister of Aviation announced in the House of Commons that no restrictions were to be imposed by the government on such charter operations. Naturally IT flying quickly boomed producing a serious effect of BEA's own traffic to holiday destinations like Spain and Majorca. No less than nine independent airlines applied to the ATLB for licences to Palma for IT flights, and despite BEA's objections they all succeeded. The problem grew even larger in the years to come, and eventually BEA formed its own charter airline, BEA Air Tours, to compete with the independents. In the same House of Commons statement there was one crumb of comfort for BEA, the Minister indicated the government was not prepared to see a second British operator on international routes, or to grant any increases to the frequencies permitted to the independent carriers on the domestic trunk routes.

BEA Helicopters was fully occupied with the service to the Scillies, and the gradual development of oil support work. Even so it did undertake an unusual charter between November 1965 and February 1966. An S.61 (G-ASNM) was chartered to BEA itself to operate an air-bridge between Jersey and Guernsey. Jersey's runway was to be resurface, meaning the airfield would be closed between 09.00 and 17.00. To maintain a midday link between the Island and London, a Viscount flew into Guernsey and the passengers were taken on to Jersey in the helicopter. Two or three helicopter flights were required to carry a full Viscount load between the two Islands. While the helicopter link was operating, it carried 4,306 passengers. During its stay in the Channel Isles the S.61 visited Alderney on a crew training flight, being the first aircraft of BEA's to land there since the airline had withdrawn Alderney services in April 1956. G-ASNM also visited Sark, which does not permit cars, let alone aircraft. The purpose of the visit was to evacuate a seriously ill woman and fly her to Guernsey's hospital. The helicopter's engineering needs in Jersey were catered for by one BEAH engineer on detachment from Gatwick. Having just one person able to sign the aircraft out as servicable almost lead to the grounding of the helicopter one day. Just before it was due to depart for Guernsey, the helicopter engineer fell off a platform and was knocked unconscious. An ambulance was summoned, but the Captain was stuck. Without the engineers signature he could not fly G-ASNM. Company legend has it that he could be seen bending over the engineer in the ambulance, technical log and pen in hand, imploring him to wake up and sign the log. Fortunately he did, and the aircraft was able to depart. The closure of the runway in Jersey meant all BEA services from the Island had to be rescheduled for the winter. Just before 09.00 there were Viscount departures to Guernsey/Gatwick, Bournmouth and Heathrow. The Viscount that flew to Heathrow was used to operate the midday Guernsey service to connect with the S.61. The other two aircraft remained idle on the ground at Gatwick and Hurn all day. In the early evening they returned to Jersey arriving just after 17.00, though quite often the contractors had not finished the days work on the runway and the aircraft had to wait to land. In the evening there were departures to Heathrow and Guernsey.

Across in West Germany demand for seats to and from West Berlin was so high over the Christmas period that seventy nine extra flights were laid on, many being operated by a Viscount V.701 chartered from Cambrian.

BEA's Commercial Branch concluded a useful contract with Cyprus Airways during the year. Cyprus Airways had been using BEA Comets to fly its routes.

However it wanted to expand its network and believed Comets were too large for many of the new routes. Consequently it chartered two BEA Viscounts to fly local services from Nicosia to places like Cairo, Tel Aviv, Jerusalem and Rhodes. The London-Nicosia flights continued to be operated by Comets under the BE/CY flight prefix. The Viscounts allocated to Cyprus Airways were G-AOYJ and G-AOYK. They began to fly Cyprus Airways routes from November 1st and were both painted in Cyprus Airways colours. The lease continued until 1969/70, when Cyprus Airways obtained its own Tridents. G-AOYJ was returned to BEA late in 1969 when the first Trident (5B-DAA) arrived in Nicosia, and G-AOYK returned after the delivery of the second Trident (5B-DAB) in May 1970. When G-AOYJ arrived back with BEA it was immediately placed into service due to aircraft shortages, and flew in Cyprus Airways colours with BEA titles for some time. G-AOYK did not fly for BEA again, being stored at Cambridge on its return from Cyprus, and eventually sold.

The freighter network continued to be expanded with the opening or re-introduction of several routes. From May 3rd a thrice weekly London-Rome service was recommenced using Viscounts, on Tuesdays, Wednesdays and Fridays. Unlike Milan, which was currently booming as a freighter destination, Rome was not popular, and the service ended in October. An entirely new route was a direct Manchester-Paris cargo schedule on Wednesday, Thursday and Saturday, but again it was not very popular and ceased in October 1966. Cargo services to Scandinavia improved with the provision of a six times weekly Argosy service, routing London-Copenhagen-Gothenburg-London. Vanguards began to make a limited appearance on freight services in 1965. On the routes between London and Dublin, Frankfurt, Glasgow, Paris and Turin some Vanguards flew in a mixed configuration, carrying up to eight tons of freight in the forward cabin and seventy one passengers at the rear. Viscounts, similarly modified to accommodate three tons of cargo and thirty six passengers, were occasionally used too.

Just as BEA was beginning to enjoy the benefits of the larger Argosy 222s (the first service being on March 1st) and less than a month after the fifth and final aircraft had been delivered (G-ASXP), the airline lost one of the fleet. One July 4th G-ASXL hit high ground about seventy miles from Milan while inbound from London. It was a complete write off, and both pilots were seriously injured. The loss of G-ASXL left the Cargo Unit short of capacity, and Argosy 101, G-APRM, was leased back from Hawker Siddeley to compensate, while a replacement aircraft was ordered. It was allocated the registration G-ATTC and arrived in November 1966. Just over a year later G-ASXP was lost in a training accident at Stansted. This time no replacement was ordered.

By 1965 BEA was beginning to give very serious consideration to its future requirements for a wide bodied jet suitable for use on both high density tourist and business routes. The events leading up to an order were long drawn out, and highly political. To begin with, BEA was interested in the possibility of buying the European Airbus, a projected twin engined jet built by a consortium of European nations, including Britain who were to build the wings and perhaps supply the engines. The aircraft would not be ready for some time, so BEA needed something else too. It favoured the projected BAC 2-11, which was a development of the 1-11, first announced as a firm proposition in 1967; able to seat two hundred and eight passengers, with a range of 1,500 miles, a wing span of just over 120 feet, and a length of 156 feet. BEA envisaged the need for about twelve such aircraft, though as the European Airbus went gradually out of favour, the

BEA leased two Viscount V.806s to Cyprus Airways between 1965 and 1970. G-AOYK is pictured ready for delivery to Nicosia. *(BA)*

number was revised upwards to between thirty and forty. The 2-11 was not, however, the only contender. There were three other types on offer: chief among these being the Boeing 727. Before the 2-11 was announced BEA favoured buying this aircraft. The second contender was a stretched version of the VC10, able to carry two hundred and thirty passengers. Anthony Milward disliked the VC10 option most of all. The VC10 had not been developed to operate in the high density market, and he considered a stretched version to be an unsatisfactory attempt to make it suitable, as the manufacturers were desperate to get some sales for the type. At about this time there was even talk of the government pressurizing BEA to buy some surplus VC10s, the product of a reduced order by BOAC. The third option to emerge was the Trident 3, a further refinement of the Trident family, capable of seating one hundred and forty six passengers. BEA had nothing against the Trident, already operating the Trident 1, and having fifteen Trident 2s on order, but it was not keen on the design specification of the Trident 3 because its capacity was considerably below what the airline had in mind, by about sixty seats.

A great deal of thought was given to the question of which aircraft to purchase, with the government putting pressure on in the direction of the VC10 as an immediate purchase, and the European Airbus as the ultimate order for a new generation of jet. The airline's technical evaluations eventually concluded the BAC 2-11 fitted the short term needs best. Immediately a snag was encountered; the government had not yet decided whether to fund the 2-11 project, and BAC could certainly not pay for its development themselves. BEA was kept waiting while the government decided what it should do. Eventually on December 15th 1967, the Minister announced, in the House of Commons, that there would be no public funding for the 2-11 project, as he believed the market to be insufficient for the type. His decision was formally communicated to BEA on January 12th 1968. BEA made it clear it wanted to buy the Boeing 727 instead. The government did not permit that either as it was anxious not to spend any unnecessary dollars, and permission to buy the '727 was refused. BEA was instructed to buy the Trident 3. The airline was most unhappy, claiming the government was limiting its commercial freedom for political reasons. Even the promise of compensation did not reconcile the situation. The 1967/68 Report and Accounts summed up the airline's view about the Trident 3 "an excellent aircraft from the passengers point of view, but basically too small for BEA's needs." The die was cast, and BEA had little alternative but to order Trident 3s. The order was officially placed on 16th August 1968, providing for a fleet of twenty six with an option (never exercised) on another ten. The Trident 3 would be fitted with an RB162 booster engine to enable it to operate with full loads out of small or hot airfields, giving the aircraft an extra 15% take-off trust, for only 5% extra weight. The order was worth £83 million, and was the largest, at that time, single order to be placed with a British aerospace company. The government offered BEA £25 million compensation for not being able to buy the '727, with the possibility of another £12½million to follow. Needless to say the airline accepted!

Meanwhile four contenders had now emerged for the eventual wide bodied jet order, the European Airbus, the BAC 3-11, the Lockheed L.10, and the DC-10. Of these BEA felt the BAC 3-11 was the most promising. Again based on a development of the BAC 1-11, the 3-11 could accommodate two hundred and twenty passengers over a distance of 2,000 miles, powered by two Rolls Royce RB2-11.47 engines. The design was later improved to incorporate the more advanced RB2-11.S61 engines. BAC announced it required an order for fifty aircraft to open a production line. BEA issued a letter of intent to buy twenty, and both Court Lines and Laker Airways indicated they wished to buy the aircraft too. By 1970 BAC had letters of intent for forty three, and things looked quite hopeful. At the Farnborough Airshow in September 1970 BEA formally placed an order for twenty 3-11s, with an option on another ten. However despite the promising signs, the airline was once again to be disappointed. Like the 2-11, the 3-11 needed government funding, and before the end of 1970 Frederick Corfield, Minister of Aviation Supply, announced that the government had decided not to proceed with funding of the BAC 3-11. The decision was purely political. The government was anxious to show itself as pro-European, and wanted to encourage BEA, Court Line and Laker to buy the European Airbus. BEA greeted the news with gloom, believing the 3-11 to be ideal for its needs.

The three remaining contenders were given an in depth evaulation. The Airbus was considered to be insufficiently flexible to meet BEA operational requirements. It would not be equally at home on the long distance services, like London-Tel Aviv, and the short high density routes to Paris, Amsterdam and so on. The DC-10 was regarded as a little too big. In any case it did not have any major British components and the airline felt the government might even refuse permission for it to buy the type as a result. That left the L.10, now called the Tristar, which could operate quite efficiently over the long and short routes, and had the advantage of being powered by Rolls Royce RB2-11 engines. An order was eventually placed with Lockheed for six aircraft, with an option on a further twelve on September 26th 1972. The aircraft cost BEA £60 million to buy, and another £20 million to purchase spares and ground equipment. The Tristar could accommodate three hundred and thirty six economy and eighteen first class passengers, and would be fitted with automatic landing equipment like the Tridents. BEA wanted to have the L.10 in service in early 1975. Tristars never actually flew in BEA colours since by the time they were delivered the airline had been merged with BOAC to form British Airways. However, one Tristar, N305EA destined for Eastern Airlines in the USA, did carry the BEA logo on its forward fuselage when it appeared at the 1972 Farnborough Airshow.

One cannot help wondering what might have happened to the British aircraft industry if the government had been a little more adventurous and funded the 3-11. But as so often happens in aviation purely political considerations overruled all else.

BEA

1966

Although Argosy 222s had not been in service very long, the Cargo Unit was already considering the possibility of larger freighter aircraft, because the cargo services were becoming so popular. As a short term solution the airline obtained extra capacity by chartering a DC-4 from Air Ferry. Its use continued into 1967, the aircraft flying many of the London and Manchester-Dusseldorf and Frankfurt schedules, and some London-Zurich flights. Unfortunately the charter ended in disaster, because on January 21st 1967 the DC-4, G-ASOG, crashed on approach to Frankfurt killing its crew. In the longer term BEA was considering the possibility of buying Boeing 727 freighters. As has already been noted the airline was not allowed to order the '727, and instead BEA began to investigate the possibility of converting some Vanguards to all-freighter work. The Vanguard conversion plan was very attractive as the airline already owned the aircraft, which were becoming surplus to requirements with the delivery of Tridents, and the capacity of a Vanguard freighter was nearly double that of the Argosy. A firm decision was taken to convert some Vanguards in 1969, the 'new' aircraft being named the Merchantman. In the meantime Vanguards did make a limited appearance in a pure freighter role in 1966, operating a weekly Saturday night newspaper charter from Manchester to Belfast. The schedule provided for a 23.05 departure from Manchester (BE7930F), and an arrival at Belfast at 23.55. The aircraft positioned back to Ringway in the early hours.

For 1966 a number of new all-cargo routes were commenced by BEA. From May 7th a service to Nicosia, via Athens, was flown by Argosy once a week. Departure from Heathrow occurred on Saturdays at 22.45, arrival at Nicosia being at 12.20 the next day. The Athens-Nicosia sector was operated in conjunction with Cyprus Airways. The London-Athens segment was the longest non-stop route flown by Argosys in BEA service. On November 1st two more all cargo routes were opened: London to Madrid, and London to Vienna. Both were flown weekly, Argosys operating the Madrid schedule, and Viscounts the Vienna one, though from April 1967 they were replaced with Argosys. Finally a joint freighter operation between Manchester and Dusseldorf and Frankfurt was mounted with Lufthansa. The route was flown on Wednesdays and Saturdays using an Argosy or sometimes the leased Air Ferry DC-4. One of the Cargo Units most unusual consignments in 1966 was London Zoo's Giant Panda Chi Chi. Chi Chi was flown to Moscow in an attempt to mate with Moscow Zoo's Giant Panda An An. Comets were normally used on the Moscow service, but they were not large enough to accommodate Chi Chi's crate and a Vanguard was substituted instead, the Panda travelled in the front part of the cabin. Unfortunately the attempt to mate the two failed and another Vanguard substitution occurred to bring Chi Chi back from Moscow.

Plans to build a new Cargo Centre on the south side at Heathrow were well advanced. Costing £10 million, the building would be jointly used by BEA and BOAC. It could handle up to 1,000 tons of cargo a day, having the latest technology. Up to six thousand parcels and one hundred and fifty other items could be catered for in an hour. Each airline had separate facilities, but a direct conveyor link would allow much speedier interchange of cargo. The BEA part of the new building was to have eleven aircraft parking stands to be used by its freighters and those of the companies it handled. Construction of the cargo terminal began in July 1967, with a target for completion of late 1969. To link the complex with the central area a new tunnel was dug under the airfield.

Apart from the launching of two new international routes from London (to Faro and Tangier both flown by Comets), the main emphasis over the summer was the improvement of passenger services chiefly from the Midlands and North to the continent. Tridents commenced a thrice weekly Manchester to Amsterdam, and a thrice weekly Manchester-Copenhagen schedule from April, and from June 1st nearly all the international services out of Manchester were worked by the Tridents. At Birmingham, the dormant route to Amsterdam was revived being flown twice a week by Viscounts. Out of London, Tridents began to appear on flights to Basle, Cologne/Bonn and Hanover from April 1st, and from May 1st on the longest route in the route in the network from London to Ankara via Rome, Athens and Istanbul.

On the domestic trunk routes BEA was becoming increasingly worried about the competition of British Eagle's 1-11s from Heathrow, and British United's from

Gatwick, and a new form of competition came from British Rail who began running fast electric trains to Scotland. All this added up, in BEA's mind, to the conclusion that jets would have to be placed onto these routes. The economics of jet operations were not very encouraging, especially for the Comet. Tridents could operate a little more successfully, but they were required for the prestige European routes. It was, therefore, with some reluctance that the airline introduced Comets on the London-Glasgow route where there was most competition. From May 2nd a twice daily Comet service ran, with departures from London at 07.30 (BE5010) and 17.30 (BE5052). The jet shaved fifteen minutes off the Vanguards schedule, but because of congestion at Heathrow the flights were often no quicker in the end. As competition mounted, BEA made more and more use of jet services to Glasgow, and added Edinburgh and Belfast as well in 1967. Belfast, with its shorter runway, was not suitable for Comets and benefited from having Tridents on the London service right from the outset of jet operations.

From May 2nd 1966 BEA services to and from Glasgow began to use the new airfield at Abbotsinch. Abbotsinch was an ex-Fleet Air Arm station which had been extensively modified and given a new terminal building incorporating two finger piers. Once Abbotsinch was ready, Renfrew Airport was closed. BEA had served Renfrew since 1947, and the transfer to the new airport was a nostalgic occasion for many staff. Facilities were certainly far superior at Abbotsinch, and nowhere better than in the Engineering Section. The airline constructed a new purpose built Engineering Base on the airfield, costing over £1 million, equipped to carry out minor servicing of Viscounts and Vanguards, and all maintenance on the Herons. Unfortunately the Base was not ready until October 5th meaning engineering work had mainly to be conducted in the open from May to October. The first BEA aircraft to land at Abbotsinch was a Herald which positioned from Renfrew on the evening of May 1st. Although BEA was seeking to improve services from Glasgow, it did not neglect Aberdeen. During the year a second daily non-stop Aberdeen-London Viscount flight was commenced. The two services left Heathrow in the late afternoon and early evening respectively, with one aircraft returning from Aberdeen in the evening, and the other night-stopping to provide an early morning south bound flight. The summer timetable ended on October 31st, a date marked by the retirement of the Heralds from service in Scotland, with Viscounts taking over all Herald routes.

At the other end of the UK, BEA returned to Southampton for its South coast to Jersey link. Southampton Airport had been purchased by a private company, owned by Mr. Nat Somers, and a 5,509 foot concrete runway had been laid. Once ready for use, BEA gladly moved back to Southampton from Bournemouth (Hurn). Hurn had never been as popular with passengers as Southampton, being too far west in the region. Southampton proved an immediate success, with BEA laying on many extra flights in addition to the thirteen that were scheduled each week. The first service into Southampton was flown by Viscount G-AOYO on April 1st. The Airport, like Gatwick, had its own railway station with an hourly fast train to Waterloo, and the facility helped promote traffic even more. It was almost as quick to travel from Jersey to the centre of London by flying to Southampton and using the train, as to fly to Heathrow and catch the coach to WLAT, and it was a lot cheaper! BEA's Station Superintendent at Southampton was Peter Van De Velde, who had been at Hurn until the transfer. All services from Southampton to Jersey were flown by Viscount, but increasingly Vanguards were making an impact on other routes into Jersey. In the summer there were nineteen Vanguard flights from Heathrow, nine from Manchester and two from Gatwick, compared with only two flights a week in the summer of 1965. Services to both Channel Islands were severely interrupted, over both the Easter and Summer Bank Holiday periods, by fog. Fog was quite a common problem in the Islands, but this time it came and stayed, and over the busiest week-ends of the whole year. Countless passengers found themselves travelling to the Islands, not by Viscount or Vanguard but by British Rail steamer from Weymouth!

BEA's network of services from West Berlin faced increasing competition from Air France Caravelles and Pan American Boeing 727s. As yet the Corporation did not have sufficient jet capacity to enable it to use jets, but something had to be done. As a stop gap measure the 'Silver Star' service was launched, using Viscounts equipped with fifty three Comet seats giving extra luxury and leg room. Passengers were offered a much improved standard of in-flight catering too. 'Silver Star' began on May 1st, but it could not really match the competition from Air France and Pan Am. The aircraft, for all its comfort and better catering, was still only a Viscount. A step towards really effective competition was taken in November 1966, with BEA deciding to order a fleet of BAC 1-11.500 jets, some of which would be used in Germany. The order, formally signed on January 27th 1967, was for eighteen aircraft valued at £30 million. It included an option on another six, to be taken up if the States of Jersey and Guernsey decided to improve their runways sufficiently to allow operations of fully loaded 1-11s. Jersey did eventually lengthen its runway, but Guernsey has never done so and the option on the six extra 1-11.500s was never exercised. BEA had favoured the Boeing 737 rather than the 1-11 but the government would not grant it permission to buy the type. The airline toyed with the idea of leasing some smaller BAC 1-11.300s for use in Germany until the 1-11.500s were ready. In the end the costs of such a plan made the airline decide against the idea.

The summer of 1966 was not a particularly successful time. Vanguard schedules were thrown into confusion by a spate of failures with the Tyne engines. The failure ratio reached 1.25 per 1,000 flying hours; about twice the normal rate. The difficulty was traced to the failure of bearings in the high pressure compression chamber, and the demand for spare engines soon outstripped the supply. Aircraft lay idle for several days simply because there were not enough spares to re-engine them. The problem reached a peak during May and Rolls Royce worked flat out to speed up delivery of the Tyne engines to BEA. As if that was not bad enough, a further crop of problems arose with Tridents. In their case it was not engines that were to blame, but faults with the aircraft's hydraulic system. To cap it all pilots began another phase of their long running protest over pay and conditions. Four hundred of them signed a vote of no confidence in the airline's management, partly over its handling of the problems with the Vanguards and Tridents, but mainly because of the poor promotion prospects for First Officers. BEA countered with a claim that most First Officers could expect to become Captains within ten years. Such assurances did not prevent more than a few First Officers leaving the airline to obtain commands elsewhere. Henry Marking was given the unenviable task of cooling things down. Tempers were anything but cool! On one occasion a Captain delayed departure because he found an engineer's footprint on the aircraft's cabin carpet! Eventually Marking did succeed in damping down the situation, but that did not prevent BEA receiving much adverse publicity. One positive thing to emerge out of the trouble was a new in-house publication called 'BEA News'. 'BEA News' was published weekly from October 28th for staff, with the expressed aim of improving communications between management and staff. The monthly BEA Magazine continued to be issued, increasingly becoming a promotional aid for the airline.

The publication of the winter timetable showed several route improvements, but no new services were opened. Improvements included the wider use of Tridents, and the stepping up of flights to Gibraltar and Malta. Frequencies to Gibraltar were raised from four to six a week, and to Malta from five to ten a week. One station previously only served in the summer received a winter service: Bordeaux. A twice weekly Viscount service was scheduled between London and Bordeaux. Gibraltar Airways did launch a new route, Gibraltar to Casablanca via Tangier. From November 2nd G-AMFV flew to Casablanca twice weekly. Loads were rather poor and the extension to Casablanca was soon scrapped. At home, BKS announced it planned to withdraw from the Teeside- London service on October 31st. Pending the award of the license to a new operator, BEA and BKS mounted a joint bridging service. Two flights a day were flown, one in the morning and the other in the evening. BKS HS748s were used for some services, but BEA Viscounts also appeared on the route because BKS did not have enough capacity of its own. The ATLB eventually awarded Autair the licence, and the airline flew to Teeside with a mixture of HS748s and Heralds. Like BKS, however, Autair found traffic returns poor and they too gave up the route, leaving it to British Midland to make the service viable.

The winter months found BEA facing an uphill economic struggle. The government introduced a £50 foreign currency restriction which had an immediate effect of discouraging passengers from holidaying abroad. Loads to Nice fell by 30%, Switzerland by 6% and Spain/Portugal by 5%. Sterling Area destinations like Gibraltar, Malta and Cyprus were unaffected by the currency limitations and BEA began to redouble efforts at promoting holidays there, spending some £140,000 extra on advertising.

With all this going on the completion of Phase Two of 'Beacon' went almost unnoticed. However from Tuesday November 2nd all BEA services, including those in Germany, were included in the computer and full details of passengers and their special requirements were recorded. By then two hundred and eighty six reservations staff manned the WLAT telephone sales switch board, in shifts, covering six days a week. They handled anything up to 15,000 calls a day, as well as several thousand telex messages. At the other end of the scale BEA opened its first off-line sales office in Japan on June 1st. While WLATs sales staff numbered nearly three hundred, BEA Tokyo numbered just one, Mr. Oto Katsumi. Like most overseas off-line sales offices, the Tokyo office was not open to the general public.

BEA was busy promoting IT work through Silver Wing holidays, by selling seats on scheduled services to tour operators, and offering whole aircraft charters to them. The most popular destinations were Barcelona, Djerba, Palma and Tunis. The 20% reduction in charter rates, announced in 1965, had enabled the airline to win much of the traffic. IT flights were generally flown at night or at the week-ends. Over the financial year 1966/67 receipts from IT work were 359% higher than those for the previous year! The growing popularity of this sort of holiday ensured BEA a ready source of income for some time to come providing its charter rates remained competitive with those of the independent airlines. The winning of IT contracts was no easy matter, with airlines like BUA, Channel Airways, Dan Air and British Eagle all offering highly competitive rates.

The long running battle with British Eagle over the Heathrow-Glasgow route was finally settled in 1966. When Eagle's services had begun, BEA had appealed to the ATLB, which had upheld Eagle's right to operate. Then Eagle applied to increase frequencies on the grounds that BEA had a superior position by virtue of its greater frequencies. The debate went on for some time, until eventually the ATLB Commissioner, Sir Harold Kiel, upheld the Eagle case for more flights. Once BEA knew it was faced with regular competition on the route it did all it could to improve services to keep its share of the market. More than one passenger commented how much BEA's standard of service had improved with regular competition from Eagle.

The training of aircrew continued to be a major activity within BEA. In 1965/66 10,554 hours of simulator 'flying' were carried out and 3,325 hours of actual flight training. Stansted remained the main training base for Comets and Argosys, while Vanguards used Malta, Tridents Shannon and Viscounts Jersey and Dinard. However in 1966 the airline decided to move as much flight training as possible outside Great Britain because fuel costs and landing fees were generally lower abroad. Malta, Nicosia and Shannon were the main foreign airfields. BEA continued to sell its training expertise to other carriers and during the year pilots from Olympic Airways, Kuwait Airways, Middle East Airlines, Sudan Airways and the RAF all made use of the Comet simulator, while Iraqi Airways used the Trident simulator; and Cyprus Airways, BUA, BKS and Cambrian the Viscount simulators. The sale of simulator time netted an additional £164,179 for the Corporation. Simulators had been greatly improved by 1966. They incorporated a visual display outside the cockpit windows; produced first by the use of closed circuit TV and later, as technology increased, by the use of computers. The visual image provided either an airfield or en route flying conditions, greatly adding to realism. Demand for pilots was extremely high, and the College of Air Training could not keep pace. Consequently BEA decided to use the CSE Aviation training school at Oxford to supplement its intake of aircrew. CSE were contracted to train fifty pilots annually over a five year period.

Autoland development flying was steadily building up experience with the equipment. By January 1966 G-ARPB had made over one thousand autoland test landings and a further three hundred and sixty eight autolands had been made on regular commercial services in good weather. Real progress was made between November 4th and 24th, when G-ARPB made a series of test landings at Heathrow in dense fog. The first occurred on November 4th, when landings were made with a runway visual range of between 50 and 100 yards, and a cloud base of no more than 100 feet. A series of ten trial landings were made between November 4th and 24th. On November 24th 'RPB flew north to Manchester to collect Henry Marking, whose London bound flight had diverted to Manchester because of the fog. It brought him back to Heathrow where he was treated to a fully automatic landing. The aircraft was flown by Hawker Siddeley's test pilot, Captain Phillips. Sir Anthony Milward, commenting after the test landings, said "The recent very impressive landings by our Trident, G-ARPB, carried out in thick fog at Heathrow were a really convincing demonstration of the effectiveness of this wonderful equipment, and our intent to be the world's first operator to use this in day to day operations." Success with these tests helped BEA decide to equip the new Trident 3Bs with autoland for Category 3B operations. Category 3B enabled landings to be made with a zero ceiling, and an RVR of 50 metres, visibility of any less making it impossible to see to steer the aircraft once it was on the ground. There was much work still to be done before commercial operations down to Category 3B could be contemplated, and development flying continued unabated. In April 1967 G-ARPB spent a week flying scheduled BEA services, making automatic landings on every possible occasion, but still only in good weather. The aim was to test the equipment under the rigours of regular operations and use. Over the week 'RPB made twenty seven automatic landings at fifteen different airfields in Britain and Europe, and the whole experiment went without a hitch.

One anomoly cleared up in 1966 concerned staff travel on BOAC flights. BEA had granted BOAC staff cheap rebated tickets on its services for some time. However BEA staff did not receive the same level of concessions on BOAC. The staff considered it rather unfair, especially as BOAC flew to all those exotic places! They pressed the airline's management to rectify the situation which they did. From November 1st a new staff travel agreement between the two Corporations enabled staff of both airlines to travel cheaply on the services of the other. BEA staff received generous rebated travel conditions within the Corporation. Once a staff member had served with the airline for a year he was entitled to as many 90% discount tickets as he wanted, the only condition being that the tickets were issued on a 'sub-load' basis. In other words he would only be accepted for a flight if there was a seat available at the time of departure. Firm bookings were offered to staff who had worked for the airline for a little longer, though generally they were limited to only one flight a year. Travel perks did much to encourage recruitment to the airline.

Herald G-APWD outside the new engineering accomodation at Abbotsinch. *(BA)*

BEA

1967

For a number of years BEA had been a shareholder in Cambrian and BKS, owning 50% of Cambrian's share capital, and 30% of BKS's. Neither company was thriving, and could not afford to raise the necessary capital to buy more modern aircraft. BEA was anxious neither Cambrian or BKS went out of business, so in 1967 the BEA Board decided to assist them more fully. On February 2nd a new holding company was formed called British Air Services (BAS). BAS was formed by reviving the dormant Railway Air Services, and changing the company name to British Air Services. BAS then purchased all the share capital of both airlines, making them totally BEA owned. The move gave Cambrian and BKS access to more financial aid, both directly and indirectly, from BEA. The first Chairman of BAS was Henry Marking. When he became Chairman of BEA soon afterwards, Cyril Herring succeeded him at BAS. Cambrian and BKS kept their separate identities, but their aircraft were painted in a common livery, with the title 'British Air Services' along the cabin top. The Cambrian or BKS motif was painted on the tail to identify which company the aircraft belonged to. The colour scheme did not last long, with the title 'British Air Services' soon being removed from the cabin top and replaced by either 'Cambrian' or 'BKS'. A small 'BAS' sign was then carried on the forward lower fuselage side. Even that did not prove acceptable, and a totally new scheme was devised for both airlines. Cambrian aircraft had a bright orange top, white cheat line and grey underside, while Northeast (as BKS had by then become) aircraft had a bright yellow top, white cheat line and grey underside. There was even a proposal to paint BEA Scottish and BEA Channel aircraft in similar colours, Scottish having a green top and Channel a blue one. Apart from a few models appearing like that, Scottish and Channel aircraft remained in the normal BEA colour scheme until they became part of British Airways. On the equipment side, Cambrian and BKS began to receive a number of surplus Viscount V.806s from BEA. The first of these, G-AOYL, went to BKS on May 28th 1968, and between then and 1970 BKS received another five (G-AOYH, 'OYO, 'OYR, 'PEX, 'PEY) Cambrian received eight V.806s between April 1970 and November 1971 (G-AOYG, 'OYI, 'OYJ, 'OYM, 'OYN, 'OYP, 'OYS, and 'PIM). They largely replaced the Viscount 700s operated by both airlines.

Under Captain Cameron's direction, BEA Helicopters was rapidly expanding its involvement in gas and oil exploration support. During 1967 a new base was opened at Aberdeen with a single S.61. The growth of oil exploration off the Scottish coast meant the base at Dyce quickly expanded, and a second base was opened at Sumburgh in the Shetland Islands, again initially with a single S.61. Oil and gas support flying continued off the East Anglian coast too, and to improve its facilities for the task BEAH purchased a small corner of the old RAF airfield at Ellough, near Beccles, to build a heliport. Demand for North Sea support had developed to such an extent that BEAH had expanded its S.61 fleet to eight, and the company even toyed with the idea of buying up to ten Russian Mi-2 helicopters for the North Sea. Government pressure, coupled with possible problems over the supply of spares, meant the order was never placed.

Oil Rig supply flying was (and still is) a very demanding activity. The North Sea is notorious for extremes of weather; ranging from Force Ten gales, to driving rain, fog which can blot out rigs for days at a time, and icing. BEAH's S.61s could fly in light icing conditions, down to a temperature of -5°C, providing the aircraft were fitted with guards over the air intakes, heated cockpit windows and an ice detector. Landing on a rig in calm weather is demanding enough, but in a full gale it is very tricky indeed. The normal procedure was for the First Officer to fly the helicopter until the rig was sighted and then the Captain would take over to manoeuvre the aircraft onto the helideck. The co-pilot watched the instruments and checked clearances with things like the rig's tower. Landings were not usually made if the wind speed exceeded seventy knots as such speeds could quite literally blow someone off the helideck. At wind speeds above fifty knots rotors were often started and stopped in a hangar because the wind could cause the blades to flayle and strike the fuselage. Pilots were assisted in finding the rig by NDB navigation beacons and the Decca Flight Log system. Even so it was not unknown for a landing to be made on the wrong rig. BEAH was not immune from such errors. Its senior pilot once landed his Bell 212 on the wrong gas rig off the East Anglian coast, something that he never lived down! On flights out to rigs all passengers had to wear brightly coloured immersion suits, designed to allow a person to keep warm in the water. Survival time without such a suit in the winter was a matter of minutes, whereas with one it was possible to stay alive in the sea for up to two hours. The suits also helped people to float. The early models were not without problems, experiments showed that the air inside tended to rush to the bottom of the suit, causing the wearer to float but upside down! Fortunately the value of the suits were never actually put to the test in BEAH days. One S.61, G-ASNM, did ditch in the sea in November 1970 following the failure of the gearbox lubrication system, but all the passengers were rescued without even getting their feet wet.

BEA was always anxious to ensure its organisation was as up to date as possible, and in 1966 it had appointed the Tavistock Institute to undertake a full review. Its report, received in mid 1967, suggested the airline be divided into a number of small divisions supported by some centralized departments. It received the backing of Henry Marking and was implemented in November. Three Divisions were created, Traffic and Sales, Operations and Scottish, supported by central departments covering Finance, Personnel, Public Relations and Air Safety. Each Division would be a 'profit centre' meaning it was responsible for making a profit in its particular area. BEA made it clear that it would like to extend the idea, and the first step was taken in 1969 when the German internal network was created a Division and profit centre.

The 1966/67 Report and Accounts, besides recording that profits had fallen to just £708,296 mainly due to poor economic conditions, also provided a summary of the operations of each type in the fleet:

Type	Number in Fleet	Revenue Hrs.Flown	Cost per Flying Hr.	Revenue Earnt
Trident I	23	41,175	£361	£25.4m.
Comet 4B	13	30,032	£299	£16.2m.
Vanguard	19	46,600	£295	£23.1m.
Viscount	39	80,321	£113	£18.1m.
Argosy	5	13,635	£155	£2.4m.
Herald (to 31.10.66)	3	2,216	£95	£214,000
Heron	2	1,817	£72	£157,000

In 1967, for the first time, BEA allowed payment for tickets by credit card and it also began a new sales gimmick, the 'Timesaver' ticket, which passengers wrote out themselves. The tickets could be used on domestic services, and were only available to customers with a credit account. They saved the passenger the time involved in going to a sales office or travel agent, he simply looked up the flight he wished to catch, telephoned his booking to 'Beacon' and then wrote out his own ticket.

In February BEA launched a joint venture with Cunard (the shipping line). Passengers for certain Cunard cruises would fly out to join their ship at Gibraltar on a BEA flight. At the end of their cruise BEA would bring them home from Gibraltar. The first load of cruise passengers were flown out to Gibraltar on February 22nd on Vanguard G-APEM to join the S.S. Sylvania. Such loads provided a useful boost to traffic.

Getting in and out of Gibraltar's North Front airfield became even more difficult from June. The Spanish, stepping up their claim to sovereignty of the 'Rock', introduced a prohibited area in Algeciras Bay through which aircraft landing at Gibraltar were not allowed. Gibraltar's approach path came within a mere two hundred yards of the area, demanding considerable skill on the part of the crews. On occasions BEA aircraft were shadowed by Spanish Air Force jets, and for a time the RAF Hunter detachment at Gibraltar escorted BEA arrivals and departures. Once or twice BEA aircraft breached the prohibited zone, and BEA was fined £12 by a Spanish court for one such violation! Gibraltar Airways DC-3, G-AMFV, faced the same problems, but its smaller size and lower speeds made it easier for it to avoid the exclusion zone. G-AMFV earned some extra revenue for Gibraltar Airways by operating a series of charters between Gibraltar and Tetuan in 1967, and the airline found its loads to Tangier were rising because the hydrofoil link between the two cities had been cut during the year.

Back at home BEA was planning several new routes for the summer season. Two new destinations in Spain were to come on line, Alicante and Gerona. Alicante was to have a thrice weekly Trident service, and Gerona was to be served by four Comet and five Vanguard flights a week. The Comets were to operate by day and the Vanguards at night. However, with the Spanish more relaxed attitude to life, neither airfield was ready for use by BEA when the summer season began. Consequently the entire programme for Alicante was scrapped, while the night flights to Gerona were cancelled and the day flights flown to Barcelona. Alicante did eventually receive BEA services from November 1st, and Gerona in April 1968.

More successful were plans to improve services to Cyprus, Malta and Palma. From June 3rd BEA began its first non-stop London-Nicosia service. Flights were scheduled to leave London at 22.40 (BE/CY296) on Tuesday, Wednesday and Saturday. Malta gained a new route to Manchester, flown once a week on a Tuesday. Both routes were Comet operated. A weekly direct Glasgow-Palma service was flown between May 27th and October 14th using a Vanguard. There were also two flights a week from Glasgow to Palma via Manchester. One other route commenced in 1967 was a route from London to the Hungarian capital Budapest. BEA had briefly served Budapest in 1961/62, but from April 10th a non-stop Comet service flew the route on Mondays and Fridays.

However BEA ended its direct flights between Birmingham and Barcelona at the end of the summer. The timetable had provided for a once weekly service, but the growth of IT charters from the Midlands had taken great chunks of traffic away from the route, and the last service operated on Saturday September 23rd. Dinard, too, was dropped from the network the last Dinard-Heathrow sector being flown by a Viscount on Saturday September 30th. Dinard was still used by Viscounts for training flights, and for the occasional diversion from Jersey or Guernsey. BEA's resident Representative there, Monsieur Store´e, moved to Bordeaux to become Station Superintendent.

Tridents continued to make history, snatching several records for the fastest journey time. On one day in mid July G-ARPG, operating BE049 from Madrid to Heathrow, completed the journey in a record one hour thirty eight minutes. Later, a Trident flew from London to Brussels in just thirty one minutes. The whole Trident fleet was now in operation, except for G-ARPB which remained on lease to Hawker Siddeley for development flying. In that guise it visited Jersey in July, being the largest jet to land at the Island's airport to date.

BEA's other Channel Island destination, Guernsey, handled its first Vanguard on July 18th when Captain Maclannahan flew G-APEA into the Island on a flight from London in place of a Viscount. The visit was designed as a route proving flight, and afterwards Vanguards occasionally visited Guernsey. Only in the summer of 1971 did the type operate scheduled services into the Island, and then on a very limited scale, with one flight a week, (on a Wednesday between June 1st and September 19th). Vanguards did not see more regular use at Guernsey because of the runway's low bearing strength, which limited the type to only one hundred and twenty two landings a year. Once Merchantman freighters began to visit the Island (which they did from April 1970 G-APEK operating the first flight on April 5th) most of the allocation was given over to the freighters. BEA Guernsey got a new Station Superintendent in July, Peter Van De Velde, who had previously held that position at Southampton. He replaced Mr. Nicholls who was posted to Palma in place of George Borney who had been moved to Moscow. Doug Lo Bao, Senior Traffic Officer, Jersey, moved to Southampton as Station Superintendent to complete the chain of airport management moves.

One of Mr. Lo Bao's earliest duties at Southampton was to attend an emergency landing at Bournemouth. One Sunday early in August, Comet G-ARCO departed from Heathrow for Faro. A few minutes after take off the crew were alerted by a fire warning light in one engine, and they decided to make an emergency landing at Hurn, Southampton's runway being too short to accommodate a Comet in such circumstances. At that time Hurn was officially closed on a Sunday. But the Bournemouth Zone Controllers who worked from Hurn, opened up the Tower and alerted the Christchurch fire brigade. The aircraft made a safe landing and the problem was traced to a faulty warning light. Mr. Lo Bao was summoned by London Operations to supervise the handling of the flight, and coaches were arranged to take passengers back to Heathrow to catch another aircraft. When they had departed, the staff called in to attend the incident were treated to a meal from the aircraft's catering stock, as were a number of on lookers, the author included.

In Scotland services to Inverness and Wick were improved during the summer. The evening Glasgow-Inverness, and early morning Inverness-Glasgow Viscount flights began to call at Edinburgh, while the late evening Glasgow-Aberdeen flight was extended north to Wick on Monday, Wednesday and Thursday. The aircraft was scheduled to arrive at Wick at 22.20 (BE8126) where it night-stopped. Early the next morning, at 06.35, it departed for Glasgow via Aberdeen. Neither the call at Edinburgh or the extension to Wick generated much traffic, and both were abandoned in September 1968, much to the relief of the airline's small team at Wick who had to work very long hours to handle the services.

The second version of the Argosy used by BEA was the AW222, G-ASXL is here seen at Stansted during a training sortie. (BA)

BEA used Stansted for much of its Trident Training. G-ARPM lines up for take off from Stansted on another training flight. (BA)

To improve efficiency and co-ordination between Check-In and Load Control Departments, a new system called Passenger Acceptance and Load Control(PALC) was introduced in 1967. The system was first installed in Jersey, Manchester, Edinburgh and Berlin. Experience gained from its use in those locations lead to some modifications being made before it was installed at Heathrow and the West London Air Terminal during 1968 and 1969. The airline's Operations Department was developing its own sophisticated system called FIND (Flight Information and Display). FIND was a computer programme linked into 'Beacon' which carried details of the location of each aircraft, crew hours and rosters and so on. Like PALC it took some time to develop to a really adequate level, and was not commissioned at Heathrow until 1969. Other Operations Offices were linked to it as 'Beacon' spread out from London. 'Beacon' itself was re-equipped in 1968 with the Univac 494 computer to allow it to handle five times more work. Such expansion was necessary to accommodate FIND and a number of other computer projects which were in hand. The engineers, too, had a new computer which recorded the purchase, store and use of over 18,000 aircraft parts and 400,000 other components.

Operations had to cope with the loss of two aircraft during the summer. The first accident involved Viscount, G-AOYO, on July 18th. The aircraft was on a training detail for Cyprus Airways flying from Glasgow. BEA Training Captain Openshaw was giving instruction to Cyprus Airways First Officer O'Shea. The Viscount had made six touch and go landings, but on the seventh it overran the runway at Glasgow and was substantially damaged. The damage was too severe for the engineers at Glasgow to undertake a repair, so the Viscount was dismantled and taken to Marshalls of Cambridge by road for a rebuild which lasted from December 1967 to May 1968. The second incident was far more serious, involving Comet G-ARCO. On October 12th 'RCO was flying a London-Nicosia service when it was destroyed by a terrorist bomb while between the Greek coast and Cyprus. All fifty nine passengers and seven crew were killed. It transpired that the Cypriot leader, Archbishop Makarios, was expected to have travelled on the flight and the bomb was aimed at him. Fortunately for him, though not the other passengers and crew, he had cancelled his reservation at the last minute.

BEA still regularly carried members of the Royal Family. Back in 1965 Lord Snowden and Princess Margaret had been flown by Viscount from Dublin to Heathrow on November 10th, and on November 14th 1967 the Queen and Prince Philip travelled to Malta on Trident G-ARPX. A number of other VIPs also flew BEA. The Prime Minister, Harold Wilson, used a Trident on March 6th 1965 to visit Berlin, and over the next few years he flew in Tridents for visits to Paris, Vienna and Moscow. In March 1966 the Archbishop of Canterbury, Dr Ramsay, flew to Rome in a BEA Comet, for his historic meeting with the Pope.

August 1st 1967 marked BEA's twenty first birthday. The airline had certainly come a long way since 1946. From a staff of 1,600 or so and a fleet of DC-3s, and Vikings, serving only a handful of destinations, the airline had expanded its staff to 21,560 and had a large fleet of jets and turbo-prop aircraft serving eighty eight destinations in the UK and Europe. To mark the birthday a book was written outlining the history of the airline, called 'The Challenge of BEA.' Its author, Garry May, concluded by looking forward to what things might be like on BEA's fiftieth birthday in 1997. Such an event was destined never to occur. Long before 1997 BEA and BOAC were merged into British Airways. Indeed as BEA celebrated, the first moves towards the merger began, with the government announcing the establishment of an Inquiry into Civil Air Transport under Sir Ronald Edwards.

1968

By 1968 BEA's well known black and red colour scheme had been used on its fleet for almost ten years and the airline's marketing men decided the time had come to give a fresh look to the aircraft. Henrion Design Associates were contracted with the job of designing the new look, which was eventually unveiled on August 20th. The new colours were to consist of a white aircraft top, light grey underside and a dark blue cheat line. The initials 'BEA' appeared in red and white on the forward fuselage top, while the tail was to be dark blue with a striking red and white half Union flag. Red wings would be retained mainly to keep the costs of re-painting down. Even so, the airline calculated the re-painting of the fleet would cost at least £100,000. To carry out the task a hangar at Heathrow was converted into a paint shop, and individual aircraft were re-painted when they went into the Base for a major overhaul. High quality materials were used so that aircraft would not need re-painting for at least five years. The first proper glimpse of the new colours was afforded at Gatwick within days of the unveiling of the new design, when S.61 G-AWFX was rolled out from a major check, resplendent in the new livery. Coupled with the new look to the aircraft, there was a new look for cabin staff uniforms too. Designed by Hardy Amies, the new uniforms had a very distinctive bright red overcoat for stewardesses.

New image or not, BEA's financial performance for 1967/68 was less than encouraging. The balance sheet showed the dreaded minus sign, indicating another loss. Difficult economic conditons were the main explanation. In the first four months of the summer of 1967 (April to July) traffic was lower than the same period in the previous year, something which had hardly ever happened before. Over the whole of the summer (April to October) a profit of just £5½ million was achieved, far too small to

G-ARPC represents a BEA Trident in the airline's last livery. (BA)

Trident 2 G-AVFA in the black and red colour scheme. *(BA)*

be able to cover the large winter losses. Currency restrictions were still depressing traffic to foreign holiday resorts, although Silver Wing Holidays were trying to promote holidays to Sterling Area sun traps, like Malta, Cyprus and Gibraltar. Losses were further increased by the effect of the Arab-Israeli Six Day War and a coup in Greece. Both of these political events, in 1967, had severely interrupted traffic and loads were slow to pick up again. About the only consolation was that BEA managed an average load factor of 58.1%, whereas the average for all the European carriers was only 53%.

On a number of occasions BEA had employed television advertising to try to boost traffic, and in the course of its TV advertising campaign in 1968 the airline won the distinction of being the first to use colour advertising when it screened a colour advert on West German TV. The advert was for Windsor Holidays (package tours to the UK), and besides being the first colour TV advert, it also won for the airline the advertising industries coveted 'Golden Tulip' award. Windsor Holidays was a very useful money earner for BEA, being specially successful in Germany.

BEA's fleet expanded in 1968 with the coming of the Trident 2. The first Trident 2 to fly had been G-AVFA which flew at Hatfield on July 27th 1967. A period of development flying followed and a C or A was awarded to the Trident 2 early in 1968, after which deliveries began, with G-AVFD being the first to arrive on April 16th. By August another four Trident 2s had arrived, G-AVFB, 'VFE, 'VFF, 'VFG. To begin with the Trident 2s were used on an ad-hoc basis replacing Comets and Trident 1s, with G-AVFD flying the types first commercial service. On June 1st regular Trident 2 schedules began to Dublin, Madrid, Milan and Stockholm, and gradually the type began to take over the longer distance services to places like Athens, Moscow and Tel Aviv, previously the prerogative of the Comets.

A second new type was delivered to BEA in 1968, the BAC 1-11.500 called the Super 1-11 by BEA. G-AVMJ was handed over to the airline on August 29th, with another six aircraft following by December. After a period of crew training the 1-11 began to appear on some routes on an ad-hoc basis just as the Trident 2 had done a few months earlier. Regular Super 1-11 schedules commenced on November 17th on some German internal services and the London-Manchester route. Use of the 1-11 to Manchester was part of an attempt to win back traffic from British Rail's fast electric trains. In Germany the appearance of the 1-11 was not the first use of jet equipment on services from Berlin. Since August 1st a single Comet had been employed, flying a daily service to Frankfurt, two flights a day to Dusseldorf and a daily Berlin-Hanover-Bremen service, that continued on to London. The arrival of the Trident 2s meant there was sufficient spare Comet capacity to mount the services and as more Tridents arrived, so BEA increased the use of Comets in Germany. For the winter of 1968/69 they flew fourteen daily services on the Berlin-Dusseldorf, Frankfurt, Cologne/Bonn and Munich routes. BEA did not intend to use Comets in Germany for long and once sufficient 1-11s were operating the Comets would be withdrawn. Overall the summer of 1968 was a boom time for air travel into Berlin because the East Germans clamped down on surface links to the city from July 1st. BEA laid on no less than four hundred and ninety five extra services up to October 31st to cope with demand.

Delivery of the Trident 2s and Super 1-11s produced a surplus of Comets and Viscounts. A decision was made to sell off ten of the twelve Comets and to reduce the Viscount fleet by selling of the V.806s. Many of the aircraft went to various associate companies. BEA Air Tours took most of the Comets, and Cambrian and BKS most of the Viscounts. However, some Viscounts found new homes far away, in the service of Lao Airlines, Mandala Airlines and Winner Airways of Taiwan. The remaining twenty Viscounts were kept busy on domestic routes, some services to Eire, the London-Salzburg flight, local services from Malta and some of the German internal network. The sale of the surplus fleet was handled by BEA's Contracts Department.

Once again 1968 saw expansion and contraction of the network. Expansion involved beginning a number of new routes at home and abroad:

London to Minorca.	One Vanguard flight weekly on Fridays. The route did not succeed and was dropped in September 1969.
London to Rhodes.	One Night Tourist service weekly on a Friday, flown by Comet.
Manchester to Edinburgh.	Five times weekly Viscount service.
Birmingham to Malta.	Once weekly Friday evening flight by Comet, in co- operation with the Malta Airlines.
London to Bremen.	Daily Comet service.
London to Inverness.	A Daily except Sunday flight with Viscounts, via Aberdeen.

BEA services to France were modified from April 1st when the airline began to fly London-Paris services to Orly as well as Le Bourget. Five flights daily operated in Orly and twelve to Le Bourget. Eventually all services transferred to Orly but not for several years. From April 1st the Glasgow-Birmingham-Paris route became Trident operated. The popularity of Malta is indicated not only by the opening of a service from Birmingham, but also by the doubling of the Manchester-Malta frequencies to twice weekly.

On the other hand some routes were withdrawn in 1968. On September 3rd the last BEA aircraft departed from Biarritz at 18.15 (BE085), while on October 13th a Vanguard operating BE503, left Klagenfurt at 17.20 for Munich and London, marking the end of BEA services to Klagenfurt. A third international route to cease was London-Bordeaux with the last flight being flown on October 31st by a Viscount (BE093). All these routes were taken over by BKS, who had been flying some Bordeaux and Biarritz services in co-operation with BEA for several years. One domestic route closed too, Belfast to Jersey. Services ceased on September 29th with a departure from Belfast at 14.20 and Jersey at 16.40. Connections between Belfast and Jersey were still available over Manchester and London. Down in the South West, the helicopter service from Penzance to the Scillies was doing very well. On October 2nd the S.61 carried its 250,000 passenger. A survey of the first four

BAC 1-11,500 G-AVMH photographed just after its roll out from the production line at Hurn (BA)

Trident 2 G-AVFI captured in flight. *(BA)*

year of helicopter operations to the Scillies showed loads rising from 41,804 in 1964/65 to 55,690 in 1967/68, producing an overall load factor of 83.5%. All this was achieved by a single S.61 without an on site back up, and was a tremendous tribute to the reliability of the Sikorsky design and the ability of the small engineering team at Penzance.

One of BEA's enduring difficulties was the problem of late departures, especially at Heathrow. The Corporation decided to make a sustained effort to improve things. Better co-ordination was arranged between Operations, traffic and engineering staff by the widening of the job of the Traffic Dispatchers to control of all aspects of arrivals and departures. The change was reflected in a new title for the Dispatchers, they became Aircraft Dispatchers. Punctuality began to improve significantly. Unfortunately the summer programme was seriously hampered by incidents involving three Tridents and a Viscount. On June 14th Trident 1 G-ARPR was severely damaged at Shannon on a training flight, and was out of service for six weeks while engineers repaired damage caused by a heavy landing. Then on July 3rd a BKS Ambassador freighter (G-AMAD) crashed when landing at Heathrow on a Bloodstock flight. The Ambassador slew into the aircraft parking area, slicing the tail off Trident G-ARPT, and severely damaging G-ARPI. Viscount, G-APJU, loaded with passengers and about to depart for the Channel Isles, was also damaged. Engineers decided G-ARPT was a write off, but 'RPI was repaired over several months, and 'PJU was out of service only for a short time. The loss of the two Tridents could have produced a serious operational problem, but for Hawker Siddeley coming to BEA's aid by speeding up the delivery of the Trident 2s, with G-AVFC and G-AVFG arriving early to fill the gaps.

At the beginning of the winter another unpleasant event occurred, the financial collapse of British Eagle. On November 6th Eagle ceased trading and was declared bankrupt. Though BEA took no pleasure in seeing Eagle's large staff made redundant, it was pleased that competition from British Eagle on the domestic trunk routes and on one or two other routes, had ceased. A number of ex-Eagle staff were taken on by BEA, BKS and Cambrian, and the airlines picked up several routes previously operated by Eagle. BEA obtained routes from London to Pisa and Stuttgart, and BKS was awarded the London-Luxembourg licence. One ex-Eagle route BEA was keen to obtain was to Tunis. The ATLB gave BEA a dispensation to fly the route after Eagles collapse, pending the awarding of the licence to another operator. Comets served Tunis on a twice weekly basis. To the Corporation's great regret, the ATLB decided to give the licence to British United, and the temporary BEA flights to Tunis ceased at the end of March 1969.

Even with the demise of British Eagle, BEA still faced considerable competition from charter operators on holiday routes, and the airline set up a study group to consider how best to respond. Their report suggested that BEA should establish a subsidiary company to operate IT charters. It was a case of 'if you can't beat them, join them'. The Board considered the recommendation and in February 1969 agreed that it was the best solution. The way was paved for the formation of BEA Air Tours at Gatwick, on April 24th 1969. Initially Air Tours had a staff of two hundred, mainly recruited from BEA, and it was managed by Captain W. Ballie. The new company proposed to operate surplus BEA Comets, and planned to commence flying in 1970. Beforehand, a great deal of effort went into securing contracts with tour operators.

Training had become a key aspect of the airline's activity. Too often training is thought of as merely the training of air crew, but in practice the Corporation ran a whole series of training schools covering almost all aspects of operations. On the air crew side new pilots continued to be trained at Hamble and Oxford, and in service training began again to use Prestwick and Stansted, as the British Airports Authority agreed to reduce charges for such flights. In 1969 BEA began using Teeside for the training of Super 1-11 crews, having being offered favourable rates by the airport authority. On the ground, the General Apprenticeship Scheme recruiting school leavers for administration, continued to flourish. Since the scheme had begun in 1957, two hundred and ninety trainees had completed their course. A parallel scheme, called the Administrative Trainee Scheme, was run for graduates, recruiting four to six a year, for senior management posts. Courses for the General Apprentices, Graduate Trainees and other staff were run from the training centre at Heston, while existing senior managers were able to attend a variety of short courses at the East Burnham Staff College.

The Engineers ran their own apprenticeship scheme for school leavers, and each year three or four of the intake were sponsored by the airline to go to University to take a degree in engineering. A number of others took a diploma in engineering. In 1968 there were fifty five engineering apprentices at varying stages of the three year course, and four at University. In 1968 BEA and BOAC decided to co-operate in the training of engineers by setting up a joint training school in a new building at Cranebank. It came into use in 1969. Other airlines made use of the superb training facilities offered by the Engineering Training Branch. In 1967/68 sixty engineers from a variety of airlines passed through the Heathrow Base for some sort of training. The final major area of training was that given to cabin staff. Recruits were given a five week course covering matters as diverse as personal appearance, catering and emergency drills. In 1967/68 two hundred and twenty nine new cabin staff were trained for BEA flying. Induction courses were only a small part of cabin crew training. Existing staff had to take regular refresher courses, conversion courses from one aircraft type to another; and, for the lucky ones, promotion courses. Over a thousand refresher courses were taken, and another three hundred and two cabin staff underwent type conversion or promotion training in 1967/68. Most of the work was carried out at Heston, where there was a dummy fuselage of a Trident for the staff to practice in. Again cabin staff training facilities were used by other airlines, including BKS, Cyprus Airways and Kuwait Airways.

In October the first Vanguard to be converted to an all-cargo configuration was flown to Southend to be modified by Aviation Traders. The aircraft chosen was G-APEM. Conversion required the cutting of a large freight door in the forward left hand side of the cabin. The door was 139 inches long and 80 inches high. In addition the cabin floor was strengthened and the cabin windows blanked out. The cabin floor was fitted with rollers to allow pallets to be easily moved inside the aircraft. Five Vanguards were initially earmarked for conversion, the first two being modified by Aviation Traders, and the remainder by BEA itself using kits supplied by Aviation Traders. Each conversion would cost about £128,000. G-APEM flew, as a Merchantman, at Southend on October 10th 1969, just a year after it had arrived there. The other aircraft to be converted at Southend, G-APEO, was complete on February 1st 1970.

S.61 G-ATBJ airlifting a cannon from Penzance Heliport to the Scillies. *(D. & J. Wills)*

The first of the type to be modified by BEA itself was G-APEK. It took the airline's engineers about 60,000 man hours to complete the work, a job lasting some nine months.

As a prelude to Merchantman operations one Vanguard was stripped of its seats and began to operate some all-cargo services. It flew services to Copenhagen, Milan and Paris, and had the front airstairs removed to allow loading of freight in the cabin. G-APEL was initially used, but gradually most of the Vangaurds had their front airstairs removed so they could operate frieght services. The fleet of Merchantmen were designed to replace the Argosys, which had never made a profit in BEA service even though they were worked very hard. In 1967/68 the type flew 14,764 revenue flying hours, giving each aircraft a daily utilization of eight and a half hours. The problem with the Argosy was that it was expensive to maintain, and compared with the Merchantman, its capacity was small.

Between 1967 and 1970 the Cargo Unit developed a number of new all-cargo routes:

All-Cargo Services Commenced between 1967 and 1970

1.4.67	Manchester-Dusseldorf-Frankfurt.
1.4.68	London-Belfast.
1.10.69	London-Dublin.
1.11.69	London-Malta (an old route resurrected).
1.11.69	London-Turin.
7.2.70	London-Stuttgart (an old route resurrected).
1.11.70	Manchester-Amsterdam.

Most of the routes just about managed to establish themselves as viable, but the only really successful ones were to Stuttgart and Turin. The success of the Stuttgart flights was in marked contrast to its poor performance when BEA had tried the route fifteen years or so before. With the arrival of the Merchantmen in 1970, BEA began to operate the London-Zurich joint BEA/Swissair cargo service. Since its inception in 1964 it had been flown by Swissair (usually with DC-4). However as the Merchantman offered a much larger load, BEA and Swissair decided it would be better employed on the route than a DC-4. The practice of flying cargo routes in conjunction with other carriers was gradually expanded in the early 1970s. Some routes were flown by BEA aircraft on behalf of the foreign operator, and some by the particular foreign airline on behalf of BEA. By 1971 Alitalia DC-9 freighters were flying a joint Manchester-Birmingham-Milan schedule for BEA, SAS DC-9s a Manchester-Birmingham-Copenhagen route, TAP a joint Lisbon-London service with a Boeing 727 freighter, Iberia a joint Barcelona-London route with a DC-4, and Finnair a London-Manchester-Helsinki schedule using Kar Air's DC-6. BEA aircraft operated a number of joint routes, including those between Manchester and Germany, London and Gothenburg, Stockholm, Zurich, Nicosia and Brussels.

Argosy G-ASXO unloading cargo outside the new Cargo Centre Europe at Heathrow. *(BA)*

BEA

1969

On May 5th 1969 the long awaited Edwards Report (or to give its full title 'The Report of the Committee of Inquiry into Civil Air Transport' Cmmd 4018) was published. Like many government reports it was rather wordy, running to about 300,000! But its main proposal was simple: British civil air transport would be best served by the establishing of a National Air Holdings Board to supervise the activities of BEA, BOAC and BAS. The airlines should not be merged, but retain their own identity. A strong independent airline, to be a second force to the nationalized airlines, should also be encouraged with the National Air Holdings Board having a share in its ownership. BUA and Caledonian were suggested as possible suitable candidates to form the second force.

BEA greeted the report with some caution. It believed the existence of a Holdings Board would blur responsibility. Who would be responsible for the future direction of the airline, the BEA Board or the National Air Holdings Board? What would happen when there was a disagreement between the two? Anthony Milward was anxious to avoid this problem and argued that ultimate responsibilty must rest with just one body. He was also fearful that, although the Edwards Report did not recommend a merger with BOAC, the existence of a Holdings Board might provide an excellent vehicle for the government to use to merge the two. In the 1969/70 Report and Accounts he said: "At the present moment we think it is fair to say that the two national airlines (BEA and BOAC) are probably the most prosperous airlines in their respective spheres in the world today. This position has not come about by accident, but we believe, by efficient management and staff, good aircraft, good operating ability, enterprising marketing, and above all a concentrated effort by each airline in its own specialized field. This being so, we see little merit in any proposal to change for changes sake."

The government largely accepted the Edwards Report, and created a National Holdings Board, entitled the British Airways Board. It became a legal entity on August 5th 1971, with nine members under the Chairmanship of David Nicolson. The Board immediately sought to try to co-ordinate the activity of the two Corporations to avoid duplication and waste. But the government was not finished with BEA and BOAC. Though Edwards had not recommended merger, the politicians certainly favoured it, and the British Airways Board was encouraged to consider the question of how it might be best achieved.

BEA's own finances for 1968/69 reflected Milward's comments about the prosperous nature of the airline. From a loss of just over £1¾ millions in 1967/68, a profit of £3,536,000 was achieved. Milward should have retired as the airline's Chairman at the end of the 1967/68 financial year, but the government asked him to stay on for another year while it considered the Edwards Report and decided what action to take. He agreed to do so, although at the same time he was grooming his likely successor, Henry Marking.

One area of BEA activity, not so far recorded, is its involvement in the hotel business. That an airline should be involved in hotels might seem a little odd at first sight, but BEA soon came to realize that the hotel trade was a natural extension of the airline business. After all if you flew them there, you might as well put them up when they arrived! Naturally BEA was not experienced in hotel management, so it looked around for those who were, leading to the formation of a new joint company with the experienced caterers and hoteliers, Fortes. The company was known as BEA Fortes Hotels, and was organised as a subsidiary of Airport Catering Services, which BEA and Fortes already jointly owned. Several hotels came under control of the new enterprise, including the Excelsior in Manchester and its counterpart in Birmingham. Abroad, the Phoenicia and Imperial in Malta, the Plaze Athenee, George V and Le Tremoille in Paris were also owned by BEA Fortes Hotels. The company began the construction of new hotels in Glasgow and Cyprus. BEA also became involved in a second chain of hotels through the formation of the European Hotel Corporation, and joint venture between BEA, BOAC, Alitalia, Lufthansa, Swissair and a number of hotel companies. It planned to build some new hotels in several cities around Europe, offering a good standard of accommodation at a reasonable price. Lastly, in 1969 BEA acquired an interest in the Schipol Hotel at Amsterdam Airport. It soon became apparent to BEA that its involvement in hotels could be much better organised if these three strands were all brought under one roof. Consequently another new company was formed to manage all BEA's hotel activities in March 1970. It was called Sovereign Group Hotels Limited.

Back in the air, BEA planned two new routes for the summer, from London to Pisa and Stuttgart, both ex-British Eagle routes. Pisa should have come on line on May 1st, but services did not commence until the following summer because of a crop of problems. There was more success with Stuttgart, with a daily Trident service beginning on July 1st. The summer timetable recorded the recommencement of a twice weekly non-stop service to Tel Aviv, but from the historical point of view the most important feature of it was the much wider use made of the Super 1-11 jets. They operated most services from Manchester and nearly all the German internal network. Increased use of the aircraft allowed the withdrawal of the Comets from Germany, with the last flight occurring on April 30th from Berlin to London via Hamburg. Over the summer the Super 1-11s began to appear on the Glasgow-Birmingham-Paris, and Birmingham-Dublin schedules, and quite a few of the London to Germany services. The Royal Family travelled in a Super 1-11 for the first time in May; when The Queen, Prince Philip and Princess Anne flew to Vienna in G-AVMP at the beginning of their state visit to Austria.

Still in Germany, a significant development occurred in April with the coming of an operating arrangement with Air France (AF) covering services between Berlin and Frankfurt and Munich. For some years Air France had been using Caravelles to fly a limited schedule from Berlin's Tegel Airport to those destinations in competition with BEA and Pan American. With declining traffic as travel through East Germany became easier BEA and Air France concluded it made sense to pool their services. Therefore Air France gave up its Tegel operation entirely and a joint service was flown from Tempelhof to Frankfurt and Munich using BEA Super 1-11s. Flights operated under a BE/AF or AF/BE flight prefix. Naturally Air France was none too keen on its passengers flying in an aircraft painted in full BEA livery, and because BEA used the 1-11s elsewhere it was not happy about painting an Air France title or symbol on the aircraft. A compromise was reached by which the Super 1-11s were painted in a revised BEA livery which excluded the BEA logo and Union flag on the tail. Some of Super 1-11s were re-painted in the new colour scheme, but those aircraft still to be delivered were painted by BAC prior to delivery to the airline.

While BEA opened new routes in most years, there always seemed to be a corresponding, if smaller, closure of routes. Thus on September 13th BEA services to Stavanger ceased with a round trip by a Viscount. Stavanger was reconnected to the route system by British Airways. Manchester-Zurich services were withdrawn too, again to be revived by British Airways. Without doubt the most surprising route to vanish was Jersey to Guernsey. On March 31st BEA gave up carrying passengers between the two Islands, a route continuously operated since April 1947. In the days of Rapides up to ninety five flights a week had linked the two, though in the Viscount era there were generally only two a day, supplemented in the summer. The distance between the two Islands was only twenty one miles, making Viscount operations rather expensive. The opportunity to cease flying the route came because of the existence of Aurigny Air Services, an Alderney based airline established in March 1968. Aurigny flew the Alderney-Guernsey and Jersey and Alderney-Southampton link, and was anxious to expand its Guernsey-Jersey services to an hourly walk on frequency, giving BEA the opportunity to withdraw its service in favour of Aurigny. The last inter Island flight was between Jersey and Guernsey, departing at 20.15 (BE3484). The closure of the route meant the withdrawal of the winter Jersey-Gatwick service, because the midday flight from Jersey to Guernsey went on to Gatwick. Summer direct flights from Jersey to Gatwick continued, and a daily year round Guernsey-Gatwick flight was flown by an aircraft which arrived at Guernsey from Heathrow. After March 31st BEA flew Jersey-Guernsey services only as positioning flights, although in the summer of 1973 a Jersey-Guernsey-Amsterdam service was flown. The aircraft did not carry any inter-Island traffic however.

One of the most important developments to BEA services out of Heathrow was the opening of Terminal One on May 7th. Initially only international flights were transferred to the new building, but by the end of the year domestic services had moved in too, together with the flights of BKS, Cambrian, Aer Lingus and Cyprus Airways. The move into Terminal One did not go entirely without hitches. There were problems with the baggage handling equipment, and the PALC system. Once they were sorted out Terminal One became a great asset to BEA, giving plenty of space for passengers, and a system of pier gates with nose in parking for aircraft. The gates were equipped with extending gangways allowing passengers to board or disembark straight into the Terminal, without the use of passenger steps. However some aircraft, most noteable the Viscounts, were unable to use these gangways. Back in Terminal Two, BEA retained a handling unit to cater for the needs of those European airlines it handled, ranging from Aeroflot through Icelandair to Swissair. Such handling contracts were very important items of revenue, not only at Heathrow but also at other stations like Gatwick, Birmingham, Manchester and Jersey.

BEA computer technology continued to be improved with the full introduction of the computerized FIND Operations system at Heathrow. FIND gave Operations staff a continuous presentation of arrivals and departures, the whereabouts of every aircraft in the fleet, data on the availability of aircrew, crew hours flown and a host more. Reservations computers were updated too in 1969. Since 'Beacon' had come into use it handled 12 million reservations and it was vital to keep the system up to date to maximise the benefit from it. The increased memory capacity of the computer enabled staff personnel records to be computerised in a programme called 'Profile'.

'Cleared to push back.' G-AVMV begins another service from Heathrow. (BA)

'Profile' allowed Personnel staff to have instant access to the staff records of all 22,185 staff. Some staff were rather afraid of the development. Easy access to records via a computer was seen as a step towards '1984'and the 'big brother' approach. Personnel staff were not all happy either. It took hours and hours to type the staff records into the computer, and various early malfunctions meant it often took hours and hours to get it out again!

Operationally BEA faced several hiccups. Early in the year a number of industrial disputes bought chaos to Scottish Division services. The action did not affect BEA staff, but those employed by the airport authorities. Problems began at Glasgow in October 1968, and lasted on and off for a year. In that time Glasgow was closed for various periods, with flight being diverted to Prestwick. In January firemen at Aberdeen and Edinburgh went on strike, closing Aberdeen between January 15th and 30th, and Edinburgh between January 18th and February 3rd. The disputes caused severe disruption to operations and inconvenience to passengers. January was at least a happy time for one UK station, Southampton, which handled its first Vanguard early in the month. G-APEG was chartered by Cunard to carry passengers from Southampton to Liverpool. The passengers had been on board a trial voyage of the new liner the Queen Elizabeth II.

Later in the year domestic trunk routes out of London faced a new threat from Channel Airways. Channel applied to the ATLB for licences to operate services from Stansted to Belfast, Edinburgh and Glasgow. Channel's application was turned down, but BUA did gain permission to increase its frequencies between Gatwick and those points. International services did not escape problems either. In September the Libyan revolution halted all flights to Tripoli for ten days. When they resumed it was deemed prudent not to night-stop aircraft at Tripoli, and the Malta service had to be rescheduled. From November services to Naples were suspended for several months because of runway subsidence, and BEA's entire Turkish operation to Istanbul and Ankara was suspended from November 1st until March 31st 1970 due to a political dispute between the British and Turkish governments. The Turkish national airline, THY, had applied to operate into London and had been allocated Gatwick as its London terminal. Neither THY nor the Turkish government were happy, believing as a national carrier THY should be allowed into Heathrow. When the British refused to change their mind the Turk's responded by banning all BEA services into their country, leaving the small BEA traffic handling unit at Istanbul with no work at all, except the handling of the once weekly Cyprus Airways service from Nicosia. Further talks took place, and eventually THY was allowed into Heathrow in return for the ban on BEA services into Istanbul and Ankara being lifted.

By 1969 autoland development flying had forged ahead, and as a result of its success Tridents were cleared to operate commercially in Category 2 conditions, with a decision height of 100 feet and an RVR of 400 metres. Permission was granted in late 1968, but it was not until February 14th 1969 that the ILS facilities at Cologne/Bonn, Hamburg, Paris and Zurich were officially upgraded to Category 2 standard, becoming the first airfields so equipped in Europe. Heathrow was upgraded to Category 2 shortly afterwards. During the remainder of 1969 and into 1970, many other airports throughout Europe were upgraded. At last BEA was able to reap some benefit from the vast sum of money invested in autoland. Landings in Category 2 conditions were not the ultimate goal. The airline was working towards Category 3 landings, with initial development flying aimed at securing commercial operations in Category 3A conditions; a decision height of 12 feet and an RVR of 300 metres. It set the winter of 1972/73 as the target date for commercial use of autoland under those conditions. Beyond lay the ultimate goal of Category 3B landings, with an RVR or only 50 metres. In recognition of the tremendous achievement of the autoland project BEA was awarded the Queens Award to Industry for Technological Achievement in April 1970, a fitting reward for twelve years hard work.

1969 was an important year for BKS and Cyprus Airways, as both airlines took delivery of their first Tridents. BKS purchased two ex-Channel Airways Trident 1Es early in 1969, G-AVYD being delivered to them on March 6th, and 'VYC on April 4th. The first Cyprus Airways Trident was formally handed over on September 19th. Both the BKS and Cyprus Airways aircraft would be maintained by BEA at Heathrow. BKS used their Tridents on IT charters from Newcastle, as well as on some schedules from London to Newcastle, Luxembourg, Bilbao and Bordeaux. Cyprus Airways Tridents were to fly the London-Nicosia route, and some local services from Cyprus to the Middle East.

Ever on the look out for free publicity BEA organised a rather unusual staff competition in the summer; a round UK Air Race. Staff had to work out the quickest possible time required to visit all the BEA stations in the UK and Channel Isles using only BEA scheduled services. The winner was Senior Traffic Officer Copenhagen, Tom Weihe, who calculated it could be done in four days, one hour and fifty minutes. BEA dispatched him around the stations to prove it! Despite one or two nearly missed connections Tom succeeded. Several local papers and TV channels carried to story, giving the airline the hoped for publicity.

Nine Vanguards were converted to Merchantman freighters. G-APES is seen at Nicosia wearing BEA Cargo Division livery. *(BA)*

1970

On March 6th 1970, BEA's new charter subsidiary; BEA Air Tours, commenced operations. The first commercial flight was between Gatwick and Palma, flown by Comet G-ARJL. Air Tours had purchased seven Comets from BEA, with an eighth G-APME, being operated for a time on lease from the Corporation. Routes flown for the summer of 1970 were Gatwick to Alicante, Gerona, Ibiza, Malaga, Nicosia, Palma, Pisa, Rimini, Tenerife, Trieste and Venice, and a weekly Birmingham-Palma service. Tour companies who had contracted the services of Air Tours included Exchange Travel, Hickie-Borman, Cooks, Inghams, and the National Union of Students Travel Service. Air Tours entered its first season with 375 staff, 111 of whom were aircrew. The summer proved such a successful time for the airline that in November it decided to purchase some larger aircraft. At first Air Tours seriously contemplated buying ex-American Airlines Boeing 707.123s, but this was not acceptable to the BEA Board, who were under some pressure from the BOAC Board to persuade Air Tours to buy surplus BOAC Boeing 707.436s, powered by Rolls Royce Conways. Consequently the American Airlines deal was dropped and BEA Air Tours ordered several ex-BOAC aircraft, G-APFK being the first to arrive in December 1971. The winter brought the normal tail off in charter work, but Air Tours found a number of different outlets to keep the aircraft busy: Comets were leased to BEA to cover aircraft shortages caused by the late delivery of the Trident 3s, and to BKS between October 13th and November 18th to operate the BKS Trident schedules because the BKS Tridents were being re-painted in a new colour scheme ready for the airline's change of name to Northeast Airlines. BKS officially became Northeast on November 15th.

As Air Tours was being born, another well established BEA subsidiary, Cambrian Airways (part of British Air Services) was coming into the jet age with the purchase of three second hand BAC 1-11.400 aircraft from the receivers of Court Lines. The three aircraft were G-AVOE, 'VOF and 'VGP. One was leased to BEA to operate some of the German internal services, and later a Cambrian 1-11 appeared on some BEA services between Manchester, Birmingham and Dublin. The lease lasted until March 1972, by which time Cambrian had purchased a fourth 1-11, G-AWBL. All four appeared, at various times, on these BEA routes.

British Air Services itself was engaged in researching the possibility of opening a network of commuter services around the UK using short take off and landing (STOL) aircraft. Evaluation of the ST.27, Twin Otter and Short Skyliner was undertaken, and a system of routes mapped out. The first plan consisted of a network of services from Birmingham to Leeds and Hull; Blackpool and Liverpool; Manchester and Newcastle; Bristol and Exeter; Southampton; and Heathrow. Later a more ambitious plan was issued with four networks each centred on a hub. The four hubs were to be Cambridge, Birmingham, Bristol and Sheffield. From each hub a network of services radiated:

Cambridge to:
Norwich; Hull; Sheffield; Birmingham; London and Southampton; Bristol.

Birmingham to:
Southend; Heathrow; Southampton; Liverpool; Blackpool; Manchester and Newcastle; Leeds and Hull.

Bristol to:
Southampton; Bournemouth; Exeter and Plymouth; Cardiff and Swansea; Liverpool; Wolverhampton; and the Surrey Docks (a STOL port to be built in the heart of London's dock-land).

Sheffield to:
Newcastle; Teeside; Hull; the Surrey Docks; Birmingham; Wolverhampton; Bolton; Preston; Carlisle.

Several of the cities on the projected network, like Sheffield and Bolton, did not have suitable airfields and BAS proposed the construction of purpose built STOL ports. The project was given the name 'Interstol', and in September Skyliner G-ASZJ was leased from Shorts, to make a publicity tour around many of the cities involved, and some that were not! The tour lasted five days, the full programme being:

Day 1;
Cambridge-Peterborough-Norwich-Hull-Leeds.

Day 2:
Leeds-Teeside-Blackpool-Newcastle-Edinburgh.

Day 3
Edinburgh-Glasgow-Prestwick-Carlisle-Liverpool.

Day 4
Liverpool-Birmingham-Heathrow-Swansea-Cardiff.

Day 5
Cardiff-Exeter-Plymouth-Southampton-Bristol-Heathrow.

Short demonstration flights took place at all the stops, except Prestwick and Heathrow. BAS proposed to introduce 'Interstol' in stages, beginning with the Birmingham network. It even got as far as producing a timetable, providing for seven flights a day to Heathrow and Southampton; six to Leeds; four to Manchester and Newcastle; three to Bristol and Exeter; and two each to Liverpool and Hull. Later in September G-ASZJ was used to fly part of the schedule to test its feasibility. 'Interstol' was a very ambitious scheme, but sadly the economic conditions in the country were just not suitable to its launch, and reluctantly BAS shelved the whole plan –for good as it turned out. Skyliners did eventually see regular service with BEA in Scotland, as replacements for the Heron.

In Gibraltar a chapter of aviation history closed on March 30th, when Gibraltar Airways finally retired its DC-3 G-AMFV. 'MFV had been used continuously on the link to Tangier since 1963, and had completed many thousands of crossings of the Straits in the process. The aircraft had conveyed its passengers in absolute safety and had become something of an institution in Gibraltar. 'MFV had acquired the nickname 'YOGIBAIR' (from the cartoon character Yogi Bear) after a very wild party one night at which somebody chalked 'YO' in front of 'Gibair' on the aircraft's fuselage. The nickname stuck, and the Dakota was referred to as 'Yogibair' by most of the Rock's residents for the remainder of its career there. Gibraltar Airways, now trading under the more catchy name of Gibair, believed the time had finally come to retire the DC-3 and use more modern equipment. G-AMFV was sold to C.47 Aviation, who resold it to Kestral Aviation. In its place Gibair chartered a BEA Viscount, a case of history repeating itself, since prior to the introduction of 'MFV Gibraltar Airways had leased BEA Viscounts for the Tangier service. The passing of the Dakota meant the closing of the final chapter of BEA links with the type.

Back in the UK the 1969/70 Report and Accounts was presented to the House of Commons on July 17th. The document showed BEA was still the world's seventh largest airline, the other six all being in the USA. Once again the Corporation was the world's second largest international carrier, in terms of passengers flown. In 1969/70 international traffic grew by 13%, aided by the raising of the foreign currency allowance from £50 to £200 in January 1970. Traffic on services to Spain, Portugal, Italy and Southern France lept up with the higher allowances. Over the whole financial year BEA sold £126 million worth of seats. £73 millions worth was sold by UK sales offices and travel agents, £45 million through sales outlets in Europe, and the remaining £8 million from overseas sales outlets. Overall the Corporation flew 8,475,856 passengers and produced a profit of £6,532,000, nearly double that of the previous year. Never before had such a high profit been made, and with one exception – the last year of BEA's existence –never again would it be. Still, not everything was happy. Domestic services lost over £1 million despite efforts at economies during the summer and autumn of 1969. In Scotland they took for form of withdrawal of the late night Aberdeen-Wick service, and removing Edinburgh as a stop on the late evening Glasgow-Inverness schedule, and its return early the next morning. In the Channel Isles there was a general reduction in frequencies on most routes, a typical example occurring on the Jersey-Southampton service. Normally there were up to thirteen flights a week in the summer, but for the summer of 1969 only seven were scheduled.

Cargo, too, did not have an entirely successful year, with the total weight carried falling from 132,422 tons in 1968/69 to 130,758 tons in 1969/70. The drop resulted from the industrial disputes at Heathrow in the autumn, and the teething troubles with the new Cargo Centre Europe. 1970 did included some encouragement for the Cargo Division, with the final retirement of the Argosys and introduction of the Merchantmen. The last scheduled Argosy services should have been on March 31st, between Dusseldorf and London and Guernsey/Jersey and London; but late delivery of the Merchantmen meant the Argosy continued flying throughout April. Its last service was actually on April 30th between Jersey and Heathrow. Since 1965 the Argosy 222s had flown 51,415 hours for BEA. The four surviving aircraft continued their flying careers on the other side of the Atlantic in the service of Midwest Airlines. The first commercial Merchantman flight occurred on February 7th with G-APEM flying a London-Stuttgart-Vienna schedule, which coincidentally was also the inauguration of the new service to Stuttgart. Later in the year, in May, BEA's Paris cargo operations were re-organised with the re-routing of services into Orly instead of Le Bourget. A small Cargo Centre for BEA's use was opened at Orly.

Of greater significance than the opening of a new cargo terminal at Orly was the opening of the new Cargo Centre at Heathrow. The building had been handed over to BEA on December 9th 1969, and the airline's Cargo Unit moved in at the end of March and beginning of April 1970. On May 22nd the Duke of Edinburgh officially opened the Centre, although it had already been in use for some time. The building, known as Cargo Centre Europe, used the latest technology, although there were a few teething problems. Cargo got lost, or was routed to the wrong storage area, or could not be retrieved from the storage area, or got stuck just a new feet from the waiting customer but could not be reached! There were many red faces at the Centre for several weeks, both on the part of the embarrassed staff and irate customers. BEA began to lose trade and the airline's cargo chief, J.L.

Guy, made vigorous attempts to iron out the faults and improve staff training on the new equipment. Once these problems were sorted out, the Centre settled down the BEA slowly began to win back traffic.

The opening of Cargo Centre Europe was one of the last major events to be overseen by Anthony Milward. On December 31st he retired as BEA's Chairman, a post he had held since 1964. His successor, as widely expected, was Henry Marking the current Chief Executive. Marking was the second consecutive Chairman to have been appointed from within BEA, demonstrating the government's confidence in the airline's senior management. Marking's abilities were well proven, especially through his careful handling of the pilots industrial disputes. He freely admitted a great deal of his knowledge and style was inherited from Lord Douglas, and as Chairman Marking would often ask himself 'what would Sholto have done?'. Lord Douglas's influence lived on, despite the fact he had died on October 29th 1969. Marking's first task was to appoint a new Chief Executive and he selected Ken Wilkinson, the airline's Chief Engineer, and another long time employee.

As Wilkinson left the Engineering Department to take up his new duties, the engineers were busy changing the system used for aircraft maintenance checks. The old system of Check Ones, Twos, Threes and Fours performed after so many flying hours, was gradually phased out on all types, except Herons and Viscounts. The new system provided for three checks, Service A, Service B and Service M. Service As were performed on each aircraft every twenty four hours, and Service Bs were to be carried out at between 200 and 250 flying hours. Service Bs, which were roughly equivalent to the old Check Two, could be performed at Heathrow, Manchester, Glasgow or Berlin. The Service M was a major overhaul, which for Tridents, Super 1-11s and Vanguards/ Merchantmen would be carried out on completion of 4,000 flying hours, and for Comets after 3,400. In 1971 the time between Service Ms was increased 6,000 flying hours for Trident 2s, Trident 3s and Super 1-11 and to 5,000 hours for Trident 1s. Vanguards remained at 4,000 and Comets at 3,400. If any aircraft had not completed this number of flying hours in a two year period, then a Service M would be performed after two years. The longer gaps between Service Ms was the product of greater reliability of aircraft structures and components, and the system of Progressive Maintenance already in use.

Rather unusually 1969/70 recorded an increase in flying training hours to 4,895. Over many years the number of flying hours on training details had been falling thanks to the greater sophistication of the flight simulators. The rise in 1969/70 was mainly because of the sale of the Comets, Viscounts and Argosys. As part of the package BEA undertook to train some crews from the purchasing airlines, and the countryside around Stansted once again resounded to the noise of the BEA (or perhaps technically ex-BEA) Comets and Argosys pounding round the circuit. BEA's Simulator Unit now boasted seven simulators covering all the main types in use, including the forthcoming Trident 3 which was the latest in simulator technology, incorporating a colour TV visual

Comet 4B G-ARJL climbs away from Gatwick on an Air Tours charter flight. *(BA)*

flight attachment. It was so good that the airline was able to use it to train pilots for Category 3A all weather approaches and landings, ready for the time when Tridents could use the system commercially.

If 1969/70 was a profitable year for BEA, its independent rival, British United, was finding the going rather tough. BUA's management made approaches to Laker Airways, Caledonian Airways, and even BOAC concerning the possibility of mergers. Eventually the Caledonian bid was accepted and a new airline was conceived, Caledonian/BUA, later renamed British Caledonian. BEA was not directly involved in any of the talks, but seeing the posibility of BUA going bankrupt, the Corporation did apply to the ATLB for BUA's European destination licences, including:- London to Rotterdam, Genoa, Tunis, Ibiza, Madeira and the Canary Islands. Naturally these applications came to nothing as BUA did not cease to trade. Failure to win those licenced did not stop BEA expanding its route network in other directions.

A number a new destinations in Eastern Europe were connected to the network. New services were launched to Belgrade, Sofia and Bucharest. From June 2nd a twice weekly Trident flight linked London with Sofia, via Belgrade. The inaugural service was flown by a Trident 2. Bucharest was added to the network by extending the Mondays and Fridays London-Budapest service. The first flight to Bucharest occurred on April 6th, again by a Trident 2. Two new staff positions were created by the expansion in Eastern Europe, BEA Representative Bulgaria, and BEA Repesentative Yugoslavia. Ex-Aircraft Dispatcher V. Lesbirel was appointed to the post in Bulgaria, and M.D. Goodwin went to Belgrade as Representative Yugoslavia, he also covered the seasonal service to Dubrovnik. Operations to Bucharest were supervised by BEA Representative Hungary. Another Eastern European nation to be served by BEA in 1970 for the first time was East Germany. Twice a year a major trade fair was held in Leipzig, and BEA began operating a daily service from London to Leipzig for the duration of the fair. The first period of operation was between February 28th and March 11th, using Vanguards. The link was very popular with businessmen travelling to the trade fairs, and was put on for most subsequent trade fairs in Leipzig.

Away from Eastern Europe, BEA services to North Africa were expanded by the opening of a London-Marrakech schedule from November 7th. A weekly service was operated by Trident 2 via Gibraltar. Marrakech would be served throughout the year, apart from the months of June to September. Between those months day time temperatures at Marrakech were so high it not only put off tourists wanting to visit the resort, but severely limited the take off performance of the Trident. At the end of the summer season services to Gerona were abandoned, as was the Glasgow-Manchester-Palma route. The last service from Gerona to London operated on October 31st being flown by a Vanguard. A few days previously, on October 25th, the last round trip between Glasgow and Manchester and Palma had taken place. Both routes were given up as a direct effect of competition from IT charter traffic. The ending of the Glasgow and Manchester to Palma service did not lessen BEA's commitment to the development of scheduled services from the provinces direct to Europe. Over the previous ten years the airline had put a great deal of effort into these, and by the summer of 1970 quite a comprehensive network had been built up, using mainly Tridents and Super 1-11s, although Viscounts still flew the links from Birmingham to Amsterdam and Dusseldorf. However BEA soon found that the degree of effort put in to promoting these routes did not always generate the levels of traffic it might have. Passengers seemed to be quite happy to fly from the provinces to Europe via London, even though there were direct flights, probably because there was a much higher level of frequencies from London. Plans existed to extend the services from the provinces even further, especially from Manchester. Routes in mind included Manchester to Milan, Munich, Geneva and Zurich, some of which had been operated in the past. The economic conditions, however, precluded their launch in 1970.

BEA Routes from the Provinces to the Continent (Summer 1970)

Birmingham To	Glasgow To	Manchester To
Amsterdam (Viscount)	Dusseldorf, via Manchester (Super 1-11)	Amsterdam (Super 1-11) Brussels (Super 1-11)
Dusseldorf (Viscount)	Malta, via Birmingham (Trident)	Copenhagen (Super 1-11) Dusseldorf (Super 1-11)
Malta (Trident)	Palma, via Manchester (Super 1-11)	Malta (Trident) Palma (Super 1-11)
Paris (Super 1-11)	Paris, via Birmingham (Super 1-11)	Paris (Super 1-11)

For 1970 the domestic, or Inter-Britain network as it was now called, saw the provision of a non-stop London-Inverness flight. Previously there had been a through service between the two points, but the aircraft called at Aberdeen on route. From April 1st a daily direct flight operated. BE5708 was scheduled to leave London at 08.15 and to arrive at Inverness at 10.25. From Inverness the Viscount flew the Scottish internal service from Inverness to Stornoway, Benbecula and Glasgow. A second Viscount operated the sectors in reverse, Glasgow-Benbecula-Stornoway-Inverness, and then flew the service from Inverness to Heathrow being scheduled to land at London at 20.10. For the crews operating this circuit a great variety of airfields and facilities were experienced. At one extreme was Heathrow with all its ATC complexity and sophisticated landing aids. At the other extreme was Benbecula with its single Air Traffic Controller, no Radar, ILS or VOR. The contrast of facilities within BEA was equally great. At Heathrow there were different departments for just about every aspect of the airline's work. At Benbecula just three staff looked after everything. At Heathrow engineers abounded, at Benbecula there were none, and not even a ground power unit. Viscounts had to start up using their own batteries. The lack of ground power units at most Scottish stations meant the Viscounts operating on the network were fitted with additional batteries to enable them to start off their own power.

1971

BEA's organisational structure was completely changed in 1971. Henry Marking was a keen advocate of the profit centre concept (the breaking up of the airline into small units each with the responsibility for making a profit), and several profit centres already existed, such as the Scottish Division. Marking took the decision to extend the concept to the whole airline, and from April 1st ten new divisions were created each with the responsibility for making a profit.

The largest of the divisions was BEA Mainline. Mainline operated all the international schedules from London as well as the domestic trunk routes from London to Belfast, Edinburgh and Glasgow. For the task it used all the Trident ICs, 2s and 3s, two remaining Comets (G-APMA and 'PMG) and a handful of Vanguards. Chief Executive Ken Wilkinson became the Director of the Divison.

The second division, entitled the 'Super 1-11 Division' flew the fleet of eighteen BAC 1-11.500 aircraft from a base at Manchester. All international routes from Manchester were the responsibility of the Division, plus the domestic services from Manchester to all points except the Channel Islands. The German internal services from West Berlin were also placed under the management of the Divison. Roy Watts was put in charge of the operation.

Next there was the Scottish Airways Divison, created out of the existing Scottish Division. Using Viscounts and the two Herons, it worked all the Scottish internal routes, plus the Aberdeen and Inverness to London schedules and the Glasgow-Belfast services. R.M. McKean became its Director and eight Viscounts were allocated to it. They were G-AOJB, 'OJC, 'OJE, 'OJF, 'OHH, 'OHI, 'OHL and 'OHS. These aircraft and the two Herons (G-ANXA and 'NXB) had the word 'Scottish' painted on the fuselage top alongside the BEA logo. Schedules for the Division normally required two of the Viscounts to night-stop at Heathrow to operate early morning flights to Inverness and Aberdeen, two to night-stop at Aberdeen, one at Inverness and the remainder together with the Herons at Glasgow.

After divisionalisation, Viscount V.802 G-AOHS displays BEA Scottish titling. *(BA)*

The fourth division also had a very definite regional identity, being called the Channel Islands Airways Division. Its sphere of operations was a little wider than the title suggests, as it not only flew all Channel Islands services, but the network of domestic and international routes out of Birmingham. Operations from Birmingham were not considered sufficiently large to warrant a divison in their own right, so they were conveniently lumped together with the CI routes to form the Division. Ian Scott Hill became the Director of BEA Channel Islands Airways, and he had twelve Viscounts assigned to him; G-AOJD, 'OHG, 'OHJ, 'OHK, 'OHM, 'OHN, 'OHO, 'OHR, 'OHT, 'OHV, 'OHW, and 'ORD. These aircraft had 'Channel Islands' painted on the fuselage top next to the BEA logo. Though Scottish and Channel had their own aircraft, it was by no means unusual to see Channel Islands Airways aircraft operating Scottish services, and vice versa. One day, in September, the author clearly remembers seeing two of the BEA Channel Viscounts on the apron at Sumburgh, the northern most point on the Scottish network! The interchange of aircraft was an operational necessity, but it did cause passengers a little confusion. For example at Southampton, the British Caledonian service to Glasgow departed at the same time as a BEA flight to Jersey. When the BEA service was operated by a Scottish aircraft, BCAL passengers sometimes tried to board the Viscount, because it said 'Scottish' on it and that's where they wanted to go! No one actually ever boarded the wrong aircraft, although one day a passenger did arrive at Southampton on the evening flight from Jersey who was booked on an Aer Lingus Jersey-Dublin aircraft. The twelve Channel Islands Viscounts were normally allocated as follows: five in Birmingham, four in Jersey, one in Guernsey, one in Gibraltar on lease to Gibair and the last on standby or maintenance. The Gibraltar aircraft was rotated periodically.

Apart from stopping BCAL passengers joining Jersey flights and dealing with mis-routed Dublin passengers, BEA at Southampton handled its first Trident 2 on September 30th when G-AVFK commanded by Captain Stone landed at Eastleigh Airport. It brought Southampton Football Club back from a match in Bilbao. Viscount G-AOHG had taken the team out to Spain and should have returned them, however, the aircraft went unserviceable at Bilbao and despite all the efforts of the BEA engineer who travelled with the Viscount, it could not be repaired until spares were flown out from London. The Trident flew the necessary parts and some more engineers out to Bilbao and then brought the 'Saints' home. Originally Operations decided to send the aircraft to Hurn because Southampton's runway was regarded as a little on the short side. However, as there was to be no outbound load from Southampton, Operations were persuaded to allow 'VFK to land at Eastleigh, which it duly did about 20.00.

BEA Travel Sales Division formed the fifth of Marking's divisions, whose task was to sell seats to the public on the other divisions passenger flights. For that it took responsibility for all the airlines sales offices at home and abroad, co-ordinated the work of the Sales Representatives and ran the airline's advertising campaign. Travel Sales also looked after the management of Silver Wing Surface Arrangements who organised inclusive tour holidays. Mr. P.C.F. Lawton, formerly Traffic and Sales Director, took control of the Division.

Division number six was British Air Services, which continued much as before, co-ordinating the operations of Cambrian and Northeast. The seventh division was BEA Cargo managed by J.L. Guy. BEA Cargo took control of the airline's cargo operations, principally through the operation of the all-freighter services by Merchantmen from the new Cargo Centre Europe at Heathrow. BEA Cargo quickly busied itself with researching the potential for new cargo routes, London to Helsinki and London to Lisbon emerging as potentially viable. BEA Air Tours was the eighth division and BEA Helicopters the ninth. Air Tours had completed its first year of operations on March 31st. It had carried 650,000 passengers and chalked up a small profit of £154,140, a hopeful sign for the future but an indication that the profit margins on charter flying were very small. The fleet of Comets had flown 16,800 revenue hours on IT flights and charters to BEA and Northeast. BEA Helicopters continued passenger services to the Scillies, and oil and gas field support flying. The bases at Aberdeen and Sumburgh were becoming increasingly busy with the hotting up of exploration work. From November 1st the company began to operate an Air Sea Rescue service from Aberdeen using an S.61. One helicopter had to be provided on standby for a call out twenty four hours a day throughout the year. It was equipped with a winch and specially trained crewmen who BEA recruited from the Royal Navy. The service was provided under contract to the Department of Trade. Engineers developed a portable winch that could be fitted to any of the S.61 fleet, giving BEAH Operations staff the flexibility to allocate any of the S.61s to the Search and Rescue duty. Before 1971 BEAH had been occasionally involved in Air Sea Rescue work. In 1968 an S.61 from Beccles had rescued the crew from an oil rig 110 miles off Flamborough Head when it broke away from its moorings in a Force Ten gale.

The tenth and final division was Sovereign Group Hotels, dealing with BEA's hotel interests. The ten divisions were served by a number of central departments covering areas like Finance, Public Relations, Air Safety, Personnel and Planning. Marking had high hopes that the new divisions would considerably increase the efficiency of the airline, because to put it in his own words; "People work better in small units." Rather than being a small cog in a very large wheel staff became larger cogs in smaller wheels!

One of the few European capital cities still outside the BEA network was the Icelandic capital, Reykjavik. From April 7th BEA remedied that by commencing a twice weekly service from London to Reykjavik. However for the winter schedules were reduced to a once weekly flight, on Sundays. The aircraft landed at the USAF base at Keflavik as the airfield at Reykjavik was too small for regular Trident flying. Icelandair was appointed as BEA's handling agent, and Tony Wadlow became BEA Representative Iceland and Greenland. He was assisted by two staff, a Station Superintendent and a Sales/Secretarial Assistant. BEA had to share an airport office with SAS, but a small town office was opened in Reykjavik. Winter conditions at Keflavik caused the airline some problems. One Captain remembers having to climb up a gantry to check the 'T' tail of his Trident 2 was properly de-iced in a Force Eight gale and driving sleet. He came down soaked to the skin, but very thankful he had been wise enough to bring a spare uniform with him. Loads to Iceland were never very large, and the route was axed soon after the formation of British Airways.

Three other new destinations were served from the beginning of the summer: Zagreb was linked with London twice a week from April 1st, Crete once a week from April 3rd and Leningrad (again once a week) from May 2nd. BEA did hope it may have been possible to serve further destinations in the Soviet Union, but such hopes were never fulfilled. The Leningrad route did not prove a great success, and like the one to Reykjavik it ceased soon after the emergence of British Airways.

When the summer schedules ended, on October 31st, several historical events occurred. The first of these was the ending of BEA services to Le Bourget. BEA had been flying into both Orly and Le Bourget since 1968, and gradually more and more services had been transferred to Orly. Now the time had come to entirely withdraw from Le Bourget, and the last movements were the arrival and departure of a Trident from London. BEO54 arrived at Le Bourget at 20.10, and departed as BEO57 at 20.40. The airline's staff at Le Bourget were transferred across to Orly. BEA Air Tours and Cambrian still flew into Le Bouget, their services being handled by Caledonian/BUA.

The second historic event was the retirement of the Comets from scheduled services. Since 1969 Comet operations had been greatly scaled down with the coming of the Trident 2s. By the summer of 1970 there were no scheduled Comet services at all, though G-APMA was retained as a standby aircraft. In the winter of 1970/71 aircraft shortages lead to G-APMA flying five services a week from London to Dublin, two a week to Bergen and one each to Malta and Paris. In addition Air Tours Comets were leased at various times due to the late delivery of the Trident 3s. For the summer of 1971 the airline was still short of capacity and G-APMA was retained, operating a limited programme of schedules to Dubrovnik, Glasgow, Helsinki and Malaga, amounting to a grand total of six flights a week. The swansong of Comet services took place on October 31st with a round trip between London and Malaga flown by G-APMA. The aircraft left London at 12.30 (BE130) arriving at Malaga at 15.10. Departure from the Spanish resort was at 15.55 (BE 131) with an arrival at Heathrow at 18.30. G-APMA was withdrawn from use and eventually scrapped at Heathrow,

The third significant event on October 31st was the withdrawal of Viscounts from the German internal network. By the summer only three Viscounts remained based in Berlin to fly services to Hamburg and Hanover. From November 1st Super 1-11s took over their commitments and the Viscounts returned to England. The last scheduled Viscount service was between Hanover and Berlin, flown by G-AOJB. Departure was at 20.40 (BE1380). However that was not quite the end of the Viscount story in Germany, because on November 1st G-AOJB flew an extra service from Berlin to Hanover as BE1351A. The aircraft then positioned direct to England. The withdrawal of the Viscounts from Germany improved BEA's competitive position on the routes, but it was sadly lamented by the Viscount crews who had always enjoyed their tours of duty in Berlin.

Earlier in the year the airline had begun to receive its new fleet of Trident 3s. The first to be delivered was G-AWZC on February 18th, followed by G-AWZB on February 24th, and 'WZD on March 26th. Much crew training was undertaken at the RAE airfield at Bedford, where G-AWZC was damaged in an incident just one day after its delivery. While 'WZC was on the runway another aircraft attempted to land and collided with the Trident damaging both aircraft. Even so on March 1st commercial operations with the Trident 3 began, with G-AWZB flying a London-Orly service. By November the Trident 3 fleet was serving a variety of destinations including Orly, Madrid, Milan, Palma, Pisa, Zurich, Geneva, Copenhagan, Oslo, Nice, Rome and Malta, the aircraft also flew the Birmingham-Malta services. Trident 3s could carry up to one hundred and forty passengers in an all economy class role, or one hundred and nineteen economy class and eighteen first class passengers. BEA and Hawker Siddeley were currently studying another version of the Trident able to carry two hundred passengers and use 3,000 foot airstrips, to be called RTOL (Reduced Take Off and Landing Aircraft). Like many other projects it did not see the light of day. Trident 3s were delivered equipped for Category 3B autoland, but the airline had yet to receive clearance to use the equipment under those conditions on commercial services.

BEA was particularly worried by the new of Rolls Royce bankruptcy. Apart from the Herons and helicopters the entire fleet was powered by Rolls Royce engines. The Viscounts had Darts, the Vanguards/Merchantmen Tynes, the Tridents and Super 1-11s Speys and Air Tours Comets Avons. The bankruptcy could mean a drying up of new engines and spares spelling disaster for the Corporation. Fortunately the problem did not materialize as a new company called Rolls Royce 1971 Limited was founded to carry on the engine production and development which had made Rolls so famous.

BEA's first fatal accident, since the loss of Comet G-ARCO in 1967, occurred on October 2nd with the loss of Vanguard G-APEC near Ghent. All fifty five passengers and eight crew were killed. The aircraft was flying the London-Salzburg schedule when it suffered a failure of the rear pressure bulkhead which triggered off a series of events leading to the flight controls to be tail being cut and the aircraft dived into the ground. As an immediate precaution all Vanguards were restricted to a cruising altitude of no more than 10,000 feet, or a cabin differential pressure of not more than three lbs per square inch. The fleet was checked for signs of corrosion around the rear bulkheads between October 8th and 10th and a modification was made, enabling the Vanguards to return to normal operations. Investigators found 'PEC's bulkhead had failed due to corrosion from a leaky rear toilet.

For some time the travelling public had complained that fares especially to Europe were too high. Consequently BEA launched a new type of excursion fare - APEX - or Advanced Purchase Excursion Fare. Bookings had to be made well ahead of the intended date of travel, but with APEX fares about 50% cheaper, who would worry? The success of APEX fares was immediate, and many other forms of special excursion fares followed, like IPEX (Instant Purchase Excursion Fare). From 1972 IPEX tickets were issued for passengers who were willing to wait to purchase a ticket until the day of departure. For those prepared to take the risk of a seat being available, even greater savings than with APEX were possible. Initially IPEX fares were offered to Paris, Amsterdam and Brussels. Like APEX, they were very successful and soon extended to include other destinations too. Other special saver fares were offered on particular routes, for example a £27.70 week-end return to Cologne/Bonn and a whole series of cheap fares to Scandinavia. They had to be booked two months prior to the date of travel, and a minimum stay of ten days was required. Typical examples were £43.70 return between London and Bergen, and £76.30 return between London and Helsinki. The only difficulty with all the new fares was the airline's reservations staff had to be on the ball to ensure passengers got the best fare for their particular circumstances. Fortunately 'Beacon' displayed all the options. However that was little help to the many sales offices still not connected to the computer. Travel agents encountered the same bewildering problem which only got worse as more and more airlines began offering various excusion fares. One agent complained that the whole system was as complicated as the Department of Health and Social Securities Benefit claims forms!

BEA's flights were threatened by a further round of industrial problems between aircrew and the management. BOAC pilots had recently gained a pay rise which greatly widened the differentials in pay between the two airlines. BEA crews decided that they should have parity with their BOAC colleagues, and put in for rises of between 35% and 60%. Management refused to agree, and the dispute escalated with a work to rule being imposed and the threat of a strike. The strike, planned for June, was averted and the dispute settled by a compromise by which the crews got large rises but not quite parity with BOAC. While the dispute was building up, another caused disruption. Engineers began a work to rule in support of a pay and conditions claim in December 1970 which lasted into January 1971, and culminated in a three day strike at London which effectively grounded all BEA flying from its main base. A few Heathrow bound flights were re-routed into Southampton with Viscount G-AOHT operating a round trip from Guernsey with London bound passengers, and Viscounts G-AOHH, 'OYN, and 'OJB flying similar trips from Jersey. Operations from Birmingham, Manchester, Glasgow and Berlin continued as normal. The loss of revenue caused by the strike, even though the dispute was soon settled, was substantial.

Poor time keeping had for a long time been a problem, especially at Heathrow. There was no doubt it caused passengers to switch to rival carriers, and equally there was no doubt that a lot of it was avoidable. Disembarkation was frequently held up by the slowness of the ramp staff to fetch the steps, and on time departures were often not achieved as the baggage handlers were slow to load baggage or the cargo or catering arrived late, or the traffic staff were slow in getting the flight boarded or a thousand and one other things. The airline decided to have a purge on punctuality, not only at Heathrow but at every station, and improvements were made. In the last quarter of 1970/71 only 78% of services had left their stand at Heathrow on time, but by May 1971 nearly 95% were doing so. The main ingredients in the purge were a publicity campaign to alert staff to the dangers of letting standards slip, and a competition to find the most punctual station. Several leagues were established for stations, depending on the number of flights they dealt with, and awards were given to the winner in each league. The urge to win did improve things, but it also lead to some 'cooking of the books'. Air Traffic delays were not counted because they were beyond the control of the airline, and it was amazing how many Air Traffic delays began to occur at stations where there had never been many before!

The year ended with BEA beginning to feel the effects of the new second force independent airline, Caledonian/BUA (later renamed British Caledonian). The government granted the company a licence to fly from Gatwick to Le Bourget from November 7th, using BAC 1-11 aircraft. Caledonian/BUA were permitted to operate up to four daily frequencies. Because of an agareement with the French over the total number of services allowed to be flown by British airlines from London to Paris, BEA had to give up four of its frequencies to allow Caledonian/BUA to operate much to its disgust. BEA complained to the government, without result. It was really this which finally made BEA pull out of Le Bourget and concentrate on Orly. Caledonian/BUA was also allowed to increase its schedules on the trunk routes from Gatwick to Edinburgh, Glasgow and Belfast, and the punctuality campaign at Heathrow took on a new urgency. Developments with Caledonian/BUA really brought home to the Corporation the need to put its own house in order as quickly as possible if it was to avoid losing large segments of its traffic on key routes. Yet BEA continued to have one major advantage over its rival, it flew from the more popular Heathrow with the vast array of inter-line connections, while Caledonian/BUA was confined to Gatwick.

1972

From its inception the British Airways Board had been busy investigating all apsects of BEA and BOAC operations to decide how best the two airlines could be managed. The product of their deliberation was three reports, published during the year. The first, issued in July, proposed the establishment of seven operating divisions under the overall management of the British Airways Board. The seven would be:

The BOAC Division.
The BEA Division, subdivided into Mainline, Super 1-11, Cargo and Air Tours.
The BAS Division, including Cambrian, Northeast, Scottish and Channel.
British Airways Helicopters (Formerly BEAH).
British Airways Engineering.
British Airways Associate Companies, to include all BEA and BOAC associate companies.
International Air Radio.

The report was accepted by the government, and the seven divisions became functional on September 1st. With the change, the position of BEA Chairman became less important. It was still necessary for BEA to have a Chairman because the airline was a legal corporation, but the Chairman of the BA Board was the more significant figure. The authority enjoyed by London Douglas and Anthony Milward had gone, and several changes in

Trident 3 G-AWZB at Heathrow's Terminal One. *(BA)*

A very clear photo of BEA Channel Islands V.802 G-AOHK at Heathrow. *(BA)*

Chairman occurred in quick succession. In September Marking left to become Group Managing Director of BA, and was succeeded by Ken Wilkinson. He stayed only until November, leaving BEA to become Managing Director of Rolls Royce 1971 Ltd. Wilkinson was followed by P.C.F. Lawton who continued as BEA Chairman and Chief Executive until January 1974. For the last three months of the Corporation's legal existence Roy Watts held the posts of Chairman and Chief Executive. The adoption of the new structure of seven divisions did not affect BEA operations very much, with the only real changes being that Helicopters, Channel and Scottish were no longer formally part of the airline. For the purposes of this book, however, mention will still be made of these three as they had been a part of BEA since 1947.

The second of the BA Board's reports was made in November. It simply suggested the single trading name of British Airways be adopted by BEA, BOAC, BAS and Helicopters. BEA would be British Airways European Divison, BOAC British Airways Overseas Division, and BAS British Airways Regional Division. Again the report was accepted by the government, and the single name came into use on September 1st 1973. The final report, also published in November, recommended that BEA, BOAC and BAS should be merged into one single airline, to be called British Airways. There it was .... after years of rumour and counter rumour the idea of merger had finally be proposed, and it was eagerly welcomed by the government. Target date for the merger was April 1st 1974, and the ensuing months saw a great deal of effort going into the question of how to accomplish such a massive task.

One immediate problem concerned a colour scheme. Clearly a single airline needed a new one, but in order to reflect the fact BA was a combination of BEA and BOAC it was thought desirable to include elements of each airlines existing colours. Negus and Negus were employed to come up with a suitable livery. When unveiled it included a white fuselage top and dark blue underside. The title 'British Airways' would appear on the forward cabin roof, as would a Speedbird reflecting the BOAC element. On the tail there appeared a quarter Union flag, based on the old BEA tail emblem. Some BEA staff felt aircraft should have red wings as BEA's had done, and a Manchester based First Officer Graham Faulkner (who was tragically killed in a road accident in 1986) drew up a petition to 'save and red wings', alas to no avail. The first BA aircraft to sport the new livery was BOAC Boeing 707 G-AXXY. In December 1973 the first BEA aircraft appeared in the new colours, Trident 3 G-AWZC. As a temporary measure BEA and BOAC aircraft had 'British Airways' painted on their fuselage tops instead of 'BEA' or 'BOAC'.

Though steps to merge BEA and BOAC were underway, BEA's own history was not quite ended. The 1971/72 Report and Accounts recorded a slim profit for the BEA Group of just £181,000. The poor performance was blamed on the level of inflation and the generally bad economic conditions. For the first time each of the airline's divisions had its own section in the Report and Accounts giving full details of its activities. Scanning the individual reports shows developments were still occurring on many fronts. The Super 1-11 Division took a step nearer all weather operations when its fleet of 1-11s received authorization to use their automatic landing equipment in Category 2 conditions. Meanwhile the Cargo Divison managed to regain some lost custom and increase revenue by 17%. Its route network was expanded to include Lisbon, and a through pallet service from Glasgow, Manchester, Birmingham and Dublin to Europe, via London. British Airways Cargo was to eventually extended this service to cover other British cities such as Bristol, Liverpool and Leeds. Bristol, Leeds and Liverpool did not become ports of call for the Merchantmen freighters. Instead the cargo was collected from the cities in large lorries, and in the process BA became the operator of a long distance road haulage fleet! Channel Islands Airways section in the Report recorded a welcome growth in passengers travelling on international services from Birmingham. The airline attributed the growth to the use of jets, in the shape of a Super 1-11 leased from the Super 1-11 Division, and a Trident IE, G-AVYE. The Trident had been delivered to Channel Islands Airways in January 1971, and generally flew the scheduled services from Birmingham to Paris and Dusseldorf, as well as some IT flights. Strangely enough the Division's headquarters was not at Birmingham, or even in Jersey, but at Hodford House in Hounslow. Hodford House also served as head office for BAS, and eventually became the head office for British Airways Regional.

BEA Travel Sales Division managed to earn 62% of the airline's passenger revenue from its sales outlets at home and abroad. Within the UK, twenty two sales shops were open to the public, and there was generally a sales office in each European town served by the airline. BEA had divided the UK into eleven sales districts, each with its own sales representative and sales shops. Each sales district was a mini profit centre. The moves towards the merger of BEA and BOAC were reflected in the opening of some joint sales shops, such as those at Croydon and Coventry, and the combining of sales offices in Birmingham, Newcastle, and London's Cheapside. By 1972 quite a few of the European sales offices were connected with 'Beacon', including those in Germany, Italy, Belgium, Sweden and Spain. About two hundred computer terminals were used by these offices. BEA still had the aim of connecting all the European sales shops to 'Beacon'. To improve sales facilities in key areas of the UK, a twenty four hours a day reservations service was made available. Direct phone lines to 'Beacon' were offered in London, Southampton, Bristol, Cardiff, Cambridge, Manchester, Leeds, Liverpool and Newcastle, and they were continuously manned on a shift system. The efficiency of 'Beacon' was improved by the addition of a facility to show an alternative flight if the flight on which a passenger was seeking to make a booking was full. Shortly before departure time the computer printed out a full passenger list, including any special information such as the need for a special meal or a wheelchair, and the lists were sent by telex to the appropriate station. The Travel Sales Division was responsible for the marketing of BEA's inclusive tours. Holidays from Europe to the UK, marketed under the title of Windsor Holidays, continued to be popular; but major expansion of IT packages from Britain to Europe took place with the formation of Sovereign Holidays. BEA had marketed a limited range of IT holidays under the Silver Wing banner for several years, but Sovereign Holidays was to offer a much more extensive range of holidays. First departures by 'Sovereign' occurred in November of 1971, although it was not until April 1972 that its full programme was launched. 'Sovereign' aimed to provide up market package holidays using BEA scheduled services, and its success was immediate. Sales were a full 100% above the target figure for the first year of operation! Few companies in any field could boast such a beginning. The success of 'Sovereign' lead BEA to start a second scheme of quality holidays, but at cheaper hotels, called 'Enterprise'. Enterprise Holidays used either BEA scheduled services, or capacity on Air Tours charter flights, and it too proved extremely successful.

The nearest thing to BEA Tristar, N305EA wearing BEA's logo at the 1972 Farnborough Air Show. *(BA)*

The 1971/72 Report and Accounts contained brief details of the operations of BEA Air Tours and BEA Helicopters. Air Tours flew 746,000 passengers and recorded a profit of £145,686. During 1972 its 'new' Boeing 707s began to operate trans Atlantic charters to the USA and Canada. Helicopters recorded a small operating profit on the Penzance-Scillies service for the first time. The company was building a new Engineering and Operations block at Aberdeen to cater for the boom in its oil related work, and had on its books a fleet of seven S.61s, a Bell 212, and a Jet Ranger. Six of the S.61s were used on oil support flying from Aberdeen, Sumburgh and Beccles, while the seventh operated the Isles of Scilly services. The Bell 212 generally resided at Beccles, and the Jet Ranger was available for general charters. However it spent much of its time carrrying Captain Cameron to the various stations from Helicopter's base at Gatwick.

BEA's associate company, Gibair, found it increasingly difficult to make ends meet with Viscount operations between Gibraltar and Tangier, and was very glad to receive some unexpected charter business in 1971/72. Its Viscount was chartered by Royal Air Maroc. The Moroccan airline was short of aircraft to operate domestic services, and leased the Viscount to fill the gap. As Gibair's requirments for flying were only in the morning and evening, the aircraft was free for most of the middle of the day, and it was in that time Royal Air Maroc used it. Because Gibair's aircraft was a BEA Channel Viscount on lease, BEA aircraft and crews found themselves operating into some most unusual airfields. BEA Mainline crews also found themselves flying into an unusual Moroccan airfield, when the Division launched a weekly Trident service from London to Agadir, via Gibraltar. Flights began on November 5th! Apart from the Agadir route a number of other new services were launched:

Date	Route	Frequency	Type	Division
April 1st	London to Marseilles	Three times weekly	Trident	Mainline
April 1st	Manchester to Geneva	Three times weekly	S.1-11	S.1-11
April 1st	Manchester to Munich	Three times weekly	S.1-11	S.1-11
May 3rd	London to Cagliari	Once weekly	S.1-11	Mainline
May 7th	Jersey to Amsterdam	Once weekly	Viscount	CI

On the debit side Ankara disappeared from the network with the departure of BE477 to Istanbul and London on Tuesday October 31st. Ankara had been served since 1946, and BEA did hope that traffic might soon improve to allow it to be re-connected to London. This hope finally materialized in 1988! The airline, did however, keep a sales office in the Turkish capital. Also on October 31st the operating agreement with Air France on the German internal network came to an end, the last joint flight being between Frankfurt and Berlin (BE/AF1856). BEA reverted to flying the services to Frankfurt and Munich in its own right, and the Super 1-11 fleet was gradually re-painted in the new British Airways colour scheme as each aircraft came up for overhaul.

During the course of the year, BEA ended first class travel on domestic services. A limited number of first class seats had been available on certain Vanguard and Trident services from London to Belfast, Edinburgh and Glasgow. Demand for the service had been tailing off and on March 31st BEA ended the facility. As a concession to those requiring a little bit of extra leg room and comfort, some flights offered bookable seats in the rear compartment of Vanguards and the forward cabin of Tridents. A £2 supplement was charged, unless a passenger was travelling on from London first class, in which case he received one free. The Vanguards and Trident 2s offered eight bookable seats, the Trident 1 twelve and the Trident 3 fourteen.

The months of June to September brought the traditional summer rush, complicated by ATC congestion over Europe. Such was the volume of aircraft flying through French and Spanish airspace that ATC facilities were swamped. A system of rationing was imposed allowing only so many aircraft per hour into their airspace. Each flight was given a slot time for entry into French or Spanish airspace, often leading to long delays in departure times. At busy week-ends passengers were kept waiting for up to five hours, and BEA schedules were thrown into confusion.

In this peak period, the blackest day in BEA's history occurred with the loss of Trident 1 G-ARPI. On June 18th 'RPI was scheduled to operate BE548 from London to Brussels, with a 16.45 departure. The Captain for the service was Stanley Key, and with him in the cockpit were two Second Officers, Jeremy Keighley and Simon Ticehurst. The flight was fully booked, and departure was briefly delayed while some cargo was off loaded to provide sufficient extra weight to take on a positioning crew, who travelled on jump seats in the cabin and cockpit. Eventually at 17.08 'RPI departed, but only three minutes later it plunged into the ground near the Crooked Billet roundabout on the Staines by-pass, and all on board died. Investigation showed the Trident's leading edge droop flaps had retracted too soon, causing the aircraft to enter a deep stall from which recovery is impossible in a 'T' tailed aircraft like the Trident. Why the droop flaps were retracted has never been established. Captain Key was possibly suffering from some heart pain and may have made a mistake, or one of the other pilots may have retracted them without the others noticing, or there may simply have been a mechanical fault. Certainly the accident highlighted the need to give crews more thorough training in the whole matter of stalls, and the use of the aircraft stick shaker system. The stick shaker system was designed to warn of a stall and push the control column forward to stop it. The loss of 'RPI did not deter the Queen, Prince Philip and Princess Anne from flying in a Trident 3 (G-AWZV) in October to commence their state visit to Yugoslavia. Exactly a year before, in October 1971, the Royal family had begun a state visit to Turkey by flying from London to Ankara in a BEA Trident 2, the aircraft used being G-AVFE, commanded by Captain Charles Owen.

BEA

1973

January 1st dawned with thick fog blanketing much of the country. It was so thick at Heathrow that the Tridents and Super 1-11s could not use their autoland equipment because visibility was below even Category 3A requirements. Two days before, on December 30th, aviation history had been made when a Trident 3 made an automatic landing on a commercial service in Category 3A conditions for the first time. Flights were diverted mainly to Birmingham and Manchester, though Southampton received five Viscounts from Channel Isles and a Vanguard (G-APEH) from Belfast. When the Vanguard landed there were already two Viscounts on the apron and the Corporation's small staff were full stretched. Some off duty soldiers travelling on the Vanguard were enlisted to help unload its baggage!

Unfortunately January had worse in store for the airline, with the loss of Viscount G-AOHI in Scotland on the 19th of the month. The aircraft had undergone maintenance at Abbotsinch and took off for a test flight, with a crew of four on board. During the flight 'OHI crashed into the side of Ben More mountain and all four lost their lives. The cause was not technical malfunction, but pilot error in misreading the altimeter. G-AOHI was the last aircraft of the old BEA Group to be lost before the merger with BOAC.

On a more happy note, BEA handled its first wide bodied jet at Heathrow on January 8th; when the Turkish airline THY used a DC-10 on its Istanbul-London flight. No problems were encountered in handling the aircraft (TC-JAV), and the THY DC-10s became regular visitors to London in the months ahead. Handling the DC-10 was a useful exercise for BEA staff, who were preparing for the delivery of their own wide bodied jet, the Tristar. Later in the month a Channel Islands Viscount visited two airfields rarely used by the BEA Group, Leeds and Norwich. The aircraft was chartered by Leeds United Football Club to fly the team across to Norwich for a match.

The last new type to enter service with the BEA Group before the merger with BOAC was the Short Skyliner, which replaced the Herons in Scotland in the spring. On March 8th the first of two Skyliners, G-AZYW, arrived at Abbotsinch and began crew training. It flew the type's first commercial service on Monday April 2nd when it worked the 08.30 (BE8746) Glasgow to Tiree schedule. Later in the morning 'ZYW flew a direct Glasgow-Barra service. Until the second aircraft (G-BAIT) arrived on April 20th, the schedule of a daily direct service to both Tiree and Barra was maintained by G-AZYW. Once the second aircraft was in service, the Skyliners took over flights to Campbeltown and Islay. The full programme for the aircraft in the summer of 1973 was:

Aircraft 1

Glasgow (09.05)-Campbeltown-Glasgow (10.40).
Daily except Sunday.

Glasgow (11.10)-Barra-Glasgow (13.45).
Daily except Sunday.

Glasgow (12.10)-Barra-Glasgow (14.45).
Sunday.

Glasgow (14.15)-Islay-Glasgow (15.55).
Monday and Friday.

Glasgow (16.25)-Islay-Glasgow (18.05).
Daily except Sunday.

Aircraft 2

Glasgow (09.25)-Islay-Glasgow (11.05)
Daily except Sunday.

Glasgow (11.35)-Tiree-Glasgow (13.45).
Daily except Sunday.

Glasgow (14.15)-Tiree-Glasgow (16.25).
Monday and Friday.

Glasgow (16.55)-Campbeltown-Glasgow (18.30).
Daily except Sunday.

After November 1st Skyliner schedules were modified to include Aberdeen and Inverness:

Aircraft 1

Glasgow (07.55)-Aberdeen-Glasgow (10.10).
Monday to Friday.

Inverness (11.15)-Glasgow (12.15).
Sunday.

Glasgow (10.40)-Tiree-Barra-Tiree-Glasgow (14.30).
Monday to Friday.

Glasgow (15.05)-Aberdeen-Glasgow (17.20).
Monday to Friday.

Glasgow (19.30)-Inverness (20.30).
Saturday.

Aircraft 2
Glasgow (08.10)-Islay-Glasgow (09.50)
Daily except Sunday.
Glasgow (10.20)-Campbeltown-Glasgow (11.55).
Daily except Sunday.
Glasgow (12.55)-Islay-Glasgow (14.35).
Daily except Sunday.
Glasgow (16.30)-Campbeltown-Glasgow (18.05).
Daily except Sunday.

Unlike the Herons the Skyliners were not used on air ambulance duties, as Loganair took over ambulance flying on April 1st. Also unlike the Herons the Skyliners did not last long in BEA/BA service. Herons had served for eighteen years, but the Skyliners managed only four before they were sold off in Norway. Nevertheless in their short time of operation with Scottish Airways they did provide a faster, smoother and more comfortable ride than the Herons.

BEA's Vanguards were gradually being phased out of passenger work over the course of the year. By the end of the year G-APEA, 'PEB and 'PED had been scrapped, and G-APEF and 'PEN had both been sold to Templewood Aviation for resale. G-APEI was earmarked for leasing to Silver City Airways, though the lease fell through and it joined G-APEH, 'PER and 'PEU on passenger work. The remainder of the Vanguard fleet had been, or was in the process of being converted to Merchantman standard. Summer scheduled passenger flights by Vanguard were few and far between. The only international services were a Wednesday, Saturday and Sunday London-Salzburg flight, and a Sunday London-Gibraltar flight. On the domestic network there were twelve Vanguard flights a week between London and Belfast, eleven from London to Jersey, seven from London to Edinburgh and seven from Jersey to Birmingham. After November 1st the programme was even more restricted, with only three scheduled Vanguard flights a week, one to Gibraltar and two to Edinburgh. The rest of the time the four aircraft acted as standby aircraft for Tridents or operated charters. However the final passenger service to be flown with a Vanguard did not occur until after BEA had ceased to exist. The event took place on June 16th 1974 with G-APEU flying a round trip between Heathrow and Jersey. It was a tribute to the versatility of the Viscount that despite being older than the Vanguard it outlived the Vanguard in passenger service.

The 1972/73 Report and Accounts was, for the first time, produced under the British Airways title, with a section dealing with BEA finances. It showed BEA (excluding Scottish and Channel) had made a profit of about £477,000, a minute figure when compared with the total revenue of £173,866,000. Even so it was nearly four times the profit of the previous year, and the Corporation was gratified to find its average passenger load fact had crept up to 57%. The results were achieved without the handicap of Scottish and Channel Islands services, the traditional loss makers. Their losses of about £1.7 million would have more than wiped out the profit of the other divisions, had they been included. Despite its loss of £750,000 Scottish Airways was not despondent because loads were up 15%, a continued benefit from the oil boom in Scotland. Scottish costs were kept high by the need to maintain traffic handling units at stations which only received one or two flights a day, like Barra, Benbecula and Tiree. Further difficulties were created by the weather, and the poor navigation aids. Viscount flights out of Sumburgh were still uneconomic, despite the oil boom, because of the runway limitations. With hills at either end of the runway, approaches to Sumburgh were never easy, aircraft normally having to fly a curved approach path. Sumburgh's other speciality was 'gale force fog', blotting out the airfield for days at a time, and making operations impossible. Weather problems were by no means confined to Shetland. With only basic navigational aids at most of the Scottish Island airfields (only Stornoway had ILS) pilots adopted unusual tactics to beat the weather. At Islay, for example, bad weather approaches were made by following the Island's main road until it passed the airfield. The author experienced this in action on a wet windy summer's morning. After a short delay at Campbeltown while the crew obtained the latest Islay weather, the Viscount took off for the short hop across to Islay. It flew below the cloud at a height of well below 1,000 feet. When the coast of Islay was crossed, the aircraft banked round and picked up the main road which ran along the coast. The road was followed, still at well below 1,000 feet, until the airfield was sighted. A tight circuit followed and a successful landing was made. Once on the ground mail, newspapers and urgently needed cargo was off-loaded as well as twenty or so passengers, illustrating the vital social service provided by BEA Scottish.

The Report and Accounts highlighted a further area of concern, the German internal services. The financial year produced a 14½% drop in passengers, partly through competition from Pan American, but mainly thanks to the East German government relaxing its controls on surface links to West Berlin. If the results in Scotland, the CI and Germany were poor, the Cargo Division presented something of a contrast. BEA Cargo carried an extra 28,000 tons of freight in 1972/73, bringing the total uplifted for the year to 140,000 tons. Merchantman loads were good, and planning was well in hand for the opening of a number of new all-cargo routes, including London to Barcelona, Hamburg and Hanover.

In line with normal practice the Report and Accounts contained comprehensive data on operations. It showed BEA Mainline and Super 1-11 Division had collectively offered 18 million seats for sale, of which 10½ million had been purchased, to give the 57% load factor. Flight simulators had 'flown' 16,800 hours and the sale of time on them to other airlines had produced an additional £160,000 income for the airline. Most flight training was now being done at Prestwick, Bedford and Nicosia for Trident, and Teeside for the Super 1-11. Aircraft utilisation for Mainline, Super 1-11 Division and Cargo Division was as follows:

Type	Average Hours Flown per Aircraft	% Variation on 1971/72
Trident 3	2,150	+ 4%
Trident 2	2,408	–11%
Trident 1	2,084	– 2%
Super 1-11	2,538	– 2%
Vanguard	2,007	– 6%
Merchantman	1,825	+ 2%

BEA Air Tours reported a profit of £88,007 rather lower than in the previous year and a further proof of the risky nature of IT charter flying. Air Tours year included the company's first round the world charters, using Boeing 707s. Over the winter of 1972/73 two such charters were completed, one lasting a month, and the second three weeks. One aircraft was used for each charter, and one crew remained with the aircraft throughout, resting at the various stop over points. On October 31st 1973 Air Tours retired its Comets from service. The final Air Tours Comet charter was a round trip from Gatwick to Le Bourget for the National Union of Students Travel Service. The aircraft used a G-ARJL, which had inaugurated Air Tours flying three years before. The Comet fleet was sold off, mainly to Dan Air who got another ten years flying out of the type.

BEA role in Malta's civil air transport underwent a major change in 1973. For nearly thirty years BEA had been a major shareholder in Malta Airlines, and had always operated services for the company. In 1973 the Maltesse government decided to re-organise its airline activity and it purchased BEA's shares in Malta Airlines. It wound up Malta Airlines, and replaced it with an entirely Maltesse owned airline called Air Malta. Shares in Air Malta were held partly by the Maltesse government and partly by private business interests. National pride and a growing anti-British feeling were the main reasons behind the move. Air Malta was to buy its own aircraft, although in the short term while the necessary finances were arranged and purchases made, BEA was contracted to operate services for Air Malta. They would be flown under a joint BE/KM flight prefix, and for the winter of 1973/74 provided for a daily service from Malta to Rome, six flights a week to London, two to Tripoli and one to Manchester. Air Malta's own Boeing 720s eventually arrived in 1975 and the British Airways (as BEA had by then become) involvement ceased.

The poor financial performance for 1972/73 did not deter the various parts of the BEA Group from commencing of new services:

Date	Route	Frequency	Type	Division
April 1st	London to Thesalonika	Three times weekly	Trident	Mainline
April 2nd	London to Casablanca (via Gibraltar)	Twice weekly	Trident	Mainline
April 2nd	Manchester to Milan	Four times weekly	S. 1-11	S. 1-11
May 3rd	Guernsey to Amsterdam	Once Weekly	Viscount	CI
May 4th	London to Catania	Once Weekly	Trident	Mainline
June 1st	Berlin to Sylt	Four times weekly	S. 1-11	S. 1-11

The Manchester-Milan service was technically not a new route, but an old one revived, while the Berlin-Sylt schedule was a holiday route for Berliners. Sylt is part of the Frisian Islands and a popular holiday destination with Berliners. The Sylt service was not the first holiday route to be planned from Berlin. Back in the 1960s there had been talk of a Berlin-Klagenfurt holiday service, and a schedule was even produced, though the service was never actually launched. The Casablanca service lasted only until October, as BCAL appealed against the awarding of the licence to BEA. BCAL's appeal succeeded, and the route was transferred to BCAL.

Some thought was given to up dating existing services too. New through flights, via Manchester, from Belfast to Geneva and Edinburgh to Amsterdam began. Travellers from Birmingham on Channel Islands Airways Division flights to the continent benefitted from the greater use of BAC 1-11s, initially Super 1-11s leased from the Super 1-11 Division, but after November BAC 1-11.400s operated by the CI Division. The British Airways Board had ordered three 1-11.400s for the regional network from Birmingham; and the first, G-BBMG, entered regular service on November 1st. Once it had arrived the Trident 1E used by the CI Division on its Paris and Dusseldorf routes out of Birmingham was transferred to Northeast Airlines. Scottish Airways also entered the jet scene with the operation of a Super 1-11 on one of its week-day London to Aberdeen schedules. The Super 1-11 offered a thirty five minute time saving over the Viscount, which still flew twenty of the twenty five weekly flights between London and Aberdeen.

Severe competition from IT charter traffic was continuing to affect loads on BEA's scheduled services to holiday destinations. Services had been progressively trimmed back to reduce losses, producing a marked effect on some routes. For example in 1968 the airline had flown eighteen services a week from the UK to Palma, but by 1973 the number had been cut to only seven. A similar story existed in the case of Malta where the frequencies dropped from thirty six to twenty flights a week over the same period. Some routes had entirely disappeared, like Birmingham-Barcelona and Manchester-Palma. At the end of the summer season in 1973 two others joined them, with the ending of the twice weekly Trident service to the Norwegian holiday centre of Bergen, and the weekly Birmingham-Malta services. Of course the existence of BEA Airtours did enable BEA to gain some traffic back by having a share in the IT marked, but increasingly BEA itself was chartering aircraft to tour companies for night flights to holiday destinations. Sometimes a rather bizarre situation arose, with one division of BEA competing against another or Airtours for IT contract work. The other way adopted to counter competition from charter operators was to sell even more seats on scheduled flights to tour companies, 'Sovereign' and 'Enterprise' being the obvious targets.

As the Commercial Departments were busy looking for tour work, the Reservations Unit continued to extend the use of 'Beacon'. The most significant extension to the reservations system was the centralizing of telephone reservations into four regional centres linked direct to the computer. The four regional centres were Belfast, Glasgow, Manchester and London. Those wanting to make telephone reservations in Northern Ireland 'phoned a Belfast number, those in Scotland a Glasgow number, those in the North of England a Manchester number, and those in the South a London number. The numbers took them direct to 'Beacon', and the 'phone calls were only charged at local rates, BEA paying the GPO a sum to cover the rest of the costs. In Germany a similar system was used, with a 'phone link to Berlin. Next the computer was adapted to print out passenger tickets, producing a considerable saving in time and improving accuracy. The scheme was an unqualified success, and the airline began to install printers linked to the computer in sales offices. The computer could print out a ticket in a matter seconds, and in time it took to write out a single ticket 'Beacon' printed out half a dozen. BEA was promoted in a most unlikely location during the year, Peking. BEA's Japanese Sales Representative attended a British exhibition in Peking to spread the BEA message, though it is doubtful he generated much traffic since China was still very restrictive about allowing its citizens to travel abroad. The value of having an off-line Sales Office in Tokyo was, however, enormous; because Japanese businessmen made frequent trips to Europe and there was plenty of demand for BEA services.

From September 1st, BEA began to trade as British Airways European, while Scottish Airways, Channel Islands Airways, Cambrian and Northeast traded as British Airways Regional. Apart from the change in name there was little obvious effects on day to day operations. The biggest problem faced by the whole British Airways group occurred late in the year, and was once again the result of a situation totally outside the control of the airline. The crisis was a severe shortage of fuel and soaring prices for what was available. Fuel prices rose in some places by almost 300%. The reason for the shortages and rising prices was the Arab-Israeli dispute. As part of their campaign the Arabs decided to restrict oil supplies to the West in retaliation for the West's support of Israel. Soon there was not enough fuel to go round, and the government ordered all airlines to reduce their consumption by 40% between November 20th and December 31st. BEA had to cancel many flights, re-route others, and combine still more. To try to save fuel the airline experimented by shutting down the third engine on Tridents while cruising. All that did was to raise the temperature, and shorten the life, of the other two and the idea was quickly abandoned. A small saving in fuel was achieved by reducing cruising speeds. The four remaining passenger Vanguards came into their own, being much more fuel efficient than Tridents. They were substituted for Tridents on as many domestic trunk services as possible. BEA put in for an increase in fares to cover the rising fuel costs, and Air Tours levied a £3 surcharge on all passengers to help cover its costs.

The situation quickly became chaotic, with fuel supplies actually running out at some stations. Operations Departments in each section of BA set up special units to monitor the situation and route flights via those airfields where fuel could be picked up. Things became so bad that Henry Marking, speaking for the BA Group as a whole, warned that the airline could not guarantee to carry all those passengers who had bookings over the Christmas period. Eventually by careful fuel management passengers were successfully moved, all be it sometimes at different times, on different routes and by different aircraft types from those envisaged. The fuel crisis eased at the beginning of 1974 although there were two lasting effects from it; firstly fuel prices did not go down to the pre-crisis levels, and secondly neither did air fares. Purchasing of aviation fuel became the airline's chief expense after the oil crisis, and many schemes were evaluated to try to reduce the bill by making fuel go as far as possible. Operations staff worked out, in great detail, the most economic cruising speeds and heights for each type; and Air Traffic Control did all it could to reduce delays and give flights more direct routing wherever possible.

1974

The last three months of BEA's legal existence commenced with the withdrawal of check-in facilities at West London Air Terminal from January 1st. Since BEA had begun flying in August 1946 a town terminal check-in service had been provided in London, although the location had changed on several occasions. The airline's Board had made a study of the use of West London's check-in facilities in 1973 and concluded the service could be scrapped as the number of passengers using it was falling. The ever widening ownership of private cars and the improving coach links from the suburbs of London help to explain the decline in the use of WLAT. With the removal of passenger check-in went the removal of a specific coach departure from WLAT for each flight. Coaches continued to run to Heathrow but passengers could join any coach they liked. They were offered a frequent service with coaches running at ten minute intervals between 06.20 and 22.00. For the handful of flights outside those hours, a specific coach departure was laid on leaving WLAT just over an hour before take-off time. Overall the number of coach journeys was reduced by about 20%, producing a useful saving in petrol costs, which like aviation fuel, had rocketed in price thanks to the 1973 oil crisis.

BEA purchased two Skyliners to replace Herons, G-AZYW in basic BEA Scottish livery, but with British Airways titles, is seen near Tiree.
(Short Brothers.)

At Heathrow passengers on domestic services had been checking-in at the departure gate since April 1973, using the check-in desks in the main hall only to deposit heavy baggage. As the experiment had produced encouraging results in reducing delays and speeding up departures, it was decided to extend it to international flights too. From January Paris passengers checked-in at the gate, and from April 1st all international passengers did. The system worked well for all but those who arrived at the airport too late to deposit their heavy baggage at the normal desks. They had to take their cases to the gate themselves, which could be quite a walk – or run! The baggage trolleys provided by the British Airports Authority were turned into racing machines as passengers hurtled through the Terminal en route for their gate, and not a few innocent bystanders, who did not get out of the way quickly enough, got the backs of their legs quite bruised by collisions with the racing trolleys and their drivers.

The work load for airline staff in Terminal One was tremendous. Between April 1972 and March 1973 BEA staff there dealt with 7½ million passengers flying on BEA, Cyprus Airways, Malta Airlines, and British Midland flights. With such figures the odd item of misrouted baggage is perhaps a little easier to understand, but the poor passenger who arrived at his destination to find his case was not on board was not usually the most understanding person. BEA ran a Lost and Found Unit to trace missing cases, which had the habit of turning up in the most amazing places. The prize for missing baggage must go, however, not to Temrinal One but Jersey. On one busy summers afternoon a Vanguard departed for Heathrow with about one hundred passengers on board. When it arrived and the baggage holds were opened, they were found to be empty. All the cases were still on the back of a lorry in Jersey!

A major customer services improvement being contemplated by the airline in the early months of 1974, was the opening of a shuttle service between London and Glasgow. The idea had been around for some time, as noted earlier, but now active steps were taken to introduce it. The shuttle concept was to provide for an hourly departure from London and Glasgow, with no prior reservations being necessary. Passengers simply turned up to join the flight. To ensure all who did turn up could be accommodated, back up aircraft would be available for each departure. Tickets were to be sold by the cabin crew on board, and a seat was guaranteed to anybody who arrived at least ten minutes before take off time. The aim was to offer a no frills service with fares being as low as possible. No shuttle service began before BEA was disolved, but they did come soon afterwards. British Airways launched the London-Glasgow shuttle on January 12th 1975, and its success lead to the beginning of a similar service to Edinburgh in April 1976, Belfast in April 1977 and Manchester in 1979. Some international routes, chiefly London-Amsterdam and Paris, seemed good candidates for shuttle services too, although considerable difficulties have been encountered in trying to bring in international shuttle operations. At the time of writing (1988) none had commenced, and neither are there any immediate plans for them to do so.

Alongside preparations for the beginning of domestic shuttle services, went preparations for the entry into service of the L.10 Tristar. A complex flight simulator was being built in Britain and a basic cockpit procedure trainer was also under construction. The engineering training programme was well underway, and engineering facilities at the Heathrow Base had been extended to accommodate the large aircraft. Lockheed planned to deliver the first L.10 at the end of 1974, and they kept their word, enabling BA to commence Tristar operations of January 12th 1975 with a London-Malaga service. The engineers devised a plan to convert one of the Merchantman freighters into a swing tail aircraft to carry spare RB 2-11 engines for stranded Tristars. The scheme no doubt owed something to the memory of the purchase of the Bristol 170 in 1950 to carry spare Elizabethan engines. A swing tailed Merchantman would certainly have been a unique Vanguard. However the conversion never took place, because a cheaper alternative was found - agreements with foreign airlines to use their spares. The Merchantman fleet did make a number of trans Atlantic crossings in connection with the Tristar programme, going out to America to fetch Tristar seats and spares. These flights occurred after the merger with BOAC. Like the Tridents and Super 1-11s the Tristars were equipped with automatic landing facilities meaning a substantial proportion of the BA short haul fleet could now beat most of the winter weather. By March 1974 the Tridents had notched up a grand total of 27,000 commercial automatic landings proving the value of the system.

The financial results for 1973/74 showed a profit of £6,699,000 excluding the results of Scottish Airways, and Channel Islands Airways, both being part of BA Regional. The profit, the largest ever made by BEA, was earned despite the fuel shortages, dramatic rise in fuel prices and continued inflation. The airline recorded an increase in passengers carried from 8,199,121 to 8,743,031, an extra 543,910 which was more than the total number of passengers carried by BEA in its first full year of operations! Some routes showed a very healthy growth, London to Istanbul topping the league with a 140% rise in passengers carried. A more modest, but still very encouraging, growth of 24% was recorded on international services out of Manchester. Though cheered by that figure, the Super 1-11 Division was very concerned with a continued fall in passengers on the German internal network, with the continued aggresive competition from Pan American coupled with the easier surface access to West Berlin. Eventually traffic slumped for both airlines to such a degree that they were forced to reach an operating agreement to share out the traffic. BA gave up flights from Berlin to Frankfurt, Hamburg and Munich leaving Pan Am as the sole carrier, and Pan Am gave up its Berlin-Cologne/Bonn, Dusseldorf and Hanover services.

Scottish and Channel Islands operations continued to be grossly unprofitable. Both airlines made extensive use of Viscounts and as these aircraft were coming up for twenty years old some thought had to be given to a replacement for them. Just as with the issue of replacing the Rapide, it was no easy task to select a type to replace the Viscount, and in the end British Airways came up with a dual solution. Most of the Viscount routes in Scotland were taken over by HS748 aircraft, and most of the remaining Viscount routes flown by Channel, Cambrian and Northeast were simply given up. The BA Board placed an order for two forty four seater HS 748s in May 1974, the first step towards the operation of a larger fleet. The 748 had the advantage of being able to carry a full load out of Shetland and use the crosswind runway there, neither of which the Viscount could achieve. From 1975 until 1982 Viscounts and 748s operated alongside each other in Scotland, but in May 1982 the Viscounts were finally retired and replaced with more 748s. Outside of Scotland, most British Airways Viscount routes were closed down on March 31st 1980. The entire Channel Islands network went, with the exception of London-Jersey and Manchester-Jersey flights. For the first time since 1947 the nationalized airline did not fly into Guernsey or Southampton. Also closed on March 31st 1980 were the ex-Cambrian and Northeast route networks from Cardiff, Bristol, Leeds, Liverpool, and the Isle of Man; and services from Newcastle were severely curtailed. A slight reversal of the trend had occurred by 1987, with direct services to Jersey operating from Aberdeen, Edinburgh and Dusseldorf as well as London and Manchester, and Southampton had been re-connected to the network with an HS748 schedule to Aberdeen via Birmingham (since abadoned).

At midnight on March 31st 1974 BEA (and BOAC) formally ceased to exist under the terms of the Air Corporation's (Disolution) Order 1973. Just as the birth of the Corporation went virtually unnoticed in August 1946, so did its death. No publicity marked the event, there was no ceremony, and no record even appears to exist of which aircraft flew the final service. The timetable suggests it was a Trident operating BE943 from Dublin which landed at London Heathrow at 23.30. The absence of any attempt to mark the occasion is easily explained, BEA was simply continuing to operate as British Airways, and of course its services had been flown as BA European Division anyway since September 1973. The airline had come full circle, it emerged in 1946 out of BOAC and ended up in 1974 merging with BOAC.

There are many fascinating comparisons between the state of the airline in 1946 and 1974. If the fleets of BA Scottish, BA Channel and BAH are included, the airline had one hundred and twenty two aircraft on its books on March 31st 1974; sixty one Tridents, nineteen BAC 1-11s, twelve Vanguard/Merchantman, nineteen Viscounts, two Skyliners and nine helicopters. In 1947, after the merger with the AAJC companies, the number was not dissimilar standing at one hundred and twenty five aircraft; twenty nine Vikings, twenty two DC-3s, thirty nine Rapides, ten JU52s, thirteen Avro 19s, seven communications aircraft and five helicopters. While the fleet size may have been roughly equal the passenger carrying capacity was not. In 1947 the total fleet could produce about 2,000 seats daily, whereas in 1974 the total was more like 10,000. Passengers carried had risen from 511,522 in BEA's first full year of operations (1947/48) to 8.7 million in the last and revenue had gone up accordingly from £3.5 million to £212.8 million, although inflation helps to explain some of the magnitude of the increase.

The comfort in which passengers travelled had changed greatly over the course of the years. In 1946 Vikings chugged along at between 6,000 and 8,000 feet and at a speed of about 120 mph, catching the worst of the weather and turbulence. In 1974 a Trident whisked passengers to their destination at 30,000 feet and 600 mph far above the worst of the bad weather. Gone were the rugs, needed in the early days to keep passengers feet warm, and the aircrews plastic macs needed to keep rain off their legs as it dripped into the cockpit of the Vikings or DC-3. Gone too was the noise and vibration of the old piston types. Everything was now smooth, quiet and slick. There had been great progress, as flying turned from a rich man's game to an accepted part of everyday life for millions. The increased popularity of air travel is well illustrated by comparing the number of BEA departures from Northolt on a typical Wednesday in August 1947, with the number of BEA departures from Heathrow on a typical Wednesday in August 1973. In 1947 there were twenty five departures from Northolt to twenty destinations at home and abroad, fifteen flown by Vikings, and the rest by DC-3s. In 1973 the equivalent day had one hundred and sixty departures to sixty destinations, one hundred and twenty six flown by Tridents, seventeen by Viscounts, ten by Super 1-11s and the remaining seven by Vanguards. (For a full comparison of the movements at Northolt and Heathrow for the months of August 1947 and August 1973 see Appendix 6). Most passengers approved of the progress. A few, however, lamented the passing of the very personal attention the passengers received in the early days and of the piston driven aircraft, regarding jet travel as a little like hurtling through the sky in a small narrow metal tube!

With the improvements in aircraft, journey times had become considerably quicker in 1974 as the table shows:

Typical Flying Times (Hours and Minutes)

Route	**1947 (Viking)**	**1958 (Viscount)**	**1974 (Trident)**
London to Amsterdam	1.20	1.05	.55
London to Athens	11.05	6.35	3.25
London to Berlin	4.45	3.25	1.40
London to Copenhagen	3.20	2.25	1.40
London to Gibraltar	7.55	4.20	2.35
London to Istanbul	26.30 (including a night-stop)	8.50	3.35
London to Oslo	5.00	2.55	1.55
London to Paris	1.30	1.05	1.00
London to Rome	6.30	3.20	2.15
London to Stockholm	5.25	4.35	2.15

Quicker flights did not necessarily mean quicker city centre to city centre journey times, especially on shorter routes. Roads to and from the major airports, especially London, were becoming increasingly busy and congested. Half an hour might have been saved on the flight to Paris by the use of a jet, but more than likely it would take over an hour to reach London Airport and another good hour to reach the centre of Paris. With such decreases in flying time the utilization of aircraft was much higher in 1974. In 1947 one Viking could just about manage to operate one round trip to Rome in a day, whereas by 1974 a Trident could operate a return service over the same route and still be available for another two or three sectors. This helps to explain why the fleet size was roughly similar at the beginning and the end, and yet the network so much larger in 1974.

The tremendous expansion of the airline meant staffing levels had rocketed. In 1946 there had been just 1,641 staff, increasing to 5,731 once the AAJC companies were absorbed. In 1974 there were a grand total of 24,403, including those working for Scottish, Channel and Helicopters. In keeping with the growth, the Board had expanded from six members to eleven, although none of the founding Board members were still serving by 1974. It will be the memory of the personnel involved in BEA that will remain in peoples minds. There were certainly some very able men and women employed at all levels in the airline. Lord Douglas and Peter Masefield probably stand out as the two who did most to get the Corporation on a stable foundation but they were by no means alone. There was Ken Wilkinson in Engineering, Roy Watts in Sales and later managing the Super 1-11 Division, 'Jock' Cameron at Helicopters, Anthony Milward and Henry Marking in the Chairman's seat; to mention just a few more. Many of these people gave most or all of their working lives to BEA, and some went on to use their considerable talents to try to solve the problems facing BA. However BEA consisted of a whole host of ordinary folk who generally gave devoted service and without whom BEA could never have been made what it was. But the there were the characters, of which BEA had its fair share. There was Kattie Macpherson in her wellies wading across Barra's beach to check if it was dry enough for the daily Heron arrival, Geoff Giddings and his 'smog like' pipe which reduced visibility in the Jersey Duty Officer's office to zero, Captain Wellman and his tricks on unsuspecting Rapide passengers, Reggie Marshal and his infamous bike at Southampton.......To many it will be the memory of those sorts of people who will spring to mind, for many years to come, when BEA is mentioned.

BEA had come and gone. Over twenty eight years the Corporation had developed from a weak fledgling into one of the foremost airlines in the world. It had coined the slogan 'Number One in Europe' to promote itself and surely that was no idle boast as this book has tried to show. It was now up to British Airways to take on that mantle something it found rather hard, largely because of the problems encountered in trying to merge two airlines ... but that's another story.......

THE BOARD OF BRITISH EUROPEAN AIRWAYS IN 1946

Sir Harold Hartley	(Chairman)
Mr G. D'Erlanger	(Managing Director)
Sir Patrick Dollan	(Chairman of the Scottish Advisory Council)
Mr W.A. Edmenson	(Chairman of the Northern Ireland Advisory Council)
Mr I.J. Hayward	
Mr. A.H. Measures	

THE BOARD OF BRITISH EUROPEAN AIRWAYS IN 1974

Mr R. Watts	(Chairman and Chief Executive)
Captain E.W. Lowden	(Deputy Chief Executive)
Captain W. Ballie	(Director British Air Tours)
Mr J.E. Garton	(Chief Engineer)
Mr J.L. Guy	(Director Cargo)
Captain C.A. Owen	(Flight Operations Director)
Mr E.E. Pell	(Planning Director)
Captain R.E. Preston	(Director Super 1-11 Division)
Mr R.A. Spencer	(Financial Director)
Mr C.R. Stuart	(Marketing Director)
Mr R.J. Wyatt	(Personnel Director

BEA's GENEALOGICAL TREE 1946 to 1974

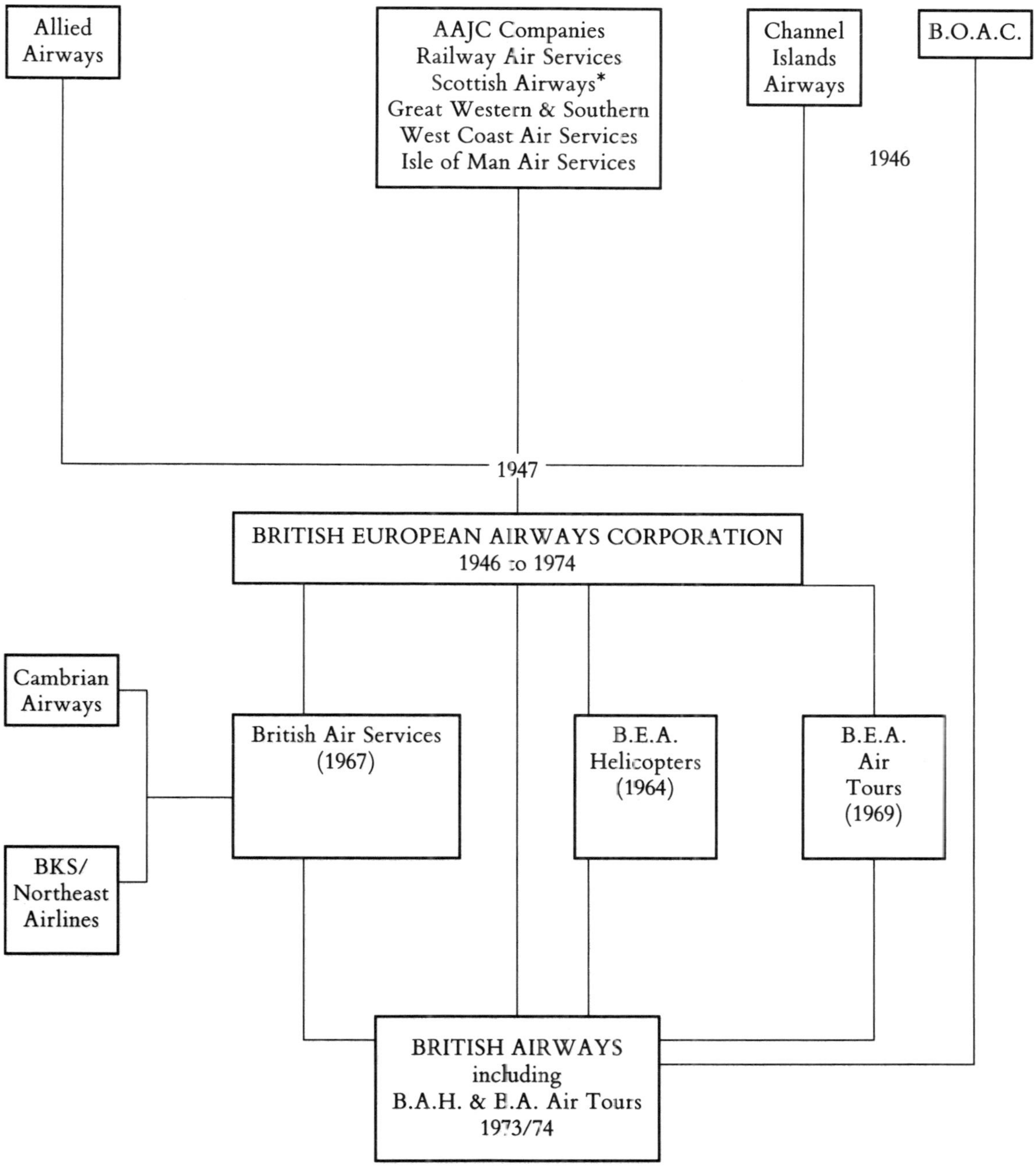

(*Scottish Airways includes Highland Airways and Western Isles Air Services)
Also included was the dormant North Eastern Airways

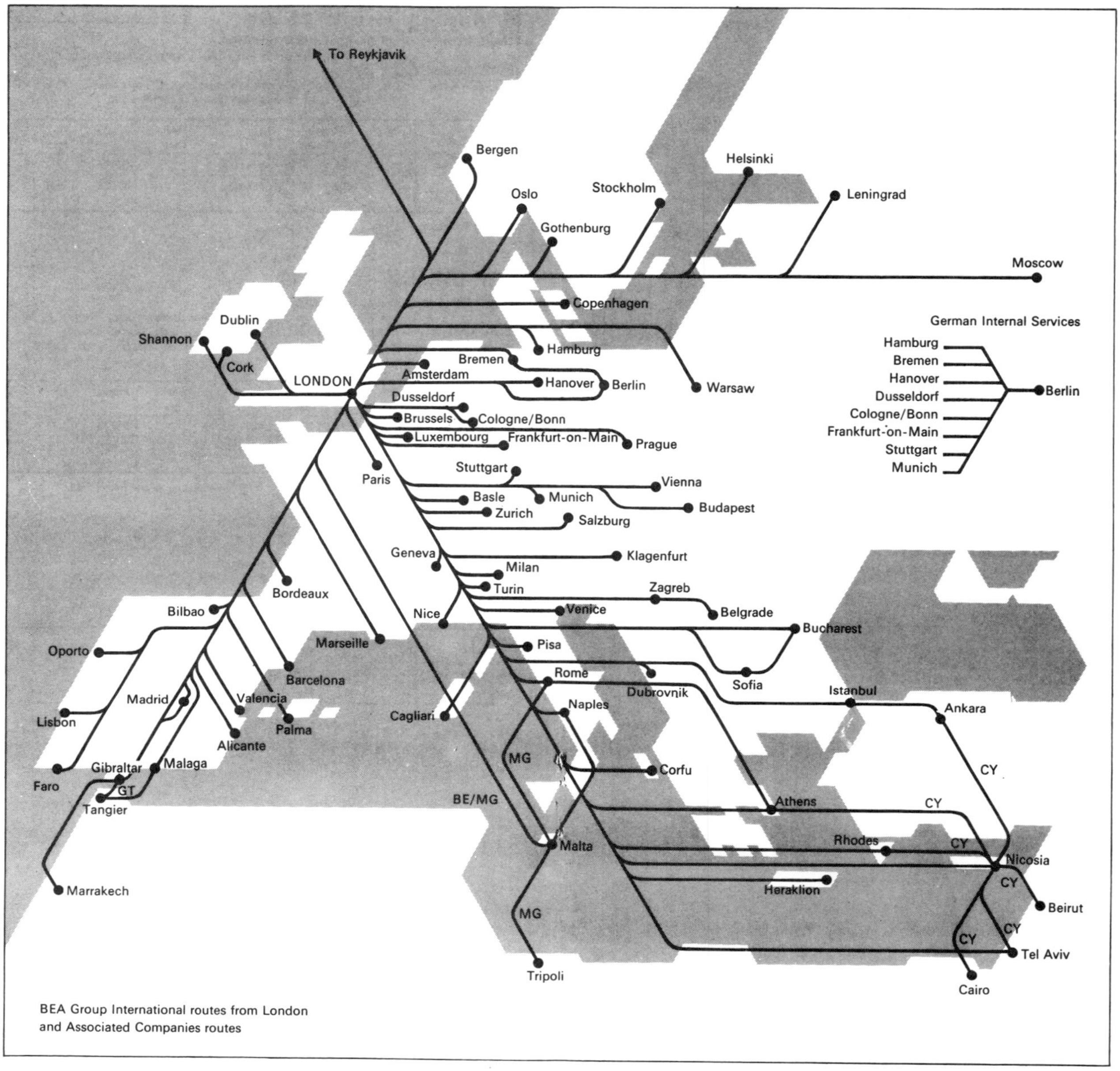

BEA Group International routes from London
and Associated Companies routes

Appendix 1

Summary of All-Cargo Scheduled Services Operated by BEA

This section contains details of all known passenger scheduled services operated by BEA. Routes are listed under the point of origin, eg London to Lisbon appears only under London To. Multi sector routes are also generally only listed under the point of origin, so Malta-Tripoli-Benghazi-Cairo is listed only under Malta To. Some routes were seasonal and this is not shown, and some were suspended at various times. The dates of such suspensions are not shown unless they were for significant periods or of special importance.

ABERDEEN TO

Inverness	1.11.68 to 31.10.70.
Jersey (Via Edinburgh)	9.6.57 to 30.9.60.
Orkney (Some via Wick)	1.2.47 to British Airways.
Shetland (Some via Wick and Orkney)	1.2.47 to British Airways.
Wick	1.2.47 to British Airways.

ALDERNEY TO

Gatwick	28.4.50 to 20.10.52.
Southampton	1.4.47 to 20.4.56.

BELFAST TO (Nutts Corner)

Carlisle (Some via Isle of Man)	1.7.47 to 6.10.47.
Newcastle (Via Carlisle)	1.7.47 to 6.10.47.

BERLIN TO

Services operated from Gatow airfield between August 1946 and May 1951. From May 8th 1951 they were transferred to Tempelhof.

Bremen (Some via Hanover)	1.4.64 to British Airways.
Cologne/Bonn	1.1.51 to British Airways.
Dusseldorf (Some via Colgone/Bonn)	14.11.49 to British Airways.
Frankfurt	1.1.51 to 31.3.54, and 1.4.59 to British Airways.
Hamburg	1.2.47 to British Airways.
Hanover	1.1.51 to British Airways.
Munich (Some via Dusseldorf)	1.1.51 to 31.3.54, and 1.4.60 to British Airways.
Stuttgart	1.6.65 to British Airways.
Sylt	1.6.73 to British Airways.

BIRMINGHAM TO

Amsterdam	1.4.60 to 31.10.61, and 1.4.66 to British Airways.
Barcelona	1.4.60 to 23.9.67.
Belfast (Some via Manchester or Liverpool)	1.5.50 to British Airways.
Dublin	15.4.57 to British Airways.
Dusseldorf	23.4.56 to British Airways.
Edinburgh (Some via Manchester	19.4.53 to British Airways.
Glasgow	1.4.56 to British Airways.
Guernsey	13.5.50 to British Airways.
Jersey	13.5.50 to British Airways.
Leicester (Via Nottingham)	2.7.56 to 10.11.56 Helicopter Service.
Liverpool	1.11.61 to 31.3.62.
Malta	1.4.68 to 27.10.73.
Milan (Malpensa	1.4.58 to 31.10.58 and 22.4.61 to 31.10.61. (Linate in 1961).
Nottingham	2.7.56 to 10.11.56 Helicopter Service.
Paris	11.4.49 to British Airways. (Orly from 1.4.69.)
Zurich	20.4.52 to 31.3.65.

BRISTOL TO (Whitchurch)

Southampton	1.2.47 to 6.10.47.

CARDIFF TO (Pengam Moors)

Bristol	1.2.47 to 6.10.47.
Liverpool	11.4.49 to 1.10.49.
Liverpool (Some via Wrexham)	1.6.50 to 31.3.51 HELICOPTER SERVICE.
Weston Super Mare	1.2.47 to 6.10.47.
Wrexham	1.7.50 to 31.3.51 HELICOPTER SERVICE.

COLOGNE/BONN TO

Frankfurt	Exact dates have not been traced, but a service did operate for a time in 1951.

CROYDON TO

Belfast (Some via Liverpool or Manchester)	1.2.47 to 18.5.47.
Deauville	1.4.47 to 30.9.49.
Guernsey	1.4.47 to 1.11.47.
Helsinki (Via Amsterdam, Copenhagen, Gothenburg and Stockholm)	23.4.47 to 6.10.47.
Jersey	1.4.47 to 20.4.47.
Liverpool	1.2.47 to 5.10.47.
Manchester	1.2.47 to 5.10.47.

DUSSELDORF TO

Frankfurt	25.3.49 to 1.11.49.

EDINBURGH TO

Aberdeen	1.2.47 to British Airways.
Inverness	1.4.67 to 30.9.69.
Jersey	9.6.57 to British Airways.
Orkney (Via Aberdeen and Wick)	1.2.47 to British Airways.
Shetland (Via Aberdeen, or Aberdeen, Wick and Orkney)	1.2.47 to British Airways.
Wick (Via Aberdeen)	1.2.47 to British Airways.

GATWICK TO

Cologne/Bonn	15.5.59 to 31.10.59.
Dinard	15.5.59 to 31.10.63.
Guernsey	9.6.58 to British Airways.
Hanover (Via Cologne/Bonn)	15.5.59 to 31.10.59.
Jersey	9.6.58 to British Airways.
London (Heathrow)	1.11.54 to 16.4.55 HELICOPTER SERVICE.
Paris	1.4.61 to 31.10.61.

GIBRALTAR TO

Including services operated by Gibraltar Airways/Gibair.

Agadir	5.11.72 to British Airways.
Casablanca	2.11.66 to 31.7.67 Gibraltar A/W.
Casablanca	2.4.73 to 31.3.74.
Madrid	1.8.46 to British Airways.
Malaga	1.6.50 to 30.9.50 Gibraltar A/W.
Marrakech	7.11.70 to British Airways.
Seville	1.6.50 to 30.9.50 Gibraltar A/W.
Tangier	30.8.47 to 31.3.74 Gibraltar A/W.
Tetuan	1.6.50 to 30.9.50.

GLASGOW TO

Services operated from Renfrew until 1.5.66 and then from Abbotsinch.

Aberdeen (Some via Edinburgh)	1.2.47 to British Airways.
Barra (Some via Tiree)	1.2.47 to British Airways.
Belfast	1.2.47 to British Airways.
Benbecula (Some via Tiree)	1.2.47 to British Airways.
Campbeltown	1.2.47 to British Airways.
Copenhagen	11.8.47 to 1.12.47.
Edinburgh	1.2.47 to British Airways.
Guernsey	4.6.55 to British Airways.
Islay (Some via Campbeltown)	1.2.47 to British Airways.
Isle of Man	21.4.47 to 31.10.54. (Suspended 10.48 to 1.4.51)
Jersey (Some via Guernsey)	1.4.51 to British Airways. (Suspended 30.9.52 to 1.6.55).

Malta (Via Birmingham)	1.4.69 to 27.10.73.
Orkney (Via Inverness and Wick, or Edinburgh, Aberdeen and Wick)	1.2.47 to British Airways.
Palma (Some Via Manchester)	1.4.64 to 25.10.70.
Paris (Via Manchester or Birmingham)	28.4.50 to British Airways. (Orly from 1.11.69).
Perth	1.7.50 to 31.8.50.
Shetland (Via Inverness, Wick and Orkney, or Aberdeen, Wick, Orkney,	1.2.47 to British Airways.
Stornoway (Some via Inverness or Benbecula)	1.2.47 to British Airways.
Tiree (Some via Islay)	1.2.47 to British Airways.
Wick (Via Inverness, or Edinburgh and Aberdeen)	1.2.47 to British Airways.

GUERNSEY TO

Alderney	1.4.47 to 20.4.56.
Amsterdam	3.5.73 to British Airways.
Dinard (Some via Jersey)	11.6.49 to 20.4.56.
Southampton (Some via Jersey)	1.4.47 to 20.4.56.

INVERNESS TO

Benbecula (Some via Stornoway)	1.2.47 to British Airways.
Orkney (Via Wick)	1.2.47 to British Airways.
Shetland (Via Wick and Orkney)	1.2.47 to British Airways.
Stornoway	1.2.47 to British Airways.
Wick	1.2.47 to British Airways.

ISLE OF MAN TO

Belfast	1.2.47 to 31.3.63.
Blackpool	21.4.47 to 6.10.47.
Carlisle	1.2.47 to 6.10.47.
Newcastle (Via Carlisle)	1.2.47 to 6.10.47.

HAMBURG TO

Dusseldorf	25.3.49 to 30.11.49.
Frankfurt (Via Dusseldorf)	25.3.49 to 30.11.49.

JERSEY TO

Alderney (Some via Guernsey)	1.4.47 to 20.4.56.
Amsterdam (Some via Guernsey)	7.5.72 to British Airways.
Bournemouth	20.3.61 to 31.3.66.
Belfast	1.6.56 to 29.9.68.
Dinard	11.6.49 to 20.4.56.
Guernsey	1.4.47 to 31.3.69.
Liverpool	1.4.52 to 4.9.55.
Paris	1.4.47 to 6.10 47 and for a few weeks in the summer of 1951.
Rennes	1.4.47 to 10.6 49.
Southampton (Some via Guernsey)	1.4.47 to British Airways. Suspended 20.3.61 to 31.3.66.

LAND'S END TO

Isles of Scilly (St Mary's)	1.2.47 to 31.8.64 HELICOPTER SERVICE FROM 2.5.64

LIVERPOOL TO

Belfast (Some via Isle of Man)	1.2.47 to 31.3.63
Chester	11.4.49 to 1.10.49
Isle of Man	1.2.47 to 31.3.63
Valley (Via Chester)	11.4.49 to 1.10.49

LONDON TO

Services generally operated from Northolt until October 1954, and then from Heathrow, though they were progressively transferred from Northolt from April 1950, and all Elizabethan and Viscount flights operated from Heathrow.

Aberdeen (direct)	1.11.63 to British Airways.
Agadir (Via Gibraltar)	5.11.72 to British Airways.
Ajaccio	23.4.55 to 30.9.61.
Alghero	5.6.60 to British Airways.
Alicante	1.11.67 to British Airways.
Amsterdam	1.8.46 to British Airways.
Ankara (Via Rome, Athens, Istanbul)	17.9.46 to 31 10.72.
Athens (Some via Nice, Marseilles, Dusseldorf, Munich, Geneva, Milan, Rome or Thesalonika)	1.8.46 to British Airways.
Barcelona	22.10.50 to British Airways.

Basle	2.5.50 to British Airways.
Belfast	19.5.47 to British Airways.
Belgrade (Via Zagreb or Zurich)	4.6.57 to 31.3.62 and 2.6.70 to British Airways.
Benghazi (Via Malta and Tripoli)	7.1.51 to 31.3.63.
Bergen (Some via Stavanger)	15.6.56 to 27.10.73.
Berlin (Some via various West German stations)	1.9.46 to British Airways.
Beruit (Some via Rome, Athens, Nicosia)	13.4.54 to 28.3.71.
Biarritz (Some via Bordeaux)	28.5.54 to 3.9.68.
Birmingham (Haymills Rotor Station)	4.6.51 to 9.4.52 HELICOPTER SERVICE.
Birmingham (Elmdon)	1.4.53 to British Airways.
Bordeaux	1.8.46 to 31.10.68 (Technical stop only 1.8.46 to 14.7.50)
Bremen	1.4.68 to British Airways.
Brussels	1.8.46 to British Airways.
Bucharest (Some via Zagreb)	6.4.70 to British Airways.
Budapest (Some via Prague or Zurich)	1.4.61 to 31.10.62, and 10.4.67 to British Airways.
Cagliari	3.5.72 to British Airways.
Cairo (Some via Malta, Tripoli, Benghazi, others via Munich, Athens)	7.1.51 to 31.10.64. (frequently suspended)
Casablanca	2.4.73 to 31.3.74.
Catania	1.5.73 to British Airways.
Cologne/Bonn (Some via Amsterdam or Brussels or Hanover)	1.1.51 to British Airways.
Copenhagen	1.8.46 to British Airways.
Corfu	3.4.65 to British Airways.
Crete	2.4.71 to British Airways.
Deauville	1.4.51 to 30.9.51.
Dinard	13.6.49 to 30.9.58, and 1.4.64 to 3.9.67.
Dublin	14.4.57 to British Airways.
Dubrovnik	1.5.65 to British Airways.
Dusseldorf (Some via Amsterdam or Brussels)	5.6.49 to British Airways.
Edinburgh	19.5.47 to British Airways. Suspended 10.47 to 3.48.
Faro	1.4.66 to British Airways.
Frankfurt	2.9.46 to British Airways.
Geneva	19.5.47 to British Airways.
Gerona	1.4.68 to 31.10.70.
Gibraltar (Some via Bordeaux or Madrid)	1.8.46 to British Airways.
Glasgow	1.2.47 to British Airways.
Gothenburg	1.8.46 to 10.48, and 22.4.56 to British Airways.
Guernsey (Some via Jersey)	1.4.47 to British Airways. Suspended 6.10.47 to 3.48, and 9.6.58 to 31.3.63.
Hamburg (Some via Amsterdam)	1.9.46 to British Airways.
Hanover (Some via Amsterdam or Bremen)	1.4.52 to British Airways.
Heathrow (From Northolt)	4.6.51 to 9.4.52 HELICOPTER SERVICE.
Helsinki (Some via Stockholm)	1.4.62 to British Airways.
Inverness (Some via Aberdeen)	1.11.68 to British Airways.
Isle of Man (Some via Manchester)	18.4.48 to 31.3.63.
Istanbul (Some via Rome and or Athens)	1.8.46 to British Airways.
Jersey (Some via Guernsey)	21.4.47 to British Airways.
Klagenfurt (Some via Munich)	6.6.59 to 13.10.68.
Leipzig (Trade Fair periods only)	28.2.70 to British Airways.
Leningrad	2.5.71 to British Airways.
Le Touquet	26.5.50 to 30.9.51.
Lisbon (Some via Bordeaux)	1.8.46 to 2.6.50; and 4.10.53 to British Airways.
Liverpool (Via Manchester)	6.10.47 to 17.4.48.
Madrid (Some via Bordeaux)	1.8.46 to British Airways.
Malaga	1.4.62 to British Airways.
Malta (Some via Marseilles or Nice or Ajaccio or Alghero or Palermo or Rome or Naples)	1.12.47 to British Airways.
Manchester	6.10.47 to 17.4.48; and 20.4.52 to British Airways.
Marrakech (Via Gibraltar)	7.11.70 to British Airways.
Marseilles	1.8.46 to 30.4.49, and 1.4.72 to British Airways.
Milan (Malpensa) (Some via Geneva)	12.2.51 to British Airways. (Linate from 1.11.60)
Minorca	1.4.68 to 30.9.69.
Moscow (Some via Copenhagen or Warsaw)	14.5.59 to British Airways.
Munich (Some via Dusseldorf)	5.6.49 to British Airways.
Naples	11.4.54 to British Airways.
Nice	1.6.48 to British Airways.
Nicosia (Some via Rome and or Istanbul, Ankara, or Rhodes or Crete)	6.10.47 to British Airways.
Oporto	1.4.61 to British Airways.
Oslo (Some via Gothenburg or Stavanger)	1.8.46 to British Airways.

Palermo	1.6.61 to British Airways.
Palma (Some via Bordeaux or Barcelona)	15.5.53 to British Airways.
Paris (Le Bourget)	1.8.46 to 31.10.71.
Paris (Orly)	1.4.68 to British Airways.
Pisa	1.5.70 to British Airways.
Prague (Some via Frankfurt)	7.8.46 to 21.3.51, and 7.10.57 to British Airways.
Prestwick	1.2.47 to 6.10.47.
Reykjavik (Keflavik)	7.4.71 to British Airways.
Rhodes	1.4.68 to British Airways.
Rome (Some via Marseilles or Nice)	1.8.46 to British Airways.
Salzburg (Some via Munich)	22.4.55 to British Airways.
Shannon	2.4.65 to British Airways.
Sofia (Via Bucharest)	2.6.70 to British Airways.
Southampton	15.6.54 to 16.4.55 HELICOPTER SERVICE.
South Bank (Waterloo)	25.7.55 to 31.5.56 HELICOPTER SERVICE.
Stavanger (Some via Bergen)	2.9.46 to 6.10.47, and 1.6.61 to 13.9.69.
Stockholm (Some via Copenhagen or Oslo or Gothenburg)	1.8.46 to British Airways.
Stuttgart	1.7.69 to British Airways.
Sumburgh (Shetland) (Via Birmingham, Edinburgh and Aberdeen)	19.5.47 to 31.10.55.
Tangier (Some via Gibraltar or Malaga)	1.4.66 to British Airways.
Tel Aviv (Some via Rome and or Athens and or Nicosia)	7.10.56 to British Airways.
Thesalonika (Salonika)	1.4.73 to British Airways.
Tripoli (Via Malta)	7.1.51 to British Airways.
Tunis (Via Malta)	.11.68 to 31.3.69.
Turin	1.4.60 to British Airways.
Valencia (Some via Barcelona)	3.5.57 to British Airways.
Venice	17.5.56 to British Airways.
Vienna (Some via Zurich)	2.9.46 to British Airways.
Warsaw	8.4.58 to British Airways.
Zagreb	1.4.71 to British Airways.
Zurich	9.9.46 to 9.12.46, and 1.11.48 to British Airways.

MALTA TO

$_4$ Services operated in conjunction with the Malta Airlines.
§ Service operated for the Malta Airlines and Gibraltar Airways.

Ajaccio	23.4.55 to 30.9.61.
Algiers§ (via Tunis)	19.6.52 to 30.9.52.
Alghero	5.6.60 to British Airways.
Benghazi $_4$ (via Tripoli)	7.1.51 to 31.3.63.
Cairo $_4$ (via Tripoli and Benghazi)	7.1.51 to .11.56.
Catania $_4$	7.1.51 to 31.3.71.
Gibraltar § (via Tunis and Algiers)	19.6.52 to 30.9.52.
Naples	19.4.53 to British Airways.
Rome $_4$ (Some via Naples)	1.12.47 to British Airways.
Tripoli $_4$	7.1.51 to British Airways.
Tunis $_4$	7.1.51 to 30.9.51.
Tunis §	19.6.52 to 30.9.52.

MANCHESTER TO

Amsterdam	1.4.52 to British Airways.
Barcelona (Some via Birmingham)	16.6.57 to British Airways.
Belfast (Some via Blackpool and the Isle of Man or Liverpool)	1.2.47 to British Airways.
Birmingham	11.4.49 to British Airways.
Copenhagen	1.4.66 to British Airways.
Dublin	16.4.57 to British Airways.
Dusseldorf (Some via Birmingham or Amsterdam)	1.4.52 to British Airways.
Edinburgh	1.4.68 to British Airways.
Geneva	1.4.72 to British Airways.
Glasgow	1.4.50 to British Airways.
Guernsey (Some via Birmingham)	13.5.50 to British Airways.
Isle of Man (Some via Blackpool or Liverpool)	1.2.47 to 31.3.63 (suspended 6.10.47 to 1.4.51).
Jersey (Some via Birmingham or Guernsey)	13.5.50 to British Airways.
Liverpool	1.2.47 to 31.3.63.
Malta	1.4.67 to British Airways.
Milan (Malpensa)	16.6.53 to 7.10.64, and 1.11.73 to British Airways (Linate from 1.11.60)
Munich	2.4.72 to British Airways.
Nicosia (Some via Brussels)	1.4.73 to British Airways.
Palma	14.5.57 to 25.10.70.

Paris (Some via Birmingham)	11.4.49 to British Airways (Orly from 1.4.69).
Zurich (Some via Birmingham)	20.4.52 to 31.3.69.

NICOSIA TO

These services were generally operated either for or in conjunction with Cyprus Airways. As far as possible the dates given are only for periods when BEA aircraft operated the routes: (This includes aircraft leased from BEA)

Ankara (Some via Istanbul)	2.2.58 to 31.3.70 (Suspended at various times)
Athens	6.10.47 to 31.3.70.
Bahrain (Via Beruit and Kuwait)	2.2.58 to 29.3.62.
Beruit	13.4.54 to 30.10.65.
Cairo	1.7.61 to 31.10.61, and 1.11.65 to 31.3.70.
Crete	1.4.71 to 31.3.72.
Doha (via Beruit, Kuwait and Bahrain)	2.2.58 to 29.3.62.
Damascus	1.2.58 to 31.3.61.
Istanbul (Some via Ankara)	2.2.58 to 31.3.70. (Suspended at various times)
Jerusalem	1.4.66 to 31.10.67.
Kuwait (via Beruit)	2.2.58 to 29.3.62.
Rhodes	1.4.66 to 31.3.72.
Tel Aviv	7.10.56 to 31.3.70.

ORKNEY TO

Services operated from Hatston Aerodrome until 1950, and then from Grimsetter.

Shetland	1.2.47 to British Airways.

PENZANCE TO

Isles of Scilly (St Mary's)	1.9.64 to British Airways Helicopters. HELICOPTER SERVICE.

PRESTWICK TO

Belfast	1.2.47 to 6.10.47.
Glasgow	1.2.47 to 6.10.47.

SOUTHAMPTON TO

Northolt	15.6.54 to 29.10.54 HELICOPTER SERVICE.

STORNOWAY TO

Barra (Via Benbecula)	1.2.47 to 30.9.52.
Benbecula	1.2.47 to British Airways.

N.B. Services to and from Belfast used Nutts Corner Airport until 23.9.63 and then transferred to Aldergrove Airport.

Frequency of Major International Routes 1947 to 1974
Number of Weekly Flights in August

ROUTE	1947	1950	1956	1959	1964	1967	1971	1973	31.3.74
London to									
Amsterdam	7	14	28	35	42	42	62	54	41
Athens	2	12	16	11	17	20	19	21	13
Brussels	14	21	21	21	21	27	32	26	29
Copenhagen	3	7	13	19	17	19	24	22	14
Frankfurt	-	5	7	10	7	21	21	20	20
Madrid	2	2	7	7	8	13	15	15	15
Paris	35	84	77	70	63	111	116	88	73
Rome	2	22	26	34	17	17	24	21	14
Zurich	-	14	30	24	17	24	26	26	19

Frequency of Major Domestic Routes 1947 to 1974
Number of flights Weekly in August

ROUTE	1947	1950	1955	1959	1963	1967	1971	1973	31.3.74
London to									
Aberdeen (direct)	-	-	-	-	-	13	17	25	25
Belfast	19	38	27	44	43	60	55	60	51
Birmingham	-	-	6	15	19	14	8	7	8
Edinburgh	12	16	17	28	39	69	52	53	42
Glasgow	12	26	34	47	58	91	72	77	83
Guernsey	21§	21	25	47_4	35_5	37_5	31_5	34_5	14_5
Inverness (direct)	-	-	-	-	-	-	6	13	13
Jersey	42	61	65	79_5	73_5	49_5	51_5	57_5	41
Manchester	14§	-	13	31	57	58	46	45	41

§ Service operated from Croydon Airport
$_4$ Services operated from Gatwick Airport
$_5$ Includes flights from both Heathrow and Gatwick

Frequency of German Internal Services 1947 to 1974
Number of flights Weekly in October

ROUTE	1947	1954	1960	1965	1970	31.3.74
Berlin to						
Bremen	-	-	-	14	28	20
Cologne/Bonn	-	7	14	21	21	21
Dusseldorf	-	7	21	28	27	28
Frankfurt	-	-	21	49	70	68
Hamburg	6	13	21	56	49	40
Hanover	-	28	28	70	77	43
Munich	-	7	7	14	35	28
Stuttgart	-	-	-	7	28	21
Sylt§	-	-	-	-	-	-

§Sylt became a destination on 1.6.73 for a seasonal service between June and September only.

Viscount V.802 G.AOHU loading passengers for the final 'Silver Wing' flight to Paris on April 30th April 1958. *(BA)*

Berlin's Tempelhof Airport, with Viscounts, Super 1-11s and a Comet in attendance (BA)

An old bird in new guise, Heron 1B G-ANXA at Abbotsinch in the new BEA colours. (BA)

Appendix 2

Summary of All-Cargo Scheduled Services Operated by BEA

All known All-Cargo scheduled services are listed in this appendix. Routes are listed under the point of origin, eg London-Milan is found only under London To. Multi-sector routes are only listed under the point of origin, eg London-Dusseldorf-Vienna-Linz will be found only under London To.

In compiling this section it has been very difficult, in some cases, to obtain exact dates; and in addition many routes were frequently suspended. Generally the dates of such suspensions are not shown.

BIRMINGHAM TO

Paris	1.4.71 to 31.10.71.

GLASGOW TO

Amsterdam (via Manchester)	1.11.70 to British Airways Cargo.
Frankfurt (via Manchester and London)	1.11.70 to British Airways Cargo.

JERSEY TO

Bournemouth	20.3.61 to 31.3.61.
Southampton	25.2.59 to 19.3.61.

LONDON TO

Services generally operated from Northolt until October 1954 and then from Heathrow.

Athens (Some via Marseilles and or Rome)	1.4.48 to British Airways Cargo.
Amsterdam	1.4.48 to British Airways Cargo.
Barcelona	1.4.73 to British Airways Cargo.
Basle	1.4.48 to 30.10.48.
Belfast	1.4.68 to British Airways Cargo.
Berlin (via Hanover)	1.4.57 to 31.3.58.
Birmingham	10.4.52 to 14.1.54 (HELICOPTER SERVICE).
Bordeaux	1.4.48 to 30.10.48.
Brussels	10.8.47 to British Airways Cargo.
Buckenburg	3.2.50 to 31.3.54.
Copenhagen	1.4.48 to British Airways Cargo.
Dublin	1.10.69 to British Airways Cargo.
Dusseldorf (Some via Frankfurt)	1.11.51 to British Airways Cargo.
Frankfurt (Some via Dusseldorf)	1.5.57 to British Airways Cargo.
Gibraltar (Some via Bordeaux and Madrid)	1.4.48 to 30.10.48.
Glasgow (Some via Manchester)	1.4.58 to British Airways Cargo.
Gothenburg (Some via Copenhagen or Stockholm)	1.11.64 to British Airways Cargo.
Guernsey (Some via Jersey)	1.4.47 to .4.49, and 1.5.63 to British Airways Cargo.
Hamburg (Some via Amsterdam, Copenhagen)	1.4.48 to 31.3.58, and 1.4.73 to British Airways Cargo.
Hanover	1.4.54 to 31.3.58.
Helsinki	1.4.73 to British Airways Cargo.
Istanbul (via Marseilles, Rome, Athens)	1.4.48 to 31.10.52.
Jersey (Some via Guernsey)	1.4.47 to .4.49, and 1.11.61 to British Airways Cargo.
Linz (via Dusseldorf and Vienna)	1.11.51 to 31.3.52.
Lisbon (Some via Bordeaux and Madrid)	1.4.48 to 30.10.48, and 1.11.71 to British Airways Cargo.
Liverpool (Some via Manchester)	1.4.48 to 31.10.49.
Lyons	1.11.51 to 31.3.52.
Madrid (Some via Bordeaux)	1.4.48 to 30.10.48, and 1.11.66 to British Airways Cargo.
Malta (Some via Rome)	3.4.49 to 31.3.55, and 1.11.69 to British Airways Cargo.
Manchester (Some via Liverpool)	1.4.48 to British Airways Cargo (Suspended 10.49 to 1951).
Milan (Malpensa) (Some via Lyons)	1.11.51 to British Airways Cargo (Linate from 1.11.60).

Nice	1.4.48 to 31.3.61.
Nicosia (via Athens)	7.5.66 to British Airways Cargo.
Paris (Some via Brussels)	1.4.48 to British Airways Cargo (Orly from 1.5.70).
Prague (via Brussels)	10.8.47 to 30.10.48.
Rome (Some via Marseilles or Nice)	1.4.48 to 31.3.61, and 1.4.65 to 30.10.65.
Stockholm (Some via Gothenburg)	1.4.65 to British Airways Cargo.
Stuttgart (Some via Vienna)	10.10.57 to 30.10.58, and 7.2.70 to British Airways Cargo.
Turin	1.11.69 to British Airways Cargo.
Vienna	1.11.51 to British Airways Cargo. (Very erratic periods of operation).
Zurich (Some via Basle)	1.4.48 to 30.10.48, and 1.11.62 to 31.3.72.

MANCHESTER TO

Amsterdam	1.11.70 to British Airways Cargo.
Belfast	12.3.51 to British Airways Cargo.
Dublin	A service operated for a period in 1957.
Dusseldorf (via Frankfurt)	1.11.66 to 30.10.67.
Frankfurt (Some via London)	1.11.66 to British Airways Cargo.
Paris	1.4.65 to 31.10.66, and 1.4.71 to British Airways Cargo.

Frequency of major All-Cargo Services 1948 to 1974

Number of Flights weekly (November)

ROUTE	1948	1955	1959	1964	1969	1973
London to						
Amsterdam	5	6	6	6	6	6
Athens	3	-	-	-	1	1
Belfast	-	-	-	-	3	5
Brussels	3	3	3	4	2	2
Copenhagen	5	6	6	12	2	6
Dusseldorf	-	7	3	6	4	4
Frankfurt	-	-	4	9	5	5
Glasgow	-	-	6	-	5	5
Gothenburg	-	-	-	3	5	4
Guernsey	7	-	-	2	3	2
Jersey	7	-	-	2	4	6
Manchester	1	-	6	4	5	5
Milan	-	1	3	9	5	5
Paris	3	6	7	9	7	7
Rome	3	4	4	-	-	-
Manchester to						
Belfast	-	7	6	6	6	5

Appendix 3

Fleet List & Details of Aircraft Owned or Operated by BEA 1946 to 1974

This section contains full details of aircraft owned or operated by BEA between 1946 and 1974. Fleet details of the BEA Helicopter Unit/BEA Helicopters, and BEA Air Tours are also included. In addition aircraft ordered before March 31st 1974 (but not yet delivered) are listed. Some information has proved very difficult to obtain or substantiate, and the author would be pleased to receive any additional details or corrections. Aircraft types are listed alphabetically under the manufacturer. A word of explanation is necessary concerning Delivery Dates and Disposal Dates. The Delivery Date shown is the date formally given in BEA records on which the aircraft was delivered to the airline. This date is usually different from the date on which the aircraft was registered to the Corporation. In a few early cases no record exists regarding delivery date, in which case the date the aircraft was registered to BEA is shown instead.

In the case of Disposal Dates the date shown is, again, the date given in official BEA records on which the aircraft was sold. This is often not the same date as the date on which ownership was cancelled with the Air Registration Board, or the date on which the aircraft was actually delivered to the purchaser.

Technical Description of Main Types Operated by BEA

MANUFACTURER	TYPE	TOTAL NUMBER OPERATED	POWER PLANT	WING SPAN	LENGTH	MTOW (lbs)	REMARKS
Airspeed	Ambassador (Elizabethan)	20	2xBristol Centaurus 601	115′	82′	55,000	
Agusta	Bell 47J	1	1xLycoming VO435	37′2″ Rotor Dia	43′4″	2,800	
Agusta	Jet Ranger	1	1xASN 250C Turbo-Shaft	33′4″ Rotor Dia	31′	3,200	Owned by BEAH
Avro	Anson	1	2xArmstrong Siddeley Cheetah IX	56′6″	42′3″	9,540	Communications aircraft
Avro	Avro 19	15	2xArmstrong Siddeley Cheetah XV	56′6″	42′3″	10,400	
Avro	Lancaster	1	4xRolls Royce Merlin T24/4	102′	76′10″	65,000	Purchased for Alitalia
Avro	Lancastrian	5	4xRolls Royce Merlin T24/4	102′	76′10″	65,000	Purchased for Alitalia
Bell	Bell 47B3	2	1xFranklin 6VA-178-B32	35′1″ Rotor Dia	31′6″	2,200	
Bell	Bell 212	1	1xPratt Whitney PT6T-3 Twin Pac	48′1″ Rotor Dia	57′2″	11,200	Owned by BEAH
Boeing	Boeing 707.436 (incl 1 Boeing 707.465)	8	4xRolls Royce Conway	145′5″	152′6″	336,000	Owned by BEA Air Tours
Bristol	Bristol 170 Mk21	1	2x Bristol Hercules 672	108′	98′4″	40,000	Cargo Aircraft
Bristol	Bristol 171	3	1x Alvis Leonides HM9	 Rotor Dia	48′6″	61′1″	5,300
Bristol	Bristol 173	1	2x Alvis Leonides 73	48′7″ Rotor Dia	78′	10,600	Loaned from Bristol's for evaluation
BAC	BAC1-11.51018		2xRolls Royce	93′6″		107′	98,000

MANUFACTURER	TYPE	TOTAL NUMBER OPERATED	POWER PLANT	WING SPAN	LENGTH	MTOW (lbs)	REMARKS
BAC	BAC1-11.510	18	2xRolls Royce Spey 512	93′6″	107′	98,000	
De Havilland	Comet 4B	14	4xRolls Royce Avon 525B	107′10″	118′	158,000	10 later operated by BEA Air Tours
De Havilland	Dragon (DH84)	1	2xGipsy Major 1	47′4″	34′6″	4,200	Communications aircraft
De Havilland	Heron 1B	3	4xGipsy Queen 30	71′6″	48′6″	13,000	
De Havilland	Mosquito PR34	2	2xRolls Royce Merlin	54′2″	41′2″	25,200	Used by the Gust Research Unit
De Havilland	Moth	1	1xGipsy 1	30′	23′11″	1,650	Communications aircraft
De Havilland	Rapide (DH89)	53	2xGipsy Queen 3	48′	34′6″	5,500	
Douglas	DC-3 (Pionair)	68	2xPratt & Whitney Twin	95′	64′5″	28,000	Another 3 aircraft were purchased for
Handley Page	Herald 101	3	2xRolls Royce Dart 527	94′9″		72′	39,000
Hawker Siddeley	Argosy 101	3	4xRolls Royce Dart 526	115′	86′9″	88,000	Cargo aircraft
Hawker Siddeley	Argosy 222	6	4xRolls Royce Dart 532	115′	86′9″	93,000	Cargo aircraft
Hawker Siddeley	Trident IC	24	3xRolls Royce Spey 505	89′10″	114′9″	115,000	
Hawker Siddeley	Trident IE	1	3xRolls Royce Spey 510	94′8″	114′9″	135,525	
Hawker Siddeley	Trident 2E	16	3xRolls Royce Spey 512	98′10″	114′9″	142,500	
Hawker Siddeley	Trident 3B	26	3xRolls Royce Spey 512, plus 1xRolls Royce RB162 booster engine	98′10″	131′2″	150,000	
Junkers	JU 52(3m)	11	3x830 (619kw) BMW 132T-2	96′	62′	20,280	
Miles	Marathon IA	1	4xGipsy Major 703	65′	52′1″	18,250	One aircraft used for evaluation, larger order cancelled
Miles	M28	1	1x Blackburn Cirrus Major 3	47′	24′	2,400	Used as the Chairman's personal aircraft
Short	Skyliner	2	2xTPE 331-2-201A	64′9″	40′1″	13,700	
Sikorsky	S.51	4	1x Pratt & Whitney R985. B4	48′ Rotor Dia	57′6″	5,300	
Sikorsky	S.61 N	8	2xGeneral Electric CT58-1101	62′ Rotor Dia	72′10″	19,000	Owned by BEAH
Taylorcraft	Auster JI	4	1xGipsy Major I	36′	23′8″	2,000	Communications aircraft
Vickers	Merchantman	9	4xRolls Royce Tyne 506	118′	122′10″	142,000	Cargo conversion of the Vanguard
Vickers	Vanguard V.951	6	4xRolls Royce Tyne 506	118′	122′10″	135,000	
Vickers	Vanguard V.953	14	4xRolls Royce Tyne 506	118′	122′10″	142,000	
Vickers	Viking IA	27	2xBristol Hercules 634	89′5″	65′4″	34,000	
Vickers (Admiral)	Viking IB Hercules 634	53	2xBristol	89′5″	65′4″	34,000	
Vickers	Viscount V.630	1	4xRolls Royce Dart 502	89′	74′6″	45,000	Loaned from Vickers
Vickers	Viscount V.700	1	4xRolls Royce Dart 504	93′8″	81′2″	56,000	Loaned from Vickers

MANUFACTURER	TYPE	TOTAL NUMBER OPERATED	POWER PLANT	WING SPAN	LENGTH	MTOW (lbs)	REMARKS
Vickers	Viscount V.701	27	4xRolls Royce Dart 505/506	93′8″	81′2″	56,000	
Vickers	Viscount V.732	1	4xRolls Royce Dart 506	93′8″	81′2″	60,000	Leased from BOAC
Vickers	Viscount V.736	2	4xRolls Royce Dart 506	93′8″	81′2″	60,000	Leased from Fred Olsen
Vickers	Viscount V.745	2	4xRolls Royce Dart 506	93′8″	81′2″	60,000	Leased from Vickers
Vickers	Viscount V.779	2	4xRolls Royce Dart 510	93′8″	81′2″	60,000	Leased from Fred Olsen
Vickers	Viscount V.802	24	4xRolls Royce Dart 510	93′8″	85′	64,500	
Vickers	Viscount V.806	19	4xRolls Royce Dart 520	93′8″	85′	64,500	
Westland	WS.55	3	1xPratt & Whitney R1340 Wasp 9	53′ Rotor Dia	62′3″	7,500	

AIRSPEED

AIRCRAFT TYPE: AMBASSADOR **BEA CLASS NAME: ELIZABETHAN**

REGISTRATION	C/N	BEA NAME	DELIVERY DATE	DISPOSAL DATE	REMARKS
G-ALZN	5212	Elizabethan	31.3.53	10.3.61	Operated first commercial service by the type on 3.9.51 between London and Paris. Sold to Overseas Aviation.
G-ALZO	5226	Christopher Marlowe	25.11.52	5.5.60	Sold to the Royal Jordanian Air Force.
G-ALZP	5213	Richard Grenville	28.2.52	13.9.60	Sold to the Royal Jordanian Air Force.
G-ALZR	5214	Sir Walter Raleigh	13.2.52	30.8.57	Sold to Rolls Royce to be used as a test bed for Tyne engines.
G-ALZS	5215	William Shakespeare	25.1.52	8.11.60	Sold in Norway.
G-ALZT	5216	Sir John Hawkins	27.1.52	5.5.58	Sold to BKS Air Transport.
G-ALZU	5217	Lord Burghley	5.3.52	-	WO Munich 6.2.58.
G-ALZV	5218	The Earl of Leicester	12.4.52	10.3.61	Sold to Overseas Aviation.
G-ALZW	5219	Sir Francis Walsingham	28.4.52	15.5.58	Sold to BKS Air Transport.
G-ALZX	5220	Sir John Norris	29.5.52	6.6.57	Sold to Butler Air Transport.
G-ALZY	5221	Sir Philip Sydney	10.7.52	26.12.59	Sold to the Royal Jordanian Air Force.
G-ALZZ	5222	Edmund Spencer	9.8.52	8.11.60	Sold to Overseas Aviation.
G-AMAA	5223	Sir Francis Knollys	5.9.52	26.1.60	Sold to Shell Aviation Division.
G-AMAB	5224	Sir Francis Bacon	4.10.52	-	WFU after accident at Dusseldorf 8.4.55.
G-AMAC	5225	Sir Robert Cecil	1.11.52	17.6.60	Sold to BKS Air Transport.
G-AMAD	5211	Sir Francis Drake	20.3.52	23.7.57	Sold to BKS Air Transport.
G-AMAE	5227	The Earl of Essex	18.12.52	6.6.57	Sold to Butler Air Transport.
G-AMAF	5228	Lord Howe of Effingham	17.1.53	10.3.61	Operated last scheduled BEA Elizabethan service on 30.6.58 from Cologne/Bonn to London. Sold to Overseas Aviation.
G-AMAG	5229	Sir Thomas Gresham	4.2.53	8.2.59	Sold to Shell Aviation Division.
G-AMAH	5230	Sir Christopher Hatton	6.3.53	6.6.57	Sold to Butler Air Transport.

AGUSTA

AIRCRAFT TYPE: AGUSTA BELL 47J | **BEA CLASS NAME: KING ARTHUR CLASS**

REGISTRATION	C/N	BEA NAME	DELIVERY DATE	DISPOSAL DATE	REMARKS
G-APTH	1058	Sir Lucan	2.4.59	2.4.65	Operated on charter to Aero Contractors of Nigeria March to December 1963 as 5N-ACP. Sold to R.A. Wade.

AGUSTA

AIRCRAFT TYPE: AGUSTA BELL 206 JET RANGER (Owned by BEAH) | **BEA CLASS NAME: -**

REGISTRATION	C/N	BEA NAME	DELIVERY DATE	DISPOSAL DATE	REMARKS
G-AWGU	8044	-	27.4.68	-	To British Airways Helicopters.

AVRO

AIRCRAFT TYPE: ANSON | **BEA CLASS NAME: -**

REGISTRATION	C/N	BEA NAME	DELIVERY DATE	DISPOSAL DATE	REMARKS
G-AHBN	NK270 (Military Serial)	-	1.8.46	26.7.48	Used as a communications aircraft. Transferred to Alitalia.

AVRO

AIRCRAFT TYPE: AVRO 19 | **BEA CLASS NAME: -**

REGISTRATION	C/N	BEA NAME	DELIVERY DATE	DISPOSAL DATE	REMARKS
G-AGUD	1275	-	1.2.47	.6.48	Inherited from RAS. Transferred to the Ministry of Civil Aviation for resale.
G-AGUX	1277	-	1.2.47	.5.48	Inherited from RAS. Transferred to the Ministry of Civil Aviation for resale.
G-AGVA	1278	-	1.2.47	.4.48	Inherited from RAS. Transferred to the Ministry of Civil Aviation for resale.
G-AHIB	1317	-	1.2.47	.4.48	Inherited from RAS. Transferred to the Ministry of Civil Aviation for resale.
G-AHIC	1318	-	1.2.47	.4.48	Inherited from RAS. Transferred to the Ministry of Civil Aviation for resale.
G-AHID	1319	-	1.2.47	.4.48	Inherited from RAS. Transferred to the Ministry of Civil Aviation for resale.
G-AHIE	1320	-	1.2.47	.4.48	Inherited from RAS. Transferred to the Ministry of Civil Aviation for resale.
G-AHIF	1321	-	1.2.47	.4.48	Inherited from RAS. Transferred to the Ministry of Civil Aviation for resale.
G-AHIG	1322	-	1.2.47	.4.48	Inherited from RAS. Transferred to the Ministry of Civil Aviation for resale.
G-AHIH	1323	-	1.2.47	.4.48	Inherited from RAS. Transferred to the Ministry of Civil Aviation for resale.
G-AHII	1324	-	.10.48	.3.50	Inherited from Airways Training. Sold to Starways.
G-AHIJ	1325	-	1.2.47	.4.48	Inherited from RAS. Transferred to the Ministry of Civil Aviation for resale.
G-AHIK	1326	-	.10.48	.3.50	Inherited from Airways Training. Sold to Starways.
G-AHXL	1352	-	.10.48	25.7.50	Inherited from Airways Training. Sold in Sweden.
G-AHXM	1353	-	.10.48	.10.50	Inherited from Airways Training. Sold to Sperry Gyroscopes.

N.B. Several of these aircraft were registered to BEA before 1.2.47, though they continued to be operated by Railway Air Services until that company became part of BEA on 1.2.47

AVRO

AIRCRAFT TYPE: LANCASTER B Mark1 — **BEA CLASS NAME: -**

REGISTRA-TION	C/N	BEA NAME	DELIVERY DATE	DISPOSAL DATE	REMARKS
G-AJWM	PP741 (Military Serial)	-	4.6.47	30.11.48	Acquired for Alitalia. Not used by BEA. Used to train Alitalia crews at White Waltham.

AVRO

AIRCRAFT TYPE: LANCASTRIAN — **BEA CLASS NAME: -**

REGISTRA-TION	C/N	BEA NAME	DELIVERY DATE	DISPOSAL DATE	REMARKS
REGISTRA-TION	**C/N**	**BEA NAME**	**DELIVERY DATE**	**DISPOSAL DATE**	**REMARKS**
G-AHBX	1292	-	.2.47	13.2.48	Purchased for Alitalia, to whom transferred. Never flew for BEA.
G-AHBY	1293	-	.2.47	12.11.47	Purchased for Alitalia, to whom transferred. Never flew for BEA.
G-AHCB	1296	-	.1.47	21.7.47	Purchased for Alitalia, to whom transferred. Never flew for BEA.
G-AHCD	1298	-	.5.47	17.12.47	Purchased for Alitalia, to whom transferred. Never flew for BEA.
G-AHCE	1299	-	.2.47	7.8.47	Purchased for Alitalia, to whom transferred. Never flew for BEA.

BELL HELICOPTERS

AIRCRAFT TYPE: BELL 47 B3 — **BEA CLASS NAME: KING ARTHUR CLASS**

REGISTRA-TION	C/N	BEA NAME	DELIVERY DATE	DISPOSAL DATE	REMARKS
G-AKFA	69	Sir Balin	24.7.47	-	WO Gatwick 4.1.55.
G-AKFB	73	Sir Balan	24.7.47	11.9.64	Sold to Autair Helicopters.

BELL HELICOPTERS

AIRCRAFT TYPE: BELL 212 (Owned by BEAH) — **BEA CLASS NAME: -**

REGISTRA-TION	C/N	BEA NAME	DELIVERY DATE	DISPOSAL DATE	REMARKS
G-BAFN	30550	-	1.11.72	-	To British Airways Helicopters.

BOEING

AIRCRAFT TYPE: BOEING 707.436 (Owned by BEA Air Tours) — **BEA CLASS NAME: -**

REGISTRA-TION	C/N	BEA NAME	DELIVERY DATE	DISPOSAL DATE	REMARKS
G-APFB	17703	-	27.3.74	-	Leased to Syrian Arab A/L from 28.3.74. To British Air Tours.
G-APFD	17705	-	16.2.73	-	To British Air Tours.
G-APFG	17708	-	31.3.73	-	To British Air Tours.
G-APFH	17709	-	15.1.72	-	To British Air Tours.
G-APFK	17712	-	30.12.71	-	To British Air Tours.
G-APFL	17713	-	1.12.72	-	Leased to Syrian Arab A/L from 28.3.74. To British Air Tours.
G-APFO	17716	-	15.11.72	-	To British Air Tours.
G-ARWD*	18372	-	15.1.73	-	To British Air Tours.

* G-ARWD was a Boeing 707.465.

BRISTOL AEROPLANE COMPANY

AIRCRAFT TYPE: BRISTOL 170.Mark 21 **BEA CLASS NAME: YEOMAN**

REGISTRATION	C/N	BEA NAME	DELIVERY DATE	DISPOSAL DATE	REMARKS
G-AICS	12762	Yeoman/ Sir George White	16.8.50	13.5.57	Leased to Silver City Airways 10.6.52 to 12.5.57, and then sold to them.

BRISTOL AEROPLANE COMPANY

AIRCRAFT TYPE: BRISTOL 171 **BEA CLASS NAME: KING ARTHUR CLASS**

REGISTRATION	C/N	BEA NAME	DELIVERY DATE	DISPOSAL DATE	REMARKS
G-ALSR	12886	Sir Gareth	9.11.51	15.10.54	Leased from manufacturer for evaluation. Not owned by BEA.
G-AMWG	13068	Sir Gaiwan	25.6.53	12.7.56	Sold to Ansett ANA.
G-AMWH	13069	Sir Geraint	30.6.53	4.8.64	Sold in England to be used as an aerial crane.

BRISTOL AEROPLANE COMPANY

AIRCRAFT TYPE: BRISTOL 173 **BEA CLASS NAME: KING ARTHUR CLASS**

REGISTRATION	C/N	BEA NAME	DELIVERY DATE	DISPOSAL DATE	REMARKS
G-AMJI	12872	Sir Bors	20.7.56	.8.56	Leased from the manufacture for evaluation. Not owned by BEA.

BRITISH AIRCRAFT CORPORATION

AIRCRAFT TYPE: BAC 1-11.408 **BEA CLASS NAME:-**

REGISTRATION	C/N	BEA NAME	DELIVERY DATE	DISPOSAL DATE	REMARKS
G-BBMG	115	-	26.9.73	-	Aircraft registered to British A/W Regional not BEA. Incuded for information only.

N.B. Another two BAC 1.11.400s were also ordered by BA in 1973 (G-BBME and G-BBMF). There were delivered in April and May 1974 respectively to British Airways Regional.

BRITISH AIRCRAFT COPORATION

AIRCRAFT TYPE: BAC 1-11.510 **BEA CLASS NAME: SUPER 1-11**

REGISTRATION	C/N	BEA NAME	DELIVERY DATE	DISPOSAL DATE	REMARKS
G-AVMH	136	-	12.6.69	-	To British Airways.
G-AVMI	137	-	2.4.69	-	To British Airways.
G-AVMJ	138	-	29.8.68	-	To British Airways.
G-AVMK	139	-	16.9.68	-	To British Airways.
G-AVML	140	-	4.10.68	-	To British Airways.
G-AVMM	141	-	25.10.68	-	To British Airways.
G-AVMN	142	-	20.11.68	-	To British Airways.
G-AVMO	143	-	27.11.68	-	To British Airways.
G-AVMP	144	-	11.12.68	-	To British Airways.
G-AVMR	145	-	5.5.70	-	To British Airways.
G-AVMS	146	-	13.1.69	-	To British Airways.
G-AVMT	147	-	28.3.69	-	To British Airways.
G-AVMU	148	-	19.3.69	-	To British Airways.
G-AVMV	149	-	21.4.69	-	To British Airways.
G-AVMW	150	-	2.5.69	-	To British Airways.
G-AVMX	151	-	20.6.69	-	To British Airways.
G-AVMY	152	-	21.7.69	-	To British Airways.
G-AVMZ	153	-	15.8.69	-	To British Airways.

DE HAVILLAND

AIRCRAFT TYPE: COMET 4B **BEA CLASS NAME: -**

REGISTRATION	C/N	BEA NAME	DELIVERY DATE	DISPOSAL DATE	REMARKS
G-APMA	06421	Edmund Halley	23.12.59	-	Operated BEA's last scheduled Comet service on 31.10.71. Scrapped LHR 6.1.72.
G-APMB	06422	Walter Gale	9.11.59	25.6.70	Operated BEA's first scheduled Comet service on 1.4.60, Tel Aviv - LHR. Sold to Channel Airways.
G-APMC	06423	Andrew Crommeun	16.11.59	12.3.70	Sold to BEA Air Tours.
G-APMD	06435	William Denning	29.3.60	31.3.70	Sold to BEA Air Tours.
G-APME	06436	John Tebbutt	10.5.60	21.2.72	Leased to BEA Air Tours 8.70 to 2.72 and sold to Dan Air.
G-APMF	06426	William Finley	27.1.60	1.4.70	Sold to BEA Air Tours.
G-APMG	06442	-	31.7.60	16.3.70	Sold to BEA Air Tours.
G-ARCO	06449	-	13.4.61	-	WO over Meditteranean 12.10 67.
G-ARCP	06451	-	19.4.61	22.5.70	Sold to BEA Air Tours.
G-ARGM	06453	-	6.5.61	31.3.70	Originally allocated registration G-AREI. Sold to BEA Air Tours.
G-ARJK	06452	-	15.5.61	5.3.70	Sold to BEA Air Tours.
G-ARJL	06455	-	31.5.61	1.3.70	Leased to Olympic A/W Summer 1964. Sold to BEA Air Tours.
G-ARJM	06456	-	26.6.61	-	WO Ankara 21.12.61.
G-ARJN	06459	-	4.8.61	25.3.70	Sold to BEA Air Tours.

In addition the following aircraft were briefly registered to BEA either prior to delivery to Olympic Airways or on disposal by Olympic:

REGISTRATION	C/N	BEA NAME	DELIVERY DATE	DISPOSAL DATE	REMARKS
G-APYC (ex SX-DAK)	06437	-	3.11.69	26.1.70	From Olympic for sale to Channel A/W.
G-APYD (ex SX-DAL)	06438	-	3.11.69	27.2.70	From Olympic for sale to Channel A/W.
G-APZM (ex SX-DAN)	06440	-	14.7.60 3.11.69	.7.60 14.5.70	From De Havilland to Olympic A/W. From Olympic for sale to Channel A/W.
G-ARDI (ex SX-DAO)	06447	-	25.3.61 6.11.69	.3.61 .4.70	From De Havilland to Olympic A/W. From Olympic for sale to Channel A/W.

DE HAVILLAND

AIRCRAFT TYPE: COMET 4B (Owned by BEA Air Tours) **BEA CLASS NAME:-**

REGISTRATION	C/N	BEA NAME	DELIVERY DATE	DISPOSAL DATE	REMARKS
G-APMC	06423	-	12.3.70	.10.73	Sold to Dan Air.
G-APMD	06435	-	31.3.70	9.9.72	Sold to Dan Air.
G-APME	06436	-	1.8.70	.2.72	Leased from BEA.
G-APMF	06426	-	1.4.70	31.1.73	Sold to Dan Air.
G-APMG	06442	-	16.3.70	.4.73	Sold to Dan Air.
G-ARCP	06451	-	22.5.70	22.10.73	Sold to Dan Air.
G-ARGM	06453	-	31.3.70	1.11.73	Sold to Dan Air.
G-ARJK	06452	-	5.3.70	1.10.73	Sold to Dan Air.
G-ARJL	06455	-	1.3.70	31.10.73	Operated Air Tours first service on 6.3.70 and last Comet service on 31.10.73. Sold to Dan Air.
G-ARJN	06459	-	25.3.70	15.2.73	Sold to Dan Air.

DE HAVILLAND

AIRCRAFT TYPE: DH84 DRAGON — **BEA CLASS NAME: -**

REGISTRATION	C/N	BEA NAME	DELIVERY DATE	DISPOSAL DATE	REMARKS
G-ACIT	6039	-	1.2.47	.1.49	Inherited from Scottish A/W. Used as a communications aircraft. Sold to Speedbird Flying Club.

DE HAVILLAND

AIRCRAFT TYPE: HERON IB — **BEA CLASS NAME: HEBRIDES**

REGISTRATION	C/N	BEA NAME	DELIVERY DATE	DISPOSAL DATE	REMARKS
G-ANXA	14044	Sir John Hunter/ Sister Jean Kennedy	23.2.55	20.11.73	Renamed in memory of the nurse killed in the crash of G-AOFY. Sold to Peters Aviation.
G-ANXB	14048	Sir James Simpson	12.2.55	25.10.73	Operated BEA's last scheduled Heron service on 31.3.73 Barra-Tiree-Glasgow. Sold to Peters Aviation.
G-AOFY	14099	Sir Charles Bell	13.4.56	-	WO Islay 28.9.57.

DE HAVILLAND

AIRCRAFT TYPE: HERON 2 — **BEA CLASS NAME: -**

REGISTRATION	C/N	BEA NAME	DELIVERY DATE	DISPOSAL DATE	REMARKS
REGISTRATION	C/N	BEA NAME	DELIVERY DATE	DISPOSAL DATE	REMARKS
G-AORG	14101	-	-	-	Neither aircraft delivered. Had been ordered in 1955 to replace DH89s on Alderney services, but when Jersey A/L took over these routes in April 1956 the and Herons were delivered to them.
G-AORH	14102	-	-	-	

DE HAVILLAND

AIRCRAFT TYPE: MOSQUITO PR34 — **BEA CLASS NAME: -**

REGISTRATION	C/N	BEA NAME	DELIVERY DATE	DISPOSAL DATE	REMARKS
G-AJZE	RG231 (Military Serial)	-	1.3.48	.12.49	Used by the Gust Research Unit.
G-AJZF	RG238 (Military Serial)	-	9.6.48	.12.49	Used by the Gust Research Unit.

DE HAVILLAND

AIRCRAFT TYPE: MOTH — **BEA CLASS NAME: -**

REGISTRATION	C/N	BEA NAME	DELIVERY DATE	DISPOSAL DATE	REMARKS
G-AAWO	1235	-	1.2.47	31.3.48	Inherited from Scottish Airways. Used briefly as a communications aircraft. Given to Captain Fresson on his departure from BEA.

DE HAVILLAND

AIRCRAFT TYPE: DH89A RAPIDE **BEA CLASS NAME: ISLANDER**

REGISTRA-TION	C/N	BEA NAME	DELIVERY DATE	DISPOSAL DATE	REMARKS
G-ACPP (DH89)	6254	-	1.2.47	.4.48	Inherited from Great Western & Southern Airlines. Sold to Aircraft and Engineering Services Limited.
G-ADAJ (DH89)	6276	-	1.2.47	.11.47	Inherited from Scottish A/W. Sold to Air France.
G-AERN	6345	-	1.2.47	.11.47	Inherited from West Coast Air Services. Transferred to Gibraltar Airways.
G-AEWL	6367	-	1.2.47	14.5.48	Inherited from Scottish Airways. Sold to C. Allen.
G-AFEZ	6408	Lord Shaftsbury	1.2.47	5.6.56	Inherited from Isle of Man Air Services. Sold to Air Views.
G-AFOI	6450	-	1.2.47	7.6.48	Inherited from Scottish Airways. Sold to Gibraltar Airways.
G-AFRK	6441	Rudyard Kipling	1.2.47	16.5.56	Inherited from Scottish Airways. Sold to Airviews.
G-AGDG	6547	-	1.2.47	21.11.47	Inherited from Scottish Airways. Sold to Air France.
G-AGDM	6584	-	12.4.47	.5.48	Inherited from Allied Airways. Sold to C. Allen.
G-AGEE	6622	-	1.2.47	.11.47	Inherited from Great Western & Southern Airlines. Transferred to Gibraltar Airways.
G-AGHI	6455	-	21.4.47	1.7.48	Inherited from Allied Airways. Sold to C. Allen.
G-AGIC	6522	-	1.2.47	20.11.47	Inherited from Scottish Airways. Sold to Air France.
G-AGIF	6509	-	1.2.47	.4.48	Inherited from Scottish Airways. Sold to Ulster Aviation.
G-AGJF	6499	-	1.2.47	-	Inherited from Scottish Airways. WO Barra 6.8.47.
G-AGJG	6517	-	1.2.47	.10.48	Inherited from Scottish Airways. Sold to Adie Aviation.
G-AGLE	6784	-	1.2.47	8.6.48	Inherited from Railway Air Services. Sold to C. Allen.
G-AGLP	6780	-	1.2.47	8.6.48	Inherited from Railway Air Services. Sold to C. Allen.
G-AGLR	6781	-	1.2.47	21.6.48	Inherited from Railway Air Services. Sold to Lees Hill Aviation.
G-AGOJ	6850	-	1.2.47	18.6.48	Inherited from Scottish Airways. Sold to Lancashire Aircraft Corporation.
G-AGPH	6889	Sir Henry Havelock	1.4.47	-	Inherited from Channel Islands Airways. Damaged Barra 6.12.51 and WFU.
G-AGPI	6885	-	1.4.47	.5.48	Inherited from Channel Islands Airways. Sold to Lees Hill Aviation.
G-AGSH	6884	James Kier Hardy	1.4.47	4.5.56	Inherited from Channel Islands Airways. Sold to Airviews.
G-AGSH	6884	Sir Baden Powell	12.1.62	2.5.64	Purchased to replace G-AKZB. Sold to British Westpoint Airlines.

G-AGSJ	6888	-	1.2.47	25.5.48	Inherited from Isle of Man Air Services. Sold to Island Air Services.
G-AGSK	6887	Lord Kitchener	1.4.47	15.12.52	Inherited from Channel Islands Airways. Sold to Gibraltar Airways.
G-AGUF	6855	-	1.4.47	18.6.48	Inherited from Channel Islands Airways. Sold to Island Air Service.
G-AGUG	6859	-	1.4.47	18.6.48	Inherited from Channel Islands Airways. Sold to Lancashire Aircraft Corporation
G-AGUP	6911	Sir Robert Peel	1.2.47	18.8.51	Inherited from Isle of Man Air Services. Sold to Jersey Airlines.
G-AGUR	6910	Lord Roberts	1.2.47	10.11.53	Inherited from Scottish Airways. Sold to C.E. Harper Aviation.
G-AGUU	6908	Sir Colin Campbell	1.2.47	1.8.52	Inherited from Great Western & Southern Airlines. Sold to Malasyian Airways.
G-AGUV	6912	General Gordon	1.2.47	6.1.53	Inherited from Great Western & Southern Airlines. Sold to Gibraltar Airways.
G-AHGF	6903	-	1.2.47	21.6.48	Inherited from Railway Air Services. Sold to Lees Hill Aviation.
G-AHGH	6934	-	1.2.47	21.6.48	Inherited from Railway Air Services. Sold to Patrick Duval Aviation.
G-AHGI	6935	-	1.2.47	21.6.48	Inherited from Railway Air Services. Sold to Patrick Duval Aviation.
G-AHKR	6824	-	1.2.47	-	Inherited from Isle of Man Air Services. WO Isle of Man 15.4.47.
G-AHKS	6812	Sir Robert Louis Stevenson	1.2.47	25.4.55	Inherited from AAJC Pool. Sold to Eagle Aviation.
G-AHKT	6811	Lord Tennyson	1.2.47	.4.53	Inherited from Isle of Man Air Services. Sold to A.J. Whittemore.
G-AHKU	6810	Cecil John Rhodes	1.2.47	2.5.64	Inherited from Isle of Man Air Services. Operated last scheduled passenger DH89 flight for BEA from Scillies to Land's End on 1.5.64. Sold to British Westpoint Airlines.
G-AHKV	6792	Sir James Outram	1.2.47	.4.53	Inherited from Isle of Man Air Services. Sold to A.J. Whittemore.
G-AHLL	6576	Sir Henry Lawrence	1.2.47	-	Inherited from Scottish Airways. Damaged Land's End 21.5.59 and WFU.
G-AHLM	6708	-	1.2.47	.3.48	Inherited from Scottish Airways. Sold to Marshalls of Cambridge.
G-AHLN	6754	-	1.2.47	.4.48	Inherited from Scottish Airways. Sold to Ulster Aviation.
G-AHXV	6747	-	1.2.47	-	Inherited from AAJC Pool. WO North Ronaldsay 15.1.49.
G-AHXW	6782	John Nicholson	1.2.47	13.3.53	Inherited from AAJC Pool. Sold to A.J. Whittemore.
G-AHXX	6800	Islander	1.2.47	4.6.52	Inherited from AAJC Pool. Sold to Malasyian Airways.
G-AHXY	6808	-	1.2.47	-	Inherited from AAJC Pool. WO Renfrew 27.12.48.
G-AHXZ	6825	Charles Dickens	1.2.47	-	Inherited from AAJC Pool. WO Renfrew 28.8.51.
G-AIHN	6498	-	1.2.47	.11.47	Inherited from Railway Air Services. Transferred to Gibraltar Airways.
G-AJCL	6722	Sir Henry Lawrence	12.6.59	2.5.64	Purchased to replace G-AHLL. Flew last commercial Rapide service from Scillies to Land's End on 1.5.64, an ambulance charter. Sold to British Westpoint.
G-AJSK	6500	Lord Lister	1.5.49	30.12.52	Sold to Gibraltar Airways.
G-AJXB	6530	William Gilbert Grace	17.12.48	25.4.55	Sold to Eagle Aviation.
G-AKDX	6898	-	25.8.47	.7.49	Sold to Adie Aviation.
G-AKZB	6790	Sir Baden Powell	8.2.49	-	WO Land's End 12.12.61.

N.B. It seems probable that some of the aircraft inherited on 1.2.47 never actually flew for BEA and were stored pending delivery to their new owners in 1947/48.

DOUGLAS

AIRCRAFT TYPE: DC-3 DAKOTA 3 **BEA CLASS NAME: PIONAIR**

Notes: A: Aircraft converted to Pionair Leopard Class. B: Aircraft not converted to Pionair Standard.

REGISTRATION		C/N	BEA NAME	DELIVERY DATE	DISPOSAL DATE	REMARKS
G-AGHH	(B)	9187	-	24.1.49	10.2.49	Leased from BOAC.
G-AGHJ		9413	Albert Ball	1.8.46	28.3.61	Sold to Jersey Airlines.
G-AGHL		9407	Lanoe Hawker	1.8.46	23.3.60	Sold to Field Aircraft Services.
G-AGHM		9623	Edward Maitland	21.2.51	26.8.64	Leased to Cambrian A/W from 16.4.61, and sold to them.
G-AGHP	(A)	9408	Bert Hinkler	17.12.48	-	WO Chateney (France) 16.5.58.
G-AGHS		10099	Horace Short	1.8.46	1.5.63	Leased to Cambrian A/W from 2.3.61, and sold to them.
G-AGHU	(B)	9863	-	17.8.46	9.7.47	Leased from BOAC.
G-AGIO	(B)	11907	-	1.8.46	28.7.47	Leased from BOAC.
G-AGIP		11903	Horatio Phillips	1.8.46	7.2.61	Leased to Cambrian A/W from 31.1.60, and sold to them.
G-AGIS		12017	Ross Smith	1.8.46	8.9.53	Sold to Aero Services London Ltd.
G-AGIT	(B)	11921	-	1.8.46	30.7.47	Leased from BOAC.
G-AGIU		12096	Edward Busk	20.9.46	21.3.61	Sold to Ministry of Aviation for Air Mali.
G-AGIW	(B)	12186	-	1.8.46	-	WO Mill Hill (London) 17.10.50.
G-AGIX	(B)	12053	-	1.8.46	-	WO Sywell 30.7.48.
G-AGIZ	(A)	12075	Oliver Swann	22.6.49	1.2.54	Damaged Guernsey 22.9.53, repaired, and sold to Field Aircraft Services.
G-AGJV		12195	John Porte	1.8.46	2.12.60	Sold to Derby Airways.
G-AGJW		12199	Wilfred Parke	1.8.46	5.11.58	Sold to BOAC Associate Companies.
G-AGJZ		12054	John Stringfellow	1.8.46	22.3.60	Sold to Field Aviation Services.
G-AGNF (Dakota 4)	(B)	26979	-	1.8.46	14.10.49	Sold to Field Aviation Services.
G-AGNG (Dakota 4)	(B)	26997	-	1.8.46	20.5.48	Leased from BOAC.
G-AGNK (Dakota 4)		15540	Edward Mannock	29.3.51	26.5.61	Sold to East Anglian Flying Services.
G-AGYX		12472	George Holt Thomas	1.8.46	21.4.61	Sold to Autair.
G-AGYZ	(A)	12278	Charles Kingsford Smith	1.2.47	29.3.54	Sold to Eagle Aviation.
G-AGZB		12180	Robert Smith Barry	1.2.47	8.12.60	Operated last BEA Scheduled Pionair flight ex LHR on 31.10.60. Sold to East Anglian Flying Services.
G-AGZC		12222	Samuel Cody	19.8.46	26.2.61	Sold to the Ministry of Aviation for Air Mali.
G-AGZD		12450	Percy Pilcher	1.8.46	26.7.60	Sold to East Anglian Flying Services.
G-AGZE	(B)	12416	-	19.8.46	16.9.47	Leased from BOAC.
G-AHCS	(B)	12348	-	1.8.46	-	WO Oslo 7.8.46.
G-AHCT		12308	Hiram Maxim	1.8.46	29.3.54	Sold to Eagle Aviation.
G-AHCU	(A)	13381	Charles Ulm	1.8.46	18.5.62	Sold to East Anglian Flying Services.
G-AHCV		12443	George Cayley	1.8.46	8.6.61	Sold to East Anglian Flying Services.
G-AHCW	(B)	13308	-	1.8.46	-	WO Near Coventry 19.2.49.
G-AHCX	(A)	13335	Spencer Grey	1.8.46	27.6.62	Sold to Yemen Airlines.
G-AHCY	(B)	12355	-	1.8.46	-	WO Near Oldham 19.8.49.
G-AHCZ		11924	Charles Samson	1.8.46	9.1.61	Leased to Cambrian Airways from 2.3.59, and sold to them.
G-AHDA	(B)	12177	-	3.9.46	-	Purchased for spares only. Scrapped at Liverpool.

G-AHDB	(B)	12077	-	3.9.46	-	Purchased for spares only. Scrapped at Liverpool.
G-AHDC	(B)	13481	-	3.9.46	-	Purchased for spares only. Scrapped at Liverpool.
G-AIWD		13475	John Dunne	26.2.51	17.5.60	Sold to BKS Air Transport.
G-AJDE		13182	David Henderson	1.1.51	6.2.61	Sold to Martin Air Charters.
G-AJHY		13388	William Henson	23.8.47	20.6.61	Sold to Westpoint Aviation.
G-AJHZ		12421	Bentfield Hucks	10.7.47	28.3.61	Sold to Jersey Airlines.
G-AJIA		12208	John Alcock	24.6.47	22.3.61	Sold to Ministry of Aviation for Air Mali.
G-AJIB		9624	Griffith Brewer	30.7.47	26.2.60	Sold to East Anglian Flying Services.
G-AJIC		9487	Roy Chadwick	22.5.47	29.3.61	Sold to Autair.
G-AKJH		13164	Edward Hilman	29.11.50	17.4.61	Sold to Derby Airways.
G-AKNB		9043	Sefton Brancker	13.11.50	11.12.59	Sold to Silver City Airways.
G-ALCB	(B)	9878	-	.6.50	-	Purchased for spares only.
G-ALCC		10106	Harry Hawker	12.4.49	13.9.63	Leased to Cambrian A/W from 2.4.61 and sold to them.
G-ALLI		19351	Samuel Instone	17.5.49	4.3.60	Sold to Travelair.
G-ALPN		12158	Godfrey Paine	17.11.50	18.11.59	Sold to Silver City Airways.
G-ALTT	(A)	12000	Charles Grey	5.7.49	13.11.62	Operated last scheduled BEA Pionair flight, Islay-Campbeltown-Glasgow on 19.5.62. Sold to Autair.
G-ALXK (Dakota 4)		16080	Rex Pierson	2.6.50	8.7.61	Sold to North South Airlines.
G-ALXL (Dakota 4)		16487	Charles Rolls	19.5.50	13.4.62	Leased to Cambrian A/W from 3.5.60, and sold to them.
G-ALXM (Dakota 4)		16465	William Rhodes Moorhouse	26.4.50	1.7.60	Sold to Martin Air Charters.
G-ALXN (Dakota 4)	(A)	14661	Henry Royce	22.9.50	25.5.62	Converted to Dart DC-3 between 14.1.51 and 8.6.51. Operated first Dart DC-3 service 15.8.51. Reconverted to standard Pionair Leopard 11.53. Sold to East Anglian Flying Services.
G-ALYF		19350	Pionair	9.12.50	22.3.61	Operated first Pionair service on 24.1.51, a charter London-Dublin. Sold to Westpoint Aviation.
G-AMDB	(A)	14987	Claude Johnson	10.10.50	16.3.62	Converted to Dart DC-3 between 14.1.51 and 5.9.51. Reconverted to standard Pionair Leopard 11.53. Sold to Westpoint Aviation.
G-AMDZ		12911	Frank Barnwell	21.1.51	4.4.60	Sold to East Anglian Flying Services.
G-AMFV		10105	Richard Howard	11.12.50	2.6.60	Leased to Cambrian A/W from 16.3.59 and sold to them.
G-AMFV	(B)	10105	-	4.3.63	1.6.70	Purchased for Gibraltar A/W. Did not fly for BEA. Sold to C.47 Aviation.
G-AMGD		9628	George Brackley	3.11.50	8.4.60	Originally allocated registration G-AJXL, changed to avoid confusion with G-ALXL. Sold to Autair.
G-AMJX (Dakota 4)		15635	Reginald Mitchell	11.5.51	2.6.60	Leased to Cambrian A/W from 20.3.59 and sold to them.
G-AMJY (Dakota 4)		16808	James McCudden	11.5.51	11.11.59	Sold to Air Ceylon.
G-AMKE (Dakota 4)		14483	Frederick Lanchester	11.6.51	4.7.61	Sold to Air Links.
G-AMNV (Dakota 4)	(A)	16833	Eric Geddes	14.1.52	21.6.62	Sold to Tyne Tees Air Charters.
G-AMNW (Dakota 4)	(A)	14177	Frank Searle	14.1.52	29.5.62	Sold to East Anglian Flying Services.
G-AMYB (Dakota 4)	(B)	33346	Lord Hood	.4.56	.11.56	Leased from Eagle Airways.

N.B. In addition the following DC-3s were registered to BEA prior to delivery to Cyprus Airways, though they did not fly for the Corporation:

G-AKII	(B)	12299	-	18.9.47	15.12.47	Transferred to Cyprus Airways.
G-AKIJ	(B)	13304	-	18.9.47	3.3.48	Transferred to Cyprus Airways.
G-AKIK	(B)	13487	-	18.9.47	17.12.47	Transferred to Cyprus Airways.

HANDLEY PAGE

AIRCRAFT TYPE: HERALD **BEA CLASS NAME: —**

REGISTRATION	C/N	BEA NAME	DELIVERY DATE	DISPOSAL DATE	REMARKS
G-APWA	149	-	.1.62	.4.62	Loaned from Handley Page to be used on Duke of Edinburgh's tour of South America.
G-APWB	150	-	10.3.62	28.11.66	Operated first BEA Herald service 16.4.62 Glasgow-Shetland, and last Herald service on 31.10 66, Islay-Campbeltown-Glasgow. Sold to Autair.
G-APWC	151	-	9.1.62	28.11.66	Used on Duke of Edinburgh'sSouth American tour 1962. Sold to Autair.
G-APWD	152	-	30.4.62	28.11.66	Sold to Autair.

NB: None of the Heralds were owned by BEA, but G-APWB, 'WC, 'WD were leased to BEA by the Ministry of Supply.

HAWKER SIDDELEY

AIRCRAFT TYPE: ARGOSY 101 — **BEA CLASS NAME: —**

REGISTRATION	C/N	BEA NAME	DELIVERY DATE	DISPOSAL DATE	REMARKS
G-AOZZ	6651	-	21.12.61	27.7.65	Returned to Hawker Siddeley in part exchange for Argosy 222s.
G-APRM	6653	-	29.11.61	22.3.65	Returned to Hawker Siddeley in part exchange for Argosy 222s. Leased back from Hawker Siddeley 23.7.65 to 11.8.66 to cover loss of G-ASXL.
G-APRN	6654	-	6.11.61	3.5.65	Returned to Hawker Siddeley in part exchange for Argosy 222s.

HAWKER SIDDELEY

AIRCRAFT TYPE: ARGOSY 222 — **BEA CLASS NAME: —**

REGISTRATION	C/N	BEA NAME	DELIVERY DATE	DISPOSAL DATE	REMARKS
G-ASXL	6800	-	28.1.65	-	WO Costalba (Italy) 4.7.65.
G-ASXM	6801	-	2.3.65	15.6.70	Sold to Midwest Airlines.
G-ASXN	6802	-	26.3.65	26.6.70	Sold to Midwest Airlines.
G-ASXO	6803	-	28.4.65	4.4.70	Sold to Midwest Airlines.
G-ASXP	6804	-	16.6.65	-	WO Stansted 15.12.67.
G-ATTC	6805	-	21.11.66	29.4.70	Purchased to replace G-ASXL. First service LHR-Manchester-Glasgow on 22.11.66. Sold to Midwest Airlines.

HAWKER SIDDELEY

AIRCRAFT TYPE: HS748 — **BEA CLASS NAME: —**

REGISTRATION	C/N	BEA NAME	DELIVERY DATE	DISPOSAL DATE	REMARKS
G-BCOE	1736	-	-	-	Ordered in 1973 by BA Regional. Delivered after dissolution of BEA. Included for information only.
G-BCOF	1737	-	-	-	Ordered in 1973 by BA Regional. Delivered after dissolution of BEA. Included for information only.

HAWKER SIDDELEY

AIRCRAFT TYPE: TRIDENT IC — **BEA CLASS NAME: —**

REGISTRATION	C/N	BEA NAME	DELIVERY DATE	DISPOSAL DATE	REMARKS
G-ARPA	2101	-	18.8.65	-	To British Airways.
G-ARPB	2102	-	30.6.64	-	Leased to Hawker Siddeley for autoland development flying 1964-1967. To British Airways.
G-ARPC	2103	-	9.9.64	-	To British Airways.
G-ARPD	2104	-	8.1.65	-	To British Airways.
G-ARPE	2105	-	10.7.64	-	To British Airways.
G-ARPF	2106	-	31.3.64	-	To British Airways.

G-ARPG	2107	-	19.2.64	-	Operated BEA's first commercial Trident service on 11.3.64, LHR-Copenhagen. To British Airways.
G-ARPH	2108	-	25.3.64	-	To British Airways.
G-ARPI	2109	-	2.5.64	-	Out of service due to damage at LHR 3.7.68 to 14.2.69. WO Staines 18.6.72.
G-ARPJ	2110	-	26.5.64	-	To British Airways.
G-ARPK	2111	-	26.6.64	-	To British Airways.
G-ARPL	2112	-	6.8.64	-	To British Airways.
G-ARPM	2113	-	9.10.64	-	To British Airways.
G-ARPN	2115	-	4.12.64	-	To British Airways.
G-ARPO	2116	-	31.1.65	-	To British Airways.
G-ARPP	2117	-	25.2.65	-	To British Airways.
G-ARPR	2119	-	12.4.65	-	To British Airways.
G-ARPS	2120	-	1.6.65	-	Damaged by fire (possibly arson) LHR 29.7.69, and WFU.
G-ARPT	2121	-	9.7.65	-	WO LHR 3.7.68.
G-ARPU	2122	-	25.8.65	-	To British Airways.
G-ARPW	2123	-	15.10.65	-	To British Airways.
G-ARPX	2124	-	25.5.66	-	To British Airways.
G-ARPY	2126	-	-	-	WO Felthorpe 3.6.66 on test flight prior to delivery.
G-ARPZ	2127	-	1.7.66	-	To British Airways.

HAWKER SIDDELEY

AIRCRAFT TYPE: TRIDENT IE — **BEA CLASS NAME: —**

REGISTRATION	C/N	BEA NAME	DELIVERY DATE	DISPOSAL DATE	REMARKS
G-AVYE	2139	-	20.1.71	1.11.73	Operated by BEA Channel. Transferred to Northeast Airlines, subsequently to British Airways Regional.

HAWKER SIDDELEY

AIRCRAFT TYPE: TRIDENT 2E — **BEA CLASS NAME: —**

REGISTRATION	C/N	BEA NAME	DELIVERY DATE	DISPOSAL DATE	REMARKS
G-AVFA	2140	-	23.12.69	-	To British Airways.
G-AVFB	2141	-	6.6.68	19.6.72	Sold to Cyprus Airways.
G-AVFC	2142	-	6.8.68	-	To British Airways.
G-AVFD	2143	-	16.4.68	-	Operated first BEA commercial Trident 2 service. To British Airways.
G-AVFE	2144	-	8.5.68	-	To British Airways.
G-AVFF	2145	-	30.5.68	-	To British Airways.
G-AVFG	2146	-	4.7.68	-	To British Airways.
G-AVFH	2147	-	1.8.68	-	To British Airways.
G-AVFI	2148	-	27.11.68	-	To British Airways.
G-AVFJ	2149	-	21.12.68	-	To British Airways.
G-AVFK	2150	-	17.1.69	-	To British Airways.
G-AVFL	2151	-	18.2.69	-	To British Airways.
G-AVFM	2152	-	25.4.69	-	To British Airways.
G-AVFN	2153	-	22.5.69	-	To British Airways.
G-AVFO	2156	-	23.6.70	-	To British Airways.
G-AZXM	2154	-	28.6.72	-	To British Airways.

HAWKER SIDDELEY

AIRCRAFT TYPE: TRIDENT 3B **BEA CLASS NAME: —**

REGISTRATION	C/N	BEA NAME	DELIVERY DATE	DISPOSAL DATE	REMARKS
G-AWYZ	2301	-	23.3.72	-	To British Airways.
G-AWZA	2302	-	11.5.71	-	To British Airways.
G-AWZB	2303	-	24.2.71	-	Operated first commercial Trident 3 service on 1.3.71 from LHR to Orly. To British Airways.
G-AWZC	2304	-	18.2.71	-	To British Airways.
G-AWZD	2305	-	26.3.71	-	To British Airways.
G-AWZE	2306	-	8.4.71	-	To British Airways.
G-AWZF	2307	-	11.5.71	-	To British Airways.
G-AWZG	2308	-	12.6.71	-	To British Airways.
G-AWZH	2309	-	15.7.71	-	To British Airways.
G-AWZI	2310	-	9.8.71	-	To British Airways.
G-AWZJ	2311	-	16.9.71	-	To British Airways.
G-AWZK	2312	-	16.10.71	-	To British Airways.
G-AWZL	2313	-	25.11.71	-	To British Airways.
G-AWZM	2314	-	16.12.71	-	To British Airways.
G-AWZN	2315	-	20.1.72	-	To British Airways.
G-AWZO	2316	-	16.2.72	-	To British Airways.
G-AWZP	2317	-	21.3.72	-	To British Airways. First Service LHR-Glasgow 24.3.72.
G-AWZR	2318	-	13.4.72	-	To British Airways. First Service LHR-Glasgow 22.4.72.
G-AWZS	2319	-	5.5.72	-	To British Airways.
G-AWZT	2320	-	6.6.72	-	To British Airways.
G-AWZU	2321	-	10.7.72	-	To British Airways. First Service LHR-Glasgow 17.7.72.
G-AWZV	2322	-	8.8.72	-	To British Airways. First Service LHR-Glasgow 12.8.72.
G-AWZW	2323	-	29.11.72	-	To British Airways. First Service LHR-Manchester 9.12.72.
G-AWZX	2324	-	23.3.73	-	To British Airways.
G-AWZY	2325	-	-	-	Re-registered G-AYVF before delivery.
G-AWZZ	2326	-	19.4.73	-	To British Airways.
G-AYVF	2325	-	14.3.73	-	To British Airways.

JUNKERS

AIRCRAFT TYPE: JU52 (3M) **BEA CLASS NAME: JUPITER —**

REGISTRATION	C/N	BEA NAME	DELIVERY DATE	DISPOSAL DATE	REMARKS
G-AHBP	6750	-	1.2.47	.2.48	Inherited from RAS. Scrapped Castle Bromwich.
G-AHOC	501441	-	1.2.47	.2.48	Inherited from RAS. Scrapped Warrington.
G-AHOD	131150	-	1.2.47	-	Inherited from Scottish Airways. Used for spares only.
G-AHOE	SH.8C	-	1.2.47	.2.48	Inherited from RAS. Scrapped Warrington.
G-AHOF	8685	-	1.2.47	.2.48	Inherited from RAS. Scrapped Warrington.
G-AHOG	3317	-	1.2.47	.2.48	Inherited from RAS. Scrapped Warrington.
G-AHOH	641364	-	1.2.47	.2.48	Scrapped Warrington.
G-AHOI	641227	-	1.2.47	.2.48	Scrapped Warrington.
G-AHOJ	500138	-	1.2.47	.2.48	Scrapped Warrington.
G-AHOK	2298	-	-	-	Was to have been inherited from Scottish A/W, but damaged at Glasgow 26.1.47, and WFU.
G-AHOL	741213	-	1.2.47	.2.48	Scrapped Warrington.

N.B.: Several of these aircraft were registered to BEA before 1.2.47, but continued to be operated by RAS on behalf of BEA.

LOCKHEED

AIRCRAFT TYPE: L10 TRISTAR **BEA CLASS NAME: —**

REGISTRATION	C/N	BEA NAME	DELIVERY DATE	DISPOSAL DATE	REMARKS
G-BBAE	1083	-	-	-	These aircraft were ordered by the British Airways Board on behalf of BEA, but delivered to BA European after the dissolution of BEA. Included for information only.
G-BBAF	1093	-	-	-	
G-BBAG	1094	-	-	-	
G-BBAH	1101	-	-	-	
G-BBAI	1102	-	-	-	
G-BBAJ	1106	-	-	-	

MILES

AIRCRAFT TYPE: MARATHON IA **BEA CLASS NAME: CLANSMAN**

REGISTRATION	C/N	BEA NAME	DELIVERY DATE	DISPOSAL DATE	REMARKS
G-ALUB	101	Rob Roy	.4.51	.9.51	Loaned to BEA for trials only.
G-AMGW	127	Clansman	-	-	Aircraft not delivered as order cancelled.
G-AMGX	128	MacLeod	-	-	Aircraft not delivered as order cancelled.
G-AMHR	129	MacDonald	-	-	Aircraft not delivered as order cancelled.
G-AMHS	130	MacNeil	-	-	Aircraft not delivered as order cancelled.
G-AMHV	133	MacGregor	-	-	Aircraft not delivered as order cancelled.
G-AMHW	134	MacKenzie	-	-	Aircraft not delivered as order cancelled.
G-AMHX	135	MacDuff	-	-	Aircraft not delivered as order cancelled.

MILES

AIRCRAFT TYPE: MILES M.28 **BEA CLASS NAME: —**

REGISTRATION	C/N	BEA NAME	DELIVERY DATE	DISPOSAL DATE	REMARKS
G-AHAA	6268	-	1.8.46	.3.48	Used as a communications aircraft, and the Chairman's personal aircraft. Sold to K. E. Millard & Company.

SHORT

AIRCRAFT TYPE: SKYLINER **BEA CLASS NAME: —**

REGISTRATION	C/N	BEA NAME	DELIVERY DATE	DISPOSAL DATE	REMARKS
G-AZYW	SH1903	-	8.3.73	-	Operated first commercial BEA Skyliner service on 2.4.73, Glasgow-Tiree. To British Airways Regional.
G-BAIT	SH1908	-	20.4.73	-	To British Airways Regional.

SIKORSKY

AIRCRAFT TYPE: S.51 **BEA CLASS NAME: KING ARTHUR CLASS —**

REGISTRATION	C/N	BEA NAME	DELIVERY DATE	DISPOSAL DATE	REMARKS
G-AJHW	5117	Sir Baudwin	8.8.49	12.7.53	Purchased to replace G-AKCU. Sold to Autair Helicopters.
G-AJOR	5132	Sir Owen	26.8.47	16.7.53	Sold to Autair Helicopters.
G-AJOV	5135	Sir Lamorak	13.10.47	9.6.54	Sold to Autair Helicopters.
G-AKCU	5128	-	9.10.47	-	WO Croesor Dam (North Wales) 24.5.49.

SIKORSKY

AIRCRAFT TYPE: S.61N (Owned by BEAH) **BEA CLASS NAME: —**

REGISTRATION	C/N	BEA NAME	DELIVERY DATE	DISPOSAL DATE	REMARKS
G-ASNL	61220	-	28.1.64	-	Operated first commercial BEAH S.61 service on 2.5.64. Leased to BEA-Schreiner Helicopters 1968/69 as PH-SBH. To British Airways Helicopters.
G-ASNM	61221	-	5.2.64	-	Leased to BEA-Schreiner Helicopters 1969 as PH-SBC. WO North Sea 15.11.70.
G-ATBJ	61269	-	8.4.65	-	To British Airways Helicopters.
G-ATFM	61270	-	8.10.65	-	Inherited when BEA took full control of International Helicopters. To British Airways Helicopters.
G-AWFX	61216	-	5.9.68	-	To British Airways Helicopters.
G-AYOM	61143	-	7.1.71	-	To British Airways Helicopters.
G-AYOY	61476	-	22.2.71	-	To British Airways Helicopters.
G-AZCF	61488	-	22.8.71	-	To British Airways Helicopters.

TAYLORCRAFT

AIRCRAFT TYPE: AUSTER JI **BEA CLASS NAME: —**

REGISTRATION	C/N	BEA NAME	DELIVERY DATE	DISPOSAL DATE	REMARKS
G-AGVM	1872	-	3.7.47	13.3.48	Used by the BEA Aero Club. Sold to the Bristol & Wessex Aero Club.
G-AGYO	2006	-	9.8.47	27.7.48	Used mainly as a communications and training aircraft. Sold to Speedbird Flying Club.
G-AHCN	1980	-	19.7.47	13.3.48	Used by the BEA Aero Club. Sold to the Bristol & Wessex Aero Club.
G-AIBR	2151	-	19.7.47	9.3.48	Used mainly as a communications and training aircraft. Sold to Brooklands Aviation.

NB: From delivery until December 1947 all four aircraft were formally registered to the BEA Flying Club. Formal change of ownership to BEA occurred on December 1st for G-AGVM and G-AHCN, and on December 16th for G-AGYO and G-AIBR.

VICKERS

AIRCRAFT TYPE: MERCHANTMAN (VANGUARD CARGO CONVERSION) **BEA CLASS NAME: —**

REGISTRATION	C/N	BEA NAME	DELIVERY DATE	DISPOSAL DATE	REMARKS
G-APEG	710	-	23.7.71	-	To British Airways Cargo.
G-APEJ	713	-	31.7.73	-	To British Airways Cargo.
G-APEK	714	-	17.1.70	-	To British Airways Cargo.
G-APEL	715	-	18.10.70	-	To British Airways Cargo.
G-APEM	716	-	13.10.69	-	Operated first scheduled commercial Merchantman service on 7.2.70, LHR-Vienna-Stuttgart. To British Airways Cargo.
G-APEO	718	-	23.2.70	-	To British Airways Cargo.
G-APEP	719	-	8.3.71	-	To British Airways Cargo.
G-APES	721	-	21.4.70	-	To British Airways Cargo.
G-APET	722	-	.10.72	-	To British Airways Cargo.

VICKERS

AIRCRAFT TYPE: VANGUARD V.951 **BEA CLASS NAME: —**

REGISTRATION	C/N	BEA NAME	DELIVERY DATE	DISPOSAL DATE	REMARKS
G-APEA	704	Vanguard	27.3.61	-	Scrapped LHR 1.1.73.
G-APEB	705	Bellerphon	17.3.61	-	Scrapped LHR 6.6.73.
G-APEC	706	Sirius	14.1.61	-	WO Arselle (Belgium) 2.10.71.
G-APED	707	Defiance	30.1.61	-	Scrapped LHR 5.1.73.
G-APEE	708	Euryalus	2.12.60	-	WO LHR 27.10.65.
G-APEF	709	Victory	13.12.60	27.4.72	Operated BEA's first commercial Vanguard service on 17.12.60, LHR-Le Bourget. Sold to Templewood Aviation.

VICKERS

AIRCRAFT TYPE: VANGAURD V.953 **BEA CLASS NAME: —**

REGISTRATION	C/N	BEA NAME	DELIVERY DATE	DISPOSAL DATE	REMARKS
G-APEG	710	Arethusa	19.5.61	-	Converted to Merchantman 1971.
G-APEH	711	Audacious	21.6.61	31.3.74	Sold to Merpati Airlines.
G-APEI	712	Indefatigable	20.7.61	-	To British Airways.
G-APEJ	713	Ajax	16.8.61	-	Converted to Merchantman 1973.
G-APEK	714	Dreadnought	16.9.61	-	Converted to Merchantman 1970.
G-APEL	715	Leander	7.10.61	-	Converted to Merchantman 1970.
G-APEM	716	Agamemnon	8.11.61	-	Converted to Merchantman 1969.
G-APEN	717	Valiant	14.11.61	18.12.73	Sold to Templewood Aviation.
G-APEO	718	Orion	27.11.61	-	Converted to Merchantman 1969/70.
G-APEP	719	Superb	13.12.61	-	Converted to Merchantman 1970/71.
G-APER	720	Amethyst	16.1.62	-	To British Airways.
G-APES	721	Swiftsure	24.1.62	-	Converted to Merchantman 1970.
G-APET	722	Temeraire	23.2.62	-	Converted to Merchantman 1972.
G-APEU	723	Dauntless	30.3.62	-	To British Airways.

VICKERS

AIRCRAFT TYPE: VIKING IA **BEA CLASS NAME: —**

REGISTRATION	C/N	BEA NAME	DELIVERY DATE	DISPOSAL DATE	REMARKS
G-AGON	104	-	2.5.47	19.8.47	Used for training only. Transferred to Ministry of Supply for use by RAF.
G-AGRM	105	-	16.6.47	15.8.47	Used for training only. Transferred to Ministry of Supply for use by RAF.
G-AGRN	106	-	17.6.47	22.8.47	Used for training only. Transferred to Ministry of Supply for use by RAF.
G-AGRO	107	-	11.6.47	2.2.48	Transferred to Ministry of Transport who sold aircraft to James Stuart Travel.
G-AGRP	108	-	18.6.47	2.2.48	Leased from Ministry of Supply.
G-AGRS	110	-	14.8.46	19.2.47	Sold to BSAA.
G-AGRU	112	Vagarant	9.8.46	2.2.48	Sold to BSAA.
G-AGRV	114	Vallie	11.8.46	29.7.48	Transferred to Ministry of Transport who sold aircraft to James Stuart Travel.
G-AGRW	115	Vagabond	8.8.46	2.2.48	Transferred to Ministry of Transport who sold aircraft to James Stuart Travel.
G-AHON	116	Valentine	15.8.46	10.1.48	Sold to Trans World Charters.
G-AHOP	117	Valarie	19.8.46	2.2.48	Operated first commercial Viking service on 1.9.46, Northolt-Copenhagen. Transferred to Ministry of Transport who sold aircraft to British Netherlands A/S.
G-AHOR	118	Valet	29.8.46	2.2.48	Transferred to Ministry of Transport, who sold aircraft to James Stuart Travel.

G-AHOS	119	Valiant	7.9.46	2.2.48	Sold to BSAA.
G-AHOT	121	Valkyrie	2.9.46	10.1.48	Sold to Trans World Charters.
G-AHOU	122	Valley	27.9.46	2.2.48	Sold to BSAA.
G-AHOV	123	Valour	1.10.46	2.2.48	Transferred to Ministry of Transport who sold aircraft to James Stuart Travel.
G-AHOW	124	Vanessa	11.10.46	2.2.48	Transferred to Ministry of Transport who sold aircraft to James Stuart Travel.
G-AHOX	125	Vanguard	21.10.46	10.9.47	Transferred to Ministry of Supply for use by the RAF.
G-AHOY	128	Vanity	7.11.46	2.2.48	Transferred to Ministry of Transport who sold aircraft to James Stuart Travel.
G-AHOZ	129	Vantage	12.11.46	10.11.47	Transferred to Ministry of Transport who sold aircraft to British West Indian A/W.
G-AHPA	130	Varlet	23.11.46	15.8.47	Transferred to Ministry of Supply for use by RAF.
G-AHPB	132	Variety	20.11.46	2.2.48	Transferred to Ministry of Transport who sold aircraft to Field Aircraft Services.
G-AHPC	133	Vassal	21.11.46	2.2.48	Transferred to Ministry of Transport who sold aircraft to Field Aircraft Services.
G-AHPD	134	Vampire	3.12.46	2.2.48	Transferred to Ministry of Transport who sold aircraft to Field Aircraft Services.
G-AHPE	137	Vandal	6.12.46	2.2.48	Transferred to Ministry of Transport who sold aircraft to British West Indian A/W.
G-AHPF	138	Vedette	7.12.46	2.2.48	Transferred to Ministry of Transport who sold aircraft to British West Indian A/W.
G-AHPG	139	Velocity	-	-	Resold to Central African A/W prior to delivery to BEA.
G-AHPH	141	Velox	-	-	Not delivered.
G-AHPI	142	Velet	-	-	Not delivered.
G-AIJE	127	-	10.3.48	12.2.51	Loaned from Ministry of Supply, for de-icing trial.

VICKERS

AIRCRAFT TYPE: VIKING IB **BEA CLASS NAME: ADMIRAL**

(Note A: Not converted to Admiral Standard.)

REGISTRATION		C/N	BEA NAME	DELIVERY DATE	DISPOSAL DATE	REMARKS
G-AHPK	(A)	148	Veracity	15.4.47	-	WO Ruislip 6.1.48
G-AHPL		149	Verdant, Lord Anson	14.4.47	10.4.53	Sold to Central African Airways.
G-AHPM		152	Verderer, Lord Rodney	26.4.47	15.7.53	Sold to Eagle Aviation.
G-AHPN	(A)	155	Ventnor	24.3.47	-	WO Heathrow 31.10.50.
G-AHPO		157	Venturer, Sir Edward Howard, Lord Dundonald	12.3.47	21.4.53	Sold to Eagle Aviation for spares.
G-AHPP		160	Venus, Sir Charles Saunders Sir Peter Parker	15.4.47	-	WO Nuremburg 20.12.53.

G-AHPR		164	Verily, Prince Rupert	28.4.47	16.11.55	Sold to Field Aviation Services.
G-AHPS		167	Verity, Sir Doverton Sturdee	14.5.47	29.2.56	Sold in West Germany.
G-AIVB		215	Vernal, Robert Blake	16.5.47	2.12.55	Sold to First Air Trading Company.
G-AIVC		216	Vernon, Lord Collingwood	16.5.47	3.6.54	Sold to Eagle Aviation.
G-AIVD		217	Veteran, Lord Duncan	16.5.47	3.2.54	Sold in West Germany.
G-AIVE	(A)	218	Vestal	31.5.47	-	WO Largs (Scotland) 21.4.48.
G-AIVF		219	Vibrant, Sir James Somerville	30.5.47	29.2.56	Sold in West Germany.
G-AIVG		220	Viceroy, Sir George Rooke	30.5.47	-	Damaged Le Bourget 12.8.53, and WFU
G-AIVH		221	Vicinity, Lord Howe	30.5.47	14.5.53	Sold to Eagle Aviation.
G-AIVI		222	Victor, Viking	4.6.47	14.11.55	Sold to First Air Trading Company.
G-AIVJ		223	Victoria, Lord Jellicoe	18.7.47	13.2.56	Sold in West Germany.
G-AIVK		224	Victory, Lord Keyes	23.6.47	16.4.55	Sold to British International Airlines.
G-AIVL		225	Vigilant, Lord Hawke	25.6.47	25.4.55	Sold to Eagle Aviation.
G-AIVM		226	Vigorous, George Monck	8.7.47	15.12.55	Sold in West Germany.
G-AIVN		227	Violet, Sir William Penny Edward Boscawen	27.7.47	2.9.54	Sold to Central African Airways.
G-AIVO		228	Vilain, Edward Vernon	18.8.47	7.6.53	Sold to Eagle Aviation
G-AIVP	(A)	229	Vimy,	9.8.47	-	WO Berlin 5.4.48.
G-AIVR	(A)	230	-	-	-	Not delivered. Resold to Iraqi A/W.
G-AIVS	(A)	231	-	-	-	Not delivered. Resold to Iraqi A/W.
G-AIVT	(A)	232	-	-	-	Not delivered. Resold to Iraqi A/W.
G-AJBM		239	Vincent, Sir Charles Knowles, Sir Charles Watson	7.8.47	26.1.56	Sold to the Argentinian Air Force.
G-AJBN		240	Vindictive, Lord Nelson	11.9.47	5.1.55	Sold to the Argentinian Air Force.
G-AJBO		241	Vintage, John Benbow	12.9.47	18.5.53	Sold to Eagle Aviation.
G-AJBP		242	Vintner, Sir Hyde Parker	16.9.47	9.12.55	Sold to First Air Trading Company.
G-AJBR		243	Virginia, Sir Bertram Ramsay	24.9.47	5.11.54	Sold to BKS Air Transport.
G-AJBS		244	Virgo, Air Cloudsey Shovel	25.9.47	26.1.56	Sold to the Argentinian Air Force.
G-AJBT		245	Viper, Sir Thomas Trowbridge	19.9.47	18.4.55	Sold to Central African Airways.
G-AJBU		246	Virtue, Lord Bridport	16.1.48	16.11.55	Sold to Field Aviation Services.
G-AJBV		247	Viscount, Sir Henry Morgan	23.1.48	22.5.55	Sold to Iraqi Airways.
G-AJBW		248	Vista, Sir Willian Cornwallis	21.1.48	25.4.55	Sold to Eagle Aviation.
G-AJBX		249	Vital, Sir Edward Hughes	27.1.48	1.6.54	Sold to Eagle Aviation.
G-AJBY		250	Vitality, Sir Richard Strachan Lord Torrington	10.1.48	26.1.56	Sold in West Germany.
G-AJBZ	(A)	251	-	-	-	Not delivered. Resold to Air India.
G-AJCA		252	Vixen, Sir John Leake	7.2.49	12.6.54	Sold to Misrair.

G-AJCB	(A)	253	-	-	-	Not delivered. Resold to Air India.
G-AJCD		255	Vizor, Lord Barham	17.2.49	15.7.53	Sold to Eagle Aviation.
G-AJCE		256	Vivacious, Lord Exmouth	23.3.48	6.12.54	Sold to Eagle Aviation.
G-AJDI		258	Volatile, Sir Christopher Cradock, Lord Keith	25.4.49	26.1.56	Sold to the Argentinian Air Force.
G-AJDJ		259	Volley, Lord Beatty	1.3.49	9.6.54	Sold to Misrair.
G-AJDK		260	Volunteer, Richard Kempenfelt	22.3.49	11.9.53	Sold to the Jordanian Air Force.
G-AJDL		262	Vortex, Lord St Vincent	30.3.49	-	WO Belfast 5.1.53.
G-AJJN		289	Vulcan, Sir Charles Napier	13.12.49	13.12.54	Sold to BKS Air Transport.
G-AKBG		263	Votary, Sir Richard Bickerton Sir Thomas Hardy	25.5.49	21.4.55	Sold to Hunting Clan
G-AKBH		264	Voyager,	25.4.49	8.4.53	Sold to Eagle Aviation.
G-AMGG		290	Sir Robert Calder	20.3.51	1.4.55	Sold to Eagle Aviation.
G-AMGH		293	Sir John Duckworth	22.3.51	4.10.55	Sold in West Germany.
G-AMGI		297	Sir Henry Harwood	17.4.51	29.6.55	Sold to Eagle Aviation.
G-AMGJ		295	Sir John Warren	6.4.51	2.12.55	Sold to First Air Trading Company.
G-AMNJ		296	Lord Fisher	27.5.52	2.11.55	Sold in West Germany.
G-AMNR		291	Lord Charles Beresford	8.8.52	25.4.55	Sold to Eagle Aviation.
G-AMNS		294	Sir Dudley Pound	8.8.52	26.1.56	Sold to the Argentinian Air Force.
G-AMNX		292	Philip Broke	17.7.52	25.4.55	Sold to Eagle Aviation.

VICKERS

AIRCRAFT TYPE: VISCOUNT V.630 — **BEA CLASS NAME: —**

REGISTRATION	C/N	BEA NAME	DELIVERY DATE	DISPOSAL DATE	REMARKS
G-AHRF	1	-	28.7.50	23.8.50	Loaned from Vickers. Operated world's first commercial turbo-prop service from Northolt to Le Bourget on 29.7.50.

VICKERS

AIRCRAFT TYPE: VISCOUNT V.700 — **BEA CLASS NAME: DISCOVERY**

REGISTRATION	C/N	BEA NAME	DELIVERY DATE	DISPOSAL DATE	REMARKS
G-AMAV	3	Endeavour	.8.52	.2.53	Loaned from Vickers from route proving flights.
			.10.53	.11.53	Loaned again from Vickers for the London to New Zealand Air Race.

VICKERS

AIRCRAFT TYPE: VISCOUNT V.701 — **BEA CLASS NAME: DISCOVERY**

REGISTRATION	C/N	BEA NAME	DELIVERY DATE	DISPOSAL DATE	REMARKS
G-ALWE	4	Discovery	3.1.53	-	WO Manchester 14.3.57.
G-ALWF	5	Sir John Franklin	13.2.53	6.12.63	Sold to Channel Airways.
G-AMNY	6	Sir Ernest Shackelton	20.2.53	-	Operated first sustained Viscount service on 18.4.53 LHR-Athens-Nicosia. WO Malta 5.1.60.
G-AMNZ	20	James Cook	3.10.53	28.12.62	Sold to Cambrian Airways.
G-AMOA	9	Sir George Vancouver	17.4.53	6.12.63	Sold to Channel Airways.
G-AMOB	11	William Baffin	24.4.53	30.8.62	Sold to VASP.
G-AMOC	13	Richard Chancellor	4.6.53	6.12.63	Sold to Channel Airways.
G-AMOD	15	John Davis	26.6.53	30.8.62	Sold to VASP.
G-AMOE	17	Sir Edward Parry	13.7.53	20.1.65	Leased to Channel A/W 13.3.64 to 26.3.64, leased to British Eagle 26.3.64 to .12.64. Sold to Cambrian Airways.
G-AMOF	19	Sir Martin Frobrisher	8.8.53	30.8.62	Sold to VASP.
G-AMOG	7	Robert Falconer Scott	27.3.53	26.6.63	Sold to Cambrian Airways.
G-AMOH	21	Henry Hudson	14.10.53	6.12.63	Sold to Channel Airways.
G-AMOI	22	Sir Hugh Willoughby	5.11.53	23.3.63	Sold to VASP.
G-AMOJ	23	Sir James Ross	30.11.53	6.12.63	Sold to Channel Airways.
G-AMOK	24	Sir Humphrey Gilbert	5.12.53	19.2.63	Sold to LAV.
G-AMOL	25	David Livingstone	1.1.54	28.12.62	Sold to Cambrian Airways.
G-AMOM	26	James Bruce	27.1.54	-	WO Blackbushe 20.1.56.
G-AMON	27	Thomas Cavendish	5.3.54	1.3.63	Sold to Cambrian Airways.
G-AMOO	28	John Oxenham	19.12.53	14.11.66	Leased to Channel A/W .4.64 to .11.66, and sold to them.
G-AMOP	29	Mungo Park	16.2.54	6.1.63	Sold to Cambrian Airways.
G-ANHA	61	Anthony Jenkinson	19.10.54	30.8.62	Sold to VASP.

G-ANHB	62	Sir Henry Stanley	21.11.54	30.8.62	Sold to VASP.
G-ANHC	63	Sir Leo McClintock	19.12.54	-	WO Anzio (Italy) 22.10.58.
G-ANHD	64	Sir William Dampier	4.5.55	30.8.62	Sold to VASP.
G-ANHE	65	Gino Watkins	29.6.55	30.8.62	Sold to VASP.
G-ANHF	66	Matthew Flinders	11.7.55	30.8.62	Sold to VASP.
G-AOFX	182	Sir Joseph Banks	30.7.56	30.8.62	Purchased to replace G-AMOM. Sold to VASP.

VICKERS

AIRCRAFT TYPE: VISCOUNT V.700 (Other marks operated by BEA) **BEA CLASS NAME: DISCOVERY**

REGISTRATION	MARK OF VISCOUNT	C/N	BEA NAME	DELIVERY DATE	DISPOSAL DATE	REMARKS
G-ANRS	V.732	75	George Bass	19.11.55	31.3.56	Leased from BOAC.
G-AODG	V.736	77	Fridtjof Nansen	18.11.55	27.3.57	Leased from Fred Olsen (LN-FOF).
G-AODH	V.736	78	Roald Amundsen	14.12.55	22.4.57	Leased from Fred Olsen (LN-FOL).
G-APNF	V.745	225	Philip Cartaret	7.6.58	16.8.58	Leased from Vickers while BEA Viscounts undergoing spar modifications.
G-APNG	V.745	228	James Lancaster	26.6.58	6.3.58	Leased from Vickers while BEA Viscounts undergoing spar modifications.
G-APZP	V.779	250	-	26.3.60	1.3.61	Leased from Fred Olsen (LN-FOH) to cover for late delivery of Vanguards.
G-ARBW	V.779	247	-	19.6.60	6.2.61	Leased from Fred Olsen (LN-FOM) to cover for late delivery of Vanguards.

VICKERS

AIRCRAFT TYPE: VISCOUNT V.802 **BEA CLASS NAME: DISCOVERY**

REGISTRATION	C/N	BEA NAME	DELIVERY DATE	DISPOSAL DATE	REMARKS
G-AOJA	150	Sir Samuel White Baker	14.2.57	-	Originally allocated registration G-AOHA. WO Belfast 23.10.57.
G-AOJB	151	Stephen Borough	6.2.57	-	Originally allocated registration G-AOHB. To BEA Scottish 1971. To British A/W Regional 1973.
G-AOJC	152	Robert O'Hara Burke	19.1.57	-	Originally allocated registration G-AOHC. To BEA Scottish 1971. To British A/W Regional 1973.
G-AOJD	153	Sebastian Cabot	11.1.57	-	Originally allocated registration G-AOHD. Operated first V.802 service on 13.2.57, LHR-Glasgow. To BEA Channel 1971. To British Airways Regional 1973.
G-AOJE	154	Sir Alexander Mackenzie	26.1.57	-	Originally allocated registration G-AOHE. To BEA Scottish 1971. To British A/W Regional 1973.
G-AOJF	155	Sir George Somers	8.2.57	-	Originally allocated registration G-AOHF. To BEA Scottish 1971. To British A/W Regional 1973.

G-AOHG	156	Richard Hakluyt	20.2.57	-	To BEA Channel 1971. To British A/W Regional 1973.
G-AOHH	157	Sir Robert Maclure	5.3.57	-	To BEA Scottish 1971. To British A/W Regional 1973.
G-AOHI	158	Charles Montagu Doughty	11.3.57	-	To BEA Scottish 1971. WO near Perth 19.1.73.
G-AOHJ	159	Sir John Mandeville	27.3.57	-	To BEA Channel 1971. To British A/W Regional 1973.
G-AOHK	160	John Hanning Speke	5.4.57	-	To BEA Channel 1971. To British A/W Regional 1973.
G-AOHL	161	Charles Stewart	17.4.57	-	To BEA Scottish 1971. To British A/W Regional 1973.
G-AOHM	162	Robert Machin	27.6.57	-	To BEA Channel 1971. To British A/W Regional 1973.
G-AOHN	163	Alexander Gordon Laing	1.5.57	-	To BEA Channel 1971. To British A/W Regional 1973.
G-AOHO	164	Samuel Wallis	4.5.57	-	To BEA Channel 1971. To British A/W Regional 1973.
G-AOHP	165	James Weddel	17.5.57	-	WO Copenhagan 17.11.57.
G-AOHR	166	Sir Richard Burton	4.6.57	-	To BEA Channel 1971. To British A/W Regional 1973.
G-AOHS	167	Robert Thorne	22.6.57	-	To BEA Scottish 1971. To British A/W Regional 1973.
G-AOHT	168	Ralph Fitch	3.7.57	-	To BEA Channel 1971. To British A/W Regional 1973.
G-AOHU	169	Sir George Strong	11.7.57	-	WO Heathrow 7.1.60.
G-AOHV	170	Sir John Barrow	25.7.57	-	To BEA Channel 1971. To British A/W Regional 1973.
G-AOHW	253	Sir Francis Young Husband	1.8.57	-	To BEA Channel 1971. To British A/W Regional 1973.
G-AORC	254	Richard Lander	17.8.57	-	WO Craigie (Scotland) 28.4.58.
G-AORD	171	Arthur Philip	13.9.57	-	To BEA Channel 1971. To British A/W Regional 1973.

NB: Aircraft originally registered G-AOHA to G-AOHF were re-registered G-AOJA to G-AOJF to avoid confusion with V.701 aircraft G-ANHA to G-ANHF

First into Malaga, V.802 G-AOHG opening scheduled services from LHR in April 1962.

VICKERS

AIRCRAFT TYPE: VISCOUNT V.806 **BEA CLASS NAME: DISCOVERY**

REGISTRATION	C/N	BEA NAME	DELIVERY DATE	DISPOSAL DATE	REMARKS
G-AOYF	255	Michael Faraday	-	-	WO Johannesburg 20.10.57, prior to delivery to BEA.
G-AOYG	256	Charles Darwin	29.3.58	8.9.70	Sold to Cambrian Airways, later becoming British A/W Regional.
G-AOYH	311	William Harvey	23.12.57	31.7.68	Operated first V.806 service on 27.1.58, LHR-Glasgow. Sold to BKS, later becoming British Airways Regional.
G-AOYI	257	Sir Humphrey Davy	2.1.58	15.7.70	Sold to Cambrian Airways, later becoming British Airways Regional.
G-AOYJ	259	Edward Jenner	8.1.58	15.10.70	Leased to Cyprus A/W 28.10.65 to .5.70. Sold to Cambrian A/W, later becoming British A/W Regional.
G-AOYK	260	Edmund Cartwright	12.2.58	16.5.70	Leased to Cyprus A/W 20.10.65 to 16.11.69. Sold to Mandala Airlines.
G-AOYL	261	Lord Joseph Lister	14.2.58	28.5.68	Sold to BKS, later becoming British Airways Regional.
G-AOYM	262	John Loudon McAdam	19.3.58	8.11.71	Sold to Cambrian Airways, later becoming British Airways Regional.
G-AOYN	263	Sir Isaac Newton	26.3.58	30.12.71	Sold to Cambrian Airways, later becoming British Airways Regional.
G-AOYO	264	Adam Smith	3.4.58	30.5.68	Damaged Glasgow 18.7.67, back in service 29.5.68. Sold to BKS, later becoming British A/W Regional.
G-AOYP	265	John Napier	16.4.58	7.1.71	Sold to Cambrian Airways, later becoming British Airways Regional.
G-AOYR	266	Sir Richard Arkwright	13.6.58	29.12.69	Sold to BKS, later becoming British Airways Regional.
G-AOYS	267	George Stephenson	13.6.58	14.10.71	Sold to Cambrian Airways, later becoming British Airways Regional.
G-AOYT	268	James Watt	2.5.58	8.5.69	Sold to Winner Airways of Taiwan.
G-APEX	381	John Harrison	24.6.58	29.12.69	Sold to BKS, later becoming British Airways Regional.
G-APEY	382	William Murdock	18.7.58	2.4.68	Sold to BKS, later becoming British Airways Regional.
G-APIM	412	Robert Boyle	23.6.58	3.11.71	Sold to Cambrian Airways, later becoming British Airways Regional.
G-APJU	413	Sir Gilbert Blane	2.8.58	8.8.70	Sold to Mandala Airlines.
G-APKF	396	Michael Faraday	12.7.58	20.9.69	Purchased to replace G-AOYF. Sold to Lao Airlines.
G-APOX	418	Isambard Brunel	11.4.59	21.6.70	Sold to Mandala Airlines.

WESTLAND

AIRCRAFT TYPE: WS.55 **BEA CLASS NAME: KING ARTHUR CLASS**

REGISTRATION	C/N	BEA NAME	DELIVERY DATE	DISPOSAL DATE	REMARKS
G-ANFH	WA15	Sir Ector	2.11.54	13.8.68	Sold to Bristow Helicopters.
G-ANUK	WA39	Sir Kay	10.12.54	14.5.57	Sold to C.H.R. Salverson Ltd.
G-AOCF	WA56	Sir Lionel	29.8.55	24.10.66	Sold in Libya.

BEA took part in the 1953 London-New Zealand Air Race using Viscount V.700 G-AMAV. *(BA)*

The first ex-BOAC Boeing 707 to be delivered to Air Tours, G-APFK, arrives at Gatwick on December 31st 1971. *(BA)*

Vanguard G-APEH showing the last BEA livery to be worn by the type. *(BA)*

Appendix 4

Summary of main Incidents involving BEA Aircraft 1946 to 1974

Incidents included in this list caused substantial damage to the aircraft involved, or are of an unusual nature. Unless otherwise stated the damaged aircraft was repaired and evenutally returned to service.

1946

7th August	G-AHCS. DC-3. Near Oslo. Seven killed, five injured. The aircraft crashed short of the runway at Gardermoen airfield while attempting to land. It was destroyed in the incident.
18th November	G-AGBE. DC-3. Near Sons Le Saunier (France). Four injured. Following technical difficulties 'GBE made a forced landing in a field and was written off. The aircraft was owned by Skyways, operating under charter to BEA.

1947

15th April	G-AHKR. Rapide. Isle of Man. Seven injured. Flew into high ground while letting down to land at Jurby Airport in bad weather, and was written off.
6th August	G-AGJF. Rapide. Barra. The aircraft was destroyed at Barra, but the circumstances are unclear.
9th November	G-AIVP. Viking. Gothenburg. The Viking overran the runway after the throttle cables iced up, and was substantially damaged.

1948

6th January	G-AHPK. Viking. Northolt. One killed, eight injured. While attempting to land in fog, the aircraft crashed and was written off. The cause was largely attributed to an incorrect altimeter pressure setting.
5th April	G-AIVP. Viking. Near West Berlin. Fourteen killed. G-AIVP collided with a Soviet fighter aircraft while inbound to Berlin Gatow, and was destroyed on impact.
21st April	G-AIVE. Viking. Near Largs (Scotland). Thirteen injured. Flew into the Irish Law mountain in bad weather, and was destroyed.
30th July	G-AGIX. DC-3. Sywell. Following engine trouble, while en route Edinburgh to Northolt, the aircraft made an emergency belly landing and was written off.
27th December	G-AHXY. Rapide. Renfrew. The aircraft was destroyed at Renfrew, but the details are unclear.

1949

15th January	G-AHXV. Rapide. North Ronaldsay (Orkney Isles). Severely damaged when landing on a water logged grass strip while on an air ambulance flight. The aircraft was declared a write off.
19th February	G-AHCW. DC-3. Near Coventry. Ten killed. 'HCW was operating a scheduled Northolt-Glasgow service, when it collided with an RAF Anson and crashed. Aircraft destroyed.
24th May	G-AKCU. S.51. Croesor Dam (North Wales). The helicopter was caught in a downdraft coming off nearby mountains, and crashed. It was written off in the incident.
19th August	G-AHCY. DC-3. Oldham. Twenty four killed, eight injured. While attempting to land at Manchester in bad weather the aircraft crashed killing all on board, and several on the ground. It was operating the 11.50 Belfast-Manchester service, and was destroyed in the accident.
9th November	G-A. Viking. Blackbushe. An engine failed on landing, resulting in a heavy landing causing the undercarriage to collapse, and severe damage.

19th December	G-AHPK. Viking. Wisley. A belly landing was made at Wisley, following the failure of the undercarriage to retract on take off from Northolt. Severe damage caused.
1950	
13th April	G-AIVL. Viking. Near Hastings. One injured. A bomb exploded in the toilet injuring the stewardess. The aircraft returned safely to Northolt, but suffered some damage from the bomb.
17th October	G-AGIW. DC-3. Near Northolt. Twenty eight killed, one injured. Following an engine failure on take off, the aircraft crashed while trying to return to Northolt, and was written off.
31st October	G-AHPN. Viking. Heathrow. Twenty eight killed, two injured. The Viking failed to gain height when attempting an overshoot, and crashed. Thick fog hampered fire vehicles reaching the scene quickly enough to rescue passengers trapped in the burning wreckage.
1951	
17th January	G-A. DC3. Isle of Man. Aircraft taxied into earth excavators. Undercarriage collapsed , and propellors torn off.
28th August	G-AHXZ. Rapide. Glasgow. Aircraft burnt out, circumstances of the accident unclear.
1st November	G-AJBY. Viking. Madrid. Left undercarriage leg snapped off on following a tyre burst. 'JBY was substantially damaged as a result.
6th December	G-AGPH. Rapide. Barra. Withdrawn from use following damage on landing.
1953	
5th January	G-AJDL. Viking. Belfast. Twenty seven killed, eight injured. While trying to land at Nutts Corner in bad weather at night, the aircraft hit an approach light and then collided with a building, and was written off.
10th July	G-ALZO. Elizabethan. Blackbushe. Undercarriage collapsed as a result of a heavy landing during a training detail, causing substantial damage.
12th August	G-AIVG. Viking. Le Bourget. A tyre burst on take off resulted in an emergency belly landing. As a result of the damage, the aircraft was withdrawn from use.
22nd September	G-AGIZ. DC-3. Guernsey. Undershot on landing, pilot retracted the undercarriage, and the aircraft suffered some damage. It was operating a Jersey-Guernsey-Manchester service at the time.
20th December	G-AHPP. Viking. Nuremburg. 'HPP ran off the runway and tipped onto its nose, causing some damage.
1954	
9th August	G-AMKE. DC-3. Guernsey. One injured. On final approach the aircraft hit a baker's van, damaging the aircraft and destroying the van. The injury was to the van driver.
11th August	G-ALZN. Elizabethan. Near Paris. While flying in cloud the aircraft touched an Air France DC-4, causing slight damage.
24th October	G-AMNZ. Viscount. Rome. Following technical problems after take off from Rome for Athens and Istanbul, a return was made to Rome, where the left undercarriage leg collapsed on landing.
12th December	G-ALWF. Viscount. Blackbushe. Undercarriage collapsed on landing, during a training flight, resulting in substantial damage.
13th December	G-AMOB. Viscount. Blackbushe. Control column jammed on take off, causing the aircraft to overrun the runway, and the undercarriage to collapse. Severe damage resulted.
1955	
4th January	G-AKFA. Bell 47. Gatwick. Blown over on landing. Severely damaged and withdrawn from use.
6th January	G-AMOK. Viscount. Heathrow. Two injured. Aircraft attempted to take off on a taxiway in thick fog and collided with a barrier and a workman's hut. It was departing on a service to Rome and Athens.
25th March	G-AMOL. Viscount. Copenhagen. Hit a snow bank when caught in a strong crosswind on landing. Considerable damage caused.
8th April	G-AMAB. Elizabethan. Dusseldorf. Aircraft returned to Dusseldorf after one propeller went into reverse pitch. It stalled while attempting to land. The damage caused lead to it being withdrawn from use.
6th May	G-ALZN. Elizabethan. Orly. Aircraft diverted from Le Bourget due to weather and skidded on a wet runway leading to an undercarriage collapse.
12th December	G-AMOA. Viscount. Glasgow. Right hand undercarriage leg snapped off when the pilot turned off the runway too fast.

1956

2nd January	G-ANHF. Viscount. Bordeaux. Successful emergency landing made on one engine following fuel contamination.
20th January	G-AMOM. Viscount. Blackbushe. Three injured. Crashed during a three engined training detail. Considerable damage resulted.
27th March	G-A. Elizabethan. Near Daventry. Several injuries. While flying between Belfast and Heathrow violent evasive action had to be taken to avoid an RAF aircraft.
4th July	G-ALZW. Elizabethan. Jersey. Right hand undercarriage leg collapsed on landing.
? August	G-AKFB. Bell 47. Gatwick. Rolled over on landing. Though substantially damaged the helicopter was rebuilt over several months.

1957

20th February	G-ANXA. Heron. Coll. Damaged while landing in a strong crosswind while on an air ambulance sortie.
14th March	G-ALWE. Viscount. Manchester. Twenty two killed. On approach metal fatigue lead to a flap failure and locking of the ailerons. The Viscount crashed and was written off.
28th September	G-AOFY. Islay. Heron. Three killed. 'OFY crashed into the sea attempting to land at Islay in dreadful weather conditions to pick up a seriously ill woman.
23rd October	G-AOJA. Viscount. Belfast. Seven killed. Crashed when overshooting following a radar approach in bad weather. Aircraft destroyed.
17th November	G-AOHP. Viscount. Copenhagen. Two injured. On final approach three engines failed and the aircraft landed short of the runway. It was written off.

1958

6th February	G-ALZU. Elizabethan. Munich. Twenty three killed, twenty one injured. The Elizabethan failed to become airborn due to ice and slush on the runway and crashed. It was operating a charter for Manchester United Football Club and was destroyed in the accident.
13th April	G-AMNY. Viscount. Milan. While landing in turbulent conditions, 'MNY struck some trees and electric cables causing some damage.
28th April	G-AORC. Viscount. Craigie (near Prestwick). Five injured. Hit high ground on approach to Prestwick while on a charter to BOAC. Aircraft destroyed.
16th May	G-AGHP. DC-3. Chateney (France). Three killed. On a freight flight from Nice to Heathrow severe turbulence was encountered leading to the aircraft breaking up in mid air.
30th June	G-ALZN. Elizabethan. Rome. A nosewheel was lost on landing, damaging the forward fuselage.
22nd October	G-ANHC. Viscount. Near Anzio (Italy). Thirty one killed. Flying at 23,000 feet the Viscount collided with an Italian Air Force fighter and was destroyed on impact with the ground.
24th December	G-AOFY. Viscount. Bournemouth. Aircraft landed alongside the runway in poor weather conditions and suffered slight damage.

1959

13th April	G-AOHN. Viscount. Belfast. When landing in a strong cross wind the aircraft ran off the runway and was severely damaged.
21st May	G-AHLL. Rapide. Land's End (St Just). One injured. Aircraft overran the grass landing area suffering substantial damage. As a result it was withdrawn from use.
21st December	G-AOHI. Viscount. Edinburgh. 'OHI acquaplaned on a wet runway and overran the runway. the nosewheel then collapsed and considerable damage resulted.

1960

5th January	G-AMNY. Viscount. Malta. Four injured. Taxied into the control tower after an emergency landing following a hydraulic failure. After the incident the aircraft was withdrawn from use.
7th January	G-AOHU. Viscount. Heathrow. Nose wheel collapsed on landing inbound from Dublin. A fire broke out and the aircraft was destroyed.
11th August	G-AMOP. Viscount. Rome. Thirteen injured. Just prior to landing violent evasive action was taken to avoid colliding with another aircraft.

17th September	G-AOJC. Viscount. Jersey. On touch down there was a loud crack and the nose wheel collapsed, slightly damaging the aircraft.
31st October	G-AGZB. DC-3. Birmingham. Ran into a ditch when landing in bad weather causing considerable damage. At the time the aircraft was operating the last scheduled Pionair service from Heathrow.
1961	
30th October	G-A. Viscount. Frankfurt. Two injured. The nose wheel collapsed on landing, three propellers were torn off and other damage resulted.
27th November	G-AOYH. Viscount. Munich. Twenty injured. Aircraft encountered severe turbulence just after take off causing injury to those on board. It returned to Munich.
12th December	G-AKZB. Rapide. Land's End (St Just). When landing on a wet grass runway 'KZB overran the landing area and suffered considerable damage. It was declared a write off.
21st December	G-ARJM. Comet. Ankara. Twenty seven killed, seven injured. The aircraft stalled on take off for Nicosia and crashed. The cause was attributed to a faulty instrument.
? December	G-AMOO. Viscount. Oslo. Aircraft substantially damaged when landing on a snow covered runway. Repaired in a make shift igloo type hangar.
1962	
11th April	G-APEF. Vanguard. Edinburgh. Flew into a large flock of seagulls just after lift off. Two engines immediately failed, and the aircraft returned for an emergency landing. Just after touch down a third engine failed. Substantial damage caused.
1963	
17th March	G-AOHO. Viscount. Berlin. Touched down 200 feet short of the runway, leading to the collapse of the nose wheel.
29th March	G-APEJ. Vanguard. Dublin. Landed in a nose down attitude, causing the nose wheel to collapse, and causing some damage.
8th April	G-AOYH. Viscount. Palermo. While en route for Malta, a fire developed in one engine, and an emergency landing was made at Palermo.
2nd August	G-ARJN. Comet. Milan. Two injured. A heavy landing was made in bad weather causing some damage.
9th September	G-AOJC. Viscount. Geneva. Nose wheel collapsed on landing.
1964	
6th October	G-APEE. Vanguard. Glasgow. A heavy landing lead to the collapse of the nose wheel.
5th November	G-APMD. Comet. Malaga. Skidded off the runway while landing in heavy rain and a gale. Considerable damage resulted.
1965	
4th July	G-ASXL. Argosy. Costalba (Italy). Two injured. Crashed into high ground while letting down into Milan. Written off.
27th October	G-APEE. Vanguard. Heathrow. Thirty six killed. The aircraft hit the runway when attempting to overshoot in fog, and was destroyed. It was operating an Off Peak Edinburgh-London flight.
26th November	G-APEY. Viscount. Jersey. Nose wheel collapsed on landing and some damage resulted.
26th November	G-APEL. Vanguard. Belfast. Ran off the runway on landing, and suffered some damage.
1967	
21st January	G-ASOG. DC-4. Frankfurt. Two killed. Crashed on approach in bad weather, while operating a freight flight. Aircraft owned by Air Ferry and operating under charter to BEA.
18th July	G-AOYO. Viscount. Glasgow. Ran off the runway and hit a fence, causing severe damage. The incident occurred during a training detail for Cyprus Airways. Aircraft transferred to Cambridge by road and rebuilt.
12th October	G-ARCO. Comet. Between Greece and Cyprus. Sixty six killed. The Comet was destroyed by a terrorist bomb while inbound to Nicosia.
3rd December	G-ARPU. Trident 1. Copenhagen. Six injured. Landed short of the runway and hit a pipe. Substantial damage resulted.

G-ASXP. Argosy. Stansted. Three injured. Crashed soon after take off on a training flight, and was written off.

1968

4th February — G-ARGM. Comet. Akrotiri (Cyprus). Seventeen injured. Emergency landing made on a bed of foam, following failure of undercarriage to lock down. The aircraft diverted to Akrotiri from Nicosia to benefit from the foaming facilities. Considerable damage caused.

17th February — G-ATTC. Argosy. Le Bourget. Diverted to Le Bourget when operating a Milan-Heathrow service. Some damage caused in the emergency landing.

14th June — G-ARPR. Trident 1. Shannon. A heavy landing on a training sortie caused some damage and the aircraft was out of service for six weeks.

3rd July — G-ARPI and G-ARPT. Trident 1s. Heathrow. Both aircraft substantially damaged when a BKS Ambassador (G-AMAD) crashed into them following a flap failure. G-ARPI was repaired, but 'RPT was withdrawn from use. Slight damage was also caused to Viscount, G-APJU.

27th October — G-APEN. Vanguard. Belfast. Ran off the runway on landing in a strong crosswind. Some damage resulted.

31st October — G-AWFX. S.61. Penzance. A mechanical fault occurred just after lift off on a training detail, and the helicopter force landed on marshy ground adjoining the heliport. Some damage occurred.

1969

29th July — G-ARPS. Trident 1. Heathrow. The aircraft was destroyed by fire while parked on the apron. Arson was suspected but never proved.

26th December — G-AOHV. Viscount. Berlin. One injured. A heavy landing was made on a snow covered runway after the pilot became dazzled by the runway lights.

1970

10th January — G-AOHO. Viscount. Southampton. On landing all the aircraft's tyres burst when the brakes locked on a wet runway.

1st October — G-ARPO. Trident 1. Rome. An engine failed and disintegrated on take off, causing the take off to be aborted and some damage to occur.

15th November — G-ASNM. S.61. North Sea. While en route from an oil rig to Aberdeen the helicopter made a precautionary landing on the sea, following the failure of its transmission system. It later sank.

1971

19th January — G-AWZC. Trident 3. Bedford. 'WZC collided with another aircraft on the runway while on a training flight, resulting in some damage.

2nd October — G-APEC. Vanguard. Arselle (Belgium). Sixty three killed. Metal fatigue in the tail section lead to the aircraft breaking up in flight and crashing while en route from Heathrow to Salzburg. Aircraft destroyed.

1972

18th June — G-ARPI. Trident 1. Staines (Near Heathrow). One hundred and eighteen killed. Crashed just after departure from Heathrow for Brussels, when the drop flaps retracted too soon. Aircraft destroyed by impact.

1973

19th January — G-AOHI. Viscount. Near Perth. Four killed. Crashed into a mountain while on a test flight from Abbotsinch. Aircraft written off.

Appendix 5

Aircraft Chartered by BEA from Other Operators for Significant Periods

Aircraft Chartered from	Period of Charter	Aircraft Type	Routes used on (Passenger unless otherwise stated)
Scottish Airlines	1.2.47 to 31.7.47	DC-3 Fokker F.22	Northolt-Glasgow, Northolt-Prestwick, Prestwick-Belfast and Glasgow-Belfast
Westminster Airways	23.4.47 to 6.10.47	Consul	Croydon-Amsterdam-Copenhagen-Gothenburg -Stockholm-Helsinki
Olley Air Services	Summers of 1948 and 1949	Dove	Croydon-Deauville
Scottish Airlines	Summer 1950	DC-3	Northolt-Jersey, at week-ends
Sivewright Airways	10.50 to 3.51	DC-3	Various freight services
Air Transport Charter	Throughout 1951	DC-3	Various freight services, especially Manchester-Belfast
Scottish Airlines	3.51 to 8.51	DC-3	Various freight services
BOAC Associate Companies	19.11.55 to 31.3.56	Viscount (G-ANRS)	Various
Fred Olsen	12.55 to 4.57	Viscount (G-AODG) (G-AODH)	Various
Air Charter Limited	4.56 to 10.58	DC-3, DC-4	German internal Services
Eagle Airways	4.56 to 11.56	DC-3 (G-AMYB)	Various passenger and freight services
Eagle Airways	23.6.56 to 31.12.57	DC-3, Viking	Various freight services
Trans Air	Summer 1958	DC-3	German internal services
Dan Air	5.59 to 3.60	DC-3	LHR-Glasgow-Manchester-LHR freight service
Vickers Aircraft Limited	6.58 to 8.58	Viscount (G-APNF) (G-APNG)	Various
Skyways	Most of 1959	DC-3	LHR-Frankfurt-Dusseldorf-LHR freight service
Dan Air	21.5.59 to 31.12.61	York	Various freight services
Fred Olsen	3.60 to 3.61	Viscount (G-APZP) (G-ARBW)	Various
Dan Air	Summer 1960	Ambassador	LHR-Jersey
Derby Airways	2.2.61 to 7.61	DC-3	LHR-Amsterdam freight service
BOAC	1.4.61 to 30.4.61	DC-7C	LHR-Frankfurt, LHR-Zurich
BOAC	1.4.61 to 30.5.61	Britannia (G-AOVG) (G-AOVP) (G-AOVT)	LHR-Copenhagen, LHR-Nice
BOAC	1.6.61 to 31.8.61	DC-7C	LHR-Paris
BEA Helicopters	1.11.65 to 28.2.66	S.61 (G-ASNM)	Jersey-Guernsey
Cambrian Airways	December 1965	Viscount	German internal services

Air Ferry	1.11.66 to 21.1.67	DC-4	Various freight services, especially LHR and Manchester-Dusseldorf/Frankfurt, and LHR-Zurich
BEA Air Tours	1.11.70 to 31.3.71	Comet 4B	Various
Cambrian Airways	1970 to 1973	BAC 1-11.400	German internal services, and Manchester/ Birmingham-Dublin

On many other occasions BEA chartered aircraft on an ad hoc basis from many different airlines, covering a wide range of aircraft types.

Operating Statistics 1946 to 1974

Financial Year	Total Revenue (£,000)	Profit (+)/ Loss (-)	Total Passengers	Total Cargo (Tons)	Total Mail (Tons)	Revenue Hours Flown	Staff as at 31 March
1946/47	£1,206,045	£2,157,937-	269,678	688	510	23,200	5,731
1947/48	£3,962,475	£3,573,989-	511,522	2,610	1,558	97,400	7,249
1948/49	£5,312,654	£2,763,085-	577,122	4,426	2,981	91,400	7,145
1949/50	£6,884,935	£1,363,594-	751,512	6,093	4,168	110,700	6,479
1950/51	£8,998,821	£979,267-	939,586	10,079	5,249	143,800	7,048
1951/52	£10,817,687	£1,423,611-	1,135,579	12,500	6,489	153,500	7,978
1952/53	£13,128,080	£1,459,131-	1,400,122	14,300	6,289	171,900	8,551
1953/54	£14,773,170	£1,773,797-	1,656,779	14,600	6,582	160,900	9,020
1954/55	£17,141,314	£63,089+	1,874,316	14,900	6,964	149,100	9,143
1955/56	£21,599,494	£603,614+	2,224,747	18,600	7,895	165,100	9,570
1956/57	£23,947,774	£216,770+	2,461,065	22,500	7,541	181,300	10,439
1957/58	£28,340,725	£1,054,087+	2,765,591	24,600	7,465	190,500	10,933
1958/59	£31,761,313	£233,695+	2,828,715	28,020	7,669	194,058	11,528
1959/60	£36,536,613	£2,086,078+	3,289,606	36,395	7,848	193,790	12,190
1960/61	£42,270,467	£1,545,321+	3,990,957	41,996	8,850	195,725	13,240
1961/62	£46,368,040	£1,488,065-	4,393,378	41,042	9,325	176,821	14,493
1962/63	£51,243,861	£265,301-	4,914,927	49,290	12,115	162,535	16,010
1963/64	£59,851,871	£3,030,007+	5,604,812	58,259	12,997	165,411	16,688
1964/65	£65,858,456	£1,316,876+	6,119,134	72,561	14,069	183,258	17,685
1965/66	£76,334,282	£1,283,725+	6,842,763	92,362	15,100	195,185	18,790
1966/67	£86,382,680	£708,296+	7,323,970	110,021	16,430	215,276	20,224
1967/68	£92,279,000	£1,784,000-	7,334,962	115,932	14,791	220,969	21,560
1968/69	£108,385,000	£3,536,000+	7,728,654	132,422	15,581	217,345	22,185
1969/70	£126,038,000	£6,532,000+	8,475,856	130,758	16,436	216,250	23,228
1970/71	£133,350,000	£524,000+	8,665,824	110,605	16,683	225,832	24,868
1971/72	£178,125,000	£181,000+	9,080,801	112,300	18,300	238,200	25,348
1972/73*	£173,866,000	£477,000+	8,199,121	140,000	19,100	202,100	24,524
1973/74*	£212,794,000	£6,699,000+	8,743,031	138,631	19,522	214,700	24,403

* Excluding results for Scottish Airways and Channel Island Airways.

Appendix 6

Comparison of BEA Departures from Northolt and Heathrow

In this section a comparison is given between the number of BEA scheduled departures from Northolt for August of 1947 and from Heathrow for August of 1973. In the case of 1973 freighter departures have been left out, and so have the services of Cambrian Airways and Northeast Airlines.

The days of the week are shown by number, 1 is Monday, 2 is Tuesday and so on.

Departures from Northolt August 1947

00.55	DC-3 Freighter	BE799A	Brussels, Prague	1	2	3	4	5	6	
07.00	Viking	BE660A	Marseilles, Rome, Athens		2				6	
07.00	Viking	BE665A	Marseilles, Rome, Athens, Istanbul, Ankara			3				
07.40	DC-3	BE630A	Hamburg, Berlin	1	2	3	4		6	7
08.00	Viking	BE624A	Paris	1	2	3	4	5	6	7
08.05	Viking	BE671A	Marseilles, Rome				4			7
08.10	Viking	BE645A	Bordeaux, Madrid	1			4			
08.15	Viking	BE686A	Stavanger, Oslo	1				5		7
08.20	Viking	BE640A	Bordeaux, Lisbon	1	2		4		6	7
08.25	Viking	BE700A	Gothenburg, Stockholm		2			5		7
08.30	Viking	BE680A	Copenhagen	1		3		5		
08.35	Viking	BE730A	Prague	1		3			6	7
08.40	Viking	BE722A	Brussels	1	2	3	4	5	6	7
08.45	DC-3	BE632A	Vienna			3		5		7
08.50	Viking	BE635A	Amsterdam	1	2	3	4	5	6	7
09.00	Viking	BE652A	Bordeaux, Madrid, Gibraltar		2			5		
09.05	DC-3	BEE321A	Jersey	1	2		4	5	6	7
09.20	DC-3	BEE300A	Belfast	1	2	3	4	5	6	7
09.25	Viking	BES200N	Glasgow	1	2	3	4	5	6	
09.30	DC-3	BES201N	Edinburgh, Aberdeen, Sumburgh	1	2	3	4	5	6	
10.10	DC-3	BEE321U	Jersey							7
10.20	DC-3	BEE321P	Jersey	1	2	3	4	5	6	7
11.20	Viking	BE624B	Paris	1	2	3	4	5	6	7
12.15	DC-3	BEE300B	Belfast	1	2	3	4	5	6	
12.35	DC-3	BEE321V	Jersey							7
12.35	Viking	BES202N	Prestwick	1	2	3	4	5	6	
12.40	DC-3	BEE321Q	Jersey	1	2		4	5	6	7
13.30	Viking	BE745A	Geneva	1	2	3	4	5	6	7
13.50	Viking	BE624C	Paris	1	2	3	4	5	6	7
14.10	DC-3	BEE321R	Jersey	1	2	3	4	5	6	7
14.30	Viking	BE722B	Brussels	1	2	3	4	5	6	7
15.50	DC-3	BEE300C	Belfast	1	2	3	4	5	6	
16.20	DC-3	BEE321S	Jersey	1	2		4	5	6	7
16.40	Viking	BE624D	Paris	1	2	3	4	5	6	7
18.00	DC-3	BES201P	Edinburgh, Aberdeen	1	2	3	4	5	6	
18.10	DC-3	BEE321W	Jersey							7
18.30	DC-3	BEE321T	Jersey	1	2	3	4	5	6	7
18.50	DC-3	BES202P	Glasgow							7
18.50	Viking	BES202P	Glasgow	1	2	3	4	5	6	

20.10	Viking	BE624E	Paris	1	2	3	4	5	6	7

In addition there were the following services from Croydon Airport:
Croydon to Deauville. (Frequency unknown)
Croydon to Guernsey. (Twenty one flights weekly)
Croydon to Helsinki. (Once weekly)
Croydon to Manchester-Liverpool. (Fourteen weekly)

Departures from Heathrow August 1973

07.00	Trident	BE002	Paris (Orly)	1	2	3	4	5	6	
07.00	Trident	BE912	Dublin	1	2	3	4	5	6	
07.25	Trident	BE502	Amsterdam	1	2	3	4	5	6	
07.45	Trident	BE5006	Glasgow	1	2	3	4	5		
07.55	Trident	BE6504	Belfast	1	2	3	4	5	6	7
08.00	Trident	BE004	Paris (Orly)	1	2	3	4	5	6	7
08.00	Trident	BE914	Dublin	1	2	3	4	5	6	7
08.00	Super I-II	BE4054	Manchester	1	2	3	4	5	6	
08.05	Trident	BE5664	Edinburgh	1	2	3	4	5	6	7
08.10	Viscount	BE8306	Aberdeen	1	2	3	4	5	6	
08.15	Trident	BE538	Brussels	1	2	3	4	5	6	7
08.15	Trident	BE5008	Glasgow	1	2	3	4	5	6	
08.25	Trident	BE422	Corfu				4		6	7
08.35	Trident	BE504	Amsterdam	1	2	3	4	5	6	7
08.50	Trident	BE482	Tel Aviv	1			4	5		7
08.50	Viscount	BE3142	Guernsey	1		3	4	5	6	7
08.50	Viscount	BE8508	Inverness	1	2	3	4	5	6	
08.55	Viscount	BE3014	Jersey	1	2	3	4	5	6	7
09.00	Trident	BE006	Paris (Orly)	1	2	3	4	5	6	7
09.00	Trident	BE564	Zurich	1	2	3	4	5	6	7
09.05	Trident	BE602	Frankfurt	1	2	3	4	5	6	7
09.10	Trident	BE756	Stockholm	1	2	3	4	5	6	7
09.15	Trident	BE626	Dusseldorf	1	2	3	4	5	6	7
09.15	Trident	BE352	Rome	1	2	3	4	5	6	7
09.20	Trident	BE416	Istanbul	1	2	3	4	5	6	7
09.25	Trident	BE742	Copenhagen	1	2	3	4	5	6	7
09.30	Trident	BE5014	Glagow	1	2	3	4	5	6	7
09.30	Trident	BE306	Malta		2		4		6	7
09.30	Trident	BE326	Naples, Malta	1		3		5		
09.30	Super I-II	BE4058	Manchester	1	2	3	4	5	6	7
09.40	Trident	BE576	Geneva	1	2	3	4	5	6	7
09.40	Trident	BE622	Hanover	1	2	3	4	5	6	7
09.40	Trident	BE506	Amsterdam	1	2	3	4	5	6	7
09.45	Trident	BE456	Athens	1	2	3	4	5	6	7
09.50	Vanguard	BE6506	Belfast	1		3		5	6	7
09.50	Trident	BE734	Budapest, Bucharest							7
09.50	Viscount	BE3016	Jersey							7
09.55	Trident	BE202	Gibraltar		2				6	
09.55	Trident	BE228	Gibraltar, Casablanca	1				5		
09.55	Trident	BE234	Gibraltar, Agadir							7
10.00	Trident	BE008	Paris (Orly)	1	2	3	4	5	6	7
10.05	Trident	BE702	Vienna	1	2	3	4	5	6	7
10.10	Trident	BE612	Hamburg	1	2	3	4	5	6	7
10.15	Trident	BE366	Milan	1	2	3	4	5	6	7
10.15	Trident	BE642	Munich	1	2	3	4	5	6	7
10.15	Trident	BE916	Dublin		2		4	5		7
10.25	Super I-II	BE618	Bremen, Berlin	1	2	3	4	5	6	7
10.25	Trident	BE362	Venice	1	2	3	4	5	6	7
10.25	Viscount	BE3144	Guernsey	1	2	3	4		6	7
10.25	Viscount	BE3018	Jersey	1		3		5	6	7
10.30	Trident	BE5672	Edinburgh	1	2	3	4	5	6	7
10.30	Trident	BE376	Turin	1				5		7
10.30	Trident	BE184	Madrid	1	2	3	4	5	6	7
10.35	Viscount	BE8316	Aberdeen	1	2	3	4	5	6	
10.40	Trident	BE732	Sofia, Bucharest		2			5		
10.40	Trident	BE774	Bergen			3			6	
10.45	Vanguard	BE3022	Jersey	1	2	3	4	5	6	7
10.50	Trident	BE5016	Glasgow	1	2	3	4	5	6	7

10.50	Trident	BE672	Moscow	1				5	6	
10.50	Trident	BE262	Lisbon	1	2	3	4	5	6	7
10.55	Trident	BE6508	Belfast	1	2	3	4	5	6	7
10.55	Trident	BE688	Warsaw	1		3		5	6	7
11.00	Trident	BE012	Paris (Orly)	1	2	3	4	5	6	7
11.05	Trident	BE542	Brussels	1	2	3	4	5	6	7
11.10	Trident	BE674	Leningrad							7
11.10	Trident	BE386	Pisa		2	3	4		6	
11.20	Trident	BE132	Malaga	1	2		4		6	
11.20	Trident	BE134	Malaga, Tangier			3		5		7
11.25	Viscount	BE3146	Guernsey	1	2	3	4	5	6	7
11.25	Trident	BE782	Oslo	1	2	3	4	5	6	7
11.35	Trident	BE772	Helsinki	1	2	3	4	5	6	7
11.35	Trident	BE084	Marseilles		2		4		6	
11.35	Trident	BE972	Shannon	1	2	3	4	5	6	7
11.40	Trident	BE728	Zagreb, Belgrade	1		3		5	6	7
11.40	Trident	BE922	Dublin	1	2	3	4	5	6	7
11.40	Trident	BE692	Prague	1		3		5	6	
11.45	Trident	BE076	Nice	1	2	3	4	5	6	7
11.45	Super I-II	BE4064	Manchester	1	2	3	4	5	6	7
11.50	Trident	BE788	Keflavik			3				7
11.50	Trident	BE116	Barcelona	1	2	3	4	5	6	7
12.00	Trident	BE014	Paris (Orly)	1	2	3	4	5	6	7
12.05	Trident	BE724	Budapest	1		3		5		
12.10	Viscount	BE3026	Jersey	1		3			6	7
12.15	Super 1-11	BE616	Berlin	1	2	3	4	5	6	7
12.15	Vanguard	BE712	Salzburg			3			6	7
12.20	Trident	BE204	Gibraltar			3	4	5		
12.25	Trident	BE078	Nice			3		5		
12.25	Trident	BE508	Amsterdam	1	2	3	4	5	6	7
12.40	Trident	BE5682	Edinburgh	1	2	3	4	5	6	7
12.45	Viscount	BE3032	Jersey	1	2	3	4	5	6	7
12.55	Trident	BE604	Frankfurt	1	2	3	4	5	6	7
13.10	Trident	BE016	Paris (Orly)	1	2	3	4	5		
13.10	Trident	BE382	Naples		2		4		6	7
13.10	Trident	BE578	Geneva	1	2	3	4	5	6	7
13.15	Trident	BE472	Nicosia	1	2	3	4	5	6	7
13.25	Trident	BE138	Alicante			3	4		6	
13.25	Trident	BE276	Faro		2			5		7
13.30	Trident	BE162	Palma	1	2	3	4	5	6	7
13.35	Trident	BE6512	Belfast	1	2	3	4	5	6	7
13.35	Trident	BE5018	Glasgow	1	2	3	4	5	6	7
13.35	Viscount	BE3152	Guernsey		2					
13.45	Trident	BE566	Zurich	1	2	3	4	5	6	7
13.45	Trident	BE354	Rome	1	2	3	4	5	6	7
13.45	Viscount	BE3034	Jersey		2	3	4		6	7
14.00	Trident	BE018	Paris (Orly)	1	2	3	4	5	6	7
14.00	Viscount	BE8318	Aberdeen							7
14.05	Vanguard	BE5688	Edinburgh	1	2	3	4	5		7
14.10	Viscount	BE3038	Jersey		2					
14.15	Trident	BE458	Athens	1	2	3	4	5	6	7
14.15	Trident	BE368	Milan	1	2	3	4	5	6	7
14.20	Trident	BE484	Tel Aviv	1	2	3	4	5	6	7
14.20	Vanguard	BE6514	Belfast	1	2	3	4	5	6	7
14.25	Trident	BE142	Valencia							7
14.30	Trident	BE512	Amsterdam	1	2	3	4	5	6	7
14.30	Super 1-11	BE4074	Manchester	1	2	3	4	5	6	7
14.40	Viscount	BE3154	Guernsey					5		
14.55	Trident	BE704	Vienna	1			4			
15.00	Trident	BE5022	Glasgow	1	2	3	4	5		
15.00	Trident	BE022	Paris (Orly)	1	2	3	4	5	6	7
15.00	Trident	BE926	Dublin	1	2	3	4	5	6	7
15.05	Trident	BE426	Crete				4			
15.05	Trident	BE5694	Edinburgh	1	2	3	4	5	6	
15.10	Trident	BE432	Rhodes		2					
15.10	Trident	BE464	Thesalonika			3			6	7
15.20	Trident	BE744	Copenhagen	1	2	3	4	5		7
15.25	Trident	BE336	Cagliari			3				
15.35	Trident	BE974	Shannon		2	3		5	6	
15.35	Trident	BE272	Oporto				4		6	

15.40	Trident	BE546	Brussels			3	4	5		
15.40	Trident	BE6516	Belfast	1	2	3	4	5	6	7
15.50	Trident	BE758	Stockholm	1	2	3	4	5	6	7
16.00	Trident	BE024	Paris (Orly)	1	2	3	4	5	6	7
16.10	Trident	BE212	Madrid, Gibraltar	1						
16.10	Trident	BE644	Munich	1	2	3	4	5	6	7
16.10	Trident	BE568	Zurich	1	2	3	4	5	6	7
16.15	Super 1-11	BE624	Cologne/Bonn, Berlin	1	2	3	4	5	6	7
16.25	Trident	BE646	Stuttgart	1	2	3	4	5	6	7
16.30	Trident	BE516	Amsterdam	1	2	3	4	5	6	7
16.40	Trident	BE784	Gothenburg	1	2	3	4	5		7
16.45	Trident	BE548	Brussels	1	2	3	4	5	6	7
16.50	Trident	BE746	Copenhagen	1	2	3	4	5	6	7
16.55	Trident	BE614	Hamburg	1	2	3	4	5	6	7
17.00	Trident	BE026	Paris (Orly)	1	2	3	4	5	6	7
17.05	Trident	BE5698	Edinburgh	1	2	3	4	5	6	7
17.10	Trident	BE582	Geneva	1	2	3	4	5		7
17.10	Viscount	BE3056	Jersey	1						
17.15	Trident	BE5026	Glasgow	1	2	3	4	5		7
17.20	Trident	BE632	Dusseldorf	1	2	3	4	5	6	7
17.25	Trident	BE6518	Belfast	1	2	3	4	5	6	7
17.25	Trident	BE932	Dublin	1	2	3	4	5	6	
17.30	Trident	BE206	Gibraltar					5		
17.30	Super 1-11	BE8324	Aberdeen	1	2	3	4	5		
17.35	Trident	BE356	Rome, Malta	1	2	3	4	5	6	7
17.35	Trident	BE606	Frankfurt	1	2	3	4	5		7
17.35	Trident	BE186	Madrid	1	2	3	4	5	6	7
17.35	Trident	BE4084	Manchester	1	2	3	4	5		
17.40	Trident	BE592	Basle	1	2	3	4	5	6	7
17.50	Viscount	BE3058	Jersey				4			
18.00	Trident	BE028	Paris (Orly)	1	2	3	4	5		
18.00	Trident	BE518	Amsterdam	1	2	3	4	5	6	7
18.00	Trident	BE5032	Glasgow	1	2	3	4	5	6	7
18.10	Trident	BE278	Faro						6	
18.10	Viscount	BE8514	Inverness	1	2	3	4	5	6	7
18.20	Viscount	BE3166	Guernsey	1	2	3	4	5	6	7
18.30	Trident	BE934	Dublin	1	2	3	4	5	6	7
18.45	Trident	BE5134	Glasgow	1	2	3	4	5		7
18.45	Viscount	BE3062	Jersey	1	2	3	4	5	6	7
18.50	Trident	BE5704	Edinburgh	1	2	3	4	5		7
18.50	Vanguard	BE208	Gibraltar							7
18.55	Trident	BE032	Paris (Orly)				4	5		
19.00	Trident	BE552	Brussels	1	2	3	4	5	6	7
19.00	Super 1-11	BE4088	Manchester	1	2	3	4	5		7
19.15	Trident	BE634	Dusseldorf	1	2	3	4	5	6	7
19.20	Trident	BE082	Nice	1				5	6	7
19.20	Trident	BE266	Lisbon					5		
19.25	Trident	BE6522	Belfast	1	2	3	4	5		7
19.25	Vanguard	BE3064	Jersey			3		5	6	7
19.30	Trident	BE5036	Glasgow	1	2	3	4	5	6	7
19.35	Viscount	BE8328	Aberdeen	1	2	3	4	5	6	7
20.00	Trident	BE474	Nicosia	1	2	3	4	5	6	7
20.00	Trident	BE034	Paris (Orly)	1	2	3	4	5		7
20.00	Trident	BE454	Athens	1	2	3	4	5	6	7
20.15	Trident	BE372	Milan			3		5		7
20.20	Viscount	BE7334	Birmingham	1	2	3	4	5	6	7
20.25	Trident	BE586	Geneva		2	3	4	5		7
20.25	Trident	BE572	Zurich		2	3	4	5		7
20.45	Trident	BE5038	Glasgow	1	2	3	4	5	6	7
20.50	Trident	BE476	Nicosia				4		6	7
20.55	Trident	BE5716	Edinburgh	1	2	3	4	5	6	7
21.00	Trident	BE312	Malta	1	2	3	4	5	6	7
21.00	Super 1-11	BE4094	Manchester	1	2	3	4	5	6	7
21.05	Trident	BE428	Crete						6	
21.10	Trident	BE434	Rhodes						6	
21.15	Trident	BE6524	Belfast	1	2	3	4	5	6	7
21.30	Trident	BE944	Dublin	1	2	3	4	5	6	7
22.00	Trident	BE762	Stockholm					5		
22.40	Trident	BE748	Copenhagen					5		7
22.55	Trident	BE342	Catania					5		
23.10	Trident	BE316	Malta	1			4	5	6	

Farewell to Northolt, passengers about to board Pionair G-AHCZ for the last BEA service from the Airport, on October 30th 1954. *(BA)*

Comet 4B G-APMG at Heathrow. *(BA)*

List of Main Abbreviations Used

AAJC	Associated Airways Joint Committee.
ACS	Airport Catering Services Limited.
A/L	Airlines.
ATC	Air Traffic Control.
ATLB	Air Transport Licencing Board.
A/W	Airways.
BA	British Airways.
BAC	British Aircraft Corporation.
BAH	British Airways Helicopters.
BAS	British Air Services.
BCAL	British Caledonian Airways.
BEA	British European Airways.
BE	BEA Flight Prefix.
BEAH	BEA Helicopters.
BIH	British International Helicopters.
BOAC	British Overseas Airways Corporation.
BSAA	British South American Airways Corporation.
BUA	British United Airways.
CI	Channel Islands.
C/N	Construction Number.
C of A	Certificate of Airworthiness.
CoAT	College of Air Training.
CY	Cyprus Airways Flight Prefix.
Dia	Diameter.
DH 89	Rapide aircraft.
EEC	European Economic Community (Common Market).
FIND	Flight Information and Display.
GT	Gibralter Airways Flight Prefix.
HEU	BEA Helicopter Experimental Unit.
IAL	International Air Radio Limited.
IOM	Isle of Man.
IT	Inclusive Tour.
KM	Air Malta Flight Prefix.
LHR	London Heathrow Airport.
MN	The Malta Airlines Flight Prefix.
MTOW	Maximum Take Off Weight.
P32	Pionair Aircraft.
PALA	Passenger Acceptance and Load Accumulation.
PALC	Passenger Acceptance and Load Control.
RAE	Royal Aircraft Establishment.
RAF	Royal Air Force.
RAS	Railway Air Services.
RVR	Runway Visual Range.
STOL	Short Take Off and Landing.
Super 1-11	BAC I-II.500 aircraft.
TAP	Transportes Aereos Portugese.
USAF	United States Air Force.
WFU	Withdrawn from use.
WLAT	West London Air Terminal.
WO	Written Off.

Bibliography

This is not a fully comprehensive list, but provides a guide to the main sources consulted by the author.

Books

B. Martin and others.	The Vickers Viking Monograph.	Air Britain.
G. Cowell.	The Heron.	G. Cowell.
G. Cowell.	The Handley Page Herald.	Airline Publications and Sales
P.W. Davies.	The Vickers Viscount and Vanguard Monograph.	Air Britain
J. Godson.	The Papi India Tragedy.	Compton Press.
J.M.G. Gradidge.	The Douglas DC-3 Monograph.	Air Britain.
P. Lo Bao.	A History of British Airways Helicopters and it's Predecessors since 1947.	Air Britain
G. May	The Challenge of BEA.	Wolfe Publications.
A.C. Merton Jones.	British Independent Airlines Since 1946, Volumes One to Four.	Merseyside Avn. Soc. and LAAS.
H. Penrose.	Wings Across the World.	Cassells.
I. Scott Hill and G. Behrend.	Channel Silver Wings.	Jersey Artists.
T. Staddon	The History of Cambrian Airways.	Airline Publications and Sales.
P. St John Turner	The Handbook of the Vickers Viscount.	Ian Allen.
J. Stroud.	The Annals of British Air Transport.	Putnams.
J. Stroud.	Railway Air Services.	Ian Allen.

Magazines

Aeronautics.	1946 to 1955.
Air Pictorial.	1962 to 1974.
Flight International.	1946 to 1974.
Propliner.	

BEA Publications

BEA Magazine	1947 to 1974.
BEA News	1966 to 1974.
BEA Report and Accounts.	1946 to 1972.

British Airways Publications

Highways in the Air, The Story of British Airways.
British Airways Reports and Accounts. 1973 to 1974.